CAMBRIDGE CLASSICAL STUDIES

General editors: M.I.Finley, E.J.Kenney, G.E.L.Owen

ARISTOTLE ON MIND AND THE SENSES

Aristotle on mind and the senses

Proceedings of the Seventh Symposium Aristotelicum

Edited by
G.E.R.LLOYD and G.E.L.OWEN

CAMBRIDGE UNIVERSITY PRESS
Cambridge
London : New York : Melbourne

Published by the Syndics of the Cambridge University Press

The Pitt Building, Trumpington Street, Cambridge CB2 1RP

Bentley House, 200 Euston Road, London NW1 2DB

32 East 57th Street, New York, NY 10022, USA

296 Beaconsfield Parade, Middle Park, Melbourne 3206, Australia

© Faculty of Classics, University of Cambridge 1978

First published 1978

Printed in Great Britain by
Redwood Burn Ltd,
Trowbridge & Esher

Library of Congress Cataloguing in Publication Data

Symposium Aristotelicum, 7th, Cambridge, Eng., 1975.
    Aristotle on mind and the senses.

    (Cambridge classical studies)
    Includes index.

    1. Aristoteles--Congresses.   2. Mind and body--Congresses.
3. Senses and sensation--Congresses.   I. Lloyd, Geoffrey Ernest
Richard.   II. Owen, Gwilym Ellis Lane.   III. Title.   IV. Series.
B491.M5S95   1975   185   77-9389

ISBN 0 521 21669 9

CONTENTS

PREFACE

The triennial Symposia Aristotelica, inaugurated at Oxford in 1957, are by now well known. The seventh, whose Proceedings appear in this volume, was held at St John's College, Cambridge, from 27 August to 5 September 1975. Since the third Symposium it has been customary to focus attention on a particular group of treatises, on this occasion the *De anima* together with the *Parva naturalia*. These texts, while rich in philosophical interest, contain many particularly unyielding difficulties of interpretation. No attempt was made, of course, to cover all the major problems. In particular some traditional questions, such as the relation between the active and the passive reason, receive comparatively little discussion here. On the other hand the investigation of some topics that have much exercised scholars in recent years (such as the question of developments in Aristotle's psychology) is here advanced, and new areas of his thought are explored.

All the papers that were presented to the Symposium are included in a revised form. Those of Professor Mansion, Dr Graeser, Professor Berti and Dr Wiesner have been translated from their original languages. The editors wish to express their thanks to Dr Geoffrey Cubbin of Jesus College, Cambridge, for undertaking the translation of Dr Wiesner's paper.

It remains to thank the Faculty Board of Classics for a generous grant from the Henry Arthur Thomas Fund towards the expenses of the Symposium.

Cambridge
September 1977   G.E.R.L. & G.E.L.O.

LIST OF PARTICIPANTS IN THE SEVENTH SYMPOSIUM ARISTOTELICUM

Professor J.L.AKRILL, Brasenose College, Oxford, U.K.

Professor D.J.ALLAN, 83 Bainton Road, Oxford, U.K.

Professor P.AUBENQUE, 5 rue Berteaux-Dumas, 92200 Neuilly sur Seine,
    France

Professor E.BERTI, Via Nazareth 6, 35100 Padova, Italy

J.BRUNSCHWIG, 10 rue Bobierre de Vallière, 92 Bourg-la-Reine, France

Professor D.J.FURLEY, Department of Classics, Princeton University,
    Princeton, NJ 08540, USA

Dr A.GRAESER, Seminar für Klassische Philologie, Gesellschafts-
    strasse 6, 3012 Bern, Switzerland

Professor W.K.C.GUTHRIE, Downing College, Cambridge, U.K.

Dr W.HAASE, Philologisches Seminar der Universität Tübingen, Wilhelm-
    strasse 36, 74 Tübingen, W. Germany

Abbé Ch.LEFÈVRE, 60 Boulevard Vauban, F-59046, Lille, France

Dr G.E.R.LLOYD, King's College, Cambridge, U.K.

Professor S.MANSION, 5 Hooverplein, 3000 Leuven, Belgium

Professor P.MORAUX, Aristoteles-Archiv, 35 Ehrenbergstrasse, 1 Berlin
    33, W. Germany

Professor J.MOREAU, 34 rue de Lachassaigne, 33000, Bordeaux, France

Professor G.E.L.OWEN, King's College, Cambridge

Professor G.PATZIG, Philosophisches Seminar der Georg-August-
    Universität, Nikolausbergerweg 9C, 34 Göttingen, W. Germany

Dr D.A.REES, Jesus College, Oxford, U.K.

Dr M.SCHOFIELD, St John's College, Cambridge, U.K.

Professor J.B.SKEMP, 10 Highsett, Hills Road, Cambridge, U.K.

Dr R.SORABJI, University of London King's College, Strand, London
    WC2R 2LS, U.K.

Professor E. de STRYCKER, Prinsstraat 13, 2000 Antwerp, Belgium

P.THILLET, 3 rue de Bagno a Ripoli, 92350 Le Plessis-Robinson,
    France

Professor G.VERBEKE, de Croyplein-Winksele, 3009 Leuven, Belgium

Professor W.J.VERDENIUS, Homeruslaan 53, Zeist, Holland

Professor C.J. de VOGEL, Oosterenbanweg 24, Renesse (Zld.), Holland

Dr J.WIESNER, Mollnerweg 25, D - 1 Berlin 47, W. Germany

Dr M.WOODS, Brasenose College, Oxford, U.K.

1: SOUL AND LIFE IN THE *DE ANIMA*

S.Mansion

As the title of the treatise[1] and the content of the first chapter
indicate, the problem which Aristotle proposes to examine in the *De
anima* is: What is the soul? Other formulas such as What is man?
What is a living being? What is life?, which would perhaps better
correspond to the real content of the work, are not even alluded to.
No doubt it is the *human* soul that is primarily envisaged in such a
question; but Aristotle soon (in the form of a reproach addressed
to other philosophers) expresses his intention of not restricting
his investigation to that kind of soul (402b1-2). He is well
aware of the fact that he is not the first to have asked what the
soul is and, though he is not quite satisfied with the ancients'
approach to the question,[2] neither is he prepared to reject their
general problem. For him too, the first thing is to know what the
essence of the soul is and to this he devotes his main endeavour.

The important first chapter enumerates the various requirements
of a study of this kind, from which the following may be selected.
Apart from the fact that it is always difficult to look for the
essence of something, because for that there is no common method
(402a12-22), in the case of the soul the further question will
also have to be asked whether there exists a single *logos* for all
the types of soul (402b1-9). The danger here would be to posit a
'dialectical and empty' definition from which no account conformable
to experience could be given of the properties of our subject
(402b26-403a2; 402b16-26).

The knowledge of the soul is of great value, both because of
its dignity (402a1-4) and because this knowledge greatly contributes to the advance of truth in general and particularly to our
understanding of *nature*, 'for the soul is in some sense the
principle of animal life' (402a4-7). The contrast between the soul
itself and the soul in its function as principle for the living
being will immediately give rise to another distinction bearing on
the subject of investigation - namely the essence and nature of the

soul and everything connected with it - for a difference should be
marked here between what affects the soul itself and what belongs to
animals (living beings) on account of their soul (402a7-10, 403a3-5).
And Aristotle specifies the meaning and the implications of this
distinction: what seems proper to the soul is the activity of
thinking; now, if the latter can be exercised without the body, and
in this case only, the consequence will be that the soul will be
capable of a separate existence (403a7-12).

Thus from this simple reading of a part of chapter 1, it appears
that, for Aristotle just as for Plato and the Pythagoreans, the
(human) soul is at the same time the principle of life and something
which, in so far as it is the seat of consciousness, is distinct
from the body to such an extent that one might wonder whether it
could not subsist after death. It is clear then that Aristotle
starts thinking about the soul on the basis of ancient conceptions
about it. For it is a well known fact that the word ψυχή originally
meant the principle which distinguishes the living from the non-
living or the dead, something that was first thought of as what
leaves a man when he dies. But upon this first sense a second one
was soon grafted, which appears for the first time with ·the Orphics
and the Pythagoreans. These thinkers conceive of man as being in
his true nature an eternal and rational being to whom belongs the
task of governing a body. The soul then is in itself 'spiritual'.
Its more or less forced union with a body ceases at death. If it
succeeds in avoiding reincarnation, it maintains its existence as a
spirit.[3] Although these two ideas of ψυχή (principle of life and
principle of consciousness) do not coincide, they are far from being
opposed to one another. For it is self-evident that, even conceived
as a spirit, the soul is what animates, and gives life to, the body.
Conversely mental activities are regarded as proper to living beings.
Still it is not clear at first sight how these two 'functions' are
joined together, and one of the tasks of a philosophical reflection
about the soul will be to show how they are related to one another.

Correlatively the term 'body' is seen to have two meanings also.
If the soul is what animates, the body is that upon which this
activity is exerted. The distinction is necessary. There are two
'principles' in a living being since life can disappear without the
thing that was living being completely annihilated: the existence of

the corpse testifies that the body is something other than the soul.[4]
But there is a much more familiar distinction between soul and body,
which does not coincide with the former one: the soul being taken as
the seat of consciousness, of the inner life, the body will be what
is seen, what is perceived by other people, the external face of my
being - in a word, all that can be investigated by someone else. In
this sense, the physiological functioning *qua* event in the physical
world belongs to the body, not to the soul. Of course, we know that
it is in virtue of being animated by the soul that the body functions,
and we know also that the body plays a part in producing the
impressions the soul is aware of (the body is affected in such and
such a way); it remains nevertheless possible to distinguish the
external from the internal side of the events of our life and quite
naturally we link the first to the body and the second to the soul,
thus narrowing more or less deliberately the meaning of the latter
word. Taking things in that way, Aristotle can talk about activities
common to body and soul and of activities proper to the soul.

Since this manner of opposing the body to the soul is rooted in
our everyday experience, it is no wonder that it survives philosophical
theories and in particular the hylomorphic conception of the body-
soul relationship expounded in the *De anima* . Indeed it is a fact
that in at least one passage of the latter work and in several places
in the *Parva naturalia*, for example, the soul is identified with the
seat of consciousness and the body with the non-conscious part of our
being.[5]

So the perception of an opposition between consciousness and body
could very well have been for Aristotle, as for many others, the
phenomenological starting point of the problem. But what exactly is
this problem and what is Aristotle's exact purpose - which, he thinks,
has not been achieved by his predecessors? The methodological
chapter which opens the *De anima* with its critical review of the
opinions of the ancient philosophers (I 2-5) might enlighten us about
this. To put it quite schematically, what the philosopher regards as
essential, and blames earlier thinkers for not having achieved, is to
propose a conception of the soul applicable to all living beings,
accounting both for their various powers (in the first place movement
and perception) and at the same time for their unity - by explaining
how the body and its principle of life are adapted to one another -

in short, a conception in which both aspects of the soul designated above are harmoniously united.

In a former paper, I expressed the opinion that Aristotle did not reach the conception of life he advances in the *De anima* directly.[6] My hypothesis was as follows. Aristotle, a systematic thinker, first thought he could amalgamate the two different ideas generally held about the soul by assimilating life to consciousness. In such an outlook, where things are as it were seen from above, where the essence of life appears, so to speak, in its pure form, in the power of thinking, the difficulty is to understand the more primitive vital activities (nutrition, growth, reproduction). It seems possible only by allowing the most rudimentary living being some measure of consciousness, as Plato had done.[7] I offered some reasons for conjecturing that Aristotle did the same at the period under consideration, that is when he wrote the *Protrepticus*. But the biologist in him could not for long be satisfied with such a solution, for it does not really account for the various vital functions, which experience reveals as specific and relatively autonomous. Approaching, then, the problem from the other end and giving a fundamental definition of life through these primitive functions themselves, Aristotle tried to grasp all the other vital activities beginning from them. This led him to arrange these activities in a definite order, which manifests the progressive unfolding of the single perfection, called life, in the higher and higher degrees it can achieve. The difficulty that awaits the new theory is easy to foresee. It is the converse of that of the previous theory. It is thinking now which is difficult to conceive of as a vital activity, if the fundamental sense of the latter phrase is biological.

My intention here is neither to call attention to these two concepts of life again, nor to give fresh tokens of their presence in two successive stages of Aristotle's philosophy, but rather to examine, in the context of the *De anima*, how the old approach - that which asks what the soul is - still interferes with the new one - that which decides first to investigate what life is and then to conceive of its principle, the soul, accordingly.

Let me first indicate how such an interference is possible in the second conception of life, whereas it is less apparent in the former.

It we conceive of life as consisting essentially of consciousness,

it is possible to start, as from a relatively clear definition, from
the current idea which makes the soul the seat of mental activities.
It is not that we claim to have an intuition of the essence of the
soul, but since what is conscious is by definition immediately
accessible to us, in conceiving the soul as the source of 'the mental',
we put forward an idea of it which is directly meaningful. The soul
being thus more or less known in itself, the problem will be to link
the various manifestations of consciousness to one another[8] and to
explain how the soul animates the body, i.e. how a non-corporeal
principle can show its presence in the body through activities that
are usually recognized as characteristic of a living body (the biological functioning). The answer may perhaps be laborious and even
unsatisfactory in some measure; but the problem certainly is this:
to describe the result of the soul's presence in the body – the soul
whose nature we know, or believe we know.

From the point of view proper to the *De anima*, on the contrary,
where the soul, the principle of life, is conceived as the form of
the living being, it is on the living body that the attention is
first focused and the main effort is directed towards defining the
peculiar state of the body which distinguishes the living from the
dead, a state regarded as so essential that what it affects is
thought to change its nature, to be altered down to its very substance, when it dies. When the matter is investigated strictly from
this point of view, the old problems – concerning what the soul is
in itself – lose much of their interest, if not of their meaning.
The unity of the living being is given or presupposed: it is *its*
essence which is being investigated. To say that the soul is its
substantial form is simply to state that life is essential to it; it
is simply to take in all seriousness the formula according to which
the soul is that whereby we live.[9] But Aristotle, as is well known,
scarcely differentiates between form and essence. To say that the
soul is the form of the body, then, is more or less equivalent to
saying that the essence of the living being is its soul, a statement
that Aristotle never quite avers, but that he does not regard as
simply unacceptable.[10] Now if this is so, it will be seen that the
question 'What is soul?' is equivalent to 'What is the essence of
something which is the essence of a living being?' – a question whose
meaning is far from clear. So, strictly following the logic of

Aristotle's second conception and taking account of the identification
of form with essence, it is hard to see what question could still be
asked about the soul in itself, except in virtue of an abstraction
similar to that made when we ask what *whiteness* is or what *justice* is
while knowing very well that these are not subjects possessing an
essence of their own.[11] Unfortunately for the theory, the question
'What is the soul?' continues to have a very clear intuitive meaning,
i.e., 'What is the conscious subject?', and above all, 'What is the
thinking subject?'. If we have to reply to the latter question that
it is not the compound of matter and form which thinks, at least in
the sense that thinking is not the act of a bodily organ, we come up
against a non-material subject, having an essence of its own, which,
as form of the body, can be called the essence of the compound, a
very difficult thing to conceive. For when talking about such a
subject, we are referring both to what it is in itself and to what
the compound is: the soul, then, seems to be the essence of man
without matter,[12] something quite close to a Platonic Idea.[13]

In short, when posing the problems from the point of view of soul,
it makes sense to ask what the soul is, because it is then regarded
as a subject possessing an essence and an activity. Starting from
the notion of life, on the other hand, it is the living being which
is thought of as the true subject and the soul is only a principle
of it, a principle to which apparently one cannot properly attribute
an essence or an activity, except fictitiously, in virtue of an
abstraction.

If such is the situation, interferences are inevitable because in
establishing the second conception we are bound to come across
ordinary ways of speaking which will have to be corrected when they
are misleading (within the framework of the theory). But these
interferences can even become conflicts if it appears that there
really exists an activity of man independent of matter.

Let us come back to the first chapter. After explaining that,
with the exception of the questionable case of thinking, all the
affections of the soul are at the same time affections of the body,
and having drawn the conclusion that they are forms embedded in
matter (λόγοι ἔνυλοι, 403a25), Aristotle has a long methodological
note about the different kinds of definition (403a25-b16), which he
himself regards as a digression (403b16). The passage bristles with

difficulties; the text is not everywhere sure and various minor
emendations have been proposed by modern editors. This is not the
place to make a detailed analysis of the text and I shall limit myself to pointing out some sufficiently clear features which are of
interest to us here.

The general meaning is as follows. Since the affections in
question are as described, the only correct definition of them is a
formula which takes account both of matter and form. Now, such a
definition is what the physicist must offer. Consequently it belongs
to the physicist to study the soul, if not all kinds of soul, at
least that which is linked in this way to the body. According to the
example given (anger), the definition taken as a model differs on the
one hand from that of the dialectician,[14] expressed in mental terms
(desire for retaliation),[15] and on the other hand from that of the
physicist who, wrongly, contents himself with describing bodily
modifications accompanying the event (boiling of the blood or of the
warm stuff around the heart). Of these two definitions, the first
one gives the form only, the second, the matter only (403b1-2),
whereas, if we want to give a faithful account of the object to be
defined, we should take both principles into consideration and
explain how the form demands such and such matter for its realization.[16] That this is truly the task of the physicist and that he
cannot leave it to someone else, restricting himself to a study of
the qualities of matter[17] only, is strongly asserted afterwards: the
φυσικός must take cognizance of *all* the properties, active and
passive, of a body of such a nature and of the matter embedded in
it.[18] To the example of anger is added that of a house, according
to the usual procedure of Aristotle, who is fond of illustrating an
exposé concerning a natural being with a model - clearer for us -
taken from art. To define a house either solely by its function as
a shelter against bad weather, or solely by the materials out of
which it is built is equally unsatisfactory: one must unite the two
in a *logos* accounting for the relationship between materials and
function (403b3-8).

There is nothing very surprising in all this if we recall *Physics*
II 1-2, with which the present section is in complete agreement.
Stranger at first sight is the presence of such an explanation at
the beginning of a treatise on the soul, as also is the consequent

attribution of the study of the soul (with slight reservations) to
the physicist. Since the two other representatives of the theoretical
sciences, namely mathematics and first philosophy, are referred to at
the end of the digression in order to distinguish their object and
their mode of knowing from those of the physicist (403b14-16), we can
be sure that this attribution is important from a theoretical point
of view. In so far as the soul is the seat of phenomena inseparable
from the body, it is an object of physics. The condition under which
the soul (or any other entity) could interest first philosophy is
indicated: it is that it should be separable from matter.[19] As for
the treatment 'in abstraction' of non-separated 'psychic' phenomena,
it is explicitly discarded,[20] a fact that is easily understandable
after what we have just explained: these phenomena are 'inseparable
from the physical matter of the animals'[21] and an abstraction of the
mathematical type is not practicable in their case.[22] The entire
section is thus logically quite consistent with its own (hylomorphic)
approach. But the difficulty is precisely that this approach, which
is clearly connected with problems about life, seems ill suited to
an enquiry about the soul: it is strange to commit to the physicist
a study which, without going so far as to examine our intellectual
faculties, will nevertheless have to pronounce on the nature of
mental activities such as perception and emotion.

Our puzzlement is all the more justified when we compare with one
another the examples of definitions that Aristotle gives. As has
been noted,[23] anger and a house are not to be put on a par, because,
among other reasons, the former is at least partly a 'psychic'
process, whereas the latter is a physical object. In interpreting
the relationship between anger as an emotion and anger as a bodily
excitation in terms of end and means (i.e. form and matter), we will
not have accounted for the specific character of the feeling of
anger.[24] It is clear then that the two different ways of posing the
problems clash, not only at the level of intellect but already at that
of sensory consciousness, because the facts belonging to the latter
have a meaning peculiar to them, which must be expressed in mental
terms if we do not want to reduce them to the inferior order of the
physiological.

Faced with such a situation, shall we pronounce the Aristotelian
undertaking - which claimed to account for the whole of the soul in

conceiving it as the (formal) principle of life - a failure? Before we do so, a more thorough examination of the meaning of this undertaking is clearly necessary.

Let us call the 'biological sense' of an activity proper to a living being the way in which such an activity contributes to the carrying out of the primary ends of life: maintenance and development of its own being, production of another like itself. Aristotle's effort tends not only to discover a biological meaning for every vital activity, but also to arrange all these activities in an ascending order according to that meaning. According to this view of things, one activity will be declared higher than another both because it is conditioned by that other, without which it cannot exist, and because it makes it possible for the primary biological functions to be exerted in a more perfect manner. Such is for instance the relationship which exists between the powers of vegetative life and sensibility, or between touch and the other senses.[25] Though Aristotle's aim in proposing this order is to establish the soul clearly as the principle of unity for a variety of manifestations of life,[26] it is no less evident that he is careful to preserve the originality of each of these and of each type of soul.[27] He is quite convinced that he has achieved his purpose, thanks to the flexibility of his principles. If, indeed, what is biological in the Aristotelian theory is a condition for what is 'psychic', if the meaning of the 'psychic' is rooted in the biological, the biological, in its turn, exists only for the 'psychic'.[28] The result is that the 'psychic' possesses a meaning proper to itself, which one could not define by its biological role alone. Once we admit that perception is a vital power, that a being equipped with it realizes, thanks to it, a specific type of life, and that consequently the presence together in the same being of the θρεπτικόν and of the αἰσθητικόν is not the result of a chance meeting (it is necessary if the animal *must* live), we are prepared to understand that the soul of an animal is to be thought of as its principle of life in the sense of the (one) principle of *this specific type of life*. Under the general description of 'formal essence of the living being',[29] we will thus be able to include souls at different levels, corresponding to different degrees of life, these being determined by the hierarchically ordered powers of action which living beings possess. But, since

these powers are all vital, they do not depend on different souls but
are the different faculties of one and the same soul (II 414a29-32).
And in order to know the particular nature of these faculties, it is
their activities that must be examined, activities whose essences
will in their turn be defined by studying their proper object (415a
14-22).

Let us now turn back to the objection we raised above against the
Aristotelian undertaking in order to see whether at least a partial
answer may not be derived from the point that has just been explained. According to the logic of the theory, the facts of sensibility
must be recognized and described in their peculiar modality, which
is 'psychic' (mental). But one must not forget that even though mental they are *felt in a body*. The corporeal conditions of that type
of consciousness are thus inseparably bound up with its own being.
Further, the philosophical interpretation to be given of these facts
must not overlook their biological significance, upon which the
'psychic' significance is, so to speak, superimposed: if for instance thirst as felt is neither a simple state of physiological
deficiency nor the exact reflection of this state at the level of
sensibility,[30] if thirst has a 'psychic' finality of its own (it is
a striving for pleasure and a flight from pain), one must not forget
that such an impulse *helps* to maintain the animal alive. The same
thing can be said of the other manifestations of sensory consciousness: they possess a power of a 'psychic' nature, certain physiological conditions and a meaning (to be discerned and determined in
each case) for the life of the whole animal. The Aristotelian conception seems thus flexible enough to make room inside one and the
same vital principle for activities of various orders, which, however, can all be connected with the vital functions thanks to their
mutual concatenation.

Still, we must not turn a blind eye to the fact that the main
difficulty remains. At each stage of life a rupture exists between
the lower and the higher degree since, precisely because of the kind
of relationship they have with one another, the lower one, which is
a condition making the higher one possible, in no way helps us to
surmise what this will be. It is only afterwards, when considering
how an animal lives, that I can perceive how useful sensibility is
for the achievement of the biological functions. In itself, though,

sensibility appears to me to break with the level of physiological
mechanisms, which in no way account for it, and to initiate a new
mode of existence that is *sui generis*, that of consciousness. And
of course there is no need to emphasize that a break of a similar
kind occurs when passing from perceptual to intellectual life.
Aristotle is perfectly aware of this and often calls attention to
it.[31]

But looking more closely at the problem, we are perhaps bound to
say that a gap of the same sort already exists between means and
end in an artefact and still more between physiological mechanisms
and the being which lives thanks to them. The arrangement of
stones, bricks and timber which will make a house is significant
only for him who knows what a house is in the formal sense; the
arrangement of the parts of a plant is meaningful only for him who
is aware of the finality of its organs. At most, it can suggest
this finality by analogy with some known cases.

All this in the end amounts to saying that the teleological
explanation crops up all at once, at the moment when we perceive
the unifying principle of a multiplicity of formerly scattered
phenomena. The Aristotelian theory of life wholly proceeds from
such an intuition. What enables us to run together beings as
different in their appearance as a tree, an insect and a man is
the insight which reveals in them the presence of similar functions
(nutrition, growth, reproduction) and then synthesizes this group
of functions under the one concept of vegetative life. Now this
insight, though prepared for by observation and a descriptive knowledge of the phenomena, is not their logical consequence: we can
very well be blind for a long time to the finality of a biological
mechanism we are quite capable of describing.[32]

This indicates that there is always a distance between the form
and its corresponding matter and, if we remember this, we can perhaps account for a rather puzzling formula of Aristotle at the
beginning of the second book of the *De anima*. The philosopher has
just outlined his own definition of the soul, in contrast with the
unsatisfactory theories of his predecessors: the soul is the substance in the sense of the form of the living being. But he wants
to specify the correlative principle of such a form and he repeats
three times over: the soul is the formal *ousia*, the first entelechy

of a *natural body having life potentially in it*, that is of an organized body (412a19-21, 27-28, 412b5-6). This is a puzzling formula
for two reasons: first because a sound metaphysics seems to demand
that the correlate of a substantial form be a matter deprived of any
determination; secondly because the character of 'having life potentially' which is attributed to the organized body, that is to a body
made of various tissues and organs, is very hard to conceive. For
the very notions of tissue and organ clearly implicate life, as
Aristotle is the first to admit.[33] But the phrase can make sense if
we consider that, even after we have found the unifying principle of
the living being, which gives their specific nature to its parts,
the difference between these and the form (of the whole) does not
disappear: if it is true that they exist as organs in virtue of the
form, it is also true that the existence of the living being depends
upon them - indeed some of the organs are its indispensable condition.[34] If, then, the organized body having life potentially can in
no way be *isolated* - for clearly it at no time exists in such a
state[35] - we are still entitled to say that, *in a living being*, the
corporeal parts with their organization are but means compared with
that end which is the life of the whole, since none of them alone and
by itself carries that life into effect.[36] Aristotle's bold formula
emphasizes thus that the relation of matter to form, which is specific to life, is set up at a high level of elaboration of matter.
Understood in the right way, it does not minimize the role of form
- quite the contrary - for the form of a living being is, according
to this view, an end which shapes the very instruments of its
realization.

What lesson is to be drawn from the comparison just made between
the form of an artefact or of a living being in general and the form
of the higher living beings, endowed with consciousness? When
starting the investigation from the point of view of life, we could
regard the concept of form as broad enough to enable us to understand
the soul of an animal as the principle of its various functions. But
we meet with difficulties as soon as we perceive that sensibility,
though on this view conceived as necessary for keeping the animal
alive - even thought of as an agent of a biologically better life -
is not represented in its most characteristic and most obvious signification, that of a fact of consciousness. Are we then to give up

the 'vitalistic' approach at this point and go back to the common
idea of soul as the seat of consciousness, thus throwing away all the
advantages offered by the hylomorphic theory for the unity of the
living being? The points made above about the role of the vital form
could help us to answer this in the negative. Once we admit that the
kind of life proper to an animal, that is, sensitive life, is, according to the hylomorphic theory, essentially a mode of *life*, to acknowledge that what characterizes this particular way of living is its
mental quality introduces no inconsistency in the doctrine. For on
this view the mental belongs to the soul *as a form*. It is thus firmly
rooted in the unity of the living being. But, as was said, it is
from the point of view of the end that the necessity of the materials
and of the sequence leading to the achievement of the end is understood. If then there exists between vegetative and sensitive life
(between the physiological and the 'psychic') the relationship of
means to end that was pointed out above, it is not to the former that
we must turn in order to understand the latter, but the other way
round. Consequently the 'psychic' can only be comprehended in and by
itself. Passing from vegetative to sensitive life, one thus necessarily goes up a step, but the main point is to realize that this is
a step up the scale *of life*. The experience of sensory consciousness tells us that living can (also) be discerning differences and
striving consciously towards some goals.[37] That activities of that
type, in so far as they are felt, are not to be identified with what
constitutes their physiological aspect, is quite obvious. They thus
belong to the form of the living being (to its soul) in a much
stricter way than the other vital activities and for that reason they
can be distinguished from the former by being called *psychic*. Once
we grant this, we see that it makes sense to talk about the soul,
which is the form of an animal, as the source and seat of consciousness, without falling back, in so doing, on the soul-minded approach
to the problems that the hylomorphic doctrine wished to overcome.

But, if the preceding point is accepted, why could it not be
applied *mutatis mutandis* to the problem of the intellect and its
relationship to the soul?

We are not concerned here with the problem of the immortality of
the human soul, about which Aristotle says nothing definite (as is
well known, the νοῦς alone, not the soul, is declared immortal, III

5, 430a22-3), but rather with the question whether the idea of a
rational level of life has a meaning, as compared with that of the
sensitive level, and with whether the rational activity of man can
be connected with the soul as form, as deriving from a faculty of
the latter, without losing anything of its specific dignity. Aristotle, though showing some hesitation,[38] certainly wanted to pose
the problem of rationality in these terms. For, on the one hand,
from the start he regards thinking as proceeding from the soul (I
1, 403a3-10) and places the νοῦς, or dianoetic power, among the
faculties proper to the living being at the very moment when he
accounts for his definition of soul as form.[39] On the other hand,
the intellectual faculties are compared with the sensible ones and
their importance for the conduct of life is proclaimed for the same
reasons: the νοῦς πρακτικός, a power of discrimination, tells us
what is to be avoided or pursued, βούλησις is the appetite which
originates movement in accordance with reasoning.[40] Now, if we
were able to talk about a biological function of sensibility because
of its usefulness - even its necessity - for the survival of the
animal, can we not talk in the same way about the faculty proper to
man and admit that intelligence carries on from instinct in providing for the primordial needs of man?[41] In other words, the leading
function of the νοῦς πρακτικός for the conduct of human life appears
to be rooted in the biological nature of man. Of course, it cannot
be reduced to the function of maintaining man in existence,[42] but
it is essential, according to Aristotle's approach, to seek its
first meaning in connection with the chief end of life. That sense
once found, will it then be possible to integrate with it what remains of the significance and the value of human rationality?

   The requirements of the question are easy to perceive: in order
to be able to place rationality among the vital powers (the powers
of the soul conceived as the principle of life), the theory offers
us nothing except the idea of a 'better life'. It has just been
pointed out that the (necessary) connection of this 'better life'
with life in general can be quite easily established. The problem
is thus to provide the 'better' of the better life with a content.
This content cannot emerge from pondering on the idea of a 'better',
nor even from a mere reflection upon the previous level, that of
sensibility, for, though such a reflection could make us surmise

that a life better than the sensitive one would be a 'more conscious' life, the 'how' of this more conscious life and the 'why' of its superiority can in no way be guessed from observation of the sensitive level. The rupture indicated above between two degrees of life is present here too, and necessarily so. The question therefore is rather to know how we are to understand rationality as a better way of living *from our own experience of what it is*. Rationality must thus first be defined in itself. Now, following Aristotle in his endeavour to analyse an intellectual act and so to delineate the essence of rationality, one will say that intellection is a dematerialization and that the intellect is immaterial.[43] One is then confronted with a problem which looks very much like a deadlock: how are we to integrate this immaterial νοῦς with the living body, or even with the soul that makes it live, without giving to the word 'life' two irreconcilable meanings – animation of a body on the one hand and thought on the other?

Indeed it is well known that Aristotle says nothing definite about the way in which the intellect must be integrated with the human soul and that he has left his interpreters quite puzzled about it. I shall not try to remedy this state of affairs.

But perhaps I might be allowed to indicate by way of conclusion a direction which an Aristotelian investigation about life might take in order to get out of the difficulty.

Leaving aside the metaphysical puzzles, we should come back to human action. As a matter of fact, it is Aristotle himself who suggests this, for he gives the νοῦς πρακτικός the highest role in the government of our life. For a mortal being, whose reason is its leading faculty, the question is not to know whether reason must assume and perfect the powers which tend to the preservation of this being's existence; so much is obvious. The simple fact of being alive appears to us as a good, questionable only on second thoughts and by arguments assessed by reason. But the problem which awaits all the specialists of the good life (the moralists) is rather to decide whether the horizon of human values is absolutely limited by death, whether there is not among our values something worth sacrificing one's (biological) life for. If there is, does not such a sacrifice, lucidly accepted, testify to our possessing a kind of life that, in some manner, overcomes the loss of our biological life? That such an action could make sense for man, that it could be a reasonable way of 'conducting one's life', would then amount to affirming a will to live of which the love of terrestrial life is but a reflection. Thereby would be revealed to us the form of life proper to a mind: ἡ γὰρ νοῦ ἐνέργεια ζωή.[44]

NOTES

1 A title which most probably goes back to Aristotle himself, since he often refers to what has been said ἐν τοῖς περὶ ψυχῆς. See e.g. *Sens*. 436b10, 14, 439a8, 16, 440b28; *Mem*. 449b31; *Somn*. 455a8; *GA* 736a37, 786b25, 788b2, etc.

2 See his criticisms in chs. 2-5 of Book I.

3 Cf. I.M.Crombie, *An examination of Plato's doctrines* I (London 1962), 298-300. The use that Socrates - and Plato after him - made of such a conception of the soul is well known. For Socrates, as Prof. Guthrie remarks, the *psyche* is the true self and the body is only its instrument (W.K.C.Guthrie, *A history of Greek philosophy* III (Cambridge 1969), 469). On the history of the concept of soul and the two tendencies present in Greek psychology in the interpretation of this concept, see article 'Psyche' (by O.Gigon) in *Lexikon der alten Welt*, coll. 2468-9. Of course I do not want to say that there have been no other conceptions of the soul than those we have outlined, nor that these are definite theories about what the soul is. I simply observe that the two main functions that were attributed to the soul are the animation of a body on the one hand and the power of feeling, perceiving and thinking (the power of 'conscious-ness' in the broadest sense of the word) on the other. Now, whereas the former function seems always to have been allotted to the soul (cf. the Homeric soul), the latter was apparently only recognized later and remained distinct.

4 Compare Homer's use of σῶμα in the sense of 'corpse'.

5 *De An*. 434a27-b14; *Sens*. 436a6-10, 436b2-8, 448b26-8; *Mem*. 450a27-30, 453a14-16, b8-9; *Somn*. 453b11-14, 454a7-11; *Insomn*. 458b1-3, 13; *Juv*. 468b12-15, etc. To answer a difficulty raised by Dr R.Sorabji, let me point out that, of course, none of these passages commits Aristotle to a conception of the soul as a *separable* subject of consciousness. All that these texts show in talking about what is common to body and soul or what is proper to either, and in asking whether and how 'the soul' per-ceives something, is that Aristotle is here resorting to the familiar concept of the soul as 'what is aware of what is going on' in contrast with the body and its blind mechanisms. On the difference between this Aristotelian body-soul and the Cartesian

body-mind couple, see C.H.Kahn, 'Sensation and consciousness in Aristotle's psychology' *Archiv Gesch. Philos.* 18 (1966), 44, 48, 70.

6 'Deux définitions différentes de la vie chez Aristote?' *Rev. Philos. Louvain* 71 (1973), 425-50. I am basing my discussion on this article.

7 *Ti.* 77b-c.

8 Aristotle does that by arranging the various kinds of perception and forms of intellectual knowledge in an ascending scale, dominated by contemplative thinking. It is the cognitive aspect of consciousness which is mostly taken into account, but the 'affective' aspect (feelings, emotions) is not totally ignored; see *Protrepticus*, fr. 14.

9 II 2, 414a4: ᾧ ζῶμεν καὶ αἰσθανόμεθα; 414a12-13: ᾧ ζῶμεν καὶ αἰσθανόμεθα καὶ διανοούμεθα πρώτως. καί is clearly explicative here: perceiving and thinking are reckoned among vital activities.

10 See *Metaph.* Z, 1035b14-16, 1036a16-17, 24, 1037a7-10, 28-29; H, 1043a29-36, b2-4. On this point see J.L.Ackrill, 'Aristotle's definitions of *Psyche*', *Proc. Arist. Soc.* 73 (1972-3), 123-4.

11 Or in virtue of an abstraction analogous to that of the mathematician defining the triangle or the straight line in themselves, although knowing that they exist only in the physical world.

12 Cf. *Metaph.* Z, 1032b14.

13 See A.Mansion, 'L'immortalité de l'âme et de l'intellect d'après Aristote', *Rev. Philos. Louvain* 51 (1953), 455.

14 For the pejorative undertone of this term here (403a29), see 403a2 with Hicks' notes at both places and Ross's at 403a29. See also P.Aubenque, 'Sur la définition aristotélicienne de la colère', *Revue Philosophique de la France et de l'Etranger* 82 (1957), 302-4.

15 I shall use mental and 'psychic' (in inverted commas) as synonyms to cover the whole range of phenomena we are aware of (perceptions, feelings, emotions, thoughts, etc.), and reserve psychic (without inverted commas) to mean what belongs to the soul as such (as we shall see, it can be appropriate to say that an activity belongs to the soul even when the soul is regarded as the form of the living being, cf. below, p.13).
    Dr Sorabji asks whether Aristotle picked out mental acts as a distinct class of phenomena (in 'Body and soul in Aristotle', *Philosophy* 49 (1974), 68 sqq.). Certainly not in a Cartesian fashion, he answers, correctly. But, he goes on, Aristotle would not be prepared to accept a materialist view of things either (pp.75 sqq.). For Aristotle anger or any other feeling or perception cannot be *reduced* to a physiological process. That is all we need here.

16 403b2-3. We read: ὁ μὲν γὰρ λόγος ὅδε τοῦ πράγματος with
   Förster and Ross.

17 Of matter in the sense in which it was contrasted with the form
   in 403b1-2.

18 403b11-12: τοῦ τοιουδί σώματος καὶ τῆς τοιαύτης ὕλης. For the
   meaning of this phrase, see Hicks' note *ad loc*.

19 ᾗ δὲ κεχωρισμένα, 403b15; cf. *PA* I 641a21-b10.

20 403b19. It is another point that is made in the obscure comparison of the soul with a straight line in 403a12-15: the straight
   line *qua* straight touches a sphere at a point (a mathematical
   proposition), but, since the straight line necessarily involves
   some matter, and since that matter in its concrete existence will
   have some physical nature or other, it happens to the straight
   line (συμβαίνει: it necessarily can happen) to touch the bronze
   sphere at a point, something that would not happen if the straight
   line were separated (if it existed in the state of separation
   from sensible matter which it has in the mathematical abstraction).
   Such is also the case of the soul: if it has no activity independent from the body, it will have no existence without the body
   either.
       In our (tentative) interpretation, it is thus essential to
   keep χαλκῆς (against Ross) before σφαίρας (403a13-14), for the
   problem is that of the actual status of the soul, which in the
   case considered is necessarily united to a concrete body, just as
   are mathematical objects, which exist only in the physical world.
   Nothing is said yet in this passage of the kind of definition
   (abstract or concrete) of the soul and of its properties. But it
   is precisely that problem which is examined from 403a25 on and
   solved in the way we have indicated in the text.

21 403b17-18; cf. 403b3: ἀνάγκη δ' εἶναι τοῦτον ἐν ὕλῃ τοιᾳδί.

22 See my study: 'Τὸ σιμόν et la définition physique', *Naturphilosophie bei Aristoteles und Theophrast*, ed. I.Düring (Heidelberg
   1969), 127-8.

23 Cf. W.F.R.Hardie, 'Aristotle's treatment of the relation between
   the soul and the body', *Philos. Quart.* 14 (1964), 64. See also
   the interesting paper of P.Aubenque (*op.cit. n.14*).

24 This relationship of means to an end, moreover, is not a simple
   one. First of all, we must say that the emotion is the end of
   the bodily excitation if we accept the general idea that the
   physiological exists for the sake of the 'psychic'; further, the
   felt anger is endowed with a conscious finality of its own since
   it is a desire; and finally, this purposeful process itself
   finds room in the finality of the animal as a whole, as will be
   explained in the text.

25 On all this, see S.Mansion (*op.cit. n.6*), 440-4.

26 Cf. in particular II, 413a22-5, 413b10-414a4.

27 See for instance II, 414b19-33.

28 II, 415b18-20: πάντα γὰρ τὰ φυσικὰ σώματα τῆς ψυχῆς ὄργανα, καὶ καθάπερ τὰ τῶν ζῴων, οὕτω καὶ τὰ τῶν φυτῶν, ὡς ἕνεκα τῆς ψυχῆς ὄντα.

29 II, 412a5-6: κοινότατος λόγος αὐτῆς *sc.* τῆς ψυχῆς; 412a19-20.

30 Aristotle correctly observes this lack of an exact correspondence between the physiological and the 'psychic' in emotions and he rightly infers their psycho-somatic character from this: I, 403a 16-25.

31 I, 403a8, 408b18-19, 29-30; II, 413b24-7, 415a11-12, etc.

32 Conversely, one can have a goal clearly in mind without knowing by what means it is to be reached. That is the reason why the 'formal' definition of a house is insufficient.

33 See for instance *GC* I, 321b29-32; *GA* II, 734b24-31, 741a10-11; *Mete.* IV, 389b23-390a15. I have borrowed almost all these references from J.L.Ackrill's paper to which I refer the reader for a detailed exposition of this difficulty (*op.cit. n.10*, in particular pp. 127 sqq.).

34 Cf. *Metaph.* Z, 1035b14-28.

35 As opposed to the bronze of a statue, one is tempted to say. But let us not forget that a piece of bronze, even when 'not a statue', is not without any shape whatever. But, precisely because this shape is whatever you like, it is not noticed.
   A part that has been taken from a machine offers another misleading parallel for it keeps ˙its nature and capacity, it seems, even when separated from the whole in which it can actually function (cf. J.L.Ackrill (*op.cit. n.10*), 127-8). Could we not suggest however that the principle of unity, the form-giving principle, in this case is not the machine itself but its builder, or even more precisely, the idea in the builder's mind (ἀπὸ τέχνης δὲ γίγνεται ὅσων τὸ εἶδος ἐν τῇ ψυχῇ, *Metaph.* Z, 1032a32-b1)? The end by which a manufactured object is defined is thus in any case external to it.

36 As for the metaphysical difficulty indicated above, it could perhaps be solved by saying that the ultimate form integrates in itself the determinations of a lower order and, in so doing, gives them a new significance, prime matter alone putting up an unbreakable resistance to this integrating power of the form (cf. *Mete.* IV, 390a4-10).

37 When he considers the powers that are proper to animal soul, Aristotle classifies them in two main categories: the κριτικόν and the faculty of locomotion. The first is divided into perception and thinking (*De An.* III, 432a15-17). After some discussion, the second is distinguished into νοῦς and ὄρεξις, νοῦς being understood as imagination in animals deprived of thinking and as practical intellect for those that possess it; ὄρεξις also

comprises two levels: βούλησις, which conforms to reasoning, and ἐπιθυμία, which can oppose it (II, 433a9-26).

38 Cf. note 31.

39 II, 413a23, b12-13, 414a12-13, 32, b18, 415a7-9; see also III, 429a10-13.

40 III 9-10; see note 37.

41 Cf. *Ph.* II, 199a20-30 where a comparison between intelligent action, animal instinct and even the organization of plants is outlined on the basis of their usefulness for the living being.

42 Even animal instinct cannot be reduced to a power of survival, for it involves desire or aversion, i.e. pursuit of pleasure or avoidance of pain.

43 III 4 and 5, in particular 429b21-2: ὅλως ἄρα ὡς χωριστὰ τὰ πράγματα τῆς ὕλης, οὕτω καὶ τὰ περὶ τὸν νοῦν.

44 I wish to express my thanks to Dr Sorabji for his interesting comments on the French version of this paper. A thorough discussion of all the points he raised is unfortunately impossible here, but I have tried to take his observations into account as best I could. My thanks are also addressed to all who took part in the discussion. I found their remarks helpful for the revision of the paper. I am grateful to Prof. M.B.Crowe who kindly corrected my English.

Charles Lefèvre

La structure du *De anima* et des *Parva naturalia* ainsi que leurs
particularités doctrinales exigeraient une étude considérable.
Paulo ... minora canamus. On centrera ici l'attention sur un thème,
non négligeable au demeurant: l'âme dans son rapport à l'unité du
vivant, en vue de dégager les conclusions minimales qui concernent
la composition, voire, éventuellement, la chronologie relative.

Cette dernière formule voudrait traduire un réel scepticisme
vis-à-vis de théories évolutionnistes qui prétendraient reconstruire
dans le détail la genèse de nos textes. Mais il est devenu clair à
présent que la perspective d'une évolution chez notre philosophe
invite à mieux analyser la cohérence de ses développements et la
signification de ses doctrines. On songera notamment à l'étude
sagace et récente que Mlle Suzanne Mansion consacre à une question
proche de la nôtre: 'Deux définitions différentes de la vie chez
Aristote?'[1] Sans doute est-il rare que l'évolution du Stagirite
offre ainsi à ses interprètes des phases discernables. Mais
l'éventualité même d'une modification demande d'examiner, dans le
cas présent, ce qu'Aristote a pu juger compatible, ou non, avec
telle ou telle explication du rapport psycho-somatique.

En pratique, il convient de s'adresser d'abord au traité qui
expose *ex professo* sa théorie la plus personnelle. Soumettons dès
lors à l'analyse l'hylémorphisme du *De anima* et ses implications,
puis, en deux séries, les petits traités appelés *Parva naturalia*.

I

L'explication hylémorphique du vivant étant dans toutes les
mémoires,[2] je puis sans doute relever seulement que les divers
traits majeurs de la théorie se rattachent aisément à la définition
qui fait de l'âme une forme substantielle et, plus précisément,
l'acte premier du corps naturel organisé. C'est d'abord, bien
entendu, l'insistance sur l'unité biface, nettement psychophysique,
des phénomènes vitaux ou 'psychologiques' (à l'exception du

noétique); il n'y a pas plus à s'inquiéter de cette unité que de ce
qui unit la cire et la marque y imprimée: pour le vivant, exister,
c'est posséder ce que la forme signifie dans l'idée une d'un λόγος-
ούσία, forme dont on peut dire ce qui vaut de toute causalité formelle, à savoir qu'elle coïncide généralement avec les autres
éléments signifiants de l'être concret: les causalités finale et
motrice.[3] Ainsi règne-t-il entre le mort et le vif une radicale
'homonymie': celle de λόγοι qui ressortissent à des genres différents. Quant à la différence entre 'âmes' inférieures et supérieures,
Aristote la présente en recourant à la distinction entre le virtuel
et l'actuel: il en va comme pour les polygones élémentaires, qui
sont contenus en puissance dans les plus complexes; aussi bien
récusera-t-il en principe l'expression 'parties' de l'âme au profit
du terme 'facultés', moins suspect de voiler l'unité du co-principe
formel.

On se trouve donc bien en présence d'une doctrine riche et cohérente: la formule canonique entretient des liens d'inclusion
réciproque avec les traits majeurs rappelés à l'instant: donné psychophysique, unité substantielle, triade forme-fin-motricité,
homonymie, gradation des facultés. Ce sont, sans nul doute, autant
de façons d'exclure une 'two-substance view', c'est-à-dire un
dualisme qui fait de l'âme et du corps deux réalités, aussi con-
venablement adaptées que l'on voudra, mais pourtant distinctes.

Si un accord semble facile, sauf erreur, sur ces propos assez
généraux, il l'est moins, certes, quand il s'agit de préciser les
critères incontestables d'un tel dualisme incompatible avec l'hylémorphisme. M. Fr. Nuyens a innové courageusement en ce domaine,[4]
comme chacun sait, et ses thèses ont été soumises à un examen plus
ou moins approfondi par divers aristotélisants, qui les ont soit
rejetées (MM.I.Block, W.F.R.Hardie, I.Düring; celui-ci après une
phase d'adhésion), soit adoptées avec conviction en les vérifiant
(Mgr A.Mansion), en les rectifiant quelque peu (Sir David Ross) ou
en s'en faisant l'apologiste enthousiaste (Père R.-A.Gauthier).
Que j'aie été amené pour ma part, après avoir pratiqué diverses
contre-épreuves, à faire plutôt cause commune avec les premiers
nommés,[5] cela n'importe guère ici. Nous devons voir, je crois, si
et en quel sens la doctrine hylémorphique est compatible avec un
langage d'allure dualiste ou si, le cas échéant, le *De anima* présente

parfois, en outre, des traits *doctrinaux* dualistes qui devraient
attester en principe un stade plus ancien de l'élaboration.

Si on en croit M. Nuyens, ces traits dualistes - ceux d'un
dualisme modéré, qu'il baptise *instrumentisme vitaliste* - sont les
suivants: corps et âme apparaissent encore comme *deux* réalités qui
coopèrent à l'instar de l'instrument et de ce qui en use, l'âme est
localisée de façon plus ou moins complète dans le coeur et Aristote
discerne en elle deux *parties* principales, rationnelle et irrationnelle.[6] L'auteur, faut-il le dire, ne relève rien de semblable
dans notre traité. Mais peut-être convient-il de situer plus
soigneusement quelques textes par rapport aux trois traits cités à
l'instant. On s'occupera ensuite du passage célèbre de II 4 sur
la triple causalité de l'âme.

Un langage dualiste?
Pour éviter des contestations superflues, limitons ici nos emprunts
aux chapitres les plus certainement hylémorphiques, à savoir les
huit premiers du livre II.

Très énigmatique est, sans contredit, la réflexion qui clôt le
premier grand exposé hylémorphique, celui du chapitre 1. Le 'contenu
pour le moins fort inattendu' (Nuyens) de ce 'texte obscur d'Aristote'
(A.Mansion) a provoqué un déferlement de commentaires. Qu'on en juge.
Après avoir noté que, l'âme étant forme du corps, certaines facultés
- non pas toutes - sont l'acte de tels organes et dès lors 'inséparables', le philosophe déclare: 'De plus, on ne voit pas clairement si
l'âme est l'acte du corps à la façon dont le marin l'est du navire.'[7]

Estimant que ce 'curieux propos ... suggère une théorie de l'âme
complètement différente de celle que présente le reste du chapitre',
voire qu'il la 'contredit platement', Sir David Ross introduit un ἤ
devant la mention du pilote: le Stagirite se demanderait donc si
l'âme est bien, comme on l'a dit plus haut, l'acte du corps, ou si
leur rapport est celui du marin et de son embarcation.[8] Dans la
ligne de remarques émises récemment, il faut cependant noter que,
corrigé de la sorte, le texte mettrait formellement en doute ce que
tout le chapitre vient d'établir.[9] Il semble que le remède soit en
somme pire que le mal, si mal il y a; mais ne convient-il pas d'y
regarder de plus près?

On comprend aisément que le texte et le contexte immédiatement précédent aient orienté l'attention vers le problème de la 'séparabilité'. Ainsi Alexandre, auquel font écho la plupart des exégètes, repousse une hypothèse qui reconnaîtrait à la forme substantielle une indépendance au moins relative: la question posée n'évoque-t-elle point Platon plutôt qu'Aristote?[10] Mais ce dernier ne peut guère avoir déclaré indécise (ἄδηλον) une telle question, et c'est sans doute ce qui a poussé les successeurs d'Alexandre à restreindre cette séparation, ou sa possibilité, au cas de l'âme rationnelle; ainsi interprètent, avec des nuances dont nous n'avons pas à connaître ici, Thémistius (que suit fidèlement Nuyens), Philopon, Simplicius (dont s'inspire Rodier), Averroès, Albert le Grand.[11]

Mais, si considérable que soit ce concert d'opinions, je pense devoir lui opposer deux constatations. Aristote vient de déclarer que certaines parties pourraient bien être séparables et même d'expliquer pourquoi il en est ainsi;[12] pourquoi donc dirait-il qu'il n'y voit pas encore clair? D'autre part, il semble bien que l'auteur touche ici une autre question: l'expression ἔτι δέ a pour fonction classique chez lui d'annoncer des arguments ou des problèmes distincts.[13]

Ainsi peut-on penser qu'au terme d'un chapitre consacré totalement à la causalité formelle de l'âme, le philosophe indique un problème connexe: acte du corps, forme du vivant, l'âme peut-elle être encore considérée comme principe moteur? Certes, il a déjà indiqué que le corps dont il traite est un 'être naturel de telle sorte possédant en lui-même le principe du mouvement et du repos'.[14] Mais on aura reconnu ici la définition très générale de tout ce qui - le minéral compris - ressortit à la philosophie de la nature, par opposition aux objets fabriqués - la hache, par exemple - évoqués un peu plus haut; ce premier chapitre n'a rien dit encore de la causalité motrice que reconnaissaient à l'âme la plupart des philosophes. Aussi bien l'auteur indique-t-il lui-même le caractère encore schématique de ce premier exposé;[15] après une réflexion sur la définition causale, les chapitres suivants seront plus attentifs à l'ensemble du donné, notamment à cette causalité motrice.[16]

C'est dire à quelles conditions l'on peut approuver les interprètes qui songent plutôt - ou exclusivement - à ce problème. Il ne s'agit point de réfuter Platon ou ses pareils, en se demandant si l'âme pourrait n'être *que* motrice:[17] c'est ici une 'vraie question'.

D'autre part, l'auteur n'a pu combiner ce propos avec celui que
suppose l'interprétation précédente, c'est-à-dire envisager l'efficience de l'âme-acte et, en même temps, une séparation essentielle.[18]
Enfin et surtout, comme je l'ai fait observer ailleurs à M. Hardie,
on ne voit pas pourquoi il faudrait, en cette occasion ou autrement,
minimiser le sens philosophique rigoureux de l'hylémorphisme qu'Aristote applique à l'homme.[19]

Nous rejoignons ainsi, à maints égards, une interprétation que
professait A.Mansion. Selon lui, 'le philosophe veut dire: l'âme,
acte du corps, serait-elle en outre son moteur, comme le nautonnier?
Il répondra par l'affirmative.'[20] Mais ne peut-on estimer qu'une
telle formule implique une perspective instrumentiste? Il est vrai
que d'autres textes doivent auparavant nous retenir.

Au chapitre 4 du même livre II, traitant de la faculté végétative
et des fonctions qui la caractérisent (croissance, sustentation,
génération), Aristote s'explique sur les trois termes que concerne
leur exercice: l'âme 'primaire' qui est le pouvoir d'engendrer un
vivant pareil à soi, le corps qui en est le siège, enfin l'intermédiaire quelque peu mystérieux dénommé ᾧ τρέφει.[21] Ce dernier,
dit-il, 'est double, de même que "ce par quoi l'on dirige", c'est à
la fois la main et le gouvernail, celui-ci étant mû et moteur, celle-
là, motrice seulement'.[22] Et Aristote d'ajouter: 'Il est nécessaire
que toute nourriture puisse être élaborée; or, cette élaboration est
l'oeuvre du chaud; c'est pourquoi tout vivant possède de la chaleur.'[23] Quel sens précis faut-il attribuer à cette mention de la
chaleur et à la comparaison qui précède?

Dépassant les commentaires anciens dont il s'est entouré,[24] un
saint Thomas raisonne comme suit. A l'instar du gouvernail, l'ali-
ment (moteur mû) est un instrument, 'cuius forma nondum est anima'.
Or, il doit exister aussi, à l'image de la main, un 'moteur non mû',
instrument dit 'conjoint', qui sera la chaleur. 'Sicut igitur
gubernator movet temonem manu, navem autem temone, ita anima movet
calido alimentum, et alimento nutrit ... Si autem haec anima non
haberet instrumentum coniunctum, non esset actus alicuius partis
corporis; quod soli intellectui competit.'[25] La pensée de saint Thomas
ne nous concerne pas. Mais voilà une exégèse faite sur un texte
semblable au nôtre et attentive à situer les déclarations d'Aristote

dans la perspective hylémorphique du *De anima*. On pourrait ajouter
que ses explications ont simultanément une allure 'instrumentiste'
qui donne à penser en ce qui regarde la 'contradiction' entre les
deux théories: le fait de posséder un instrument (matériel) conjoint n'est-il pas présenté comme la *condition* de l'hylémorphisme?
Mais ceci ne nous dispense pas de tenter à notre tour un éclaircis-
sement, compte tenu du contexte indiqué.

On rappellera à cet égard que l'énigmatique ᾧ τρέφει suit immédiatement ce qui est dit de la faculté génératrice; comme ce propos
ne peut guère avoir quitté soudain l'esprit de l'auteur, ne doit-il
pas être pris en considération pour la suite du texte? D'autre
part, l'exégèse la plus cohérente à notre connaissance - celle qu'on
vient de résumer - offre au moins le léger inconvénient de voir dans
la chaleur vitale un κινοῦν μόνον, un moteur non mû. On pourra dès
lors remonter au coeur pour y trouver la source du mouvement[26] et
paraphraser comme suit les lignes b25-9:

> 'Venons-en au second des trois termes énumérés plus haut: ce par
> quoi opère la faculté végétative qui est chargée de la nutrition.
> Ce moyen, ᾧ τρέφει, est double: il en va du corps - le troisième
> terme - comme d'une embarcation, que contribuent à diriger deux
> facteurs: la main du pilote (solidaire de celui-ci et, à ce
> titre, moteur non mû par autre chose) et son gouvernail, mû par
> elle et déterminant le cap. Ainsi le pouvoir végétatif de l'âme
> agit-il à partir de l'organe qui en est solidaire: le coeur,
> source du mouvement et de la chaleur vitale; transmise aux ali-
> ments, celle-ci les élabore pour assurer les fonctions somatiques
> indiquées tantôt: croissance, maintien du type spécifique chez
> l'individu et transmission de ce type à la descendance.'

Certes, certains aspects de cette interprétation restent, comme
il est naturel, sujets à discussion. Mais on aura constaté que, dans
l'ensemble, ces quelques traits viennent, de facon significative,
nuancer dans un sens instrumentiste divers exposés que l'on pourrait
croire uniquement hylémorphiques.

On sera dès lors moins surpris de rencontrer, toujours au livre
II, un autre propos qui semble totalement étranger à la doctrine
dominante: l'explication que donne Aristote de la phonation. Ins-
pirer représente une nécessité, dit-il, à l'égard de (πρός) la chaleur interne:[27] l'air dessert le poumon et la région cardiaque, ce

qui explique sa pénétration profonde. Dès lors - et ici se greffe
une seconde utilité de l'inspiration - 'le choc de l'air qu'on
inspire, sous l'action de l'âme (*sc.* qui réside, ou qui agit) en
ces organes, contre ce qu'on appelle la trachée, c'est la voix'.[28]

M. Nuyens a bien vu l'allure instrumentiste de cette phrase. Il
fait appel à l'aide d'Alexandre, mais l'explication de ce dernier
se contente de développer ainsi les mots litigieux: ὑπὸ τῆς ἐν τοῖς
φωνητικοῖς ὀργάνοις δυνάμεως ψυχικῆς.[29] Or, peu importe qu'on
localise une faculté ou l'âme entière ... bien qu'Aristote parle en
fait de *l'âme*; d'autre part, le contexte invite à élargir l'identification des organes considérés, puisque le poumon et la région du
coeur, on l'a vu, entrent aussi en jeu dans l'ensemble du processus.

C'est ce qu'a compris saint Thomas, qui dit, plus fidèlement:
'Quae quidem percussio fit ab anima, quae est in his partibus, id
est principaliter in corde. Quamvis enim anima sit in toto corpore,
ut est forma animalis, tamen vis eius motiva est principaliter in
corde.'[30] Répétons que l'interprétation thomiste ne nous lie en
aucune manière. Mais Nuyens, lui, semble bien le vouloir: il cite
la seconde phrase, et elle seule, pour nous convaincre qu'il n'y a
point ici localisation de l'âme. Or, de deux choses l'une. Ou
bien 'vis motiva' n'a qu'un sens anodin et vise seulement un mécanisme secondaire; dans ce cas, saint Thomas aurait franchement
exténué le sens de la formule aristotélicienne ὑπὸ τῆς ἐν τούτοις
τοῖς μορίοις ψυχῆς. Ou bien elle équivaut à 'facultas motiva',
ce qui paraît plus conforme au texte rapporté par la première
phrase; mais alors l'exégète n'a point conçu qu'une formule instrumentiste pût contredire l'hylémorphisme. Le lecteur pourra conclure,
non sans avoir observé que ce bref passage du *De anima* semble bien
répondre, comme y tendaient déjà les deux précédents, à deux des
trois critères qui définissaient l'instrumentisme vitaliste: distinction entre le corps et l'âme analogue à celle qui règne entre
l'outil et ce qui en use, et localisation de l'âme (du moins
'principaliter') dans le coeur.[31]

Est-ce là seulement affaire de *langage*? Ou bien allons-nous dé-
créter que ces textes reflètent une *pensée* dualiste et doivent dès
lors être réputés nettement antérieurs à l'élaboration de l'hylémorphisme? Mais peut-être une telle disjonction est-elle incomplète:
n'aurions-nous pas ignoré certains aspects moins apparents de la
doctrine hylémorphique? Encore faudra-t-il d'abord analyser des

propos qui auraient quelque affinité avec le troisième trait: la
division de l'âme en parties rationnelle et irrationnelle.

Une distinction périmée?

Indiquée clairement dès le *Protreptique*,[32] ladite 'bi-partition'
se trouve-t-elle exclue, et en quel sens, par les exposés hylémorphiques? En demandant excuse de revenir sur des textes souvent
commentés déjà, je proposerais de reprendre cette question d'abord
à partir des *Ethiques*, ensuite à partir de *De anima*.

On se rappelle que la division en parties rationnelle et irrationnelle, si usuelle en 'philosophie pratique',[33] figure notamment
aux endroits qui commandent l'économie générale des *Ethiques* en
annonçant - ou en rappelant - la division entre vertus intellectuelles et vertus morales.[34] Celles-ci, dit en substance Aristote, ont
pour siège la partie qui est irrationnelle par elle-même, mais capable 'd'entendre raison' comme un fils obéit à son père; c'est 'ce
qui convoite et, d'une façon générale, désire';[35] comme l'a bien
noté Dirlmeier, la bipartition aristotélicienne se ramène pour
l'essentiel à ce rapport étroit entre les aspects intellectif et
tendanciel,[36] mais on n'oubliera pas qu'il peut régner ici des con-
flits tout autant que des relations harmonieuses: si le désir est
capable d'obéir, il peut aussi bien se rebeller contre les ordres
de la raison.

Selon divers critiques qu'appuyait récemment encore Mme Baudhuin,
une telle psychologie est 'inconciliable' avec celle du *De anima*, où
'cette division est explicitement reconnue inadéquate, tout comme la
division tripartite de Platon. Si on les accepte, on est amené à
disloquer certaines facultés de l'âme essentiellement différentes de
toutes les autres', par exemple l'ὄρεξις;[37] même si un texte de la
Politique paraît cantonner dans la partie irrationnelle de l'âme le
désir tout entier, celui-ci semble bien pouvoir normalement surgir
aussi dans la partie intellectuelle;[38] dans les traités de philosophie pratique, le désir est ainsi écartelé entre les 'parties'
rationnelle et irrationnelle, dont il chevauche la limite, alors que
le *De anima* en fait une faculté, une fonction diversifiée parmi
toutes celles qui émanent du même principe - ou co-principe - l'âme.

Que cette seconde option l'emporte, spéculativement parlant, aux
yeux d'Aristote, l'auteur lui-même a donc pris soin de nous en

assurer; qu'elle s'accorde au mieux avec une doctrine qui fait de
l'âme l'unique principe de détermination régissant le vivant hylé-
morphe, on vient de l'indiquer. Mais l'hylémorphisme exclut-il
absolument que l'accent soit mis plutôt - dans certains contextes
ou à des fins particulières - sur la différence de statut qui règne
entre les niveaux rationnel et irrationnel? J'avoue ne pas pouvoir
en décider si aisément; relisons dans cette perspective deux textes
bien connus.

En des passages parallèles de l'une et l'autre *Ethique*, Aristote
relève que le πολιτικός doit avoir quelque connaissance de l'âme et
se rappeler par exemple 'qu'un élément est irrationnel, l'autre
rationnel; qu'ils soient distincts comme les parties du corps et
comme tout le divisible, ou que cette dualité soit d'ordre logique,
inséparable par nature comme le convexe et le concave dans la cir-
conférence, cela ne nous concerne en rien à présent': tel est le
propos de l'*EN*.[39] Celui de l'*Eudémienne*, après un rappel analogue,
s'achève comme suit: 'cela ne fait nulle différence que l'âme soit
divisible ou qu'elle soit sans parties; elle a tout de même différentes puissances: celles qu'on a dites, tout comme, dans ce qui est
courbe, la concavité et la convexité sont inséparables'.[40]

En ce qui regarde la structure de l'âme, ces propos de nos *Ethiques* ne manifestent-ils pas une regrettable indécision? Il semble
cependant que le seul fait de poser la question révèle déjà la
problématique propre au *De anima*:[41] envisager que les facultés puissent ne différer *que* logiquement, à l'instar des points de vue
discernables dans un être mathématique, c'est songer non pas à une
âme-substance, mais à une âme-essence, bref, à l'hylémorphisme.[42]
Qui plus est, le second texte montre bien la nature factice de la
question: tout se passe comme si l'auteur, après avoir souligné le
point qui le concerne ici, c'est-à-dire la diversité des δυνάμεις
(qui n'importent pas toutes au moraliste), en venait à reléguer au
second plan la disjonction initiale pour déclarer sans ambages que
ces δυνάμεις ne diffèrent *que* conceptuellement.

Que penser alors des lignes qui introduisent le texte cité de
l'*EN*?[43] La 'politique', déclare en substance Aristote, exige quelque étude de l'âme; sans qu'il soit nécessaire de raffiner davantage
sur ce point, l'essentiel est exposé dans mes écrits exotériques,
notamment la bipartition ... Le Stagirite use ici d'un présent

(λέγεται), confirmant que ces écrits continuent à faire autorité pour la finalité indiquée.[44] Sans doute, puisque le texte de l'*EN* et, plus clairement encore, celui de l'*EE* supposent acquise au moins la problématique de l'hylémorphisme, l'absolution donnée à la psychologie du *Protreptique* pourrait représenter une addition due à l'auteur ou, du moins, porter la trace d'une retouche significative. Et pourtant, comme le *De anima* lui-même nous offre des formules d'allure dualiste, il semble bien que l'on puisse admettre sans réserves le sérieux et l'exactitude de la déclaration résumée ici: même après l'application de l'hylémorphisme au vivant, χρηστέον αὐτοῖς! L'unité substantielle de l'homme n'empêche pas que le problème majeur de la conduite ne revienne à pénétrer de raison l'ἄλογον.

Cette brève analyse ne nous dispense pas de la contre-épreuve annoncée, cette fois à partir du *De anima*. Aristote veut rejeter, a-t-on dit, deux 'partitions' de l'âme: ἅ τινες λέγουσι διορίζοντες, λογιστικὸν καὶ θυμικὸν καὶ ἐπιθυμητικόν, οἱ δὲ τὸ λόγον ἔχον καὶ τὸ ἄλογον. Et d'objecter aussitôt: κατὰ γὰρ τὰς διαφορὰς δι᾿ ἃς ταῦτα χωρίζουσι, καὶ ἄλλα φανεῖται μόρια μείζω διάστασιν ἔχοντα τούτων ..., c'est-à-dire, à suivre le principe de division qu'ils adoptent, on repère d'autres 'parties' beaucoup plus différentes que celles-là:[45] les principes végétatif, sensitif, imaginatif et désirant.[46] Le Stagirite semble ainsi attaquer solidairement les deux schémas; mais son argumentation tout entière les vise-t-elle l'un et l'autre? Rien n'est moins sûr.

À la division tripartite de Platon, Aristote reproche évidemment de laisser hors de compte des fonctions telles que la croissance et la sensation, marques distinctives des règnes végétal et animal, 'parties comportant des différences plus importantes', certes, que le θυμικόν et l'ἐπιθυμητικόν;[47] on ne se cachera pas la gravité d'une telle critique: l'âme ainsi conçue ne peut faire l'objet d'une psychologie générale, c'est-à-dire étendue à tous les vivants; elle ne peut davantage intégrer au sein d'une même forme hiérarchisée l'ensemble des fonctions vitales, y compris les plus humbles; bref, une telle conception est incompatible avec l'hylémorphisme.

Le même reproche vise-t-il la division en parties rationnelle et irrationnelle? Nous disposons d'un parallèle plus clair au chapitre suivant: répétant ses griefs à l'égard des 'partitions' de l'âme, le philosophe énumère à nouveau les diverses facultés qu'il reconnaît

lui-même, notant alors: ταῦτα γὰρ πλέον διαφέρει ἀλλήλων ἢ τὸ
ἐπιθυμητικὸν καὶ θυμικόν ...;[48] ce qui tantôt restait indistinct
se précise ici: seule la division platonicienne est visée. En
second lieu, la bipartition offrait certes l'inconvénient spéculatif d'écarteler les espèces du désir entre les niveaux rationnel
et irrationnel. Mais le passage cité à l'instant continue comme
suit: ὀρέξεις γίγνονται ἐναντίαι ἀλλήλαις, τοῦτο δὲ συμβαίνει ὅταν
ὁ λόγος καὶ αἱ ἐπιθυμίαι ἐναντίαι ὦσι;[49] l'écartèlement du désir
correspond ainsi, jusque dans le *De anima*, à une réalité psychologique que le Stagirite relève longuement, celle-là même que les
Ethiques décrivent elles aussi,[50] mais en proposant notamment de
surmonter cette dualité par le 'choix' vertueux.[51] Un troisième
indice a déjà été relevé de divers côtés: bien que les *Ethiques*
n'aient point à régenter le degré végétatif du vivant, elles en
font mention et prennent soin d'expliquer pourquoi elles ne s'en
occupent pas.[52] Mais peut-être n'a-t-on pas indiqué la portée
exacte de cette mention: et en effet, malgré le neutre - φυτικόν,
θρεπτικόν - qui évoque le *De anima*,[53] il n'est pas encore certain
que l'auteur veuille imposer ici le sens de 'faculté'; en revanche, on constate que ces propos figurent eux aussi aux endroits-
clés qui annoncent le plan de l'une et l'autre *Ethique* et, qui
plus est, que la vie végétative y est présentée comme faisant partie du niveau irrationnel.[54]

Une conclusion se dégage de cet examen: quand on enregistre les
refus opposés par le *De anima* à la partition ternaire de Platon et
à la division en parties rationnelle et irrationnelle, il s'impose
de n'en point confondre les raisons ni la portée. Certes, une
même critique vise l'une et l'autre division: diverses facultés,
par exemple le désir, se trouvent morcelées, l'accent étant mis,
au détriment de leur unité, sur les divers niveaux auxquels elles
s'exercent; Aristote indique en outre que ces deux partitions sont
trop sommaires, le vivant étant plus complexe qu'elles ne le supposent. Mais le parallèle s'arrête là. A la tripartition, le
Stagirite reproche de négliger les fonctions biologiques: purement
'psychologique' au sens moderne du mot, elle est inutilisable dans
une doctrine hylémorphique.[55] Au contraire, la bipartition trouve
écho dans le *De anima* lui-même: malgré ses insuffisances d'ordre
spéculatif, elle répond à un donné trop manifeste, lequel s'impose

au philosophe comme au moraliste; puisqu'elle peut englober la totalité des phénomènes vitaux, le végétatif inclus, Aristote était
fondé à l'utiliser jusqu'au bout.[56]

Dans ces conditions, on pourra considérer que le *De anima* présente avec une netteté suffisante le troisième et dernier trait déno-
tant l'instrumentisme vitaliste.   Certes, on croit saisir pourquoi
M. Nuyens y a vu une marque de dualisme: la bipartition, qui pousse
ses racines jusque dans le *Protreptique*, traduit naturellement une
anthropologie que M. E.R.Dodds appellerait 'puritaine': la vie ver-
tueuse consiste alors en ceci que notre 'vrai moi', raisonnable par
essence, tienne en bride un 'frère âne' indocile et mû par une af-
fectivité suspecte.   Mais le théoricien de l'hylémorphisme semble
bien avoir admis que son explication radicalement unitaire de l'être
vivant et de l'homme fasse une place aussi à de telles tensions
entre les niveaux du désir.   Aristote lui-même ne nous mettrait-il
pas sur la voie d'une conciliation spéculative?   C'est ce qu'il
reste à examiner.

La triple causalité de l'âme
S'il est vrai que la causalité formelle ne paraît pas poser de difficultés particulières,[57] il se pourrait que le remarquable passage
sur la triple causalité de l'âme, en II 4, appelle un examen de
l'expression: l'âme est cause également comme étant *ce en vue de
quoi*, οὗ ἕνεκεν. Rappelons le contexte.   Aristote poursuit: 'Il est
clair que l'âme est cause également à titre de fin: de même que l'intellect agit en vue de quelque chose, de même aussi la nature et cela
est son but.   De ce genre est l'âme chez les animaux, conformément à
la nature; car tous les corps naturels sont organes de l'âme et,
comme le sont ceux des animaux, ainsi également ceux des plantes;
car ils existent en vue de l'âme, et *ce en vue de quoi* a deux sens:
l'objectif et le bénéficiaire (*litt.*: le *quoi* et le *pour qui* ou *pour
quoi*).'[58]

Avant de risquer une explication, tenons compte de ce que les
derniers mots de ce passage ont reçu des interprétations divergentes.
Certes, Aristote envisage le terme *fin* en deux sens; mais auquel
songe-t-il quand il l'applique à l'âme?

Dans la logique de son exégèse hylémorphique, Nuyens raisonne
comme suit: 'En tant que forme substantielle d'un être vivant, l'âme

en est cause finale au sens de τὸ οὗ, de but. Le but auquel est
destiné l'être vivant est de se développer et de se reproduire pour
la conservation de l'espèce (cf. II 4, 415a23-6). Cette fonction
... trouve son explication dans la forme substantielle elle-même ...;
l'âme ... comme cause finale, *n'est pas* une chose à laquelle une
autre (le corps) est destinée: elle est le but à réaliser lui-même.'[59]
Ross, dont on sait qu'il épouse la thèse de Nuyens - du moins quant
à la portée et à la date de ce livre II - tranche cependant en sens
opposé pour le passage qui nous occupe: les corps existent dans l'intérêt de l'âme; celle-ci est donc τὸ ᾧ.[60]

Antérieurement, Rodier avait résumé les propos des commentateurs
anciens et suggéré prudemment un compromis: l'âme serait bien la fin
visée, tandis que le sujet auquel profite le processus, τὸ ᾧ, serait
l'animal.[61] A l'examen, cette intéressante suggestion se révèle sans
support dans le texte: c'est l'âme qui est dite *fin*, non le vivant;
c'est d'elle que les corps sont les outils, lesquels existent 'en
vue d'elle'. Mais peut-être le texte demande-t-il une synthèse, non
un compromis, ni davantage l'alternative qui sépare Ross et Nuyens.

Rappelons-nous qu'Aristote énonce en quatre endroits cette distinction explicite entre deux sens de οὗ ἕνεκα. Dans la *Physique*,
après s'être expliqué sur la finalité objective de la nature et
l'avoir comparée à l'action artisanale, il ajoute à propos de celle-
ci: 'et nous en usons comme si tout existait en vue de nous-mêmes:
en quelque sorte, nous sommes, nous aussi, *fin*, car *ce en vue de quoi*
a deux sens'.[62] Autant dire que l'auteur s'aperçoit de la signification - dérivée, en somme, dans le cas présent - qu'il vient de
donner à l'expression *en vue de*; aussi nous avise-t-il de ce qu'il
est passé du premier sens au second, celui de 'bénéficiaire'. Le
même souci d'éviter à l'auditeur une confusion regrettable se révèle
en *Metaph.* Λ: 'Que la fin (τὸ οὗ ἕνεκα) existe chez les êtres immua-
bles, l'analyse le montre: car *ce en vue de quoi*, c'est *pour* et *de*
quelque chose; de ces sens, l'un est possible, l'autre ne l'est pas.
Or, c'est comme objet de désir qu'est moteur' le Principe immuable,[63]
lequel, on le sait, ne gagne rien en cette affaire.

Dans ces deux textes, la distinction entre les deux sens de la
formule a servi à isoler l'un d'entre eux. En va-t-il de même pour
les deux autres passages? Ceux-ci figurent dans le *De anima*; le
premier précède de quelques lignes celui qui nous intéresse.

En parfait accord avec ce que dit en son début le livre II du *GA*,
le philosophe présente la génération des vivants comme 'la production
d'un autre pareil à soi ..., en sorte qu'ils obtiennent part à l'éternel (τοῦ ἀεί) et au divin autant qu'ils le peuvent; car c'est là ce
à quoi tendent tous les êtres, c'est en vue de cela qu'agit quiconque
agit selon la nature, et *ce en vue de quoi* est double: l'objectif et
le bénéficiaire. Puis donc qu'ils ne peuvent communier à l'éternel
et au divin par leur permanence - car nul être périssable ne peut
survivre tel quel dans son individualité - chacun y communie dans la
mesure où il peut y participer.'[64]

Par le truchement de la reproduction spécifique, les individus
dépassent donc les limites temporelles qui leur sont fixées et at-
teignent en quelque façon à l'éternité qui est le bien de l'espèce;
selon la signification immédiate du texte, ce bien, le οὗ ἕνεκα
auquel aspirent les vivants, est donc ici τὸ οὗ.

Mais devons-nous exclure l'autre aspect? On ne perdra pas de vue
que, reliant des réalités,[65] μετέχειν et κοινωνεῖν désignent une relation réversible: avoir part, ou communier, à la mémoire ou à la
sensation, ce n'est point recevoir partiellement une réalité qui
existerait au dehors de soi, c'est, pour sa part, *constituer* l'ordre
des êtres caractérisés par tel ou tel privilège; être membre de la
communauté politique, c'est contribuer au bien de l'ensemble comme
au sien propre: il suffit ici de faire allusion aux développements
su l'homme, ζῷον πολιτικόν.[66] D'autre part, l'homologue de l'éternel, nous le trouvons dans l'ordre des 'natures', substances porteu-
ses des traits spécifiques permanents, qu'évoquait Z 7 en parlant du
devenir naturel;[67] s'il est vrai que 'Dieu n'a besoin de rien',[68]
néanmoins, au dessous de lui, 'tous les êtres constituent un même
ordre' - à des degrés divers, certes - 'et c'est leur nature à chacun qui est un principe de ce genre'.[69]

On voit mieux dès lors qu'Aristote ne nous induit pas en erreur
en notant le double sens que revêt le terme *fin*, sans nous inviter
à choisir l'un d'entre eux: les êtres 'désirent' la durée et le divin, τοῦ ἀεὶ καὶ τοῦ θείου ... ὀρέγεται ..., et toutes les actions
naturelles ont cette fin, ἐκείνου ἕνεκα πράττει ...; or, '*ce en vue
de quoi est double*', etc. La première formule citée désigne donc
sans équivoque le οὗ, régime caractéristique des verbes de cette
catégorie, tandis que la seconde, franchement bivalente, est mise

au point par le propos qui présente les deux sens de *fin*: ces actions sont à la fois '*possessives*' et '*constitutives*' d'un ordre
permanent et, selon la mesure de chacun - ᾗ δύναται - divin; y participer, c'est aussi en élargir l'existence.[70]

Ceci nous prépare-t-il à entendre le passage directement relatif
à l'âme, cause finale, en 415b15-21?[71] Il semble en tout cas que
ce texte nous invite plus nettement à prendre au sérieux l'indication selon laquelle le sens de *fin* est double; encore convient-il
de le préciser.

Que l'âme même soit, comme le dit ce texte, 'fin', ou 'objectif'
(τὸ οὖ) de la 'nature', nous le voyons plus clairement après le vi-
goureux rappel de *Metaph*. Z 10,[72] qui caractérise l'âme comme οὐσία
et comme quiddité du vivant, mais aussi après ce qu'a exposé le *GA*
sur le développement progressif de l'embryon:[73] bien que 'toute âme
ne soit pas nature' - ainsi faut-il réserver l'intellect à une dis-
cipline supérieure[74] - c'est en tant qu'être de nature que le vivant
est lui-même, c'est-à-dire caractérisé par le principe psychique de
son espèce, à l'état actuel. Alors seulement, comme dit notre texte,
'les corps naturels sont les organes de l'âme'.[75]

Encore l'exégèse de ce premier aspect devrait-elle écarter l'un
ou l'autre malentendu possible. Si les 'corps naturels' sont bien
'en vue de l'âme' en ce sens que la nature monte vers l'âme, est-ce
à dire que cette nature dispose de quelque autonomie? Non: c'est
de nature spécifique qu'il s'agit dans tous les textes examinés, ou
encore du dessein propre à l'espèce, mis en oeuvre tandis que passe
à l'acte la forme de cette espèce.[76] - Mais, dira-t-on, n'est-ce
point là poser un devenir de la forme, en dépit d'Aristote qui la
soustrait à la génération?[77] Certes, seul le composé concret est
sujet à ce processus,[78] et cependant la genèse de l'animal, par
exemple, se caractérise par une succession de paliers, chaque stade
connaissant à son tour les degrés potentiel et actuel:[79] sans être
pour autant 'produite', cette forme n'en atteint pas moins succes-
sivement divers états, qui correspondent à la fois à des êtres connus et à l'élaboration plus ou moins avancée du substrat corréla-
tif.[80] - Peut-être ce dernier propos prêtera-t-il à une troisième
méprise, dans la mesure où il paraît donner audit substrat une sorte
de priorité incompatible avec la primauté de la forme? Il n'en est
rien, ce me semble, pour la même raison: appliqué au domaine de la

vie, l'hylémorphisme tient précisément le corps et l'âme pour co-
principes; s'il est vrai que les sécrétions sexuelles doivent pré-
exister et que celle du mâle donne le branle à la genèse du vivant,
'c'est en même temps que la nature confère à chacun la faculté et
l'organe ...; ainsi la vue ne se parfait-elle point sans yeux, ni
l'oeil sans la vue'. Oui, 'c'est comme essence des corps animés,
que l'âme est cause'.[81]

Ces précisions confirment donc ce qu'a bien vu Nuyens: 'en tant
que forme substantielle d'un être vivant, l'âme en est cause finale
au sens de τὸ οὗ, de but ..., elle est le but à réaliser lui-même'.
Il est vrai que, selon cet auteur, l'autre formule ne serait pas de
mise dans le *De anima*: faisant de l'âme 'l'être auquel autre chose
est destiné, τὸ ᾧ', elle caractériserait la 'période de transition',
c'est-à-dire un instrumentisme inconciliable avec l'hylémorphisme.[82]
Qu'en est-il au juste?

Notons d'abord qu'à nouveau Aristote ne nous invite nullement à
choisir entre ces deux équivalents: *'ce en vue de quoi est double*
...'; on relève l'analogie avec le texte sur la pérennité des générations (qui se prête en effet à ces deux lectures, τὸ οὗ et τὸ ᾧ),
mais aussi le contraste avec celui de la *Métaphysique*, qui n'en autorise qu'une, comme le philosophe l'a indiqué clairement. Au demeurant, à la ligne précédente (415b19), le terme ὄργανα prépare à
point nommé cette double lecture; 'organes' au sens d'éléments
constitutifs animés, parvenus au degré actuel de la forme spécifique (l'âme étant ainsi τὸ οὗ), les corps et leurs parties n'en
sont pas moins ses 'outils': formant des ensembles très différen-
ciés, ces instruments lui sont plus ou moins nettement indispensables (l'âme est alors τὸ ᾧ), au point qu'elle peut être dite - jusque dans le *De anima* - agir, voire résider principalement en telle
partie. D'autre part, le Stagirite va passer aussitôt à l'examen
de l'âme comme cause de mouvement local, d'altération et de croissance.[83] La bivalence de ὄργανα dans ce passage sur la cause finale, préludant à celle de οὗ ἕνεκα dans la formule litigieuse, assure donc une transition remarquable entre les réflexions sur les
causalités formelle et motrice: but auquel tendent les phénomènes
et réalités organiques (notamment la génération), l'âme 'définit'
le vivant; les utilisant comme des instruments, elle est équiva-
lemment au coeur de leur activité.[84]

Certes, on comprend sans peine que certains répugnent à reconnaître ici le second sens de la formule οὗ ἕνεκα, dans toute la mesure
où ce sens correspond à ce qu'ils appellent 'instrumentisme'. Car
cette méfiance repose sur une équivoque, que j'espère avoir tirée
au clair en concluant le paragraphe précédent: sans doute le recours
à des schèmes instrumentistes peut-il traduire une *philosophie* d'allure dualiste, assurément incompatible avec l'unité métaphysique que
thématise l'hylémorphisme;[85] mais on voit à présent que cette dernière doctrine utilise des *schèmes* de ce genre pour exprimer, précisément, l'activité motrice de l'âme, celle-ci faisant du corps son
instrument.[86] Rien n'empêche désormais d'admettre que cette seconde
perspective figure parmi celles que trace le passage dense et admi-
rablement construit sur la triple causalité de l'âme.

Conclusion

Soit dit pour synthétiser rapidement l'acquis de cette première partie, le *De anima* permet de voir comment l'hylémorphisme intègre les
traits dont on a cru qu'ils dénotent nécessairement une doctrine
différente. Cette intégration s'opère en somme à trois niveaux, re-
présentés par les trois paragraphes précédents. Même dans un tel
traité, il n'est pas inconvenant d'envisager le rôle de l'âme comme
pouvant être celui d'un nautonier, ni de la situer dans la région
du coeur en tant qu'elle commande par exemple la chaleur vitale et
la phonation. En second lieu, le *De anima* fait même place à l'opposition des niveaux rationnel et irrationnel qui sous-tend l'éthique
d'Aristote et qui remonte au temps où sa philosophie était certainement dualiste. Enfin, à qui demanderait s'il s'agit là d'un langage
anodin, ou bien peut-être de véritables reliquats d'une psychologie
dualiste, le passage synthétique de II 4 fait comprendre que le vivant est 'organique' au double sens de ce mot.

Certes, pour Aristote, à la différence des mécanicistes et des
dualistes, l'âme est la structure unitaire, intelligible et dynami-
que, que vise le *nisus* concerté des éléments organisés; ceux-ci,
trouvant dans cette insertion commune leur sens d'organes animés,
'montent' en quelque sorte vers l'âme, qui est ainsi τὸ οὗ. Mais
cette même structure, une, rationnelle et mobile, s'assujettit leur
fonctionnement, les coordonne et les utilise comme ses instruments:
elle est à cet égard τὸ ᾧ; et cette seconde perspective offre au

Stagirite l'appui philosophique souhaitable lorsqu'il entend rendre
compte des diverses fonctions, de leurs coordonnées somatiques im-
médiates et de leur enracinement dans un principe unitaire qu'il
situe, comme l'on sait, dans le coeur.[87]

Dans ces conditions, l'unité du *De anima* apparaît sous un jour
nouveau. Sans doute n'est-il nullement exclu que le traité mette
en oeuvre des éléments doctrinaux plus anciens et même que certains
morceaux aient été mis par écrit bien avant la rédaction définitive
dont nous disposons, encore que les tentatives lancées pour les re-
pérer, même en prenant d'autres critères, n'aient pas été proban-
tes.[88] L'analyse qui précède nous munit en tout cas, me semble-
t-il, d'un critère *négatif*: le langage apparemment dualiste de l'instrumentisme ne peut, à lui seul, dénoter une philosophie antérieure à l'hylémorphisme, puisque ce dernier l'a aisément intégré,
notamment pour mettre en lumière la causalité motrice de l'âme-
forme. Au total, Aristote savait où il allait lorsqu'il se deman-
dait devant ses auditeurs εἰ οὕτως ἐντελέχεια τοῦ σώματος ἡ ψυχὴ
ὥσπερ πλωτὴρ πλοίου ...

II

La situation se modifie-t-elle sensiblement lorsqu'on aborde les
Parva naturalia? Il se pourrait que ces divers petits traités présentent eux aussi une vue très unitaire de l'être vivant, accompa-
gnée elle aussi de précisions sur les mécanismes que met en oeuvre
l'action motrice du principe vital. Mais le statut de l'âme dans
l'unité du vivant pourrait se présenter différemment dans les *PN*,
soit que leur éventuel hylémorphisme y présente des traits origi-
naux, soit que l'on puisse faire la preuve de son absence. Il est
vrai que cette petite collection peut n'être pas homogène au plan
doctrinal: Nuyens, Ross et Düring relèvent des différences entre
ses composantes et jugent plus ancien le *De juventute*, en mettant
sous ce titre également ce qui le suit jusqu'à la fin des *PN*.[89]
Adoptant comme hypothèse de travail une telle division, j'envisa-
gerai d'abord les premiers traités, jusqu'au *De longitudine* inclu-
sivement, puis le *De juventute* entendu comme on vient de le dire.
Mais il semble utile de toucher un mot auparavant des références
qui lient les *PN* à d'autres traités et notamment au *De anima*; particulièrement nombreuses, elles pourraient nous éclairer sur la

situation respective des deux ensembles.

Références

Plutôt que d'examiner une par une les quelque vingt formules par
lesquelles les *PN* renvoient au *De anima*[90] ou de recenser les atti-
tudes divergentes des critiques quant à leur utilisation (depuis le
scepticisme de Jaeger jusqu'à l'extrême crédulité de P.Thielscher),
il me semble utile de noter en premier lieu qu'il nous manque une
étude permettant de *différencier* leur signification. Voici quelques rapides illustrations de ce propos.

Le *De somno* (454a11-14) note que 'l'on a disserté ἐν ἑτέροις sur
ce qu'on appelle parties de l'âme et sur le niveau végétatif que
l'on isole (χωριζομένου) des autres chez les vivants corporels'.
C'est là un point de doctrine capital pour ce traité, qui réserve
le sommeil aux vivants doués de sensations,[91] mais il le suppose
suffisamment établi par ailleurs; or, l'on sait que le *De anima* s'en
occupe longuement en II 2 et 3, et Mlle S.Mansion vient de montrer
que la gradation des facultés à partir d'un 'minimum vital' est ty-
pique de la maturité d'Aristote: cette vue biologique selon laquelle
le vivant *est* (au moins!) l'ensemble des fonctions végétatives va de
pair avec l'hylémorphisme.[92] On tendra dès lors à conclure que
cette référence a une place organique, voire logiquement indispensable, dans l'exposé qui l'encadre,[93] et que ce dernier est conçu
dans la même perspective que le *De anima*.

Que penser alors d'un renvoi tel que celui de *De memoria* 1, 449b30-
450a1, qui semble bien désigner nommément le *De anima* et en cite une
formule: νοεῖν οὐκ ἔστιν ἄνευ φαντάσματος? Il s'agit de montrer que
même la mémoire des réalités intelligibles a son siège propre dans le
sensorium commun (cf. 450a14) et, en ce sens, le renvoi est certainement pertinent; d'autre part, la proposition 'point de pensée sans
image', bien développée en *De anima* III 7-8, a un tour psycho-somatique (ou plutôt noético-somatique) très accusé. Et pourtant, la
référence ne se relie à ce qui suit, si l'on peut dire, que par une
anacoluthe très marquée: ἐπεὶ δὲ ... - συμβαίνει γάρ;[94] même si les
exposés d'Aristote présentent parfois ce genre de faille, nous pouvons croire qu'il s'agit d'un 'repentir'. Bref, *non liquet*.

Quant aux premières lignes du *De juventute* (467b13-15), leur étran-
geté ne semble pas avoir été remarquée. 'On a disserté ailleurs sur

l'âme, dit l'auteur, et il est clair que son essence ne peut être un corps; mais, qu'elle réside en un organe du corps, c'est évident.' On reconnaît certes le propos du *De anima* II 2, 414a20-2, à ceci près que ἐν σώματι est devenu ἔν τινι τοῦ σώματος μορ[ῳ: le propos emprunté à la démonstration de l'hylémorphisme s'achève ici d'une façon singulièrement instrumentiste![95] On pourrait certes y voir la confirmation pure et simple de ce que montrait l'exégèse du *De anima* développée ci-dessus. Je crains cependant que certains traits doctrinaux du *De juventute* ne s'opposent à une solution si séduisante: il faudra plus loin mettre sous les yeux du lecteur les éléments du dossier; mais on conviendra qu'en principe, tout au moins, le critère de la cohérence doctrinale doit, dans l'appréciation des références, s'ajouter aux deux précédents, c'est-à-dire la stylistique et la logique de l'exposé.

Si l'un ou l'autre de ces critères fait défaut, on admettra une insertion dont l'auteur peut être Aristote lui-même, agissant en pédagogue qui relit ses cours et marque quelque continuité dans son enseignement. Un dernier exemple nous mettra sur la voie; il provient du *GA* et semble prononcer l'antériorité du *De An.* par rapport au *De sensu*; Aristote s'explique sur l'élément constitutif de l'oeil: ... ἐστὶν ὥσπερ ἐλέχθη πρότερον ἐν τοῖς περὶ τὰς αἰσθήσεις καὶ τούτων ἔτι πρότερον ἐν τοῖς περὶ ψυχῆς διωρισμένοις, καὶ ὅτι ὕδατος καὶ δι'ἣν αἰτίαν ὕδατος, ἀλλ'οὐκ ἀερὸς ἢ πυρός.[96]

Et pourtant, -la référence doit être tenue pour adventice.[97] Même si les traités cités fournissent des explications utiles, sa suppression améliore la logique et la clarté de la réfutation que le Stagirite dirige contre Empédocle.

Selon ce dernier, en effet, (*a*) les yeux clairs sont de nature ignée, les yeux foncés plutôt de nature aqueuse; (*b*) c'est pourquoi les premiers voient moins bien le jour, les seconds la nuit; Aristote rejette ces positions (ordre inverse: *b*, puis *a*); οὐ λέγεται καλῶς, εἴπερ μὴ πυρὸς τὴν ὄψιν θετέον ἀλλ' ὕδατος πᾶσιν. ἔτι δ'ἐνδέχεται τῶν χρωμάτων τὴν αἰτίαν ἀποδοῦναι καὶ κατ' ἄλλον τρόπον , ἀλλ'εἴπερ ((ἐστὶν ... πυρός)) τὸ αἰσθητήριον τοῦτ'ἔστι, ταύτην αἰτίαν ὑποληπτέον εἶναι τῶν εἰρημένων.

Le Stagirite expliquera ensuite (ordre direct) qu'une 'humidité' plus ou moins grande rend compte en effet de la teinte des yeux (779b26-34) et de leur acuité relative (779b34 - 780a25). On constate que la formule mise entre doubles parenthèses (citée *supra*) constitue une redondance dans le raisonnement; qui plus est, la troisième mention de αἰτία (ταύτην αἰτίαν) renvoie, non pas à la seconde (celle de la parenthèse), mais à la première.

Il ne doit donc pas nous échapper que de telles clausules peuvent simplement indiquer l'ordre méthodique que le Stagirite a voulu conférer à ses écrits de philosophie naturelle, proposant aux disciples une 'séquence' qui repose sur certains principes spéculatifs ou pédagogiques et laisse dès lors au second plan d'éventuelles dissonances dans la présentation.[98] Deux indications peuvent être avancées dans ce sens. Maint critique a relevé les formules initiales ou finales des écrits biologiques, qui figurent dans tout ou partie de la tradition manuscrite, et solidement établi l'existence de trois 'cours' d'ampleur diverse; si le *De anima* n'y occupe pas toujours la même place, il est suivi des *PN*, que le *GA* ne précède jamais.[99] En second lieu, et touchant encore l'ensemble des écrits biologiques, indiquons un fait aisé à relever, mais qui ne semble pas avoir été mis en relation avec le précédent, à savoir que, sauf erreur, toutes les références se conforment à l'un ou l'autre des schémas pédagogiques évoqués à l'instant, alors qu'aucune ne déroge à leur ensemble.[100]

Puisque les renvois d'un ouvrage à l'autre amènent les interprètes à opérer des choix arbitraires dès qu'on prétend en tirer des indications chronologiques, et que, par contre, ces mêmes renvois rentrent sans difficulté dans des séquences méthodologiques, on comprendra que la plus extrême prudence me semble désormais nécessaire dans leur usage. En bref, à condition que soient respectées la stylistique et la suite des idées, nous sommes ramenés à des critères d'ordre doctrinal.

Du De sensu au De longitudine

A dire vrai, les éléments qui peuvent mettre en lumière le rôle de l'âme dans l'unité du vivant semblent ici singulièrement peu abondants. Passons-les en revue.

Vaut-il la peine de défendre contre Ross l'orientation hylémorphique du *De sensu*? On se rappelle que ce critique discerne le dualisme - 'a two-substance view' - dans la proposition qui parle de phénomènes 'communs à l'âme et au corps'.[101] Mais le *De anima* lui-

même ne renonce nullement, que l'on sache, à parler d'âme et de
corps; il souligne aussi leur interaction, justifiant par là l'interprétation métaphysique donnée à leur union. Sans doute le *De
sensu* n'avait-il point à la thématiser systématiquement, mais la
formule citée trouve écho dans cette oeuvre et dans les suivantes;
comme le note bien Nuyens, c'est le 'même monde d'idées que le *De
anima*'.[102]

Mais il convient de relever aussi une autre analogie avec ce
traité, à savoir les formules qui localisent le principe sensitif
et dont l'une, particulièrement flagrante, déclare que la mémoire
se produit, 'grâce à la sensation, dans l'âme et dans la partie du
corps qui la possède';[103] nous savons désormais que la présence de
ces traits dans un écrit hylémorphique ne compromet en rien son
unité doctrinale ou littéraire. Certes, il n'y a guère à dire du
cinquième de la série, le *De divinatione*, si ce n'est qu'il apparaît dans le sillage du *De insomniis*. Quant au *De longitudine*, il
offre des développements difficiles, parfois d'une haute portée
spéculative, mêlés à des observations très anecdotiques; au plan
psychologique, un passage me semble révéler en deux points la doctrine du *De anima*,[104] mais aussi des parallèles significatifs avec
des développements instrumentistes que nous connaissons.[105]

Sans doute cette série est-elle par excellence le domaine où
l'examen thématique conduit par d'autres symposiastes peut attirer
l'attention sur des aspects, inaperçus jusqu'à présent, de la relation psycho-somatique. Jusqu'à plus ample informé, les quelques
indications recueillies donnent à penser que, comme dans le *De anima*, une pensée hylémorphique peu explicite y assume les mécanismes
biologiques et perceptifs.

Le *De juventute*

Si les six premiers petits traités des *PN* ne semblent donc pas, du
point de vue qui nous occupe, se différencier sensiblement du *De
anima*, la perspective me paraît se modifier quand on aborde la seconde partie de la série. Convenons avec Ross et divers autres, si
l'on veut bien, d'appeler *De juventute* cet ensemble de chapitres
qui, jusqu'à la fin des *PN*, s'ordonnent tant bien que mal autour de
la respiration et où l'on a vu aussi bien une dissertation 'sur la
vie et la mort'.[106]

Sans doute cette dissertation à dominante physiologique se révèle-t-elle largement semblable, sur ce plan, au *PA* et au *GA*.[107] C'est le cas notamment pour le rôle dévolu, dans la sensation, au coeur et aux divers organes sensoriels: goût et toucher ont un lien direct avec l'organe central, mais même les autres sensations aboutissent au coeur; le *De anima* n'offre pas davantage, à cet égard, de différences marquées.[108] S'agit-il de thèses qui n'auraient guère varié chez Aristote, du moins dans les textes qui nous restent de son enseignement? Cette hypothèse plausible ne donne que plus de relief, me semble-t-il, aux différences que voici.

Même quand il s'intéresse à la genèse de l'animal, le *De juventute* n'évoque en rien la théorie aristotélicienne de la génération: 'L'être se forme lorsque dans la chaleur il commence à participer à l'âme végétative; la vie est le maintien de cet état ...'[109] Nulle allusion, on le voit, à la différenciation progressive des organes par mouvement en chaîne, aspect cinétique de toute la genèse, non seulement dans la conception, mais aussi dans le déploiement progressif du vivant. Loin de prolonger cette perspective par une mise en valeur du mouvement aux divers âges de la vie, notre écrit passe sous silence l'action motrice du coeur et suppose même que ce dernier n'est pas indispensable à cet égard: certains animaux sanguins 'survivent longtemps à l'ablation du coeur – par exemple les tortues – et se meuvent sur leurs pattes'.[110]

Au lieu de cela, le *Juv.* nous offre une dissertation centrée de façon tout à fait prépondérante sur la chaleur vitale, sa nécessité, son excès et les facteurs qui la modèrent. Mais on ne trouve ici nulle allusion au rôle d'un organe que jugent essentiel le *PA* et le *GA* pour tempérer la chaleur, à savoir le cerveau;[111] par contre, le poumon, que ces traités mettent à sa place dans l'ensemble de l'organisme,[112] reçoit dans le *Juv.* toute l'attention de l'auteur: n'était son sérieux habituel, on citerait telle comédie où un médecin d'occasion évoque le poumon à chaque tirade ...

En admettant que le sujet traité puisse expliquer en quelque mesure ce déséquilibre, on n'en devrait pas moins rester en arrêt devant des affirmations aussi singulières et aussi répétées que celles-ci.

Ayant posé que la chaleur naturelle interne a son siège dans le coeur et opère l'élaboration des aliments, l'auteur en vient à noter que 'si le coeur perd sa chaleur, la vie s'éteint complètement, car tous les organes dépendent de cette source de chaleur et *l'âme se trouve comme embrasée dans cette partie*'.[113] Plus loin, sur la θρεπτικὴ ψυχῆς δύναμις: 'celle-ci ne peut exister sans le feu naturel, car c'est au sein de ce dernier que la nature l'a embrasée',[114] et encore: 'Le refroidissement est, d'une façon générale, nécessaire à la nature des animaux, de par l'embrasement de l'âme dans le coeur.'[115]

Ἐμπυρεύειν, 'embraser' ... M.L.Couloubaritsis juge cette traduction 'exagérée'; 'ce sur quoi il faut surtout, dit-il, porter l'attention ..., c'est sur la particule qui dénote un caractère d'*inhérence*, disons plus simplement une *intégration*, en l'occurrence une intégration au feu', ce qui donne selon lui, par exemple pour le troisième passage cité, la finale que voici: 'du fait de l'intégration, dans le coeur, de l'âme au feu'.[116] Je le concède volontiers: cette traduction serre le texte de plus près. Mais ce critique semble d'accord en tout cas pour écarter un sens métaphorique; c'est d'ailleurs la préférence qu'exprime Aristote lui-même: πᾶν ἀσαφὲς τὸ κατὰ μεταφορὰν λεγόμενον.[117]

Que l'âme soit ainsi dite affectée par le feu, ou 'intégrée au feu', le fait est unique dans les traités d'Aristote. Le *GA* situe certes 'le principe psychique dans la chaleur', mais il précise bien, à propos de la chaleur fécondante, qu' 'elle n'est pas le feu ni un facteur semblable'.[118] Quant au *PA*, il déclare: 'ceux qui prennent les choses d'une façon trop grossière prétendent que l'âme de l'animal est du feu ou quelque force du même genre. Il vaut peut-être mieux dire qu'elle se constitue au sein d'un corps de cette espèce. La raison en est que rien ne seconde davantage les fonctions de l'âme que la chaleur du corps.'[119] On s'en aperçoit: en biologie, Aristote évoque le feu dans un contexte polémique, pour caractériser la position qu'il repousse ou qu'il veut corriger; exposant son point de vue personnel, il recourt à la notion de chaleur.[120]

Inversement, selon les développements classiques du *GC*, le feu est radicalement matériel, ce qu'illustrent à la fois la célèbre doctrine des transmutations d'un élément à l'autre[121] et les diverses descriptions du feu lui-même comme étant 'chaud et sec', 'excès de chaleur', 'flamme au premier chef, c'est-à-dire vapeur qui brûle - et la vapeur est faite d'air et de terre'.[122] On ne peut s'étonner, après

cela, de voir le *GC* refuser absolument que l'âme soit un des éléments ou qu'elle en soit composée, car comment expliquer alors la cul-
ture, la mémoire ou l'oubli? 'Si l'âme est feu, elle aura les propriétés qui sont celles du feu, en tant que tel; fût-elle un mixte,
elle aura celles des corps. Or, parmi elles (*sc.* celles de l'âme),
aucune n'est corporelle.'[123]

Mais lorsque le prologue du *Juv.* déclare pour sa part, on s'en
souvient, si brièvement que ce soit: 'l'essence de l'âme ne saurait
être corporelle',[124] il est permis de se demander s'il ne s'agit pas
là d'une retouche tardive, peut-être due à un interpolateur soucieux
d'édulcorer la suite. Car les propos sur l'âme embrasée au sein du
feu naturel impliquent à tout le moins une conscience philosophique
fort peu éveillée à la distinction entre ce qui est somatique et ce
qui ne l'est pas. L'auteur semble notamment n'avoir pas conçu ce
qu'un traité de physique dit si nettement: l'embrasement n'est pas
une quelconque mixtion, c'est une genèse de type strictement matériel.

On peut évidemment envisager la solution inverse, à savoir, de
maintenir l'authenticité du propos 'spiritualiste' initial et de
suspecter les autres affirmations relatives à la nature de l'âme.
Plus onéreuse, cette hypothèse offre l'inconvénient de dénaturer des
sections entières du traité, car les assertions litigieuses s'y en-
racinent profondément. Celle du ch. 4 appelle aussitôt le développement du ch. 5 sur le feu, qui s'éteint lorsqu'on ne l'alimente pas
ou qu'on l'étouffe; ceci est appliqué sans désemparer à 'la chaleur
qui est dans le principe', laquelle 'doit être rafraîchie'.[125] Celle
du ch. 14 se réclame immédiatement du même développement et force
encore le parallèle: le feu 'est étouffé plus vite si on le disperse
...; car pour le vivant également, si on le dissèque à coups d'instruments ... il y a décès'.[126] Quant à la dernière, elle figure dans
le passage qui explique le mécanisme de la respiration (ch. 21-2),
texte riche en rapprochements avec les traités anatomiques d'Aristote,[127] rien n'empêchait ici l'auteur d'attribuer à l'âme la simple
chaleur naturelle au lieu de l'ἐμπύρευσις, mais ceci ne fait que
rendre plus aiguë la difficulté: voici un maître qui, sans que le
contexte l'y invite, utilise la formule prêtant le mieux à une interprétation de type matérialiste ...

Prononcera-t-on dès lors l'athétèse du *Juv.* en sa totalité? Avant

d'en venir à cette solution extrême, examinons une hypothèse qui
semble compatible avec la singularité rappelée à l'instant, mais
aussi avec le type d'unité et l'allure aristotélicienne que l'on a
pu reconnaître, chemin faisant, à l'ensemble de cet écrit. Celui-
ci attesterait à la fois un stade relativement ancien de la doctrine et l'influence encore indiscrète d'autres penseurs; je pense
plus précisément aux doctrines qu'énonce le traité pseudo-hippocratique *Du régime*.[128]

Pour celui-ci, la nature de l'homme se compose de feu et d'eau;
'le feu enfermé au dedans est aussi le plus abondant'.[129] Mais
voici qui semble plus caractéristique: 'Quant au feu le plus chaud
et le plus fort, dirigeant et dominant toutes choses selon la nature, inaccessible à la vue et au toucher, *c'est en lui qu'est
l'âme*, l'esprit, la pensée, la croissance, le dépérissement, le
mouvement, le changement, le sommeil, le réveil.'[130]

A propos de l'âme encore: 'Elle ne croît pas chez tous pareille-
ment: dans les corps qui sont jeunes, vu la rapidité du circuit et
la croissance du corps, elle brûle (ἐκπυρουμένη), devient légère et
est utilisée pour cette croissance ...' Un second thème, à savoir
le lien de l'âme avec la semence, apparaît aussitôt: 'quant aux
corps qui sont en pleine force et à l'âge où l'on est fécond, ils
peuvent nourrir et accroître (*sc.* l'âme) ... Ceux qui peuvent nourrir le plus d'âmes sont les plus forts.'[131] Et l'auteur joint un
peu plus loin ces deux thèmes: 'Quelqu'un doute-t-il de ce que l'âme
se mêle à l'âme? S'il considère des charbons lorsqu'il en ajoute de
brûlants à ceux qui brûlent, ... homogène est le corps qu'ils vont
produire, l'un ne différant pas de l'autre ... C'est ce que subit
également l'âme humaine.'[132] Signalons enfin que le *Régime*, comme
le *Juv.*, connaît le σύμφυτον θερμόν, concept dont je ne connais
guère de formulation antérieure qui résiste à la critique;[133] en
sens inverse, l'écrit pseudo-hippocratique, qui spécule souvent sur
le chaud et le froid dans l'organisme, n'attribue à cet égard aucun
rôle appréciable au poumon.

Ces quelques données pourraient prêter appui, je crois, à une appréciation de ce genre: le traité médical pourrait bien avoir fourni, tantôt directement, tantôt *a contrario*, une première inspiration
au Stagirite lorsqu'il rédigea le *Juv.* et même - ultérieurement, par
hypothèse - le *GA*. Sur ce second point, tout d'abord, on a noté que

le *Juv.* semble ignorer la théorie aristotélicienne (si 'formelle')
de la reproduction: la γένεσις serait seulement la πρώτη μέθεξις ἐν
τῷ θερμῷ τῆς θρεπτικῆς ψυχῆς,[134] sans aucune allusion au rôle moteur
de l'apport masculin dans la transmission de l'εἶδος, ni d'ailleurs
à la distinction entre l'acte et la puissance.[135] Le *Régime*, de
tendance anaxagoréenne, ignore de façon générale cette distinction;
il met à égalité, on l'a vu, les apports masculin et féminin, mais
il pourrait avoir préparé *a longe* la doctrine du *GA* par quelques
traits.[136] Quoi qu'il en soit, à un moment où ladite doctrine
n'avait pas encore pris forme, l'auteur du *Juv.* a pu, à l'instar du
Régime, admettre une communication rudimentaire du principe vital
qui fût conditionnée principalement par la chaleur ou, comme il le
dit ailleurs littéralement, par le 'feu' vital dont la mention répé-
tée nous retient ici. Dans ce contexte plus large, en effet, ces
propos d'allure plutôt matérialiste, en tout cas dissonants par rapport au 'formalisme' de la doctrine hylémorphique, me semblent sortir quelque peu de la pénombre et l'hypothèse d'une influence exer-
cée par le *Régime* sur certains propos du *Juv.* pourrait acquérir une
relative vraisemblance.

Cette *Quellenforschung* très sommaire ne nous dispense évidemment
pas de la question principale: les particularités du *Juv.* nous orien-
tent-elles vers un instrumentisme 'à l'état pur', c'est-à-dire antérieur à l'adoption de l'hylémorphisme, ou bien la doctrine de la
maturité a-t-elle, comme dans les traités précédents, assumé les
explications instrumentistes à titre de schèmes qui explicitent la
causalité de l'âme-forme?[137] Deux réflexions me viennent à ce propos.

Il arrive au *Juv.* de mettre en lumière l'unité des vivants: alors
que des individus-colonies peuvent impunément vivre segmentés, 'ceux
des animaux qui sont le mieux constitués ne le supportent point,
parce que leur nature est la plus unifiée possible'; et plus loin:
'ceux qui n'ont pas une extrême vitalité vivent longtemps après ablation du coeur ... parce que leur organisation naturelle n'est pas
bonne'.[138] Ce lien entre la valeur d'un être et son unité - la con-
vertibilité de l'un et de l'être - dénote bien notre auteur. On
songe à ce que dit, à propos du vivant aussi, le *De anima*: 'comme
l'être et l'un se disent en des sens multiples, le principal, c'est
l'acte', c'est-à-dire ce qui caractérise l'âme-forme par rapport au

corps-matière.[139] Traitant plus haut du sectionnement des vivants,
le *De anima* applique le principe: 'c'est l'âme, semble-t-il bien, qui
fait l'unité du corps', elle est le συνέχον.[140] Mais le *Juv.* se contente de vagues recours à la 'nature' de ces vivants et n'en appelle
ni à l'acte, ni au rôle unificateur de l'âme ...

Le second indice provient d'appréciations peu flatteuses que dé-
cerne le *De anima*: 'parmi les auteurs plus vulgaires, certains décla-
rent l'âme identique à l'eau: ainsi fait Hippon; il semble le croire
parce que la semence de tous les êtres est humide. En effet, il (*sc.*
Hippon) réfute ceux qui prétendent que l'âme est du sang: la semence
n'est pas le sang, mais l'âme primaire. Pour d'autres, (*sc.* l'âme
est) le sang, ainsi Critias.'[141] Or, on sait par un témoignage plus
circonstancié d'Hippolyte que Hippon admettait comme principes à la
fois le feu et l'eau; engendré par celle-ci, le feu l'emporte sur
elle et forme le monde, et 'la semence qui se manifeste à nous existe à partir de l'humide: c'est de lui, dit-il, que provient l'âme'.[142]
Cette doxographie, plus nuancée, rapproche donc Hippon du *Régime* et,
plus curieusement, de ce que nous avons entrevu dans le *Juv.* ...

Ainsi, présentant des auteurs avec lesquels il s'était senti des
affinités, Aristote choisit désormais des formules qui ne rappellent
pas trop directement ses positions antérieures. Lui-même n'a-t-il
pas évolué depuis cette époque? Certes, il n'a sans doute jamais
admis que l'âme fût de feu, mais seulement qu'elle y trouve le milieu
qui l'embrase; à présent, il va répétant que 'l'âme au sein du feu
ne fait point l'animal'[143] et, avec pondération, il professe que la
chaleur est instrument de la vie. Probablement n'a-t-il pas davantage - pas plus que l'auteur du *Régime* ou Hippon lui-même - identifié
l'âme au sperme, mais peut-être considéré que ce dernier la communi-
que telle quelle; désormais, il enseigne que, formée à partir du sang
le mieux élaboré, la substance fécondante, porteuse de chaleur et de
pneuma, est âme en puissance; elle transmet le mouvement qui va faire
passer à l'acte la forme spécifique. Comme le propos du *PA* cité p.
44 , la doxographie déformée du *De anima* représente ainsi un démenti
infligé à une oeuvre antérieure et plus proche, en effet, d'opinions
'vulgaires'.

Dialectiquement moins élaborée, ignorant encore la théorie du feu
que creusera le traité sur les éléments, portant de surcroît des traces d'influence étrangère, la rhapsodie sur le feu vital doit avoir

reçu un début de révision: à preuves l'affirmation relative à l'âme incorporelle, ainsi que l'un ou l'autre renvoi au *De anima*. Mais certains traits n'ont pu être corrigés, peut-être parce qu'ils étaient trop liés au contexte: ainsi l'âme apparaît-elle encore en maint endroit comme une substance d'allure matérielle, logée et entretenue dans le feu intérieur, et non pas comme la forme du substrat corporel, assurant au vivant l'unité métaphysique qui est celle de l'ἐντελέχεια.

CONCLUSION

Dans les pages qui précèdent, on s'est demandé si les vues d'Aristote sur le rapport psycho-somatique permettent de discerner des ressemblances et des différences entre le *De anima* et les *Parva naturalia*.

(I) Exposant systématiquement la doctrine métaphysique, très unitaire, de l'âme-acte, forme du corps-substrat, le *De anima* recourt néanmoins à des formules d'allure dualiste peu remarquées et qui, dans d'autres ouvrages, ont paru dénoter une phase antérieure (dite 'instrumentiste') de la pensée aristotélicienne. En réalité, ce traité semble bien traduire ainsi les mécanismes biologiques, voire les tensions qui affectent la conduite humaine, sans atténuer pour autant l'unité foncière de l'être vivant. Mieux encore, Aristote suggère qu'il entend relier philosophiquement ces explications concrètes à la causalité motrice de l'âme, forme et fin du vivant.

(II) Dans ces conditions, il apparaît que de tels schèmes explicatifs, peut-être très anciens chez le Stagirite, doivent être situés, si possible, par rapport à d'éventuelles expressions de la doctrine hylémorphique. Les *Parva naturalia* ont semblé offrir un plan de clivage à cet égard. Les six premiers, dans la mesure des maigres données que j'ai repérées, semblent se situer dans l'orbite du *De anima*. Le *De juventute*, par contre, ne paraît avoir été teinté d'hylémorphisme que de façon tardive et très superficielle; divers propos, certains silences aussi, révèlent un dualisme franc, notamment ceux qui concernent la nature du principe vital.

Soit dit par mode d'appendice, les formules quelque peu rudimentaires du *De juventute* sur l'âme 'embrasée' (ou 'intégrée au feu') auraient-elles un lien quelconque avec les propos transmis par

Cicéron et qui attesteraient une période où Aristote faisait de
l'âme humaine une parente des astres animés et divins? Je ne crois
pas devoir ici faire plus qu'évoquer cette hypothèse, suspendue au
problème que pose la valeur des témoignages cicéroniens.[144] Ce dernier problème sépare, on le sait, nos éminents collègues MM. Moreau
et Moraux, et peut-être n'est-ce pas le lieu de ranimer *ueteris ues-
tigia flammae*. A choisir entre deux périls, j'ai préféré le risque
de vous infliger une dissertation soporifique; Aristote lui-même
nous assurerait que cet effet est aussi salubre qu'inéluctable (458a
29-32): ἐξ ἀνάγκης μὲν γινόμενος ... ἕνεκα δὲ σωτηρίας· σῴζει γὰρ ἡ
ἀνάπαυσις ...

NOTES

1 *Rev. Philos. Louvain* 71 (1973), 425-50.

2 Cf. récemment D.J.Allan, *The philosophy of Aristotle* (2nd ed.
Oxford 1970), 49-50.

3 Cf. *Ph.* II 7, 198a24-6; *De An.* II 4, 415b8-28; *PA* I 1, 641a27.

4 *L'évolution de la psychologie d'Aristote*, préf. de A.Mansion
(Louvain 1948 (l'original néerlandais est de 1939), réimpr.
Louvain 1973).

5 *Sur l'évolution d'Aristote en psychologie*, préf. de S.Mansion
(Louvain 1972); pour les positions des aristotélisants susnommés
(échelonnées pour la plupart entre 1961 et 1970) cf. la section
II du ch. I.

6 Nuyens (*op.cit. n.4*), 57, 159, 161, 165, 190-1; cf. Lefèvre (*op.
cit. n.5*), 77 et 106.

7 Nuyens (*op.cit. n.4*), 272-3; A.Mansion, 'L'immortalité de l'âme
et de l'intellect d'après Aristote', *Rev. Philos. Louvain* 51
(1953), 456-7; *De An.* II 1, 413a8-9: ἔτι δὲ ἄδηλον εἰ οὕτως ἐντελέχεια τοῦ σώματος ὥσπερ πλωτὴρ πλοίου.

8 W.D.Ross, *Aristotle. De Anima* (Oxford 1961), 21, 212, 214-15, et
le texte qu'il imprime.

9 H.J.Easterling, 'A note on *De anima* 413a8-9', *Phronesis* 11 (1966),
161; W.F.R.Hardie, *Aristotle's ethical theory* (Oxford 1968), 81-3;
Hardie croit que la conjecture de Ross trouve un support chez
Thémistius et Philopon, mais il n'en est rien: expliquant la question posée par le texte, ces commentateurs échafaudent deux réponses possibles, ce qui est assez naturel; mais cela ne permet

pas de conclure que la phrase d'Aristote, telle qu'ils la li-
saient, fût d'allure disjonctive.

10 A.Mansion (*art. cit. n.*7), présente longuement les commentaires
grecs (n.20, 457-8) et médiévaux jusqu'à S.Thomas inclus (458,
n.21, et 460-5), mais principalement dans le but de montrer comment ce dernier (suivi par 'des disciples fidèles, mais trop con-
fiants') a pu être amené à mettre au compte de Platon la comparaison en question. (Au passage qu' A.Mansion cite de la *Qu. De
an.*, 1c, on peut ajouter *ibid.*, 11c, début: 'Plato ... dicens
animam esse in corpore sicut nauta in navi.')

11 Références dans A.Mansion (*art. cit. n.*7) et G.Rodier, *Aristote:
Traité de l'âme*, 2 vols. (Paris 1900), II 187. A Cambridge, M.
Paul Moraux note dans le même sens que 'hors du bateau, le marin
marche par lui-même'; il s'agirait ici, dès lors, d'un 'remords
d'Aristote'. Mais cf. la suite de mon texte.

12 *De An.* II 1, 413a6-7.

13 Cf. Bonitz, *Index*, 291a13-16; *Metaph.* B *per tot.*, etc.

14 *De An.* II 1, 412b16-17. M. David Rees me suggère que le passage,
depuis 412b10, peut contenir une réminiscence de *République* I,
352e-353c, qui évoque à la fois l'oeil, l'exercice d'une fonction
et l'excellence de l'âme.

15 *De An.* II 1, 413a9.

16 Cf. *De An.* II 2, 413a23-4, b13, etc. M. Jacques Brunschwig me
signale qu'en I 3, 406a4-10, des marins sont donnés comme exemple
d'une chose mue par autre chose, c'est-à-dire 'comme de purs mobiles
passivement entraînés par le mouvement du navire, ni plus ni moins
que les marchandises arrimées dans la cale. Si l'on est fondé,
poursuit-il, à transposer les renseignements fournis par ce passage ... la question peut se poser de savoir au juste comment
l'âme, entéléchie du corps, est "mue" par ce corps dont elle est
l'entéléchie, c'est-à-dire modifiée ou affectée par les modifications qui affectent le corps. Le problème posé serait alors
celui de la sensibilité, celui des "sentiments" et des "passions",
plutôt que celui de la causalité motrice de l'âme, que l'on a
coutume de voir ici.'
   La suggestion est ingénieuse; Aristote a dû en effet se poser
la question. Mais ne l'a-t-il pas suffisamment tirée au clair
dès le livre I, aussitôt après l'avoir formulée (cf. 406a12-b25)?
Que je sache, il n'y reviendra plus par la suite.

17 *Sic* S.Thomas, *In Arist. De an.*, no 243: '... hoc nondum est mani-
festum, si anima sic sit actus corporis ... ut motor tantum'.

18 *Sic* S.Albert (cité par A.Mansion (*art. cit. n.*7), n.21 de la p.
458): '... si anima sic movet corpus totum intellectu gubernante
..., ipsa separatur tota essentialiter a corpore.' W.Theiler,
Aristoteles Über die Seele (Berlin 1959), 108: '... wie der Ma-
trose ... d.h. getrennt vom Schiff und doch in ihm und so seine
Vollendung'.

19 Recension de W.F.R.Hardie (*art. cit. n.9*) dans *Rev. Philos. Louvain* 68 (1970), 258. L'auteur avait déclaré, p.80: 'It is the connection in description rather than the causal connection which is suggested.' Ce qu'il accorde à l'instrumentisme est donc retiré à la doctrine hylémorphique, qu'il qualifie de 'indeterminate and flexible' (p.81); dévaluant les formules d'Aristote, Hardie estime de surcroît que, même à ce prix, elles ne correspondent pas aux faits (cf. 83-93 et 'Aristotle's treatment of the relation between the soul and the body', *Philos. Quart.* 14 (1964), 66): ce platonisant distingué est aussi - *salua reuerentia* - un platonicien.

20 A.Mansion, non pas dans l'*art. cit. n.7* qui ne se proposait pas de conclure sur ce point (cf. *supra*, n.10), mais dans un cours inédit de 1946-47; j'estime équitable de transcrire les notes qui m'en restent et qui concernent le point controversé.

21 *De An.* II 4, 416b20-5; pour diverses discussions textuelles et notamment (malgré Ross) le maintien de l'ordre traditionnel, cf. Lefèvre (*op.cit. n.5*), 132-3. Avec Theiler, P.Moraux préfère ᾧ τρέφεται (*Archiv Gesch. Philos.* 43 (1961), 105), ce qui est plausible, mais n'importe guère à notre propos.

22 416b25-7 (texte de Ross): ἔστι δὲ ᾧ τρέφει διττόν, ὥσπερ καὶ ᾧ κυβερνᾷ καὶ ἡ χεὶρ καὶ τὸ πηδάλιον, τὸ μὲν κινοῦν καὶ κινούμενον, τὸ δὲ κινούμενον μόνον. Comme on le voit par ma traduction, je privilégie la leçon, de loin la mieux attestée, κινοῦν μόνον. Ross (*op.cit. n.8*), 232, dit préférer κινούμενον μόνον pour assurer un parallélisme direct entre χεὶρ et πηδάλιον, d'une part, et les deux participes, d'autre part. Mais le grec offre parfois un chiasme en pareil cas, τὸ μέν renvoyant alors au *second* terme annoncé: cf. Liddell-Scott, *s.v.* ὁ, A VI, 1, et le texte de *Metaph.* Λ, cité *infra*, n.63, où τὸ δέ se rapporte manifestement au premier terme annoncé, et inversement; c'est ce qu'oublie également E.Barbotin, d'ordinaire plus avisé: son éditeur ayant adopté correctement κινοῦν, lui-même traduit: 'celle-là [la main] est motrice et mue, celui-ci (*i.e.* le *gouvernail*) est moteur seulement'.

23 416b28-9: πᾶσαν δ'ἀναγκαῖον τροφὴν δύνασθαι πέττεσθαι, ἐργάζεται δὲ τὴν πέψιν τὸ θερμόν· διὸ πᾶν ἔμψυχον ἔχει θερμότητα.

24 Leurs positions sont exposées par Ross (*op.cit. n.8*), 231-2; indiquons seulement celle du plus prestigieux, Alexandre (cité par Philopon, *De An.* 288, 5-19 Hayduck): le moteur (non mû) serait la faculté végétative; le moteur mû, la chaleur innée.

25 S.Thomas, *In Arist. De an.*, no 348 Pirotta.

26 Ross, qui allègue la chaleur vitale dans son introduction (*op. cit. n.8*, 23-4), évoque longuement le coeur dans le commentaire (231), mais en y voyant un moteur mû: on se souvient en effet qu'il adopte en fin de phrase la leçon κινούμενον μόνον, locution qu'il se voit contraint d'appliquer à la nourriture; bien qu'elles soient également celles de Rodier (*op.cit. n.11*, II 245-6) et de R.D.Hicks, *Aristotle. De Anima* (Cambridge 1907), 349, ces deux solutions paraissent toutes deux inacceptables.

27 *De An*. II 8, 420b20-1. Suit (b21-2) une référence aux ouvrages
biologiques: τὸ δ'αἴτιον ἐν ἑτέροις εἴρηται (majorité des té-
moins) εἰρήσεται (e, paraphrase de Phil., *dicetur* Guill., edd.).
Si cette seconde forme (de sens futur), plus rare, mérite en
effet la préférence, on se trouve devant un nouveau renvoi incompatible avec la chronologie de Nuyens: l'explication plus
précise des termes indiqués ici figure surtout en *Juv*. 7, 470b
24-6; 16, 475b17, 476a8; 21, 478a23-5, moins nettement en *PA*
III 6, 668b34. Mais le *GA* donne un sommaire de la théorie en
II 1, 732b28-32. On tendra dès lors à conclure qu'il s'agit ici
d'un renvoi basé sur la séquence méthodique des traités.

28 *De An*. II 8, 420b27-9 (WyH^a Φ^P atténuent ψυχῆς en ψυχικῆς δυνάμεως: δυνάμεως om. H^a): ἡ πληγὴ τοῦ ἀναπνεομένου ἀέρος ὑπὸ τῆς
ἐν τούτοις μορίοις ψυχῆς πρὸς τὴν καλουμένην ἀρτηρίαν φωνή
ἐστιν.

29 Nuyens (*op.cit. n.4*), n.77, 247-8, citant Alexandre, *Liber de
Anima*, 49, 9-11 Bruns.

30 S.Thomas, *In Arist. De an*., no 476.

31 Cf. *supra*, p.23 et n.6

32 *Protr*. frg. 6 Ross (B 60 Düring): τῆς δὲ ψυχῆς τὸ μὲν λόγος
ἐστίν, ὅπερ κατὰ φύσιν ἄρχει καὶ κρίνει περὶ ἡμῶν, τὸ δ'ἔπεται
καὶ πέφυκεν ἄρχεσθαι.

33 Voir par ex. *EE* II 1, 1219b28-32; 1220a8-10 (cf. II 2, 1220b5-7);
II 4, 1221b27-37; *EN*, I 7, 1098a3-5; I 13, 1102a27-8, b33-4; III
10, 1117b23-4; VI 1, 1139a3-5; *Pol*. I 13, 1260a16-18; VII 15,
1334b17-19.

34 *EE* II 1, *EN* I 13 et VI 1 (= *EE* V 1), indiqués à la n. précédente.

35 *EE* II 4, 1221b28-31: αἱ ἀρεταὶ ... αἱ δὲ τοῦ ἀλόγου, ἔχοντος δ'
ὄρεξιν. *EN* I 13, 1102b30-1, 1103a3: ... λόγου, τὸ δ'ἐπιθυμητικὸν
καὶ ὅλως ὀρεκτικὸν μετέχει πως ... ὥσπερ τοῦ πατρὸς ἀκουστικόν τι.

36 F.Dirlmeier, *Nikomachische Ethik* (4th ed. Berlin 1967), 294: '...
den Kern der arist. Zweiteilung, nämlich die enge Relation zwi-
schen dem Geistigen und dem "Strebenden"'. Cf.,*ibid* . et 278-9,
de bonnes indications sur les antécédents platoniciens; mais
l'auteur se méprend complètement lorsqu'il entend distinguer
(292-3) la 'partie obéissante' et une autre partie, subordonnée
elle aussi, qui serait rationnelle par nature (erreur notée par
Gauthier, II 1, 97). Sur l'intellectualisme *mitigé* de l'*EN* et
le rôle de la tendance, cf. les mises au point capitales de G.
Verbeke, 'Thèmes de la morale aristotélicienne', *Rev. Philos.
Louvain* 61 (1963), 190-5, 206-10.

37 M. Baudhuin-Van Aubel, *L'influence d'Aristote ... dans les Mora-
lia de Plutarque* (Louvain 1968), 56 et 46, commentant *De An*. III
9, 432a22 - b7; III 10, 433a31 - b4.

38 C'est alors la βούλησις. *Pol*. VII 15, 1334b22-4: θυμὸς γὰρ καὶ

βούλησις, ἔτι δὲ ἐπιθυμία ... ὑπάρχει τοῖς παιδίοις. *Contra: EE* II 7, 1223b26-7; II 10, 1225b24-31; cf. *Top.* IV 5, 126a12-13; *De An.* III 9, 432b5, III 10, 433b5, et A.Mansion, 'Le dieu d'Aristote et le dieu des chrétiens', dans *La Philosophie et ses problèmes.* Recueil d'études ... offert à R.Jolivet (Lyon 1960), 37-8.

39 *EN* I 13, 1102a27-32: τὸ μὲν ἄλογον αὐτῆς εἶναι, τὸ δὲ λόγον ἔχον. ταῦτα δὲ πότερον διώρισται καθάπερ τὰ τοῦ σώματος μόρια καὶ πᾶν τὸ μεριστόν, ἢ τῷ λόγῳ δύο ἐστὶν ἀχώριστα πεφυκότα καθάπερ ἐν τῇ περιφερείᾳ τὸ κυρτὸν καὶ τὸ κοῖλον, οὐθὲν διαφέρει πρὸς τὸ παρόν.

40 *EE* II 1, 1219b32-4: διαφέρει δ'οὐθὲν εἰ μεριστὴ ἡ ψυχὴ οὔτ' εἰ ἀμερής, ἔχει μέντοι δυνάμεις διαφόρους καὶ τὰς εἰρημένας, ὥσπερ ἐν τῷ καμπύλῳ τὸ κοῖλον καὶ τὸ κυρτὸν ἀδιαχώριστον. F.Dirlmeier, *Aristoteles Eudemische Ethik* (Darmstadt 1962), 233, estime que ceci note 'viel stärker ... dass es eben doch wesensverschiedene Teile gibt'; mais cf. la suite de mon texte.

41 *De An.* I 5, 411b5-27; II 2, 413b27-9; II 3, 415a1-12; III 9, 432a 22 - b7, avec la remarque de Simplicius (*In De an.*, *CAG*, XI 288, 17-18 Hayduck): μάχεται πρὸς τὸ διεσπασμένον καὶ τοπικῶς μεμερισμένον.

42 Ainsi le rejet thématisé de la division réelle en parties va-t-il de pair avec la réflexion sur l'âme comme être non substantiel, co-principe de nature formelle: cf. la place de la division λόγῳ, exemples mathématiques à l'appui, dans la démonstration hylémorphique en *De An.* II 2, 413b27-9; II 3, 414b20-5, 28-32.

43 *EN* I 13, 1102a23-8.

44 Cf. les formes du présent en *EN* VI 4, 1140a2; *Pol.* VII 1, 1323a 21-3; Fr. Dirlmeier, '*Physik* IV 10' (dans *Naturphilosophie bei Aristoteles -und Theophrast*, ed. I.Düring (Heidelberg 1969), 52-3).

45 *De An.* III 9, 432a24-8. - On note l'emploi de μόρια pour désigner les *facultés* que nous allons énumérer; la même observation vaut pour *De An.* II 2, 413b7; II 12, 424a33, tandis que δύναμις a parfois, même dans ce traité, le sens vague de 'pouvoir', 'force', etc.: cf. *De An.* I 1, 403a27; I 2, 404a30. On ne peut donc se fier au seul vocabulaire; cf. J.Hamesse, *Le problème des parties de l'âme* (Louvain 1964), 69-85.

46 III 9, 432a29, b7.

47 Comme le montre bien Baudhuin (*op.cit. n.37*), 46-57, notre philosophe a tendance à atténuer la distinction entre ces deux formes du désir.

48 *De An.* III 10, 433b3-4. Comme me le signale le Prof. W.J.Verdenius, citant l'*Index*, 109b44-6, l'unique τό, qui figure dans la plupart des manuscrits, ne signifie pas que les deux derniers termes doivent être pris *per modum unius*.

49 III 10, 433b5-6; cf. b6-11; III 9, 433a1-8; III 11, 434a12-15; il

ne s'agit donc pas d'une allusion isolée ni d'un 'organe-témoin'.

50 *EE* II 8, 1224a24-5: οὐ γὰρ ἀεὶ ἡ ὄρεξις καὶ ὁ λόγος συμφωνεῖ.
Cf. II 7, 1223b12-14, et, dans les 'livres communs', les longs
développements sur la 'continence' et l''incontinence'.

51 Cf. par exemple la formule justement célèbre de *EN*, VI 2, 1139b
4-5: διὸ ἢ ὀρεκτικὸς νοῦς ἡ προαίρεσις, ἢ ὄρεξις διανοητική, καὶ
ἡ τοιαύτη ἀρχὴ ἄνθρωπος, et tout ce qui concerne le mécanisme de
la décision, le syllogisme pratique, etc. - Les propos cités de
De An. III 10, 433b5-6 (*supra* et n.49), impliquent nettement
qu'au λόγος correspond un retentissement affectif du même degré:
c'est cette ὄρεξις de niveau rationnel, non la raison comme
telle, qui peut entrer en conflit avec les ἐπιθυμίαι (de niveau
irrationnel). Certains passages éthiques parallèles sont moins
nuancés, semblant mettre en cause le seul λόγος: τῆς δὲ ψυχῆς τὸ
μὲν λόγος ἐστίν ... τὸ δ'ἕπεται (*Protr.* frg. 6 Ross, B 60
Düring); οὐ γὰρ ἀεὶ ἡ ὄρεξις καὶ ὁ λόγος συμφωνεῖ ... (*EE* II 8,
1224a24-5); mais les autres textes indiqués recourent à la formule plus souple τὸ λόγον ἔχον: ce qui doit commander possède la
raison, mais ne s'y réduit pas, et ce propos laisse place aux
précisions dont fait état le *De An.* et que je relève ici.

52 C'est ce que notent, avec plus ou moins de netteté, F.Solmsen,
'Antecedents of Aristotle's psychology and scale of beings',
AJP 76 (1955), 150 et n.8, évoquant à juste titre *EN* I 13, 1102a
32 - b12; I 7, 1097b33 - 1098a3; VI 12, 1144a9-11; *EE* II 1,
1219b20-4, 36-7; Dirlmeier (*op.cit. n.36*), 278, à propos de *EN*
I 7, 1097b33 - 1098a3, estime qu'à ce moment Aristote doit avoir
déjà formulé la doctrine de *De An.* II 2. Ce même texte d'*EN* I
7, apparaît à Mlle S.Mansion comme le seul des *Ethiques* où Aristote dénie nettement aux végétaux toute puissance autre que
nutritive; cf. *art. cit. n.1*, 435-6, commentaire qui éclaire
vivement le statut du végétatif notamment dans les *Ethiques*.

53 *EE* II 1, 1219b37, b39; *EN* I 13, 1102a32, b29; cf. *De An.* III 9,
432a29; III 10, 433b2, etc.

54 *EE* II 1, 1219b31-2, 36-7, après un examen de la partie capable
d'obéir: εἰ δέ τι ἐστὶν ἑτέρως ἄλογον, ἀφείσθω τοῦτο τὸ μόριον
... ἀφήρηται δὲ καὶ εἴ τι ἄλλο ἐστὶ μέρος ψυχῆς, οἷον τὸ φυτικόν
(φυσικόν codd. ant.; corr. edd. pler., Oxf. Tr.); *EN* I 13, 1102a
32-3 (cf. b28-30): τοῦ ἀλόγου δὲ τὸ μὲν ἔοικε κοινῷ καὶ φυτικῷ.
Le Prof. Joseph Moreau m'écrit à propos de ce problème: 'La
division de l'âme en deux parties, l'une rationnelle, l'autre
irrationnelle, héritée du platonisme et adoptée dans les *Ethiques*, n'est pas en désaccord avec la psychologie du *De anima*,
où l'âme est regardée comme une hiérarchie de fonctions; elle y
trouve au contraire sa place nécessaire ...
'La faculté cognitive et la faculté motrice sont deux expressions d'une seule activité spirituelle, comme la concavité et
la convexité d'une même courbe. Mais cette activité s'exerce à
plusieurs niveaux ... C'est leur distinction qui s'exprime dans
la division de l'âme humaine en une partie rationnelle, qui commande, et une partie irrationnelle, qui obéit ...
'Ce qu'Aristote peut reprocher à la division platonicienne en
deux ou en trois parties, c'est qu'elle semble omettre complète-

ment les fonctions purement vitales de l'âme, sa partie végétative (φυτικόν), ou plus généralement physique (φυσικόν: *EE* II 1,
1219b37), et qu'elle induit à réaliser en des parties distinctes,
séparées, ce qui correspond seulement à une dualité d'aspects
(sensibilité, motricité) ou à une différence de niveau (impulsion
sensible, choix volontaire), à considérer par ex. que la raison
(λόγος) est purement cognitive, et la tendance (ἐπιθυμία ou θυμός)
pure impulsion motrice.'

On voit déjà que je suis enclin à ratifier entièrement les observations de M. Moreau, à ceci près que selon moi la critique
d'Aristote vise surtout la tripartition (cf. *supra* et n.48), tandis que la bi-partition, dont nous nous occupons ici, trouve encore sa place dans le *De anima* (cf. encore la suite de mon texte).

Quant au Dr Richard Sorabji, qui approuve en cela l'étude récente de W.W.Fortenbaugh, *Aristotle on emotion* (London 1975), il
estime que la tripartition platonicienne 'distributes emotions
among different parts of the soul', alors que le *De anima*, tout
comme les *Ethiques*, cantonne dans la partie irrationnelle l'émo-
tivité. Celle-ci peut donc être dite 'capable d'obéir à la raison' et l'on comprend que le *De anima* ne rejette pas la bipartition des *Ethiques*.

Pour ma part, je crois plutôt qu'Aristote admet en divers passages une interférence des émotions au niveau rationnel; cf. *supra* et n.38. Et je constate que le *De anima* critique aussi la
valeur spéculative de la bipartition, mais avec les réserves importantes que je crois avoir mises en lumière.

55 Cette triade survivra seulement, on le sait, comme division de
l'une des facultés aristotéliciennes, l'ὄρεξις, mais Aristote
substitue la βούλησις au λογιστικόν qui, désormais, en est déclaré le siège; cf. *supra*, n.38.

56 Ces derniers mots rappellent le texte fameux de Plutarque selon
lequel Aristote a maintenu μεχρὶ παντός la distinction entre les
parties irrationnelle et rationelle (*De virtute morali*, 442b-c).
Mme M.Baudhuin (*op.cit. n.37*), 58-62, 429 et 433, montre bien
que Plutarque fait peu état du *De An.*, peut-être parce que la
doctrine hylémorphique se prête mal à son concordisme platonico-
aristotélicien; elle conclut que la formule μεχρὶ παντός ignore
le terme de l'évolution aristotélicienne en psychologie. Il ne
me revient pas d'apprécier à nouveau l'influence éventuelle du
De An. sur Plutarque; mais on aura vu en quel sens cet auteur
pourrait avoir raison quant au maintien d'une bipartition. Sur
l'évolution de cette théorie chez Platon et Aristote, voir surtout les réflexions d' A.Mansion, 'Autour des éthiques attribuées à Aristote', *Rev. néoscol. de Philos.* 33 (1931), de P.
Moraux, *A la recherche de l'Aristote perdu: Le dialogue 'Sur la
justice'* (Louvain - Paris 1957), et de D.A.Rees, 'Bipartition
of the soul in the early Academy', *JHS* 77 (1957), 112-18.

57 Cf. *supra*, pp.21-2 et nn.2 et 3.

58 *De An.* II 4, 415b15-21 (cf. les textes de Ross et de Jannone-
Barbotin): ... διττῶς δὲ τὸ οὗ ἕνεκα, τό τε οὗ καὶ τὸ ᾧ.

59 Nuyens (*op.cit. n.4*), 245-6.

60 Ross (*op.cit. n.8*), 228.

61 Cf. Rodier (*op.cit. n.11*), II, 232-3.

62 *Ph.* II 2, 194a34-6 (considéré comme provenant du *De philosophia*, frg. 28 Ross): καὶ χρώμεθα ὡς ἡμῶν ἕνεκα πάντων ὑπαρχόντων (ἐσμὲν γάρ πως καὶ ἡμεῖς τέλος· διχῶς γὰρ τὸ οὗ ἕνεκα ...).

63 *Metaph.* Λ 7, 1072b1-3: ὅτι δ'ἔστι τὸ οὗ ἕνεκα ἐν τοῖς ἀκινήτοις, ἡ διαίρεσις δηλοῖ· ἔστι γὰρ τινὶ τὸ οὗ ἕνεκα <καὶ> τινός, ὧν τὸ μὲν ἔστι τὸ δ'οὐκ ἔστι. κινεῖ δὲ ὡς ἐρώμενον. Cf. la finale d'*EE* VIII 3, 1249b14-16: τὸ ᾧ est exclu au profit de τὸ οὗ, ces termes restant sous-entendus: ὁ θεὸς ... οὗ ἕνεκα ἡ φρόνησις ἐπιτάττει. διττὸν δὲ τὸ οὗ ἕνεκα ... ἐκεῖνός γε οὐθενὸς δεῖται.
   Cette interprétation de 1072b1-3 fut aussi, à Cambridge, celle des symposiastes qui se sont exprimés à ce propos; elle avait été soigneusement étayée par l'un d'entre eux dans une étude qui me fut révélée alors: A.Graeser, 'Aristoteles' Schrift "Über die Philosophie" und die zweifache Bedeutung der "causa finalis"', *Museum Helveticum* 29 (1972), 44-61; cf. p.51.
   Par contre, les participants sont restés divisés à propos de *Ph.* II 2: Mlle Mansion et M. Graeser (cf. son article, pp. 56-7) optent pour l'équivalent au datif, MM. Aubenque et Verdenius pour le génitif.

64 *De An.* II 4, 415a28 - b6: τὸ ποιῆσαι ἕτερον οἷον αὐτό ...,ἵνα τοῦ ἀεὶ καὶ τοῦ θείου μετέχωσιν ᾗ δύνανται· πάντα γὰρ ἐκείνου ὀρέγεται, καὶ ἐκείνου ἕνεκα πράττει ὅσα πράττει κατὰ φύσιν (τὸ δ'οὗ ἕνεκα διττόν, τὸ μὲν οὗ τὸ δὲ ᾧ). ἐπεὶ οὖν κοινωνεῖν ἀδυνατεῖ τοῦ ἀεὶ καὶ τοῦ θείου τῇ συνεχείᾳ, διὰ τὸ μηδὲν ἐνδέχεσθαι τῶν φθαρτῶν ταὐτὸ καὶ ἓν ἀριθμῷ διαμένειν, ᾗ δύναται μετέχειν ἕκαστον, κοινωνεῖ ταύτῃ.

65 Ecartons dès lors ici la participation logique - celle des espèces aux genres, par exemple - qui n'est point réciproque, ainsi que son application aux Idées, qui se déploie dans un contexte polémique.

66 Cf. notamment *Pol.* I 1 et 2, en particulier 1253a18-29, sur le bien commun et sur le besoin de participation chez l'homme digne de ce nom; VII 8, 1328a35-7, sur le bonheur visé. N'entrons pas ici dans la distinction, parfois esquissée chez Aristote, entre μετέχειν et κοινωνεῖν, ce dernier semblant connoter davantage une participation concrète aux activités: cf. IV 6, 1293a1-6; mais le sens paraît identique en *De An.* II 4, 415b3 et 5, b25 et 27, ainsi qu'en *GA* I 23, 731a32 et b1.

67 Cf. *Metaph.* Z 7, 1032a22-5: 'l'origine est nature, ce à quoi on se conforme est nature ... et l'agent, c'est la nature de même forme qui tire son nom de l'espèce: c'est elle, en un autre sujet, car l'homme engendre l'homme'.

68 *EE* VIII 3, 1249b16 (cité *supra*, n.63), écho fidèle, notamment, d'Euripide, *Hér. furieux*, 1345-6.

69 *Metaph.* Λ 10, 1075a18-19, 22-3: πρὸς μὲν γὰρ ἓν ἅπαντα

συντέτακται ... τοιαύτη γὰρ ἀρχὴ ἑκάστου αὐτῶν ἡ φύσις ἐστίν.

70 Selon K. Gaiser, 'Das zweifache Telos bei Aristoteles', dans
  Naturphilosophie bei Aristoteles und Theophrast, ed. I.Düring
  (Heidelberg 1969), 103-4, la fin rendue par l'expression au génitif (τινος) désigne l'ordre universel auquel se vouent de manière
  diverse les individus ('... die Lebewesen ... sich alle mehr oder
  weniger dem allgemeinen, göttlichen Ziel hingeben'), tandis que
  l'autre formule (τινι, c'est-a-dire τὸ ᾧ) indiquerait l'épanouis-
  sement individuel ('im Rahmen der allgemeinen Zuordnung ... wird
  jedes Lebewesen sich selbst und seine eigene Art zu verwirklichen
  und zu erhalten suchen: ... eine auf das einzelne Subjekt gerich-
  tete Zwecktätigkeit'). On ne peut que louer l'auteur d'indiquer
  nettement que notre texte voue chaque être à une réalité divine.
  Moins heureux me paraît M.P.Lerner, *Recherches sur la notion de
  finalité chez Aristote* (Paris 1969), 101: 'Le but ou la fin (τὸ
  οὗ), c'est pour le vivant de participer à l'éternel et au divin:
  mais en même temps, cette fin est pour lui (τὸ ᾧ), il y participe
  avec tout son corps.' Non, *ce n'est pas le vivant, qui est
  l'antécédent de* οὗ ἕνεκα, *mais* τὸ θεῖον! Au demeurant, on n'oubliera pas que dans le cas présent 'divin' n'implique pas nécessairement 'transcendant': la remarque d'Aristote sur le double
  sens de *fin* me semble précisément indiquer le contraire.
      Le Prof. de Strycker me fait observer aimablement: 'Grammati-
  calement, il n'est pas exact de dire que τὸ ἀεὶ καὶ τὸ θεῖον est
  l'antécédent de οὗ; car la réponse serait en grec: τὸ οὗ ἐστι
  τοῦτο οὗ ὀρέγεται. Quant à M. Gaiser, il décrit très correctement la fin οὗ; M. Lerner emploie, au lieu de τὸ ἀεὶ καὶ τὸ
  θεῖον, la formule: τὸ μετέχειν ..., et ceci est tout de même une
  formulation tolérable de la fin οὗ.'
      J'admets à la fois que l'antécédent grammatical est un démon-
  stratif et que son équivalent *ad sensum* est bien 'l'éternel et le
  divin'. Je me demande seulement ce qui autorise certains commentateurs - modernes et anciens: cf. n. /1 - à réserver cette équi-
  valence à la formule au génitif. La logique me paraît requérir
  que la formule 'l'éternel et le divin' fonctionne comme équivalent:
      - soit au génitif, désignant ainsi ce vers quoi tendent les
      vivants, leur 'objectif'; c'est l'avis de MM. Aubenque, de
      Strycker, Moreau, Patzig et moi-même;
      - soit au datif: l'éternel et le divin n'étant pas Dieu (ne
      pas confondre avec *Metaph.* 1072b1-3! cf. n. 63), mais une zone
      de l'être qui participe à certains de ses attributs, on consi-
      dère alors que cette instance est constituée notamment par les
      espèces vivantes, dans la mesure où elles ont accès à la per-
      pétuité; plus exactement, par les individus vivants, qui accè-
      dent à l'éternel par le biais de la reproduction.
      A Cambridge, cette seconde interprétation est restée sans
  écho, surtout, semble-t-il, parce que le monde du divin nous apparaît normalement comme immuable. Cela suscite en moi un doute
  peut-être salutaire sur la validité de ma suggestion. Mais je
  ne vois toujours pas que l'antécédent de οὗ ἕνεκα (ou l'équivalent
  de τοῦτο) puisse être *le vivant*, comme le suggère par exemple
  Mlle Mansion: 'Le rejeton produit par la plante ou l'animal est
  la fin-génitif, l'oeuvre faite, mais cette oeuvre elle-même est
  faite par le vivant en vue de lui-même, à son profit, ce qu'Aris-

tote explique en disant que le profit à tirer de cette production
est d'atteindre par là à l'éternité autant qu'il lui est possible.'

71 Aristote a-t-il adopté une signification unique (soit l'équivalent au génitif, soit celui au datif) pour les diverses formules
que nous avons évoquées? Mlle Mansion opte pour le datif (sauf
en *Metaph.*), MM. Patzig et Verdenius pour le génitif, M. Aubenque
de même (sauf peut-être en 415b20, qui serait bivalent). Mr
Woods rapproche les deux formules de II 4, M. Berti les oppose
pour une raison grammaticale, le Prof. de Strycker pour une raison
doctrinale à laquelle on reviendra.

On se rappelle ce que les principaux commentateurs anciens ont
pensé à ce propos. Pour 415b2, Simplicius (110, 36), Thémistius
(50, 16-17) et Philopon (270, 2-5), adoptent τὸ θεῖον comme équivalent au génitif, et, au datif, respectivement τὰ ὄντα, τὸ ἐν
γενέσει, ἡ ψυχή. Pour 415b20, Thémistius ne se prononce pas.
Simplicius (111, 33) entend par la formule au génitif l'âme,
c'est-à-dire τελείως ζῆν; Philopon (274, 16-23) hésite: les acceptions correspondant au génitif et au datif seraient l'âme et
le vivant; ou bien ce seraient la perpétuité et l'âme, ce qui
revient à son interprétation de 415b2.

72 Cf. *Metaph.* Z 10, 1035b14-16.

73 Cf. *GA* II 1, 734b19-27; II 3, 736b8-27; Lefèvre (*op.cit. n.5*),
62-73.

74 *PA* I 1, 641b9-10: οὐδὲ γὰρ πᾶσα ψυχὴ φύσις.

75 *De An.* II 4, 415b18-19: πάντα γὰρ τὰ φυσικὰ σώματα τῆς ψυχῆς
ὄργανα.

76 Cf. *De An.* II 4, 415b16-18: ὥσπερ γὰρ ὁ νοῦς ... καὶ ἡ φύσις ...
τοιοῦτον δ'ἐν τοῖς ζῴοις ἡ ψυχὴ κατὰ φύσιν.

77 Cf. *Metaph.* Z 8, 1033b11, 17.

78 Cf. la suite du même texte, 1033b17-18.

79 Cf. *GA* II 3, 736b2-3: οὐ γὰρ ἅμα γίγνεται ζῷον καὶ ἄνθρωπος.

80 Cf., pour le degré potentiel de l'âme végétative, le cas des
oeufs non fécondés (Lefèvre (*op.cit. n.5*), 70-2); et cf. *GA* II 3,
736b23-4: ταύτας ἄνευ σώματος ἀδύνατον ὑπάρχειν, οἷον βαδίζειν
ἄνευ ποδῶν.

81 *GA* IV 1, 766a5-9; *De An.* II 4, 415b11-12. S'abstenant de toute
réflexion sur l'exégèse de Nuyens, Gaiser (*art.cit. n.70*), 105,
voit au total dans les quatre textes d'*EE*, *Metaph.* Λ et *De An.*
(*bis*) la participation différenciée de chaque espèce à une vaste
scala naturae, ce qui me paraît correspondre davantage à la perspective du texte précédent sur le cycle des générations: dans le
cas présent, Aristote se préoccupe plutôt de montrer que sa définition de l'âme, entendue comme forme du corps, couvre l'ensemble
des données qu'il a convenu de rattacher à l'essence. Commentant,
dans *art.cit. n.1* (447-8), l'ensemble du passage 415b7-416a9,

Mlle S.Mansion déclare, à propos du mouvement par lequel le vivant préserve son identité formelle: 'que ce soit là la tâche
qu'il s'assigne et l'oeuvre qui est sa fin, indique qu'il est
lui-même ou - si on le prend formellement - que son âme est
elle-même fin, au second sens de ce mot: non plus comme le but à
atteindre (puisqu'elle existe déjà), mais comme l'être au profit
duquel l'action est faite (*finis cui* distingué de *finis cuius*)'.
Ce propos me paraît juste en ce qu'il affirme (on y vient dans
la suite du texte), non en ce qu'il nie: Aristote insiste trop
clairement, disais-je, sur l'avènement graduel de l'âme-forme.

82 Nuyens (*op.cit. n.4*), 245-6.

83 Troisième aspect de la causalité reconnue à l'âme: *De An.* II 4,
415b21-8.

84 Ici encore, les positions des symposiastes couvrent un spectre
très étendu, dont il importe d'indiquer quelques échantillons.
    MM. Graeser et Moreau sont ouverts à la présence des deux
significations, le premier notant que le datif est approprié à
l'exercice des fonctions, le génitif au statut de l'âme elle-
même comme fin des processus vitaux; M. Moreau relève que les
acceptions au datif et au génitif s'opposent comme le sens banal
et le sens plus philosophique.
    Quant à MM. Patzig et Verdenius, ils soulignent que ce second
sens est le seul possible à leurs yeux: puisque l'âme se définit
comme acte, c'est-à-dire comme perfection dans son ordre, on ne
voit pas qu'elle ait à gagner quoi que ce soit au processus
vital.
    La position inverse est notamment celle du Prof. de Strycker.
Le corps étant ordonné à être l'instrument de l'âme, 'un instrument est quelque chose qui sert; il sert à une fin (qui est
alors une fin οὗ; mais Aristote n'en dit rien). Mais il sert à
quelqu'un qui en fait son profit, et ce quelqu'un est alors la
fin ᾧ. L'âme est ici ce qui se sert de l'instrument.' Analogue
à certains égards est la position de Mlle Mansion, qui propose
de traduire comme suit notre texte:
    'Il est clair que l'âme est aussi cause finale. En effet, de
même que l'intellect agit en vue de quelque chose, de la même
manière le fait aussi la nature et cela (= ce en vue de quoi elle
agit) est pour elle une fin. Telle est l'âme chez les animaux
(êtres vivants) et cela par nature (ceci peut se comprendre dans
deux sens, dont je préfère le second: (1) l'âme est par nature
une fin; (2) l'âme est par nature quelque chose qui agit en vue
d'une fin), car tous les corps naturels sont les organes (instruments) de l'âme, comme ceux des animaux, ainsi aussi ceux des
plantes: ils sont en effet en vue de l'âme; mais ce en vue de
quoi se dit en deux sens, le οὗ et le ᾧ.'
    Et le professeur de Louvain commente comme suit (cf. aussi
n. 81):
    'Suivant la deuxième interprétation de τοιοῦτον, cela voudrait
dire: l'âme agit en vue d'une fin et se sert pour cela, comme
d'instrument, du corps. Mais, puisque la fin se dit dans deux
sens, il n'y a pas que la fin qu'elle poursuit (génitif), il y a
encore la fin qu'elle est elle-même, en tant que tout ce qu'elle
fait, elle le fait à son propre profit ou avantage (datif). Elle

est donc bien cause finale, mais dans ce second sens seulement.'

85 C'est bien cette antinomie que traduisait A.Mansion, 'Travaux
d'ensemble sur Aristote, son oeuvre et sa philosophie', *Rev.
Philos. Louvain* 57 (1959), 52: 'le passage de *De An.* II 4, 415b
18, où le corps se dit instrument de l'âme est écrit dans un tout
autre esprit (*sc.* que celui de la période instrumentiste); le rappro-
chement entre l'âme et la nature, qui dans les choses n'est pas
une réalité indépendante, le montre assez'. J'ai soutenu de
même cette immanence de la nature (cf. *supra* et n. 76), mais
rien ne semble empêcher que les outils de l'âme forment l'ensemble différencié décrit dans le texte et que, dès lors, le corps
soit 'instrument' au sens le plus obvie du terme. Quant à l'extension d'une 'période intermédiaire', voire à son existence,
cf. Lefèvre (*op.cit. n.5*), ch. IV.

86 C'est d'ailleurs ce qu'implique également la finale de *De An.* I
3 (407b25-6), où Aristote présente sa conviction personnelle:
'il faut en effet que, comme l'art se sert de ses instruments,
ainsi l'âme de son corps': δεῖ γὰρ τὴν μὲν τέχνην χρῆσθαι τοῖς
ὀργάνοις, τὴν δὲ ψυχὴν τῷ σώματι.

87 Ce n'est pas le seul endroit où Aristote suggère lui-même les
corollaires 'instrumentistes' de l'hylémorphisme. Ainsi le *GA*
IV 1, 765b11-14, rappelle le caractère 'formel' de la reproduction (c'est un co-principe qui est transmis, non un matériau),
mais indique clairement que l'impulsion initiale va déclencher
le mécanisme de la différenciation. Pour plus de précisions,
cf. Lefèvre (*op.cit. n.5*), ch. II, notamment 85-95.

88 On se souvient peut-être encore de l'ancienneté que l'*Aristoteles* de W.Jaeger voulait attribuer à la doctrine de l'intellect,
puis de la dissection opérée par H.Langerbeck, *Gnomon* 11 (1935),
416-23. Plus récemment, Moraux (*art.cit. n.21*) a clairement
montré l'inanité des propositions émises par W.Theiler (*op.cit.
n.18*) et, en passant, a réfuté les analyses dues à H.Dörrie,
'Gedanken zur Methodik des Aristoteles in der Schrift περὶ
ψυχῆς', dans *Aristote et les problèmes de méthode*, ed. S.Mansion
(Louvain-Paris 1961), 223-44. Quant à la relation entre l'âme
et le corps, elle inspira à Sir David Ross l'idée que seuls les
livres II et III (ch. 1 à 8) seraient postérieurs à la phase
instrumentiste (conférence de 1957, reprise dans *Aristotle and
Plato in the mid-fourth century*, ed. I.Düring et G.E.L.Owen
(Göteborg 1960), 1-17; cf. 4-5), mais il semble avoir ensuite
abandonné cette division de l'oeuvre (*op.cit. n.8*, 10-12).

89 Nuyens (*op.cit. n.4*), 163-70, 254-6; W.D.Ross, *Aristotle. Parva
Naturalia* (Oxford 1955), 17-18; I.Düring, *Aristoteles, Darstellung und Interpretation seines Denkens* (Heidelberg 1966), 562.

90 Elles sont énumerées, après l'*Index* de Bonitz et avec de menues
différences, par Nuyens (*op.cit. n.4*), 250-4, et par Ross (*op.
cit. n.8*), 8.

91 Cf. S.Mansion (*art.cit. n.1*), 435-6 et n. 26.

92 S.Mansion (*art.cit. n.1*), 440-6 et 448.

93 On sait que le Dr H.J.Drossaart Lulofs (*Aristotelis De insomniis et de divinatione per somnum* (Leiden 1947), xv-xxvi) voit dans cette première partie du *De somno* actuel (jusqu'à 455b13) une reprise du sujet, postérieure dès lors à ce qui la suit dans les manuscrits.   Je n'ai guère à discuter ici son analyse soignée, sauf en ceci que l'auteur, emboîtant le pas à M. Nuyens, appuyait le caractère ancien de la seconde partie sur sa parenté avec des écrits dits instrumentistes: *MA* (cf. 455b34-456a2) et *PA* (cf. *ibid.* et 457b27-9, avec, dans les deux cas, la formule ἐν ἑτέροις); or, il se fait que je ne puis cantonner ces traités dans une période antérieure au *De anima* (cf. Lefèvre (*op.cit. n.5*), ch. IV, 154-82).

94 Le MS P semble avoir biaisé avec la *lectio difficilior* ἐπεί en écrivant ἔτι, mais le résultat n'est guère plus heureux.

95 Les partisans d'une distinction tranchée entre ces deux 'doctrines' semblent ne s'en être pas aperçus.   Nuyens (*op.cit. n.4*), 168, déclare seulement qu'une telle 'référence doit être négligée' (ceci à propos du parallèle en 474b11-12), et ce, sans autre explication.

96 *GA* V 1, 779b21-5.

97 C.H.Kahn, 'Sensation and consciousness in Aristotle's psychology', *Archiv Gesch. Philos.* 48 (1966), 47, reconnaît en passant le caractère méthodologique de ce renvoi.   Nuyens (*op.cit. n.4*), 261, lui donne au contraire une valeur chronologique.

98 Cf. W.Jaeger, *Aristotle: Fundamentals of the history of his development*, trans. R.Robinson (2e éd. Oxford 1948), 294-5: '...the general scheme - perhaps a thoroughly late idea into which at the end of his researches Aristotle forced the mass of his detailed inquiries.   It agrees with the order as given in the best manuscripts.'

99 Cf., parmi d'autres, l'exposé fouillé de A.Mansion, *Introduction à la Physique Aristotélicienne* (Louvain-Paris 1946), 22-34, complétant diverses indications recueillies par Jaeger; on peut y ajouter ce que révèlent les catalogues d'Hésychius (v. Rose, *Ar. fragmenta* (Leipzig 1886), 16-17) et de Ptolémée (P.Moraux, *Les listes anciennes des ouvrages d'Aristote* (Louvain 1951), 297) bien qu'ici le *GA* soit suivi de *Inc.*, *Long.*, *De vita*.

100 On ne peut ici qu'effleurer les exceptions apparentes ou les particularités; à lire les données copieuses rassemblées dans Bonitz, *Index*, 97b41-104a2, on constate par exemple (100a) que le *PA* renvoie au *Inc.*, censé existant, à trois reprises: IV 11, 690b15, 692a17; 13, 696a11, alors que ce second traité *suit* l' autre dans le second schéma (A.Mansion (*op.cit. n.99*), 26).   Mais il faut observer que c'est le seul 'cours' où figure de façon certaine le *Inc.*, qui a donc pu entretenir d'autres rapports avec le *PA*; d'autre part, les chapitres de ce dernier qui y renvoient figurent en queue de l'ouvrage: ils semblent avoir été ajoutés,

car leur place normale serait plus haut, après IV 4 (cf. le plan de W.Ogle, *The works of Aristotle translated into English*, ed. J.A.Smith and W.D.Ross, Vol. V, *De Partibus Animalium* (Oxford 1912), xviii.

101 *De sensu*, 1, 436a7–8; Ross (*op.cit. n.89*), 16; l'inconséquence de Ross a été bien notée par W.F.R.Hardie (*art.cit. n.19*), 67.

102 Nuyens (*op.cit. n.4*), 251, citant les passages qui insistent sur le caractère 'corporel' des phénomènes vitaux: *Sens*. 6, 445b17–18; *Mem*. 1, 449b31–450a1; 2, 453a14–23; *Somn*. 1, 454a7–11. - Sur une divergence prétendue entre *De An*. et *PN* à propos du sensorium commun, cf. *infra* et n. 108.

103 *Mem*. 1, 450a28–9: διὰ τῆς αἰσθήσεως ἐν τῇ ψυχῇ καὶ τῷ μορίῳ τοῦ σώματος τῷ ἔχοντι αὐτήν ... (texte signalé par Ross également (*op. cit. n.89*), 16). Cf. encore *Somn*. 2, 455b34–456a1, 4: ἡ τῆς αἰσθήσεως ἀρχὴ γίγνεται ἀπὸ τοῦ αὐτοῦ μέρους τοῖς ζῴοις ἀφ'οὗπερ καὶ ἡ τῆς κινήσεως ... τοῦτ'ἐστὶ τὸ περὶ τὴν καρδίαν μέρος. *Insomn*. 3, 461a6–7: les impressions sensibles ἐπὶ τὴν ἀρχὴν τῆς αἰσθήσεως καταφέρονται.

104 *Long*. 2, 465a25–6, évoque *De An*. III 5, 430a23–4, sur l'oubli que provoque la mort; aussitôt après, l'auteur se demande si l'âme est dans le corps comme le savoir dans l'âme (c'est-à-dire d'une façon non substantielle), et sa réponse est motivée comme suit: ἐπεὶ οὐ φαίνεται τοιαύτη οὖσα ... (*ibid*. 465a30–1). Ce traité est examiné par Nuyens (*op.cit. n.4*), 163 et 169.

105 Cf. les exposés sur la chaleur, *Long*. 3,5,6, *passim*; sur le haut et le bas en 6, 467a32–4, etc. On notera que l'unité de composition de ce curieux opuscule ('ganz selbständig', note Düring (*op.cit. n.89*), 562) mérite une serieuse analyse, de même que ses relations avec la littérature médicale.

106 Cf. le catalogue attribué à Ptolémée: Moraux (*op.cit. n.99*), 296–7; Ross (*op.cit. n.89*), 3.

107 Pour les détails, cf. Ross (*op.cit. n.89*), 6–10; Lefèvre (*op.cit. n.5*), 184–5.

108 Cf. Lefèvre (*op.cit. n.5*), 185–7, où je justifie mon désaccord avec I.Block, 'The order of Aristotle's psychological writings', *AJP* 82 (1961), 50–77; celui-ci, on s'en souvient, trouve dans les *PN* une doctrine du sensorium commun beaucoup plus élaborée que dans le *De An*., où le 'sens commun', 'dépourvu d'appellation spécifique', aurait 'pour seule mission de comparer et d'unifier les sensations venues des divers sens'(63). Mais Block semble ignorer par exemple *De An*. II 12, 424a17–19, 24–8: parlant en général de toute sensation, Aristote prouve que ce phénomène consiste à recevoir les formes sensibles ἄνευ τῆς ὕλης, et il poursuit: αἰσθητήριον δὲ πρῶτον ἐν ᾧ ἡ τοιαύτη δύναμις, à savoir: le sensorium primaire - c'est-à-dire le coeur, note à bon droit Barbotin, 65 - est celui où réside une faculté de cette sorte. Voilà donc, dans le *De An*., un titre spécifique, parfaitement adéquat, et une mission importante qui prélude à celles de l'imagination et de l'intellect.

109 Juv. 24, 479a29-32: Γένεσις μὲν οὖν ἐστιν ἡ πρώτη μέθεξις ἐν τῷ θερμῷ τῆς θρεπτικῆς ψυχῆς, ζωὴ δ'ἡ μονὴ ταύτης ... En a29, comme le souligne bien W.D.Ross (op.cit. n.89, 335), θερμῷ ne saurait être régime de μέθεξις (même option chez G.R.T.Ross, The works of Aristotle translated into English, ed. J.A.Smith and W.D.Ross, Vol. III (Oxford 1908)) - qui cependant donne dans la paraphrase: 'the initial participation, mediated by warm substance, in the nutritive soul').

110 Juv. 23, 479a4-6 (cf. 2, 468b14-15).

111 Cf. PA II 7, 652b17-27; GA II 6, 743b27-9.

112 Cf. PA III 6; GA II 1, 732b28-34; II 6, 741b37-742a6.

113 Juv. 4, 469b14-16 (trad. Nuyens (op.cit. n.4), 166): τοῦ δ'ἐν ταύτῃ [sc. θερμοῦ ψυχομένου] φθείρεται πάμπαν, διὰ τὸ τὴν ἀρχὴν ἐντεῦθεν τῆς θερμότητος ἠρτῆσθαι πᾶσι, καὶ τῆς ψυχῆς ὥσπερ ἐμπε-πυρευμένης ἐν τοῖς μορίοις τούτοις.

114 Juv. 14, 474b10, 12-13: ἀδύνατον ὑπάρχειν ... ταύτην ... ἄνευ τοῦ φυσικοῦ πυρός· ἐν τούτῳ γὰρ ἡ φύσις ἐμπεπύρευκεν αὐτήν.

115 Juv. 22, 478a28-30 (in fine, Ross - cf. op.cit. n.89, 333 - lit ἐμπόρευσιν; les deux vocables sont aussi rares l'un que l'autre): καταψύξεως μὲν οὖν ὅλως ἡ τῶν ζῴων δεῖται φύσις διὰ τὴν ἐν τῇ καρδίᾳ τῆς ψυχῆς ἐμπύρωσιν.

116 Cf. note précéd. et L.Couloubaritsis, compte rendu de Lefèvre (op.cit. n.5) (dans Annales de l'Inst. de Philos. de l'Univ. Libre de Bruxelles (1973), 238-46), 245. Cette recension figure, s'il m'est permis de l'apprécier, parmi les plus soignées et les plus intelligentes que je connaisse à ce jour.

117 Top. VI 2, 139b34. Le Liddell-Scott suggère entre autres une formule qui prête à la métaphore: 'set aglow', mais on sait que la révision du grand Lexicon opérée entre 1925 et 1940 est notamment l'oeuvre de divers Oxford translators (cf. la Préface, VII-VIII, XI-XII), et telle est bien la version qu'adoptait en 1908 G.R.T.Ross pour les deux passages cités par le LSJ (469b16 et 474b13); d'ordinaire, le sens est plutôt set on fire, voire roast in, or on, a fire.

118 GA III 1, 751b6: ἐν γὰρ τῷ θερμῷ ἡ ψυχικὴ ἀρχή. II 3, 736b 34-5: τὸ καλούμενον θερμόν. τοῦτο δ'οὐ πῦρ οὐδὲ τοιαύτη δύναμίς ἐστιν; cf. P.Moraux, 'A propos du νοῦς θύραθεν chez Aristote', dans Autour d'Aristote, Recueil d'études ... offert à Mgr A. Mansion (Louvain 1955), 278, F.Solmsen, 'The vital heat, the in-born pneuma and the aether', JHS 57 (1957), 120-1, et Lefèvre (op.cit. n.5), 190 et n. 38.

119 PA II 7, 652b7-11, 13-14 (trad. Nuyens (op.cit. n.4), 159, qui toutefois donne, pour ἐν ... συνεστάναι, b9, 'elle est intimement unie'): οἱ μὲν γὰρ τοῦ ζῴου τὴν ψυχὴν τιθέασι πῦρ ἢ τοιαύτην τινὰ δύναμιν φορτικῶς τιθέντες· βέλτιον δ'ἴσως φάναι ἐν τοιούτῳ τινὶ σώματι συνεστάναι. τούτου δ'αἴτιον ὅτι τοῖς τῆς ψυχῆς ἔργοις ὑπηρετικώτατον τῶν σωμάτων τὸ θερμόν ἐστιν.

120 En réponse à une question judicieuse du Dr Sorabji, je souligne-
rais le langage de *De An*. II 4, 416a9-18: l'âme n'est pas faite
de feu, car ce dernier ne peut être que συναίτιόν πως; *ibid*. 416
b28-9: l'élaboration de la nourriture requiert la *chaleur*. Les
experts décideront du sort à réserver à l'exemple énoncé en *Top*.
V 2, 129b18-19, pour montrer que le 'propre' devant caractériser
un sujet ne peut être moins intelligible que lui (sur cette règ-
le, cf. G.Verbeke, 'La notion de propriété dans les *Topiques*',
dans *Aristotle on Dialectic*, ed. G.E.L.Owen (Oxford 1968), 265-
7): ὁ θεὶς πυρὸς ἴδιον τὸ ἐν ᾧ πρώτῳ ψυχὴ πέφυκεν εἶναι ἀγνωστο-
τέρῳ κέχρηται τοῦ πυρός. Le libellé aristotélicien n'incline
guère à penser que l'auteur évoque ici les propos d'un autre
penseur; et la désapprobation vise non pas cette thèse, mais la
faute consistant à éclairer - si on l'ose écrire à propos du
feu - *obscurum per obscurius*. En sens opposé, de telles illustrations ne peuvent nous assurer de la vraie position d'Aristote au moment où il écrit, si ce n'est lorsque le texte l'impose (cf. I.Düring, 'Aristotle's use of examples in the *Topics*',
même recueil, 203-9). Jusqu'à plus ample informé, concluons
que cet exemple, matériellement identique à ce que nous lisions
en *Juv*. 14, 474b12-13 - cf. ἐν τούτῳ [sc. τῷ πυρί] ἡ φύσις ἐμπεπύρευκεν αὐτήν - représente sans doute une position du Stagirite, mais sans que l'on puisse savoir s'il la soutient encore
à l'époque des *Topiques*.

121 *GC* II 4; cf. *Cael*. III 6.

122 *GC* II 3, 330b3-4, 25-6; II 4, 331b25-6. L'intervention du feu
n'est pas une mixtion, mais une 'génération au sens absolu,
celle du feu sous l'action du feu', c'est une 'genèse' (I 5,
322a15-16).

123 *GC* II 6, 334a13-15: εἰ μὲν πῦρ ἡ ψυχή, τὰ πάθη ὑπάρξει αὐτῇ ὅσα
πυρὶ ᾗ πῦρ· εἰ δὲ μικτόν, τὰ σωματικά· τούτων δ'οὐδὲν σωματικόν.

124 *Supra*, pp.39-40. *Juv*. 1, 467b14: δῆλον ὅτι οὐχ οἷόν τ'εἶναι
σῶμα τὴν οὐσίαν αὐτῆς.

125 *Juv*. 5, 469b21-2: μάρανσίν τε καὶ σβέσιν (même distinction en
Cael. III 6, 305a9-13), d'où nécessité de l'alimenter (b26; cf.
GC II 8, 335a17) et de le 'refroidir' (b27-9), c'est-à-dire de
l'aérer: 6, 470a6-7: δεῖ γίγνεσθαί τινα τοῦ θερμοῦ ἐν τῇ ἀρχῇ
κατάψυξιν.

126 *Juv*. 14, 474b16, 18, 19: θᾶττον σβέννυται διασπώμενον ... καὶ
γὰρ ὀργάνοις διαιρουμένου τοῦ ζῴου ... ἀποθνήσκουσιν.

127 Cf. *Juv*. 22, 478a26-8, a34-b1, qui résume *HA*, I 17 et II 17, et
y renvoie, ainsi qu'aux dissections.

128 Sur une parenté éventuelle, mais peu probable, avec le *Timée*,
certains Présocratiques ou d'autres écrits hippocratiques, cf.
Lefèvre (*op.cit. n.5*), 199-203; pour la date du *Régime* et le
contexte des propos cités ci-dessous, cf. *ibid*. 203-5.

129 *Régime*, éd. R.Joly (Paris 1968), I 7, 1; 9,3: τὸ μὲν οὖν κατα-
φραχθὲν πῦρ καὶ πλεῖστόν ἐστι.

130 *Régime* I 10, 3 (trad. de Joly, qui omet 'dominant'; F.Hüffmeier, 'Phronesis in den Schriften des Corpus Hippocraticum', *Hermes* 89 (1961), 51-84, cite ce texte, mais sans le mettre en rapport avec l'aristotélisme): τὸ θερμότατον καὶ ἰσχυρότατον πῦρ, ὅπερ πάντων κρατεῖ, διέπον ἅπαντα κατὰ φύσιν, ἄθικτον καὶ ὄψει καὶ ψαύσει, ἐν τούτῳ ψυχή, νόος, φρόνησις, αὔξησις, μείωσις, κίνησις, διάλλαξις, ὕπνος, ἔγερσις.

131 *Régime* I 25, 1-2: Αὔξεται δὲ οὐκ ἐν πᾶσιν ὁμοίως, ἀλλ'ἐν μὲν τοῖσι νέοισι τῶν σωμάτων, ἅτε ταχέης ἐούσης τῆς περιφορῆς καὶ τοῦ σώματος αὐξίμου, ἐκπυρουμένη καὶ λεπτυνομένη καταναλίσκεται ἐς τὴν αὔξησιν τοῦ σώματος ... Ὅσα δὲ τῶν σωμάτων ἀκμάζοντά ἐστι καὶ ἐν τῇσι ἡλικίῃσι γονίμῃσι, δύναται τρέφειν καὶ αὔξειν ... ὁκοῖα πλείστας δύναται ψυχὰς τρέφειν, ταῦτα ἰσχυρότατα.

132 *Régime* I 29, 2 (Littré ajoute un μή devant le second κεκαυμένους, Joly devant le premier, ce qui semble arbitraire en toute hypothèse): Εἰ δέ τις ἀπιστεῖ ψυχὴν μὴ προσμίσγεσθαι ψυχῇ, ἀφορῶν ἐς ἄνθρακας, κεκαυμένους πρὸς κεκαυμένους προσβάλλων ... ὅμοιον τὸ σῶμα πάντες παρασχήσονται καὶ οὐ διάδηλος ἕτερος τοῦ ἑτέρου ... τοῦτο· καὶ ἀνθρωπίνη ψυχὴ πάσχει.

   M. G.E.R.Lloyd me fait remarquer avec pertinence que l'identification du feu et de la chaleur vitale semble avoir été assez courante à l'époque, comme l'atteste par ex. l'Anonymus Londinensis. Le thème relevé ici ne prouve donc pas à lui seul une influence directe du *Régime* sur les opinions d'Aristote.

133 Sur une doxographie relative à Empédocle, cf. Lefèvre (*op.cit.* *n.5*), 208, n. 107. *Régime* II 62, 2; *Juv.* 4, 469b7-8: πᾶν τὸ σῶμα τῶν ζῴων ἔχει τινὰ σύμφυτον θερμότητα φυσικήν.

134 *Juv.* 24, 479a29-30; cf. *supra*, p.43 et n.109. Il s'agit bien de la *conception* (cf. G.R.T.Ross et P.Siwek), non de la *naissance* (*sic* W.D.Ross).

135 Cette distinction ne m'apparaît que deux fois dans le *Juv.* (2, 468a27-9, b3-4 et 23, 479a1-3), et seulement pour expliquer que beaucoup d'insectes puissent survivre en étant sectionnés: c'est que leur âme est potentiellement multiple. Mais cette précision pourrait être adventice: ailleurs, elle ne figure qu'en *De An.* II 2, 413b16-24. Elle peut donc avoir été ajoutée avec les références à ce traité (si c'est bien notre *De An.* qu'elles visent!) qui figurent en *Juv.* 1, 467b13 et en 14, 474b10-13, en même temps que la déclaration initiale sur l'âme incorporelle, qui précède immédiatement la première référence.

136 Rôle conjoint du πνεῦμα, du feu et de l'eau dans la fécondation (*Régime* I 7, 1; 9, 1; 16, 2; *GA* II 2, 736a1); différences entre mâles et femelles (*Régime* I 34, 1; *GA* I 19, 726b30-727a2; IV 1, 766a18-24, a34-b1); évocation du τέκτων (*Régime* I 16, 1; *GA* I 22, 730b11-13 et 30); bivalence de ὄργανα pour désigner des *outils* et des *organes* (*Régime* I 22, 1-2; *GA* ibid.; cf. *De An.* II 4, 415b 17-18, et les remarques *supra*, p.36).

137 Cette seconde option est celle de Couloubaritsis (*op.cit. n.116*), 245: 'il semblerait qu'ici aussi, comme partout ailleurs, l'instrumentisme s'intègre, en fin de compte, à l'hylémorphisme, de

sorte que l'on pourrait présumer que ce traité est contemporain du *De part.*, voire même ultérieur. En conséquence, nous croyons fermement qu'il faut aller encore plus loin que ne l'a fait l' abbé Lefèvre et supprimer toute période instrumentiste de l'évolution de la pensée d'Aristote.'

138 *Juv.* 2, 468b10-12; 23, 479a4-5, 6-7: τὰ δ'ἄριστα συνεστηκότα τοῦτ'οὐ πάσχει τῶν ζῴων διὰ τὸ εἶναι τὴν φύσιν αὐτῶν ὡς ἐνδέχεται μάλιστα μίαν. - ὅσα μὴ ζωτικὰ λίαν εἰσί, πολὺν χρόνον ζῶσιν ἐξῃρημένης τῆς καρδίας ... διὰ τὸ μὴ συγκεῖσθαι τὴν φύσιν αὐτῶν εὖ.

139 *De An.* II 1, 412b8-9.

140 *De An.* I 5, 411b7-8.

141 *De An.* I 2, 405b1-6: τῶν δὲ φορτικωτέρων καὶ ὕδωρ τινὲς ἀπεφήναντο ...

142 Hippolyte, *Philos.* I 16 (566, 20-4 Diels): Τὸ σπέρμα εἶναι τὸ φαινόμενον ἡμῖν ἐξ ὑγροῦ, ἐξ οὗ φησι ψυχὴν γίγνεσθαι.

143 *De An.* I 5, 411a9-10: ἐν ... τῷ πυρὶ οὖσα ἡ ψυχὴ οὐ ποιεῖ ζῷον ... Cf. *GA* II 3, 737a2-3.

144 Dans '"Quinta natura" et psychologie aristotelicienne' (*Rev. Philos. Louvain* 69 (1971), 5-43), je suis amené à soutenir la validité substantielle de ces témoignages; le spiritualisme d' Aristote (si nettement thématisé par le *De An.* et le *GA* II 3, notamment) serait donc moins un héritage platonicien qu'une conquête personnelle ayant valeur philosophique exemplaire.

3: ON ARISTOTLE'S FRAMEWORK OF *SENSIBILIA*

Andreas Graeser

There is a curious distinction employed by Aristotle in the course of
De anima II 6. It is designed to provide for a specification of the
various senses[1] and their functions. What this distinction amounts to
appears to be a rather clean-cut division of all *sensibilia* into two
basic kinds; it serves as a classification of what may be called
'proper' *sensibilia* and 'incidental' *sensibilia*. And it would seem
that this distinction also leaves us with some sort of rudimentary
notion concerning the basic difference between genuinely non-propositional αἴσθησις on the one side and propositional αἴσθησις on the
other.[2] But are these two fundamental classes of *sensibilia* fixed
in the sense that they are meant to be mutually exclusive? Or do
the *sensibilia* allow for being specified in either way, that is with
reference to the function(s) of the sense in question?

As the position Aristotle takes on these matters is not an altogether explicit one it may well need some clarification. Such clarification will be attempted in the course of this paper. Moreover
it is my concern to call attention to some of the fundamental issues
involved in this distinction. Yet it is only fair to say that some
of the problems that arise from this discussion require a much more
exhaustive treatment, one that would certainly go far beyond the
limited scope of this paper.

According to Aristotle there are two basic types of *sensibilia*. He
refers to them as καθ' αὐτὰ αἰσθητά (*A*-objects) and κατὰ συμβεβηκὸς
αἰσθητά (*B*-objects) respectively (418a8-9). Now it is interesting
to observe that the κοινὰ αἰσθητά so called[3] (*K*-objects) are supposed to join the ἴδια αἰσθητά (*I*-objects) under the heading *A*. The
idea behind this is not easy to grasp, particularly since it appears
to be in conflict with the statement made in III 1, 425a14-15 (ὧν
[*sc.* τῶν κοινῶν] ἑκάστη αἰσθήσει αἰσθανόμεθα κατὰ συμβεβηκός). Now
this statement has been taken as part of the hypothesis against
which Aristotle is about to argue.[4] There is good reason to assume,

however, that Aristotle is, in fact, making a point of his own (see below pp. 81-6).

But what about the basic distinction drawn between *A* and *B*? Its precise nature remains unclear since Aristotle does not choose to elaborate on the crucial function assigned to the key terms 'καθ' αὐτό' and 'κατὰ συμβεβηκός'. Anybody familiar with the writings of Aristotle knows that these terms play an important role throughout his work; much of Aristotle's philosophical achievement consists in the explanatory force that notions such as these have. Now as far as *De An.* II 6 is concerned it seems obvious that the terms in question are meant to function as intensional modifiers of the meaning attached to 'αἰσθητόν'. It is not altogether clear, however, what point, precisely, this distinction makes. For at the end of ch. II 6 Aristotle adds an important qualification: it is the class of *I*-objects only to which the term αἰσθητόν applies in its proper sense (κυρίως, 418a24).[5] And since the *I*-objects form a sub-class of *A* the qualification added in 418a24 is very likely to have some bearing on the meaning of 'καθ' αὐτό' too. In other words, among the *A*-objects some are more καθ' αὐτὰ αἰσθητά than others.[6] This complicates the whole issue considerably. And we should thus keep in mind that any ordinary rendering of the key terms in question by 'proper' and 'incidental' respectively will probably turn out to be too vague; the same will be true of 'essential' which has also been taken as the equivalent to 'καθ' αὐτό'.[7] Any such notions as those expressed by 'proper' or 'incidental' and 'essential' or 'accidental' are useful provided we take them to be merely heuristic devices. But we had better look again at what Aristotle is arguing.

What he is aiming at is to point out that some things are perceptible because of their own character, rather than because of their association with something else. And I submit that the notions of καθ' αὐτό and κατὰ συμβεβηκός are used to express something about the logical status peculiar to either kind of *sensibilia*. While *A*-objects are, in a way, independent in that they are perceptible because of their own character, *B*-objects are not; they are perceptible because of their association with something else and thus belong, in a way, to the objects they are associated with.

In fact, contextual evidence (see e.g. II 5, 417a5-6 where the elements are said to be perceived 'as such' or 'according to what

belongs to them accidentally'[8]) may be taken to suggest that the
meaning intended for 'καθ' αὐτό' in II 6 is likely to come close to
the one employed in II 7; here Aristotle makes a point concerning
the object of sight: καθ' αὐτὸ δὲ οὐ τῷ λόγῳ ἀλλ' ὅτι ἐν ἑαυτῷ ἔχει
τὸ αἴτιον τοῦ εἶναι ὁρατόν (418a30-31).[9] I am not sure whether I
have properly understood this passage. Is the καθ' αὐτὸ ὁρατόν here
colour, or is it the body or surface on which (ἐπί) colour is over-
laid? In the latter case one would probably be right to say that it
could not, after all, throw light on the sense in which *colour* (not
body or surface) is said to be a καθ' αὐτὸ αἰσθητόν in the preceding
chapter. The point would rather seem to be, on this interpretation,
that body or surface contains spatially within itself the cause of
visibility. This is presumably very different from the point in II ‹
6 that colour is visible because it is colour. And yet the analogy
is striking. The notion involved, i.e. the rather simple but not
necessarily trivial fact that *X* may be called *X* precisely on the
ground that it contains its *raison d'être* within itself, fits the
basic idea behind what is said in *Metaph.* Δ 18, 1022a32-3 (οὗ μὴ
ἔστιν ἄλλο αἴτιον). This notion can, along with the additional
statement in *APo.* I 4, 73b6-10 concerning the ontological use of
'καθ' αὐτό', account for the criterion of the independent existence
of particulars.

If we suppose that it is this notion which Aristotle has in mind
in II 6 too, we would have to infer that the *sensibilia* called καθ'
αὐτὰ αἰσθητά are called so precisely because they are meant to have,
within the framework of perceptual language, some sort of independent status. This very notion is confirmed by the fact that according to Aristotle it is the *I*-object which occupies the subject-
position in a perceptual judgement (see e.g. III 3, 428b21 *et passim*)
and the substantial particular which occupies what Aristotle wrongly
takes to be the predicate-position.

Now the assumption that there are such 'independent' objects - be
it *F*s or *F*-things - entails the idea that these objects are perceived
as such. That is to say they are perceived just simply and primarily[10] as what they are with regard to the sense in question. It is
rather obvious that all this suits the respective *I*-objects of the
various special senses. One may ask, however, (1) how this is going
to work with the *K*-objects. To be sure they are treated on a par

with the *I*-objects; this is obvious from both the statement made in
III 1, 425a27-8 (τῶν δὲ κοινῶν ἤδη ἔχομεν αἴσθησιν κοινήν, οὐ κατὰ
συμβεβηκός) and the phrase 'διὰ τὸ ἀκολουθεῖν ἀλλήλοις' in III 1,
425b8. The latter expression carries a logical force; it signifies
extensional equivalence: wherever there is colour there is size and
vice versa. However, this is not the whole story. I have already
noted that III 1, 425a14-15 probably has to be taken as a statement
of Aristotle's own position rather than as part of an hypothesis
against which he is arguing (see above p. 69). On this interpretation we would have to allow for the possibility (2) that *K*-objects
may, in some way, be specified as *B*-objects. Moreover we would
have, *mutatis mutandis*, to consider the question (3) how then Aristotle is prepared to maintain this fundamental distinction between
'dependent' and 'independent' objects if there are *I*-objects which
are perceived κατὰ συμβεβηκός (see III 1, 425a30-1) and are thus
to be specified as *B*-objects as well. We shall come back to these
points shortly, after having extended the interpretation of the
notion of κατὰ συμβεβηκός.

The term 'κατὰ συμβεβηκός' is used to indicate that *B* comprises
objects whose status differs from the one peculiar to objects assigned to *A* in that it is not independent. *Qua* αἰσθητά they are
not perceptible because of their own character. They are, therefore, not perceived 'as such' or 'immediately'.[11] Rather they are
perceived because of their association with something else. It is
the mode of speech (e.g. '...belongs to...') which deserves particular consideration:

κατὰ συμβεβηκὸς γὰρ τούτου αἰσθάνεται ὅτι τῷ λευκῷ συμβέβηκε
τοῦτο οὗ αἰσθάνεται· διὸ καὶ οὐδὲν πάσχει ᾗ τοιοῦτον ὑπὸ τοῦ
αἰσθητοῦ (418a21-4).

Now commentators tend to disagree over how to construe this sentence. Does αἰσθάνεται in 418a23 go with τῷ λευκῷ or with 'Diares'
son' and thus with the preceding τοῦτο? On syntactical grounds the
first option should be discarded.[12] It has the disadvantage of producing awkward Greek. There can be no doubt about this: and yet in
favour of this view it may be said that it helps us to get rid of a
problem that has to do with the requirement of logical consistency.
For if the object of αἰσθάνεται is not to τὸ λευκόν but rather τοῦτο
and thus 'Diares' son', consistency would require us to understand

τοιοῦτον to refer to e.g. τὸ λευκόν as the καθ᾽ αὑτὸ αἰσθητόν. This
line of thought cannot, however, be pursued seriously unless one is
prepared to argue that Aristotle meant to endow 'accidental perception' with some sort of special sense.[13]   But this is not what Aristotle meant to establish. His argument was not aimed at the thesis
e.g. that 'in the case of accidental perception the sense is not affected by the specific *I*-object as such' but rather designed to establish that 'what is true in the case of accidental perception is
that sight is not affected by the object (i.e. Diares' son) as such
but by an object that is associated with the logically preceding *I*-
object in the way an attribute is related to its subject'. This
point would come out rather well from the line of interpretation
suggested by the first option. Yet linguistic considerations do
not favour this approach and should not after all be overruled. Thus
it seems reasonable to drop the consistency-requirement and to understand: 'For sight perceives him (i.e. Diares' son) incidentally because that which sight perceives (i.e. Diares' son) belongs incidentally to the white. Therefore it does not suffer from the thing perceived as such ...'

The essential point seems to come out quite clearly. For what the
example which Aristotle employs here and elsewhere (see e.g. III 1,
425a25-6) actually suggests is that a rather large number of incidental *sensibilia* are, in fact, substantial particulars and that these
objects are treated as attributes (*sic!*) predicable of the logical
subject of a perceptual judgement. Moreover it seems obvious that
the *I*-objects which occupy the subject-position (cf. also III 3, 428b
21-2 εἰ δὲ τοῦτο τὸ λευκὸν ἢ ἄλλο τι, ψεύδεται) are not conceived of
as genuinely belonging to the category of substance. What precisely
their status is, *qua* logical subject of a perceptual judgement, may
be worth discussing.[14] Now *qua* *I*-object τὸ λευκόν ought to be considered as some sort of quality, that is to say as some *F* which is
isolated by the corresponding special sense; in other words the *I*-
object is perceived without shape, size, or any determination marking
the *F* as an *F*-thing. Yet Aristotle is aware that any αἴσθησις whatsoever does involve more than just one sense. He emphasizes that *K*-
objects such as size, shape etc., which κοινὴ αἴσθησις perceives καθ᾽
αὑτά, occur as determinations[15] of *I*-objects (III 1, 425b5-6; 8-9
(see above pp.71-2, below pp.79-81)) and therefore as perceived

because of their association with *I*-objects. They occur together and
are thus perceived along with each other. What we are to infer from
this - particularly if it is the case that the relative clause ·in III
1, 425a14-15 expresses Aristotle's own position rather than some part
of the hypothesis against which he is arguing - is that the special
sense *X* in question perceives not only the *I*-object *x* but also, κατὰ
συμβεβηκός, some *K*-object *k* that is associated with the *I*-object. On
this interpretation any special αἴσθησις of some *I*-object would result in a perception of some kind of conjunction '*x* & *k*'. The plain
F would turn out to be an *F*-thing. In fact, if a perceptual judgement
of the form '*x* is *a*' is meant to express a statement of identity, its
subject term '*x*' ought to denote some complex αἰσθητόν. It should be
considered as some kind of definite description or logically proper
name (cf. 'τὸ προσιὸν Καλλίαν [*sc.* εἶναι]' *APr.* I 27, 43a36).

In other words, if the expression 'τὸ λευκόν' occurs in the position of the grammatical subject of a perceptual judgement it is likely
to refer to some definite *F*-thing rather than to some *F*. However,
what should be kept in mind is that this interpretation is possible
only if it is the case that *K*-objects are, in fact, perceived by the
special senses κατὰ συμβεβηκός. Now leaving aside the intriguing
question of whether or not Aristotle had sufficient means to deal
with the ambiguity of such expressions as 'τὸ λευκόν', we should
realize that his framework of *sensibilia* works with what may be
called an inverse ontology. Within the framework of perceptual language genuine substances are treated as attributes and non-substances
are treated as genuine subjects. As compared to the ordinary ontological scheme that is based upon the metaphysical-grammatical distinction between subject and attribute or between subject and predicate, this division of *sensibilia* into two basic kinds, *A* and *B*, ex-
hibits an inverse structure. No doubt, according to Aristotelian
standards of scientific predication any perceptual judgement such as
'The white is Socrates' has to be taken as a specimen of what he
would call improper predication.[16]

The fundamental resemblance between certain perceptual judgements
and instances of what Aristotle understands by improper predication
is indeed striking and deserves some consideration. Among the specimens of improper predication we find statements such as 'That white
is (a) Man' (*APo.* I 19, 81b25-6 λέγω δὲ τὸ 'κατὰ συμβεβηκός', οἷον

τὸ λευκόν ποτ' ἐκεῖνό φαμεν εἶναι ἄνθρωπον, οὐχ ὁμοίως λέγοντες καὶ
τὸν ἄνθρωπον λευκόν), or 'The white is wood' (*APo.* I 22, 83a4-7 ὅταν
μὲν γὰρ τὸ λευκὸν εἶναι φῶ ξύλον, τότε λέγω ὅτι ᾧ συμβέβηκε λευκῷ
εἶναι ξύλον ἐστίν, ἀλλ' οὐχ ὡς τὸ ὑποκείμενον τῷ ξύλῳ τὸ λευκόν ἐστι).
Note that within the framework of perceptual language τὸ λευκόν
functions indeed as the ὑποκείμενον of ἃ συμβέβηκε τοῖς αἰσθητοῖς
(*De An.* III 3, 428b20). There can be no doubt about this. And it
is thus highly interesting to observe that for Aristotle one and the
same proposition (i.e. 'The white is wood') is objectionable or un-
objectionable according as its reference is ὄντα or αἰσθητά. I am
not sure that Aristotle would take this to be an accurate assessment
of his view; probably not. Yet whereas the statement 'The white is
wood' fails the test for being an instance of proper predication
precisely on the ground that it simulates fictitious ontological
configurations, that is predicative relations that do not hold true
of the πράγματα involved (cf. *Int.* 19a33), the corresponding perceptual judgement 'The white is wood' apparently does not cause trouble
or call for criticism. Why not? Is it simply because the predicative notions that are involved in phrases such as '...belongs to...',
'...holds good of...', '...follow each other...' etc. are not being
used to refer to real structures embodied in the outside world?
Must the αἰσθητά then be considered as mental entities solely? We
had better drop this issue or rather postpone it until we have completed this survey. In fact, there is another point that may throw
light on the sense in which perceptual judgements relate to what
Aristotle might call improper predication.

The statement concerned is the one in *APr.* I 27: τῶν γὰρ αἰσθητῶν
σχεδὸν ἕκαστόν ἐστι τοιοῦτον ὥστε μὴ κατηγορεῖσθαι κατὰ μηδενός,
πλὴν ὡς κατὰ συμβεβηκός· φαμὲν γάρ ποτε τὸ λευκὸν ἐκεῖνο Σωκράτην
εἶναι καὶ τὸ προσιὸν Καλλίαν (43a33-6). Here Aristotle divides ὄντα
into three classes of which one, that is the particulars, is defined
by the fact that its members occur as subject terms only.[17] Now it
is obvious that 'αἰσθητόν' carries a meaning different from the one
intended in *De An.* II 6 (κυρίως). But this point is not of much importance. What it is important to realize, however, is that Aristotle does not provide a sober account of whatever criterion he
thinks proper predications have to conform to. No more does he in
APo. I 22. And there is no way of telling whether or not he was at

all aware of the difference in logical form exhibited by statements
such as 'The white is Socrates' and 'The white is wood' respectively. I do not think he was. In any case, whereas the '*is*' in 'The
white *is* wood' represents Peano's 'ε', that is the notion of class-
membership, the '*is*' in 'The white *is* Socrates' does not signify
predication at all. It signifies identity. Therefore statements
such as 'The white is Socrates' should not be regarded as instances
of improper or incidental predication in the first place. There
are, of course, ways of making the 'is' look like a *copula*: Plato
might have recommended a minor rephrasing such as 'The white par-
takes of sameness with respect to Socrates'; and Frege would have
told us to read the statement as follows: 'The white (thing) is no
other than Socrates'. But did Aristotle grasp the point? And how
could he have done so? The statement 'The white is Socrates' cannot pass as an instance of whatever 'improper predication' may be
supposed to mean, and Aristotle is obviously at a loss to understand why this is so. On this interpretation it is not difficult
to see why Aristotle does not hesitate to treat accidental or incidental *sensibilia* as attributes of *I*-objects (or possibly rather
as attributes of a conjunct '*x* & *k*') and has their names occupy the
place of what he takes to be the position of the predicate.

So far we are left with the notion that *B*-objects are, in general,
specified as instances of the logical type *a*. They are individuals
such as Socrates or Diares' son or physical bodies such as *F*-things,
G-things, and *H*-things (i.e. pieces of wood etc.) that the *I*-objects
can be identified as. And if we confine ourselves to the example
given in *De An*. II 6 we may also infer that the respective objects
are regarded as objects of just *one* sense. This inference is sound,
I presume, since the subject of the act of perception described
here (i.e. II 6, 418a21-4) is ἡ ὄψις. No other sense is mentioned.
In III 1 we encounter a similar situation:

(a) οἷον τὸν Κλέωνος υἱόν [*sc.* αἰσθανόμεθα] (425a25).[18]

Even though it seems evident that vision or sight is the only
sense involved in the perceptual process described here and elsewhere, it is not self-evident that the *A*- and *B*-objects concerned
are of just one sense like sight. To be sure Aristotle does not
hesitate to emphasize the fundamental importance of visual percep-

tion (see *Metaph.* A 1, 980a26-7 and *Sens.* 1, 437a5-7). Yet Cleon's
son is by no means a specific object of any sense whatsoever. And
the fact that such and such an *I*-object is identified as of the logical type *a* may well be contingent. We may conceive of circumstances under which a given *I*-object *x* of the special sense *X* cannot be
identified as *a* unless there are certain criteria of identification
that do not fall within the perceptual range of the very sense, *X*,
in question. Now suppose it is dark and sight cannot function. It
may still be possible to identify the man in the shadow in the living room provided the olfactory organ and the sense of hearing are
involved. Both senses *Y* and *Z* are likely to perceive some *I*-objects
y and *z* respectively, all of which will probably contribute to establishing the perceptual fact '*x* is *a*'.[19] Such a process is complex
rather than simple. In any case it is important to realize that
Aristotle probably did not mean to say that *B*-objects occur within
the perceptual field of any particular sense. They do enter it
somehow, and yet they are definitely not what any particular sense
perceives as such.[20]

This leads us to the question whether or not Aristotle let the
matter actually rest there. The distinction he draws between *I*-
objects on the one side and *B*-objects on the other has certain advantages. But how strictly does it work? Are there not other *sensibilia* that are perceived κατὰ συμβεβηκός and that should thus be
claimed for our heading *B*? At first sight the answer seems to be
in the affirmative. For the mode of speech[21]

(*b*) ὥσπερ νῦν τῇ ὄψει τὸ γλυκὺ αἰσθανόμεθα (III 1, 425a22)
can, if necessary, be taken to mean that some *I*-object *y* of a special sense *Y* occurs as κατὰ συμβεβηκὸς αἰσθητόν of another special
sense *X*. And the statement made in

(*c*) τὰ δ' ἀλλήλων ἴδια κατὰ συμβεβηκὸς αἰσθάνονται αἱ αἰσθήσεις
    (III 1, 425a30-1)
may well, on this interpretation, be taken as an extension of what
has been said before in (*b*). The point would then be this: if some
I-object *y* of a sense *Y* occurs as a κατὰ συμβεβηκὸς αἰσθητόν of a
sense *X*, the *I*-object *x* of this sense *X* will be perceived κατὰ συμβεβηκός by another sense *Y*. However, we should not be misled by the
mere occurrence of the same phrase 'κατὰ συμβεβηκὸς αἰσθάνεσθαι' in
both (*a*) and (*c*). The circumstances involved in the cases described

as (a) and (c) differ considerably, no matter what interpretation we prefer. For the κατὰ συμβεβηκὸς αἰσθητά referred to in the case of (a) differ from the ones referred to in the case of, say, (c). ˙ They are of a different logical type. And what makes the two cases differ from one another is the fact that the objects involved in the latter case are perceived necessarily. That is to say they are perceived in their own right and because of their own character rather than because of their association with something else. (The circumstances are sufficiently specified: 425a31-b2.)[22] The κατὰ συμβεβηκὸς αἰσθη-τόν involved in cases such as the one described in (a) is, however, not perceived necessarily; it does not count as specific object of any sense whatsoever and its perceptual status is thus contingent. As it occurs as some kind of contingent attribute of some *I*-object it is perceived because of its association with some necessary object of some special sense. Now what might be important to realize with regard to the peculiar status of the *I*-objects, inasmuch as they are also perceived κατὰ συμβεβηκός in a way, is that the κατὰ συμβεβηκός-character of any *I*-object of a sense *X* in respect to another sense *Y* is functional in nature. It exists merely in the analysis of what may be called the collective functioning of several (or all) senses in the act of perceiving a conjunct of *I*-objects ('*x* & *y* & *z*'). These *I*-objects turn out to be identifiable as one and the same *B*-object, say Cleon's son or such and such a piece of wood. Only the physical body is *per se* κατὰ συμβεβηκὸς αἰσθητόν, since it cannot *qua* αἰσθητόν claim an independent status.

What emerges from this discussion is that the answer to question (3) cannot, on this interpretation, be in the affirmative. The heading *B* is probably not meant to apply to any *I*-object after all. In order to clarify further the precise nature of the distinction that Aristotle draws in *De An.* II 6 we might thus add: any κατὰ συμβεβηκὸς αἰσθητόν is perceived κατὰ συμβεβηκός; however, not everything perceived κατὰ συμβεβηκός can *ipso facto* be regarded as a κατὰ συμβεβηκὸς αἰσθητόν in the sense that it has, *qua* αἰσθητόν, a non-independent status.[23]

I believe that the above formula may also be helpful in another respect, that is with regard to the question concerning the status of the κοινὰ αἰσθητά. The common sensibles so called are specified as

A-objects and yet they are not καθ' αὐτὰ αἰσθητά in the strict sense
of the term 'αἰσθητόν' (see above, p.70). This qualification seems
to create a further problem, one that is in a way similar to the one
discussed above. For Aristotle is likely to have held that the special senses perceive K-objects κατὰ συμβεβηκός (III 1, 425a15). How
would this affect their basic καθ' αὐτό-character? Now the reason
why this problem concerning the interpretation of III 1, 425a15 calls
for attention is rather obvious. There is one thing K-objects and
B-objects do have in common; perception of them does not exclude the
possibility of error (III 3, 428b24-5; Sens. 4, 442b8). And what
we are to infer from this is also obvious. As far as perceptual
judgement is concerned K-objects ought to behave somehow similarly
to the way in which B-objects behave; and the status peculiar to B-
objects is, in this respect, characterized by the fact that they occur as predicate terms only. These are the issues which we shall
have to deal with next.

Our first question thus concerns the precise nature of the καθ'
αὐτό-character peculiar to K-objects. Their basic classification
under the heading A (see II 6, 418a8-11) cannot be doubted. In
fact, a passage in III 1, 425a27-8 (τῶν δὲ κοινῶν ἤδη ἔχομεν αἴσθησιν κοινήν, οὐ κατὰ συμβεβηκός) appears to say the very same thing.
One may note, however, that the article τήν is missing and wonder
if Simplicius and Philoponus are not right after all to suggest that
the expression 'κοινὴ αἴσθησις' does not carry its technical meaning.[24] But I do not think that we need go into this any more than
into the problems connected with the position that Aristotle takes
in III 1, 425a27-8. What he actually has in mind remains unclear,
in De anima as well as in the Parva naturalia. In particular the
opinion that there is some kind of perception (i.e. the κοινὴ αἴσθησις) to which K-objects are related καθ' αὐτά rather than κατὰ
συμβεβηκός does not tell us why K-objects should be supposed to
share the καθ' αὐτό-character peculiar to I-objects. If Aristotle
used the notion of καθ' αὐτό primarily to refer to some kind of independent status for the sensibilia concerned, there should be a
way of applying this notion to the K-objects too.

And there is. Right at the end of ch. III 1 we find two statements that indicate something about the status of K-objects with regard to I-objects. The two of them go together (425b5-6 ἢ ὅπως

ἧττον λανθάνῃ τὰ ἀκολουθοῦντα καὶ κοινὰ οἷον κίνησις καὶ μέγεθος καὶ
ἀριθμός, 425b8-9 κἄν ἐδόκει ταὐτὸν εἶναι πάντα διὰ τὸ ἀκολουθεῖν
ἀλλήλοις ἅμα χρῶμα καὶ μέγεθος). Now it is obvious that Aristotle
treats *I*- and *K*-objects on a par. There is a small point, however,
that should not be overlooked. To say of things that they are ἀκολουθοῦντα is not tantamount to asserting τὸ ἀκολουθεῖν ἀλλήλοις of
them. For whereas the expression 'τὰ ἀκολουθοῦντα' may suggest no
more than the notion of the 'is' of predication[25] as does 'ὑπάρχει'
(cf. 425b9-11 καὶ ἐν ἑτέρῳ αἰσθητῷ τὰ κοινὰ ὑπάρχει) - in which
case the statement is similar to that in *Cat.* 1a24-5[26] (see particularly a28 ἅπαν γὰρ χρῶμα ἐν σώματι) - the expression 'ἀκολουθεῖν
ἀλλήλοις' does more than just that. It signifies extensional equivalence. In other words, wherever there is colour there is size
too and vice versa. While the latter statement clearly involves
some biconditionality the former does not. According to the former
statement *K*-objects just belong to *I*-objects in the same way things
in categories other than substance have to be considered as attributes of substantial beings. According to the latter statement
both *K*-objects and *I*-objects may behave in both ways, as both subjects and attributes. Now the idea that both kinds of objects are
bound to occur together is suggestive and may help to understand
why Aristotle felt that he had to treat them on a par. Inasmuch
as their occurrence does not imply the occurrence of *sensibilia* other
than themselves both *I*- and *K*-objects seem to obtain some kind of
independent status and may thus be specified alike as *A*-objects.

The trouble is, however, that there is a metaphysical catch to
it, one that Aristotle was certainly aware of. For if it is the
case that *K*-objects occur as determinations of *I*-objects in the sense
that the former 'inhere' in the latter (425b9-11 ἐν ... αἰσθητῷ τὰ
κοινὰ ὑπάρχει) the reverse of this relation cannot hold true. Therefore the statement made in 425b8-9 (see above) cannot really
be held to allow for the possibility of regarding *K*-objects as logical subjects of *I*-objects. According to what is said in 425b5-6 and
425b9-11 the contrary seems to be the case. For further confirmation
we may look e.g. at III 1, 425a19 (καὶ τοῖς ἰδίοις [*sc.* αἰσθητοῖς
γνωρίζεται]). Although it would probably not be correct to claim (as
Simplicius does[27]) that τὰ ἴδια include the perception of all *K*-
objects alike, the point Aristotle makes is suggestive. Motion, size,

shape etc. are, *qua* κοινά αἰσθητά, to be met along with *I*-objects.
As far as perception is concerned they do not precede *I*-objects in
the sense in which *I*-objects precede *B*-objects but rather follow or
accompany them. It is thus not difficult to understand why Aristotle felt that he had to add some qualification to the main line of
the distinction after all. To say that it is only the class of *I*-
objects to which the term 'αἰσθητόν' can be applied in its proper
sense (κυρίως, 418a24 (see above p.70)). is to acknowledge the difference in their perceptual status. *K*-objects do not have the same
degree of perceptual independence.

Now that this point has been settled we may approach the second
question (2). It concerns the problem connected with the statement
made in III 1, 425a14-15. There has been some dispute over the
question whether or not the text actually says what it appears to
say. What it appears to say is that the special senses perceive *K*-
objects κατά συμβεβηκός. It has been suggested, however, that the
relative clause ὧν κτλ. is - in spite of its indicative mood - part
of the hypothesis which Aristotle is rejecting.[28] Does this really
sound plausible? If we suppose that the proposition expressed by
the relative clause (i.e. '*K*-objects we perceive by means of each
sense incidentally') as it stands is false, and has thus to be rejected, we would have to look for another proposition by which it
should be replaced. One assumption from which one might proceed,
on this interpretation, is that *K*-objects are perceived by the special senses καθ' αὐτά.[29] Yet this could not possibly be what Aristotle meant to suggest. For one thing it is definitely misleading
in that it would suggest that the size, movement, or shape of a
given object *x* can be fully grasped by any one special sense. No
special sense is capable of doing any such thing. And to imply
that it is, is to commit oneself to a proposition that is bound to
be self-contradictory for reasons of analyticity. In fact there is
nothing in Aristotle, neither in *De anima* II 6 nor elsewhere, to
suggest that he lent himself to such an opinion. In the second
place the latter version would allow for the possibility that *K*-
objects are perceived καθ' αὐτά by both the κοινή αἴσθησις and the
ἴδιαι αἰσθήσεις. It would seem very difficult to explain how this
could possibly be the case, and indeed I do not think the explana-

tion can be given.

To clarify the matter let us replace 'καθ' αὐτά' by 'οὐ κατὰ συμβεβηκός'. It is then easy to see that the latter version implies, on this interpretation, a serious confusion concerning one of the more fundamental points involved in the distinction that Aristotle offers in *De An.* II 6. For the assumption that the special senses perceive *I*- and *K*-objects indifferently must invalidate the criteria set up for 'ἰδία αἴσθησις'. From what is implied in 418a11-12 we are to infer, firstly, that a special sense is defined with reference to a set of objects none of which can be exchanged with, or replaced by, an object belonging to another *genus*, and second, that with regard to the objects concerned it is not liable to the possibility of error. Now as far as the common sensibles so called are concerned, it is obvious that they are perceived by more than just one sense. Moreover we are told that the perception of *K*-objects is, in fact, liable to the possibility of error. There is thus good reason for rejecting the assumption that it is the special senses that perceive both *I*- and *K*-objects indifferently οὐ κατὰ συμβεβηκός.

Now someone might suggest that the entire matter can be settled rather easily provided we are prepared to have the 'wrong' proposition replaced by one that is certainly 'true', that is 'τῶν δὲ κοινῶν ἤδη ἔχομεν αἴσθησιν κοινήν, οὐ κατὰ συμβεβηκός' (425a27-8 (see above p. 79)). Yet such a procedure would not be of any help whatsoever. For the assertion that the κοινὴ αἴσθησις perceives its (i.e. *K*-) objects non-incidentally raises the question how they are perceived by the special senses in the first place. The latter proposition, true as it is for Aristotle, does not tell us that the other one is 'wrong' and should thus be regarded as part of the hypothesis which Aristotle is rejecting. In fact there is nothing to suggest that they are incompatible. Therefore it seems sound to proceed on the assumption that the relative clause concerned has to be taken at its face value, that is to say it expresses Aristotle's own position, one that is likely to underlie what is said in 425a19 (see above p. 80) no less than in II 6, 418a19.

Yet there are further reasons for doubting the theory that it is a part of the hypothesis to be rejected. Let us look at the whole argument. Had Aristotle really meant the relative clause to express part of such a hypothesis he would have referred to this 'part' in

one way or another in his argument. This may be reasonably inferred
from the fact that the statement made in 425a15 must, on this interpretation, be taken to express a consequence that has to be rejected
either because it is by itself simply contrary to the real state of
affairs or because it proceeds from a wrong assumption. Looking
now at the course of the argument and the way in which it must be
supposed to relate to the 'part of the hypothesis' we are at a loss
to understand how the proposition expressed in 425a27-8 can be properly taken to pass Aristotle's verdict on the statement that has
been made at 425a14-15. That the position taken in 425a14-15 should
be rejected does not follow any more than 'No I-object of a sense X
is perceived κατὰ συμβεβηκός by another sense Y' follows from 'Sight
perceives white οὐ κατὰ συμβεβηκός.' (In fact, the contrary seems
to be the case: 425a30-1 (see above p.77).) It is obvious that
the positions taken in 425a15 and 425a27-8 are compatible.[30] And
what is obvious also is that the inference drawn at 425a27-8 (οὐκ
ἄρ' ἐστὶν ἰδία κτλ.) solely concerns the 'real' hypothesis, that is
what follows the relative clause.

Now it is important to realize that the position Aristotle arti-
culates in the relative clause has some bearing on the argument that
follows (425a20 sq.). It serves as some kind of premise. The presupposition made concerns the fact that while e.g. seeing an I-object
we also perceive some K-object. This Aristotle takes for granted.
And he is convinced that any theory concerning the nature of the
perception of K-objects must take this presupposition into account.
In other words, any assumption concerning the existence of an ἰδία
αἴσθησις in respect to the perception of K-objects must be required
to conform to the above proposition concerning the fact that while
seeing an I-object we also perceive a K-object.

The key question is thus whether or not it is at all possible to
conceive of a theory concerning a specialized perception of K-objects.
Could it possibly account for what is going on in reality and thus
meet the above requirement? Aristotle is convinced that it cannot.
His answer on this question is bound to be in the negative since
none of the alternative lines of thought that may be adopted along
with such an hypothesis can be seriously considered. They simply
fail to provide a satisfactory explanation of the fact that while
seeing e.g. white we also perceive shape or movement.

For if it were the case that K-objects are perceived by some special sense (425a14) they could not possibly be perceived along with
the perception of some I-object x by one and the same sense X. ˉAc-
cordingly, the way in which they are perceived either must be similar to that in which a sense X perceives the I-object y of another
sense Y, or else (a24 εἰ δὲ μή) it must resemble the way in which
the perception of some I-object x by the sense X evolves into the
perception of some substantial particular a. These are the alternatives.[31]

There is one thing both these forms of κατὰ συμβεβηκὸς αἰσθάνεσθαι (see above pp. 77-8) have in common, something that shows beyond doubt why Aristotle thought that the theory advanced in the
hypothesis could not possibly meet the above requirement. The pattern after which this theory would have to be modelled would be
such as to make sure that the object perceived incidentally is not
being perceived necessarily. Now as concerns the first option it
is rather obvious that the fact that while seeing the I-object x
we also see the 'I-object y' (e.g. movement) of a sense Y is contingent. It depends upon the contingent fact that both senses, X and
Y, aim in the same direction and act jointly (425a22-4 τοῦτο δ' ὅτι
ἀμφοῖν ἔχοντες τυγχάνομεν αἴσθησιν ᾗ ὅταν συμπέσωσιν ἅμα γνωρίζομεν).[32] If we decide to understand the case mentioned ((b), see
above p. 77) along the lines suggested by R.D.Hicks and the ancient
commentators,[33] the fact that some I-object y is being perceived by
a sense X would depend solely upon whether or not we remember what
we experienced before, i.e. that while perceiving some I-object x
by the sense X we perceived that x was moving etc. However, I do
not think we should settle for this line of interpretation. In any
case the hypothesis that we are endowed with an ἰδία αἴσθησις of,
say, movement (425a21 οἷον κινήσεως) does not help us to understand
how we perceive that the particular I-object x moves. For what is
perception of movement but the perception of a particular object
that is in a series of adjoining places at successive times. That
is all that motion is.[34] Seen in this light the theory concerned
cannot possibly meet the requirement stated above.

The second option is even less satisfactory. For this kind of
κατὰ συμβεβηκὸς αἰσθάνεσθαι - some commentators feel that it should
not even be regarded as 'real' perception[35] - concerns the contin-

gent fact that the *I*-object *x* of the sense *X* is being identified as
a, say Cleon's son or as some *F*-thing (e.g. a piece of wood) (see
above pp.76-7).   And Aristotle makes it quite clear that this model will not do: οὐδαμῶς ἄν ἀλλ' ἤ κατὰ συμβεβηκός κτλ. (425a24).
It does not have much explanatory force.   And *qua* explanation it
certainly cannot account for the fact that we perceive that some *I*-
object *x* is moving and that it has size, shape etc.   In other words,
the model under discussion does not explain precisely why we are
perceiving *K*-objects while perceiving *I*-objects.   (Aristotle could
have added that motion, size, shape etc. would then, on this interpretation, prove to be *B*-objects.   In this case any ἰδία αἴσθησις
of objects such as movement, size, shape etc. may well be totally
disconnected from the ἰδία αἴσθησις of the *A*-objects.)   Aristotle
has a number of good reasons to reject the hypothesis that the common sensibles so called are after all perceived by some special
sense.

Therefore there are good grounds for assuming that the statement
under discussion (i.e. 425a14-15 ὧν ἑκάστῃ αἰσθήσει αἰσθανόμεθα
κατὰ συμβεβηκός) not only is, in fact, compatible with the one made
at 425a27-8 (i.e. τῶν δὲ κοινῶν ἤδη ἔχομεν αἴσθησιν κοινήν, οὐ κατὰ
συμβεβηκός) but also conveys what Aristotle thinks is essential to
the whole matter under consideration: the κοινὴ αἴσθησις corresponding to more than just one special sense does *not* perceive its objects just κατὰ συμβεβηκός.   The individual senses defined with reference to their respective objects do, however, perceive *K*-objects
κατὰ συμβεβηκός.   Yet it is important to realize that this mode of
αἰσθάνεσθαι κατὰ συμβεβηκός differs significantly from the ones referred to in (*a*), (*b*) and (*c*) (see above pp.76-8).   It differs in
that any special sense *X* while perceiving one of its specific *I*-
objects *x* necessarily perceives some *K*-object *k* that is associated
with *x*.   As far as the perceptual field of *X* is concerned *k* belongs
to *x* necessarily.   Regarded in this light it should be obvious that
the heading *B* does not apply to objects such as the common sensibles.
Qua ἀκολουθοῦντα and ἐν ... αἰσθητῷ ὑπάρχοντα (see above pp. 80-1)
they are, in a way, internally related to the special senses because
of their being necessarily associated with some *I*-object.   Yet this
by itself does not make *K*-objects the proper object of any special
sense.   The fact that Aristotle has 'κατὰ συμβεβηκός' modify

'αἰσθάνεσθαι' clearly indicates what is obvious enough. That is to
say the special senses, defined with reference to their specific objects, are by no means capable of perceiving Ks associated with⁻
these objects in the same way as they perceive their proper objects
as such.

But what about the other point that appeared to be in need of some
clarification? Is it not the case that Ks and Bs are still very
much alike in that perception of them is liable to the possibility
of error (see above p. 79)? And are we not thus to infer that Ks
ought somehow to behave like predicate terms too? The answer to
this has to be in the affirmative. For *falsity* cannot, according
to Aristotle, occur except in connection with some kind of mental
activity involving a *synthesis* of terms.[36]   In other words, an αἴσθησις can be 'wrong' if and only if it is concerned with the perception of some complex αἰσθητόν. This notion is invoked in III 6,
430b24-30. And there is thus reason to believe that it is likely
also to underlie what Aristotle says in III 3, 428b18-25. According to this hierarchy of objects concerning which perception is liable to the possibility of error, it is the K-objects that must be
regarded as the least reliable candidates. But even the ἰδία αἴσθησις may be mistaken (428b18-19).[37] In any case, the question
concerning the logical behaviour of the common sensibles so called
raises quite a number of problems the discussion of which will probably throw light upon the fundamental distinction Aristotle draws
at II 6.

What we would like to know in particular is whether or not Aristotle, when dividing all *sensibilia* into two basic kinds, means to
imply that objects belonging to class *A* are somehow perceived *directly* whereas objects belonging to class *B* are accordingly perceived *indirectly*. (Seeing *x* as Cleon's son would seem to approximate to the notion of perceiving *a* indirectly. And as regards the
specific objects of ἰδία αἴσθησις it may be tempting to say that
they are similar to what we are accustomed to understand by 'immediate objects' or 'direct objects' (see p.94 n.11).)   Although
the question may seem inappropriate from a merely historical point
of view, the fact that this matter is not easy to decide is largely
due to the peculiar status of the κοινὰ αἰσθητά. For inasmuch as

they are perceived κατὰ συμβεβηκός (i.e. by the ἰδία αἴσθησις, III 1,
425a15) they are definitely not perceived 'immediately' or 'directly'. Yet inasmuch as they are perceived καθ' αὐτά and οὐ κατὰ συμβεβηκός (i.e. by the κοινὴ αἴσθησις, III 1, 425a27-8) it may seem
tempting to regard them as direct and immediate objects of our perception.

Now in view of Aristotle's theory concerning *error* and *falsity*
in terms of what he thinks of as a *synthesis of terms*, it would seem
possible to regard 'direct perception' as a mode of genuinely non-
propositional perceiving that is not liable to the possibility of
error (in spite of 428b18-19), and 'indirect perception' accordingly
as a mode of propositional perceiving that is liable to the possibility of error. But it is not likely that we can get away with this
distinction, since Aristotle was hardly prepared to argue along
these lines. For one thing we have to bear in mind that Aristotle,
even when talking about the perception of *I*-objects, found it possible
to employ notions such as the one expressed by 'judging perception'
(see II 6, 418a14, also *Metaph.* Γ 5, 1010b18-19). However, in the
same breath he turns to a conceptually different terminology, one
that is clearly indicative of what we understand by non-propositional
perceiving: referring to that kind of *truth* which is located in the
unerring perception of non-complex objects (*Metaph.* Θ 10, 1051b22)
he asserts that θιγεῖν and φάναι are, *ipso facto*, 'true' (see also
De An. III 7, 431a8).[38] For another thing it is important to realize
that the possible difference between the existence of some kind of
'direct perception' of *K*-objects by the κοινὴ αἴσθησις on the one
hand, and that of some kind of 'indirect perception' of *K*-objects by
the ἰδία αἴσθησις on the other, does not interest Aristotle at all.

In fact, when he discusses the senses' liability to the possibility of error he sticks to a notion of perception that is fairly general. And whereas the mode of perceiving indirectly is characterized
in terms of attributing *B*s to *I*s and thus receives a propositional
coat (428b19-21 δεύτερον δὲ [*sc.* ἡ αἴσθησις] τοῦ συμβεβηκέναι ταῦτα
<ἃ συμβέβηκε τοῖς αἰσθητοῖς>[39]), the terminology employed to point
out that perception of *K*s is liable to the possibility of error
clearly shows an assimilation of the logic of the propositional construction to that of the direct-object construction (428b22-4).

Are we then to proceed on the assumption that Aristotle's notion

of κοινὴ αἴσθησις wavers conceptually between the logic of the propositional construction and the logic of the direct-object construction? The least we can say is that the position Aristotle takes on
these matters cannot be determined precisely. In fact, his thought
displays difficulties that are all too obvious. Yet it is rather
doubtful whether Aristotle was aware of the basic inconsistency peculiar to his line of reasoning. For unsatisfactory as his position
may be in terms of the interests of contemporary philosophy, it
still seems likely to match the general framework in the back of
his mind. It is conceivable that Aristotle meant to say that κοινὴ
αἴσθησις somehow perceives its objects 'directly' and yet is liable
to the possibility of error simply because the special senses have,
from the point of view of natural teleology,[40] not been made to
perceive *K*-objects 'as such'. Accordingly they cannot be expected
to provide exact *data* in the first place. When we consider the kind
of qualification added at the end of II 6, where Aristotle says that
taken in its proper sense the term 'αἰσθητόν' applies to *I*-objects
only, it seems indeed reasonable to assume that Aristotle might have
relied on some such kind of argument. And in the light of what is
implied in II 6 the position Aristotle takes on the status of the *K*-
objects, ambiguous as it is, is likely to make sense after all.

Now it has been said that the status of the common sensibles so
called is characterized by the fact that they enter the perceptual
field of the individual senses along with *I*-objects and accordingly
(III 1, 425b8-9) may also be specified as καθ' αὐτὰ αἰσθητά. Inasmuch as it is the *I*-objects, however, that function as 'subjects'
while the *K*-objects are regarded as attributes (III 1, 425b9-11)
and non-substantial things such as size, movement, shape etc. cannot be perceived independently from the entities that they determine,
K-objects cannot possibly have the level of perceptual independence
that is peculiar to the status of *I*-objects. Some qualification has
to be made. Aristotle's position concerning the status of *K*-objects
may thus be summarized as follows: by claiming that *K*-objects share
in the general καθ' αὐτά-character peculiar to perceptually independent *sensibilia* Aristotle simply means to suggest that *K*s do not face
the κοινὴ αἴσθησις merely as κατὰ συμβεβηκὸς αἰσθητά. For it is
with reference to the genus of *K*s that κοινὴ αἴσθησις is defined.
By contrast, *K*s cannot, *qua* objects of the special senses, claim to

be καθ' αὐτὰ αἰσθητά for any such definitional reason. Even though
Ks are perceived by the special senses along with the *Is* to which
they relate in the way in which necessary attributes relate to a subject, they cannot face any of the ἴδιαι αἰσθήσεις in any other way
than as κατὰ συμβεβηκὸς αἰσθητά.[41] Yet this does not make the *K*-
objects join class *B*, the members of which cannot claim to be αἰσθητά
for any such definitional reason, but only because they are *externally*
associated with colours and with other ἴδια αἰσθητά. What Aristotle
wants us to understand is that the way in which the five senses relate to *K*-objects should still be considered in terms of an internal
relation rather than an external one. Therefore he would be entitled to reject the notion that the perception of *K*-objects, liable as
it is to the possibility of error, ought to be regarded as an instance of perceiving incidentally. Accordingly *Ks* do not have to be
considered to belong to class *B*.

     In this light the entire matter in question seems to be clarified.
For much of what has been said on the peculiar status of the common
sensibles so called simply reinforces the notion that Aristotle's
treatment of this kind of *sensibilia* is largely based upon the preliminary outline given in II 6. In particular it draws on the qualifying remark concerning the proper meaning of 'αἰσθητόν', one that
makes the basic division of all *sensibilia* into two kinds display
certain hierarchical features. *A* comprises both objects that are
sensibilia in the strict sense of the term 'αἰσθητόν' and others
that are *sensibilia* although it is not in the strict sense that the
term 'αἰσθητόν' applies to them. By contrast, *B* comprises objects
that are perceived because of their association with something else
rather than because of their own character and thus cannot really
claim to be αἰσθητά for any strict definitional reason. Thus we are
left with the notion that the kind of αἰσθάνεσθαι involved in the
perception of, say, Diares' son differs significantly from the one
involved in the perception of *Is* or *Ks*. What can be said with respect to this kind of 'non-direct' perception is that it clearly involves more than just sense perception. This is true regardless of
the problem of the precise status of *B*-objects *qua* αἰσθητά. For
the kind of αἰσθάνεσθαι involved in the perception of *a* either is
no longer, or is not merely, just an instance of what Aristotle
thinks perception really is like. The restriction that is involved

in the qualifying remark concerning the proper meaning of the term
'αἰσθητόν' reflects upon the meaning of 'αἰσθάνεσθαι'. And whereas
any *K* that is seen as *x* has to be regarded as a genuine object of
sense perception, just as the 'seeing as' is, in this particular
case, an instance of the real sense perception, the 'τὸν Κλέωνος
υἱὸν κατὰ συμβεβηκὸς αἰσθάνεσθαι' apparently approximates to a kind
of 'seeing as' that differs in category.[42] As the particular *a*
which the *I*-object *x* is 'seen as' cannot claim to be a genuine αἰσθητόν for any definitional reason, the 'seeing as' leading to this
identification cannot be regarded as an instance of genuine sense
perception. To this point of difference Aristotle seems to have
attached great importance although he did not really get to the
bottom of it.

In view of this distinction the classification attempted in the
course of *De anima* II 6 appears to concern any object to which the
term 'αἰσθητόν' is applicable. The ἴδια αἰσθητά and κοινὰ αἰσθητά
prove to be objects of genuine sense perception while the αἰσθητά
referred to as κατὰ συμβεβηκὸς αἰσθητά cannot claim to be proper
sensibilia after all. Perception of them seems to involve some
kind of association of ideas or inference and thus is likely to extend beyond the notion of genuine sense perception. But if the
latter objects cannot claim to be proper *sensibilia* the question
arises of what they are in the first place. Is what Aristotle wants
us to understand by 'Diares' son' precisely the kind of physical object which from the point of view of Direct Realism is the immediate
object of awareness while from the point of view of Representation-
alism it is quite distinct from this immediate object? Or is what
Aristotle wants us to understand by 'Diares' son' nothing more than
a construction out of the immediate objects of awareness, something
that according to the Phenomenalist's point of view does not exist
independently of perception?

Now it is rather obvious that Aristotle does not really fit in
to this picture. Taking αἴσθησις to be some kind of reception of a
sensible form without the matter he is not likely to have held that
physical existents such as Diares' son or some particular piece of
wood are the immediate objects of awareness when we perceive. Diares' son we perceive κατὰ συμβεβηκός. *Qua* αἰσθητόν he cannot be

considered as a possible candidate for what Aristotle would have meant by 'immediate object of awareness'. The expression 'κατὰ συμβεβηκὸς αἰσθάνεσθαι' points to the notion of 'perceiving indirectly' rather than to that of 'perceiving directly'. Yet if it is true that 'perceiving indirectly' involves some sort of association of ideas Aristotle may well be at a loss to assert that what we perceive in this particular case is a physical object, capable of existing independently from the immediate objects of awareness. And our perception of physical objects – or however it is that we become aware of them – is certainly no association of ideas for Aristotle.[43] There is little we know about Aristotle's views concerning the mechanism involved in what he calls κατὰ συμβεβηκὸς αἰσθάνεσθαι. And what we know is not sufficient to suggest that Aristotle was about to adopt a Phenomenalist's point of view. (As far as Aristotle's examples (*a*), (*b*) and (*c*) are concerned it is important to bear in mind that we must distinguish between what he actually said about κατὰ συμβεβηκὸς αἰσθάνεσθαι and what he ought to have said.) In any case, there is reason to assume that Aristotle could not really have been interested in the kind of answer a Phenomenalist would be likely to give. Moreover, from what has been said about the peculiar structure of perceptual judgements (see above pp.75-6), it would seem that the κατὰ συμβεβηκὸς αἰσθητά are indeed physical existents.

Finally something should be said about the view that tends to equate the ἴδια αἰσθητά and κοινὰ αἰσθητά with Locke's 'primary qualities' and 'secondary qualities' respectively. From what has been said in the course of the discussion concerning their perceptual status it would seem that they are not to be regarded as *F*-things but as *F*s, that is as colours or patches.[44] And it is certainly tempting the consider these *sensibilia* in terms of what contemporary philosophers understand by 'sense-data'. Such a comparison may prove to be helpful in various ways. In particular, it would enable us to grasp what Aristotle might have had in mind in the notion that the ἴδία αἴσθησις is practically not liable to the possibility of error. Yet as his doctrine stands it does not really qualify as a sense-data theory. Moreover it is hard to see how a sense-data theory could possibly fit into the setting of Aristotle's doctrine concerning act and potency.

NOTES

1 For some methodological points concerning the course of argument
   employed in *De anima* II 6 see R.Sorabji, 'Aristotle on demarca-
   ting the five senses', *Philos. Rev.* 80 (1971), 55-79, especially
   56; in particular I agree with his thesis that it was Aristotle's
   concern to define the senses with reference to their objects rather than the *sensibilia* with reference to the senses.

2 I am not going to discuss the question of the heuristic merits
   that an application of the modern distinction between 'propositional perceiving' (i.e. 'to perceive that *p*') and 'non-propositional perceiving' (i.e. 'to perceive *X*') (cf. e.g. R.M.Chisholm,
   Perceiving. A philosophical study (Ithaca, N.Y. 1957); D.D.
   Crawford, 'Propositional and nonpropositional perceiving', *Philosophy and Phenomenological Research* 35 (1974-5), 201-10) may
   have with respect to the interpretation of Aristotle. From his
   analysis of the alternative ἢ τῇ ὄψει αἰσθάνεσθαι ὅτι ὁρᾷ (*De
   An.* III 2, 425b12) and from what is said at b18 sqq. (ὁρᾶται δὲ
   χρῶμα ἢ τὸ ἔχον κτλ.) it seems obvious that Aristotle tends to
   assimilate the logic of the propositional construction to that
   of the direct-object construction. One may thus infer that he
   did not consider this difference as a philosophical option.
   (Plato did not either; see, however, J.Hintikka, 'Knowledge and
   its objects in Plato', in J.M.E.Moravcsik (ed.), *Patterns in
   Plato's Thought* (Dordrecht 1973), 1-30; idem, 'Plato on knowing
   how, knowing that, and knowing what', in B.Hansson (ed.), *Essays
   Dedicated to S.Halldin* (Lund 1973), 1-12 and in J.Hintikka,
   Knowledge and the Known (Dordrecht 1974), 31-49.) In any case,
   the classification outlined in *De An.* II 6, compatible as it may
   be with the notion of perception as some kind of reception of
   the form without the matter (II 12, 424a18), apparently does not
   take into account the existence of 'internal affections' that
   can also be perceived (*Mem.* 450b17-18). It also fails to provide for the possibility that we perceive *that* we perceive (*De
   An.* III 2, 425b12), *that* we think; live etc. (*EN* IX 7, 1170a29-
   b1).
      Now it is important to realize that the *modus procedendi* em-
   ployed here (i.e. the specification of the senses with reference
   to their respective objects) strictly speaking commits Aristotle
   to the position that the κοινὴ αἴσθησις has but a limited function, that is to say it ought to be confined to the perception
   of those kinds of objects with reference to which it has been
   defined in the first place.

3 To the list of κοινὰ αἰσθητά given in II 6, 418a17-18 (cf. *Sens.*
   437a9), τὸ τραχύ, τὸ λεῖον, τὸ ὀξύ, and τὸ ἀμβλύ may be added as
   species, according to *Sens.* 442b4-7 (see W.D.Ross, *Aristotle.
   Parva Naturalia* (Oxford 1955), 208). The MSS to *De An.* III 1,
   425a16 read 'unity', and from *Mem.* 450a9-10, 451a16-17 commentators have inferred that 'time' too was regarded as a member of
   the class of so-called common sensibles (see W.D.Ross, *Aristotle.
   De Anima* (Oxford 1961), 239, 270). It is usually held that Aristotle's assumption concerning the existence of κοινὰ αἰσθητά
   reflects Platonic influence, i.e. *Tht.* 185a8-186a1 (so Ross, *Ari-*

stotle. De Anima, 239). However, the subject matter discussed in the *Theaetetus* is, in my opinion, an entirely different one, and talking in terms of 'influence' does not clarify the issue. For a discussion of the meaning of κοινόν in the *Theaetetus* see H.F.Cherniss, *Aristotle's criticism of Plato and the Academy* I (Baltimore 1944), 236 n.141, F.M.Cornford, *Plato's Theory of Knowledge* (London 1935), 105-6, and J.M.Cooper, 'Plato on sense-perception and knowledge', *Phronesis* 15 (1970), 128, n.8.

4 See C.H.Kahn, 'Sensation and consciousness in Aristotle's Psychology', *Archiv Gesch. Philɔs.* 48 (1966), 53-4, n.24.

5 It should be noted that the explication of the twofold meaning (κυρίως) of this term is not related to the kind of distinction we find in II 5, 417a13 (i.e. διχῶς ... καὶ τὸ αἰσθητόν), provided we follow Ross (*Aristotle. De Anima* (*op.cit. n.3*), 235) and W.Theiler (*Aristoteles, Über die Seele* (2nd ed., Darmstadt - Berlin 1966, 117) in replacing τὸ αἰσθάνεσθαι by τὸ αἰσθητόν (cf. Alexander, *Quaestiones* 83, 6).

6 Note that this kind of qualification is interesting for other reasons too. Its formal principle contrasts with the one employed in the course of *Cat.* 5a38-9, b8 where the class of κυρίως λεγόμενα [*sc.* ποσά] is identical with the class of καθ' αὐτὰ ποσά; accordingly, the notion of 'not-κυρίως' applies to all instances of κατὰ συμβεβηκός (ποσά).

7 By 'essential' D.W.Hamlyn understands 'essential to the sense' and thus reinforces his notion that Aristotle was primarily concerned with a specification of αἰσθητά with reference to the senses (see his *Aristotle's De Anima* (Oxford 1968), 105, 108, 117). On this matter I take sides with R.Sorabji (*art.cit. n.1*).
   It may well be the case that Aristotle's position is not really clear after all. Yet it is important to keep in mind that according to *Cat.* 7b35-8a12 it is the objects of perception that are credited with priority 'κατὰ τὴν αἴσθησιν' (cf. *Cat.* 9b7). What Aristotle is saying here seems to be compatible with the notion expressed in *Metaph.* 1021a29-b3 from which we are to infer that Aristotle does not think that the relation that objects of perception and knowledge have to perception and knowledge respectively is 'relative' in the same sense as that in which perception and knowledge are relative to their respective objects. (Cf. W.D.Ross, *Aristotle. Metaphysics* I (Oxford 1924), 331.) Also see *De An.* 426a20-3 and *Metaph.* 1047a4-6. Also it is important to realize that 'κατὰ συμβεβηκός' can readily modify the verb αἰσθάνεσθαι (cf. *De An.* 425a14, also see *Mem.* 450a13-14, 24-5 and the discussion by R.Sorabji, *Aristotle On Memory* (London 1972), 77, 79) while 'καθ' αὐτό', unlike 'ἁπλῶς', cannot do so without changing its meaning. In any case, it is misleading to talk about a 'καθ' αὐτό-perception' as does I.Block, 'Aristotle and the physical object', *Philosophy and Phenomenological Research* 21 (1960), 94.

8 I recommend W.Theiler's suggestion (*op.cit. n.5*, 116-17) that the 'κατά' extends beyond the ἥ. What is perceived 'as such' is, in the case of the so-called elements, tactile qualities such

as 'warm', 'cold', 'dry', 'humid' (cf. *GC* 330a26) and 'incidentally' 'colour'. Note that the conceptual framework indicated by
Aristotle's terminology compares with the one employed in III 3,
428b18 sqq. where Aristotle no longer sticks to the particular
terminology of II 6 (see R.D.Hicks, *Aristotle. De Anima* (Cambridge 1907), 468-9, who in turn refers to I.Bywater). - The
passage II 3, 414b8-10 (... τούτων δ' αἴσθησις ἀφή, τῶν δ' ἄλλων
αἰσθητῶν κατὰ συμβεβηκός) seems to reflect the same line of conceptual thought. The meaning of this statement is probably 'The
perception of the other objects is only incidentally perception
of food' (cf. III 12, 434b18-19 and *EN* III 10, 1118a18). However, there are other ways of trying to make sense of it (cf.
Ross, *Aristotle. De Anima (op.cit. n.3)*, 222-3).

9 The only commentator to have pointed to this passage for the
interpretation of *De An.* II 6 is R.Sorabji (*op.cit. n.7*, 79-80
on *Mem.* 450a23-5). But he appears to be basically interested in
pointing out the fundamental importance of what Aristotle says
with regard to this distinction in *APo.* 73a34-b24 (also see
Philos. Rev. 80 (1971), 55 n.1). I am not convinced, however,
that the passage concerned can be read in the light of what is
stated in *APo.* 73a34-b24, particularly if 'τῷ λόγῳ' is meant to
allude to the Platonic Form (see Theiler (*op.cit. n.5*), 120; his
reference is *Metaph.* 991b3).

10 Without anticipating the discussion we may note that Aristotle
regards this kind of perception as a non-propositional or rather
'non-synthetical' grasp (cf. *Metaph.* Θ 10, and *De An.* III 4-8
with respect to the mind's grasp of non-complex entities). Aristotle thinks that the ἰδία αἴσθησις is not liable to the possibility of error (cf. *De An.* 418a11, 427b11, *Metaph.* 1010b2, 14,
Sens. 442b8-9, but also note the much disputed restriction in
428b18-19). The notion of truth employed in this particular respect, where 'true' does not function as a semantic predicate
but rather refers to some ἀληθὲς ὑπαρκτικόν and ἀληθὲς ὑποστατι-
κόν (see Sophonias, *De Anima* 123,4 ed. Hayduck), was to have a
history of its own (see K.Bärthlein, *Die Transzendentalienlehre
der Alten Ontologie* I (Berlin - New York 1972), 33-4 n.18).

11 Terms such as 'immediately' or 'directly' may be taken to signify
something like 'impossibility of doubt' or 'no inferences' respectively. See N.Malcolm, 'Direct perception', in *Knowledge and
Certainty* (Englewood Cliffs, N.J. 1963), 73-95 and D.D.Todd,
'Direct perception', *Philosophy and Phenomenological Research* 35
(1974-5), 352-62). - There is reason to suggest that such terms
may be used of what Aristotle is aiming at, *pace* Hamlyn (*op.cit.
n.7*), 105 and *Sensation and perception. A history of the philosophy of perception* (London 1963), 110. Yet it is certainly
true that the notion of indirect perception is not naturally at
home with senses other than sight (J.L.Austin, *Sense and sensibilia* (reconstructed from the manuscript notes by G.J.Warnock),
(Oxford 1962), 16).

12 See however Ross, *Aristotle. De Anima (op.cit. n.3)*, 239.

13 It is probably fair to say that S.Cashdollar's account tends in

this direction ('Aristotle's account of incidental perception', *Phronesis* 18 (1973), 160 n.10 *et passim*).

14 Cf. e.g. Block (*art.cit. n.7*), 94-6, and Cashdollar (*art.cit. n.13*), 163 n.18.

15 One is reminded of III 3, 428b24 (ἃ συμβέβηκε τοῖς αἰσθητοῖς) provided these words do, in fact, belong here (cf. Hicks (*op. cit. n.8*), 471) and not to b20 as was proposed by W.D.Ross and I. Bywater. However, it is still conceivable that the αἰσθητά under discussion here (i.e. b24) are substantial individuals after all. For a good discussion of the text see Theiler (*op.cit. n.5*), 138.

16 Some of the problems connected with *APr.* I 27 and *APo.* I 19, 22 have been reconsidered by J.Engmann, 'Aristotle's distinction between substance and universal', *Phronesis* 18 (1973), 139-55; see also G.E.L.Owen, 'Inherence', *Phronesis* 10 (1965), 97.

17 G.Patzig, *Die Aristotelische Syllogistik* (2nd ed. Göttingen 1969), 15-16 n.3.

18 For the interpretation of what follows at 425a25 it is important to take 'ὅτι' to mean 'because' in both cases (cf. Hamlyn (*op. cit. n.7*), 119). Commentators usually fail to see that in III 7, 431b5 too (i.e. οἷον, αἰσθανόμενος τὸν φρυκτὸν ὅτι πῦρ) 'ὅτι' requires the meaning 'because'.

19 It is not easy to guess what the κατὰ συμβεβηκὸς αἰσθάνεσθαι a is actually supposed to be. Is it an act of 'inference' (J.I.Beare, *Greek theories of elementary cognition* (Oxford 1908), 286) and 'something more complex and intellectual' rather than 'an act of the sense faculty as such' (Kahn (*op.cit. n.4*), 46)? See also Cashdollar (*art.cit. n.13*), 158-9.

20 Cf. Hamlyn (*op.cit. n.7*), 107, 119.

21 R.D.Hicks claimed that this statement of Aristotle clearly stands in need of correction (*op.cit. n.8*, 430; see also Ross, *Aristotle. De Anima* (*op.cit. n.3*), 271). On balance I would agree with D.W. Hamlyn who says: 'The phenomenon in question is no doubt a product of learning or experience, but this does not make it any the less a case of seeing' (*op.cit. n.7*, 119). Also cf. the wording employed in *EN* III 3, 1113a1-2.

22 From what is said we have to infer that the situation in question is such as to exclude the possibility of somebody closing his eyes, stuffing his nose or ears etc. However, it is still possible that there exists the kind of perception which Aristotle may have been thinking of in reference to (*b*) (i.e. III 1, 425a22).

23 On this point cf. Themistius, *De An.* 81,35-6 ed. Heinze: διττὸς γὰρ ὁ τρόπος τῶν κατὰ συμβεβηκὸς αἰσθητῶν· ἢ γὰρ ὅταν τῇ ὄψει κρίνωμεν τὸ γλυκύ· (82,7-9) ἕτερος δὲ ὅταν προσίοντα τὸν Κλέωνος υἱὸν θεασάμενοι κτλ.; Philoponus, *De An.* ed. Hayduck 454,15-20 φησὶ γὰρ ὅτι τὰ κατὰ συμβεβηκὸς αἰσθητὰ διττά ἐστι, ἢ τὸ ἄλλῃ αἰσθήσει ὑποπῖπτον ... ἢ ὅπερ οὐδεμιᾷ αἰσθήσει ὑποπίπτει ὡς ἡ οὐσία κτλ.

24 Cf. Simplicius, *De An.* 185,7-20; Philoponus, *De An.* 460,17-22.

25 Cf. e.g. *APr.* I 4, 26a2, 26b6; I 27, 43b4, and Patzig (*op.cit. n.17*), 20.

26 See in particular Owen (*art.cit. n.16*), 97, 99.

27 Simplicius links these words with a17 (πάντα κινήσει αἰσθανόμεθα). The parenthesis would be too long however. Cf. Hicks
(*op.cit. n.8*), 429; Ross, *Aristotle. De Anima* (*op.cit. n.3*),
270; Theiler (*op.cit. n.5*), 131, and Hamlyn (*op.cit. n.7*), 118.

28 This has been claimed by C.H.Kahn (*art.cit. n.4*), 53-4 n.24.
The point had been made before: Theiler (*op.cit. n.5*), 131, see
also Simplicius, *De An.* 182,38-183,4. A.Torstrik inserted an
οὐ before κατά, as did the *Vetus Latina*.

29 See C.H.Kahn: 'Although they are true sense objects, perceived
per se and not incidentally' (*art.cit. n.4*, 53). Some of his
observations (e.g. on p.53 n.24 on 418a8 sqq., 425a24) cannot be
substantiated by any evidence whatsoever.

30 On this matter I agree with R.D.Hicks (*op.cit. n.8*, 426-7) and
D.W.Hamlyn (*op.cit. n.7*, 117).

31 Cf. 425a28-9 - a strange repetition of what has been said in
a24-5. Cf. Theiler (*op.cit. n.5*), 131. I am not sure if the
text needs emendation. If it does not, the sentence 425a28-9
(οὐδαμῶς γὰρ ἂν ἠσθανόμεθα ἀλλ' ἢ οὕτως ὥσπερ εἴρηται) ought to
take into account either possibility (i.e. a22 and a24-5). Accordingly the words τὸν Κλέωνος υἱὸν ἡμᾶς ὁρᾶν (a29-30) would
call for deletion.

32 The ἅμα goes with γνωρίζομεν. See however Hamlyn (*op.cit. n.7*),
118

33 Hicks (*op.cit. n.8*), 430-1 (with the discussion of Simplicius,
De An. 184,22 sqq., and Philoponus, *De An.* 459,32 sqq. referring
to the interpretation advanced by Plutarch: 355,24).

34 D.M.Armstrong, *Perception and the physical world* (3rd ed. London
1966), 185.

35 Cf. Block (*art.cit. n.7*), 94; contra: Cashdollar (*art.cit. n.13*),
158 n.8.

36 Cf. *De An.* III 6, 430b1-2 (b3-4 διαίρεσις), III 8, 432a11-12, and
Metaph. Γ 7, 1012a3, E 4, 1027b25, Θ 10, 1051b3, *Int.* 16a12.

37 From this passage we are to infer that Aristotle could not really
mean his *sensibilia* to be sense-data. Cf. I.Block, 'Truth and
error in Aristotle's theory of sense perception', *Philos. Quart.*
11 (1961), 3.

38 This particular passage (*De An.* III 7, 431a8-10) which has to be
read in conjunction with *EN* VI 2, 1139a21-7) has been overlooked

by e.g. Ross, *Aristotle. Metaphysics (op.cit. n.7)*, II, 227 and
by F.Grayeff, *Aristotle and his school* (London 1974), 208. Note
that the noun φάσις may carry the same meaning (*Int.* 16b27 and
17a17), but that it rarely does so (*De An.* III 6, 430b26 and III
7, 432a10, also see *Metaph.* Γ 4, 1008a34).

39 The propositional character would not be altered, even if the
phrase ἃ συμβέβηκε τοῖς αἰσθητοῖς were not to be put in a different place. Its meaning would change, of course, but the
phrase is not 'unmeaning if it stands by itself' (Ross, *Aristotle. De Anima (op.cit. n.3)*, 288-9), for it is the same 'ontology' that also underlies the discussion in b22-4. See however
Theiler (*op.cit. n.5*), 138 and Hicks (*op.cit. n.8*), 470-1.

40 Cf. *De An.* II 6, 418a25, and Block (*art.cit. n.37*), 7 with reference to *Sens.* 442b8.

41 One may wonder why Aristotle did not express himself rather more
clearly. Apparently he felt that the matter in question was extremely difficult to express; see, *mutatis mutandis*, *De An.* III
1, 425a19-20. For some good remarks on this passage see H.Cassi-
rer, *Aristoteles' Schrift 'Von der Seele'* (2nd ed. Darmstadt
1968), 94.

42 See, *mutatis mutandis*, L.Wittgenstein's illuminating account of
'Zwei Verwendungen des Wortes 'sehen'' (*Philosophische Unter-
suchungen*, II. Teil, Abschnitt IX (Suhrkamp-Edition, Frankfurt
a.M. 1967), 227sqq.).

43 I.Block thinks that this point is indeed decisive: 'The order of
Aristotle's psychological writings', *AJP* 82 (1961), 69 n.20:
idem (*art.cit. n.7*), 96.

44 I.Block argues in favour of a 'material-object-interpretation',
cf. *op.cit. n.37*, 5sqq.

4: ARISTOTLE ON THE IMAGINATION

M.Schofield

INTRODUCTION

Every educated man knows that Aristotle invented logic. It is not
so widely known that he contests with Plato[1] the distinction of
having discovered the imagination. Men imagined things, just as
they argued correctly and incorrectly, before the birth of the Old
Academy; but it was Aristotle who gave the first extended analytical description of imagining as a distinct faculty of the soul, and
who first drew attention, not least by the ambiguities and strains
of his own account of the matter, to the difficulty of achieving an
adequate philosophical understanding of imagination. I shall not
in this essay attempt a survey of all Aristotle's uses of and pronouncements about φαντασία.[2] I shall restrict myself to a set of
fundamental problems in the interpretation of his official and principal discussion of it in *De anima* III 3. In that chapter lurk most
of the pleasures and puzzles which the student of Aristotle's views
on imagination will want to savour.

It has been doubted whether Aristotle's φαντασία should be rendered as 'imagination' at all. Plato in the *Theaetetus*[3] and *Sophist*[4] introduces φαντασία into philosophical discourse about mental
states as the noun corresponding to the verb φαίνεσθαι, 'appear';
and it is his doctrine that any belief which a man forms because of
what he perceives with his senses is an instance of φαντασία.[5] Now
a clear connection with the verb is preserved by Aristotle in talking of φαντασία in *De An.* III 3 and elsewhere. Moreover, it has
been noticed that the range of 'appearances' which Aristotle allo-
cates to the faculty includes cases which are not obviously instances
of mental imagery, but seem more like examples of direct sensory experience; and again, that in his causal explanation of φαντασία Aristotle allows that a man may have φαντασία of what he is at the moment actually perceiving (428b25-30), yet (as Wittgenstein remarked[6])
'while I am looking at an object I cannot imagine it'. Some scholars
have accordingly inferred that φαντασία is for Aristotle, at least in

some moods, a comprehensive faculty by which we apprehend sensory and
quasi-sensory presentations generally.[7] Thus his view of φαντασία is
equated[8] *pro tanto* with a view of sensory activity (or rather passiv-
ity) more typically associated with phenomenalists and sceptics; or
else he is taken to have succumbed temporarily to a Kantian conception, according to which 'sensation [i.e. sense-perception] would ...
be reduced to the level of a mere passive affection which has to be
interpreted by φαντασία before it can give any information or misinformation about objects'.[9]

Its Kantian associations might justify continuing to call the
φαντασία of this latter interpretation 'imagination'. But it is recognized that to admit such a comprehensive role for φαντασία as
either interpretation envisages is hard to reconcile with Aristotle's
treatment of the senses in Book II of *De anima*. It is widely allowed, although not universally nor by me, that Aristotle's official de-
signation of φαντασία in *De An*. III 3 as 'that in virtue of which we
say that a φάντασμα occurs to us' (428a1-2) implies that it is a faculty more narrowly but more usually named 'imagination', viz. one
in virtue of which we can have mental images.[10] And we find Ross,[11]
for example, portraying Aristotle's usual view of φαντασία, both in
De anima and in *Parva naturalia*, in terms which call to mind Hobbes'
'decaying sense' and Hume's 'faint and languid perception': its characteristic sphere, on Ross's reading, is mental imagery.

One conclusion one might draw from this apparently conflicting
evidence of Aristotle's meaning is summed up in Hamlyn's glum verdict
(*ad* 427b27): 'there is clearly little consistency here [*sc*. in *De An*.
III 3]'. My view is that the conflict in the evidence is in good
part merely apparent. For it is a bit artificial to divide the work
Aristotle assigns to φαντασία between mental imagery and the reception of sensory or quasi-sensory presentations. If we are to attribute to him a concept of imagination, then without endowing it with
a Kantian scope we can permit it to range beyond the confines of
mental imagery, as several modern authors, writing in the wake of
Ryle and Wittgenstein, would urge.[12] And although we must recognize
a proprietary connection between φαντασία and the verb φαίνεσθαι,
'appear', we need not suppose that the use of the word Aristotle
wishes to exploit is the phenomenalist appropriation of it as the
universal, basic, neutral term to report on one's any and every

sensory or quasi-sensory experience without ever yet committing oneself to a claim about how things are in the external world. Commentators who have supposed just this have been too little sensitive to
the Protean character of 'appears' and cognate expressions, so irresistibly exhibited by Austin.[13] I shall argue that in the contexts
which concern us Aristotle has his eye on the more everyday use of
φαίνεσθαι to express scepticism, caution or non-committal about the
veridical character of sensory or quasi-sensory experiences, on
those comparatively infrequent occasions when for one special reason
or another it seems inappropriate in a remark about one's own or
another's experience to claim that things are as they seem: 'it
looks thus and so (– but is it really?)'. This usage is not un-
naturally associated with the imagination, for 'imagination involves
thought which is unasserted, and hence which goes beyond what is believed'.[14]

According to the view which I shall advance, then, we need not
charge Aristotle with the radical inconsistency in his treatment of
φαντασία diagnosed by Hamlyn. Nonetheless, we should be wary about
assimilating φαντασία and imagination. Grant that a conceptual
link between imagination and a use of 'appears' can be forged: even
so, the link is not nearly as close as the morphologically grounded
connection between φαντασία and φαίνεσθαι, nor does 'appears' supply
the obvious, natural entrée to the study of the imagination which
φαίνεται provides to that of φαντασία. A little lexicography will
show that the syntactic behaviour and the semantic range of φαντασία
(not to mention φάντασμα and φαίνεσθαι) are markedly different from
those of 'imagination'.[15] And if for a moment we banish the rendering 'imagination' from our minds, then in one section of *De An.* III
3, at any rate (the discussion whether φαντασία is a faculty of
judgement, 428a1–b9), reflection on the range of phenomena Aristotle
assigns to φαντασία and on the way he introduces them into his argument suggests a rather different physiognomy for the concept from
that conveyed by 'imagination'. Aristotle seems to be concerned
with a capacity for having what I shall compendiously call *non-
paradigmatic sensory experiences*[16] – experiences so diverse as dreams
and the interpreting of indistinct or puzzling sense data, which may
be held to resemble the paradigm of successful sense perception in
one way or another, yet patently lack one or more of its central

features, and so give rise to the sceptical, cautious or non-committal φαίνεται. One merit of this interpretation of φαντασία is that
it makes immediately intelligible Aristotle's ensuing causal analysis of the faculty, which takes as its crucial premiss the fundamen-
tally sensory character of φαντασίαι, and proceeds to define them in
terms of sense perception proper, as causal traces of actual perceptions (428b10-429a2). Nor is the immediate intelligibility of that
analysis all that is salvaged. For if we read it as an account not
of imagination but of non-paradigmatic sensory experiences, it is
readily taken as a not implausible attempt to give a single general
explanation of an extremely interesting feature of human psychology,
namely the operation of our sensory equipment in a variety of non-
standard ways. As a theory of the imagination, on the other hand,
its very generality renders it disappointingly jejune, aside from
its pre-echoes of the unilluminating view of imagination familiar
to readers of the British empiricists. This is not, of course, to
deny that mental imagery would be reckoned by Aristotle as one type
of non-paradigmatic sensory experience. It is simply to argue that
the focus of his attention, in these sections of De An. III 3, is
not imagery or imagination as such.

These considerations should not lead us to abandon altogether a
direct equivalence between φαντασία and imagination. For in a passage from the opening section of his discussion of φαντασία in De
An. III 3 (427b16-24), Aristotle offers two criteria to distinguish
it from belief (δόξα) which fit the concept of imagination so perfectly, and are so fundamental to it, that it would be perverse to
take the topic to be anything other than imagination. He tells us
that φαντασία, unlike belief, is up to us when we wish, or, in modern parlance, is subject to the will;[17] and that, whereas we are
immediately affected by fear if we believe we are confronted by
something alarming, in the case of φαντασία it is merely as if we
saw something alarming in a picture.[18] I do not say that these
marks of imagination are not true also of some non-paradigmatic
sensory experiences (if not of others, such as after-images or hallucinations). But it seems pointless to invoke the latter notion
here unless the context demands it. And in the immediate context
there is no trace of the concerns characteristic of the sections we
considered briefly in the previous paragraph - the use of φαίνεται

as signally appropriate to cases of φαντασία, its emphatically sensory character (certainly φαντασία is treated at 427b16-24 as rather
like seeing,[19] but the criteria employed to distinguish it from belief make it analogous to thinking rather than to perception). Moreover, the whole section 427b6-26 bears signs of being composed separately from the sections which follow.[20] So they cannot be held to
constitute a wider context sufficiently intimately connected with
427b6-26 to require our importing the idea of non-paradigmatic sensory experience into the section. Here at least, then, there seems
every reason to identify φαντασία with imagination.

But it was no doubt Aristotle himself who was responsible for
putting together chapter 3 of *De An*. III in the form in which we
have it. He gives no sign that he is aware of changing subjects in
the course of the chapter. We owe it to him, therefore, to try to
understand how the concept of imagination which figures pretty
clearly at the beginning of the discussion of φαντασία could reasonably be treated as one and the same concept as the rather different
notion which seems to be in question from 428a1 onwards. I shall
suggest (and have already hinted) that Aristotle can be fairly interpreted as adopting different but complementary vantage points on
a more or less coherent family of psychological phenomena. But it
would be a triumph of generosity over justice to pretend that he
manages to combine his different approaches to φαντασία with an absolutely clear head.

In the body of the essay I shall devote most of my space to the
themes broached in this introduction. But first a word or two on my
method of enquiry and its limitations. In seeking to establish what
Aristotle understands by φαντασία we shall have to try to build up a
picture chiefly from relatively isolated remarks tossed off in the
course of the argument of *De An*. III 3, which must then in turn be
tested against them. In the chapter Aristotle makes many distinctions between φαντασία and other dispositions of the soul, sometimes
(but not often enough) with clearly articulated examples. What he
fails to do is to draw the threads of his discussion together, to
provide a synoptic view of φαντασία as he interprets it. This tempts
one to examine other texts in the hope of achieving a more definitive
impression of his conception, particularly from *Parva naturalia* and
elsewhere in *De anima*. But these require cautious employment. For

De An. III 3 remains Aristotle's one concentrated, extended theoretical discussion of φαντασία;[21] elsewhere he is mainly concerned
with its role in particular mental operations – dreaming, remembering, thinking, and so on. An account of his view of φαντασία which
relies too heavily on his treatment of these related phenomena runs
the risk of distortion, the risk either of taking the way φαντασία
works in memory, dreams, and so on, as its mode of operation *tout
court*, or more insidiously of putting the emphases of the description in the wrong places. Ross fell into this trap, so much so
that he was forced to doubt whether some of the more important things
Aristotle says in *De An.* III 3 really 'represent his deliberate
view'.[22] If that chapter does not give us Aristotle's considered
opinion, it is doubtful whether he had a considered opinion and certain that we could not with any confidence reconstruct it.

Of course, the persuasiveness of the account of φαντασία in *De An.*
III 3 which I am offering would be much weakened if it seemed not to
correspond with what Aristotle has in mind when he talks of φαντασία
in other contexts. In this essay I have not attempted to show that
my account will work for his handling of φαντασία elsewhere. And it
may consequently be objected, for example, that in Aristotle's theory
of animal movement φαντασία cannot be associated with sceptical,
cautious, or non-committal φαίνεται, since the point of making φαντασία a necessary condition of movement is to require that the moving
animal positively fix upon some object of desire.[23] Or, more generally, it might be thought implausible that Aristotle should wish to
specify a faculty of the soul in such negative terms, in view of the
constructive work he puts φαντασία to do not only in action but in
remembering, thinking, etc., too.[24]

I offer some general considerations in reply, in lieu of the detailed investigation which a proper answer would entail. It will be
evident from what I say in the main body of the paper, and particularly from its third section, that I take Aristotle's chief problem
in *De An.* III 3 to be that of providing conceptual room for an independent notion of φαντασία, between thinking on the one side and
sense perception on the other. If this is so, then we might reasonably expect two things: first, that Aristotle will take as fundamental to φαντασία in *De An.* III 3 features which will not necessarily
receive much emphasis in other contexts where he is not particularly

concerned with the demarcation problem of that chapter; second, that
Aristotle will elsewhere, when concerned with other problems, be
likely to emphasize features of φαντασία not given much prominence
in *De An*. III 3, or even to blur distinctions made or implied there.
Thus, to take the first point, it is principally in connection with
his attempt in *De An*. III 3 to distinguish φαντασία from sense perception as faculties of judgement that he links φαντασία so closely
with the particular use of φαίνεται which I have tried to isolate.
This aspect of φαντασία continues to attract Aristotle's attention
in contexts where he is concerned with perceptual or quasi-perceptual
judgements, as in *De insomniis*. But - and here I move to the second
point - in other contexts, notably in his accounts of thinking and
remembering, he is not concerned with φαντασία as a faculty of judgement at all. When he introduces φαντασία or φαντάσματα here, he has
in mind our capacity for visualizing, just as he does in that section
(427b6-26) of *De An*. III 3 where I interpret him as discussing the
active power of imagination.[25] I am inclined to believe[26] that much
the same aspect of φαντασία is what Aristotle chiefly has in mind
when he claims that φαντασία is a necessary condition of animal movement, although here he is certainly concerned with judgement (even if
only as assent to what one visualizes). This at any rate is suggested
by the way he develops his view in *De An*. III 9-11. For he seems to
think that movement and the desire which is its principal cause require *either* the *thought* of a desirable object *or* at least something
like thought (νόησίν τινα, 'a sort of thinking'), namely φαντασία.[27]
What he says elsewhere[28] about the connection of thought and φαντασία
makes it very likely that it is mainly imagination or visualization
that he is thinking of. Here, as in *De An*. III 3, he first suggests
that φαντασία, as opposed to νόησις, is the prerequisite of desire in
non-rational animals and in what prompts the fevered or the weak-
willed man to act (here we catch an echo of sceptical, cautious φαίνεται: 'it seems good [but principle forbids it]').[29] But later in the
same discussion Aristotle simplifies his account by making φαντασία
the crucial factor in all desire, explaining that it can be prompted
either by thought or by sense perception - evidently recalling his
doctrine that all thinking involves visualizing.[30]

I have slipped into discussion of particular issues of interpretation willy nilly. But my chief point remains this: investigation of

De An. III 3 indicates that Aristotle's φαντασία is a loose-knit, family concept. So we should expect that in its appearances else-where in his psychology its different elements are variously picked out or woven into fresh patterns. And that, I contend, is just what we would find if we carried out a detailed investigation of those contexts.

φαντασία AND φαίνεται

Ross states:[31] 'φαντασία is in its original meaning closely related to φαίνεσθαι, "to appear", and stands for either the appearance of an object or the mental act [or, we might add, disposition] which is to appearing as hearing is to sounding.' He goes on to cite a num-ber of passages in Aristotle where φαντασία seems to him to be used in this way. They and others like them constitute the evidence for holding that Aristotle at least sometimes conceives of φαντασία as a comprehensive faculty in virtue of which we apprehend sensory and quasi-sensory presentations in general. I shall argue that this evi-dence can and should be given an alternative interpretation.

The most promising text for a broad conception of the faculty of φαντασία might be thought to be a passage not in the psychological treatises but in the *Metaphysics*. For in *Metaph.* Γ 5, 1010b1-14, Aristotle introduces the notion of φαντασία in a context where the verb φαίνεσθαι is not merely used but used in a phenomenalist style to express sensory and quasi-sensory 'appearing' in general. The passage constitutes part of his argument against Protagoras' view that all φαινόμενα, appearances, are true.

It is perfectly plain that here, as indeed in the rationale of Protagoras' doctrine offered at 1009a38-b9, Aristotle is including under φαινόμενα any sensory or quasi-sensory appearances whatever. Witness the beginning of his second objection in the passage, at 1010b3-9:[32] 'Next, one may legitimately be surprised that they should find perplexing the question whether magnitudes and colours are such as they appear (φαίνεται) to those at a distance or to those nearby, to the healthy or to the sick; or whether it is what [appears so] to the weak or to the strong that is heavier; or whether it is what [appears so] to those asleep or to those awake that is true.' What directly concerns us, however, is Aristotle's first objection to the thesis that every φαινόμενον is true (1010b2-3). The text is corrupt,

but runs thus in Bonitz' widely accepted and plausible reconstruction: 'Even if perception, at least of what is special, is not false,
still φαντασία is not the same as perception.' A proponent of the
idea that a broad conception of φαντασία is to be found in Aristotle
might argue that this objection is naturally read as implying such a
conception, as follows: Aristotle is in effect accusing the Protago-
reans of fallaciously inferring from the true premiss:[33] 'All perception (or, all perception of proper objects, the fundamental sort
of perception) is true' the false conclusion: 'Every φαινόμενον is
true.' And it is clear enough that he means to challenge the inference by pointing out that it depends on an additional tacit premiss
(which is false) to the effect that every φαινόμενον is a case of
perception. But what he actually says is that φαντασία is not the
same thing as perception. The natural explanation of his putting
the point this way is that he thinks of φαντασία as the faculty in
virtue of which any φαινόμενον is experienced, and speaks here of
φαντασία rather than φαινόμενον simply because he wants to refer to
the mental disposition or act involved, and so to make the appropriate contrast with perception. Moreover, the evident influence of
Plato's *Theaetetus* in this paragraph (Plato is actually mentioned at
1010b12) and elsewhere in the chapter makes it unsurprising that
Aristotle should have used φαντασία in this broad manner. For that
is just how Plato uses the word in introducing Protagorean relativism
(*Tht.* 152a-c).

Despite its plausibility, this interpretation of φαντασία is not
the only one possible for an unforced reading of the text. This can
be made clear by an example. Aristotle is prepared to grant to Protagoras that hearing is always of sound; his point is presumably
that it is not true that wherever there is the appearance of a sound
in our ears we are actually hearing (we may be dreaming, for example)[34] – and even if we are hearing a real sound, it may appear to
us other than as it really is (as coming from the right, for example,
when it actually comes from the left).[35] Now in saying that φαντασία
is not the same as perception, Aristotle *might* mean (as someone who
held the interpretation sketched above would probably argue) that
perception (i.e. of proper objects) is only one sort of φαντασία, to
be compared with interpretation of perception, dreaming, and further
sorts of φαντασία. He would then be suggesting that, while the

φαινόμενα experienced in perception may always be true, those experienced in other sorts of φαντασία need not be. But observe that he may
equally well mean that some φαινόμενα are indeed cases of perception
of proper objects, and as such true, but that others (e.g. those we experience in dreams) involve the *coordinate* faculty of φαντασία, imagination or non-paradigmatic sensory experience, which of course admits of
falsehood. In other words, Aristotle's objection to Protagoras will be
no less forcefully and naturally expressed if φαντασία is not the genus
of which perception is a species, but a species, coordinate with perception, involved like it in the apprehension of just a part of the whole
field of φαινόμενα. Nor does the comparison with the *Theaetetus* give the
former alternative unequivocal support. For Aristotle is denying precisely what Plato makes Protagoras affirm, viz. that perception and φαντασία are one and the same. If his concept of perceiving has a different scope from Protagoras', then his concept of φαντασία may very well
do so too.[36]

We must conclude that it is hard to know how to understand the
denial that φαντασία and perception are identical without further
evidence of Aristotle's teaching about them. For that we have to
turn (as Aristotle would surely expect us to turn) to *De anima*, and
in particular to the passage in which he elaborates his reasons for
distinguishing between φαντασία and perception (*De An.* III 3, 428a5-
16). I consider first such indications as it contains that the word
φαίνεται ('appears') is a specially appropriate and significant vehicle for describing what we experience in virtue of φαντασία.

There are three occurrences of the word in the passage. In one of
these Aristotle's argument explicitly turns on the bearing of its use on
the character of φαντασία; and in consequence the other two, although
less important in themselves, gain in interest and significance. Here
is the telling example, in the fourth argument of the set (428a12-15):[37]
'Further, it is not when we are exercising [our senses] with precision
on the object of perception that we *say* that this appears (φαίνεται) to
us [to be] a man, but rather when we do not perceive it distinctly.'
Hamlyn complains that this argument 'is concerned with imagination in
the sense of appearances only and as these are perceptual phenomena they
do not serve to make a distinction from perception.'[38] But if an interpretation makes an Aristotelian point as irrelevant as that, the fault
may very well lie in the interpretation. And it is not difficult to find

a genuine contrast between perception and φαντασία expressed in Aristotle's sentence. Aristotle is surely pointing out that if we clearly *see* a man, we do not say: 'It looks like a man', since the caution, doubt or non-committal implied by that form of words is out of place. It is when our eyes let us down that φαίνεται becomes an appropriate locution; and the judgement we make by employing it is not straightforwardly a report of what we perceive, but a more guarded statement of how what we perceive looks to us, how we interpret it. 'How it looks to us', 'how we interpret it': Aristotle puts it the first way, in the language of what I am calling non-paradigmatic sensory experience, in essentially passive terms. But the appearance of 'to us' in his formulation reveals his awareness of the subjectivity of the judgement, and so suggests that he would not object to the idea that in φαντασία we consciously or unconsciously interpret the data of our senses. It is natural to assign such interpretative activity to the imagination. This is particularly the case where the interpreting is conscious. Suppose you and I are looking at a distant object in murky light: we may have to exercise our imaginations, comparing and contrasting what we *can* see with the way familiar middle-sized things of our everyday acquaintance look, before we are able to conclude that it looks like a man; we may have to try seeing it under different aspects before we succeed in seeing it as a man. 'Whatever is placed beyond the reach of sense and knowledge, whatever is imperfectly discerned, the fancy pieces out at its leisure; and all but the present moment, but the present spot, passion claims for its own, and brooding over it with wings outspread, stamps it with an image of itself.'[39] But even if the indistinctly perceived object immediately and irresistibly looks to me like a man, even if I have not consciously engaged in a moment's *reflection* about what it is that I see, there is still reason to account my judgement the product of imagination. For as in the earlier case I do not just perceive a man, but see something as a man,[40] and if I say 'it looks like a man', I employ a form of words which indicates an appreciation that I am going beyond what I actually perceive.[41] If I am wrong, I may reasonably be accused of merely imagining that it was a man;[42] right or wrong, I may be held to have *decided* what it looked like no less than if I had had to make my mind up slowly. The instantaneous character of my verdict does not tell against my having actively

engaged in imagination: imaginative leaps may notoriously occur in
the twinkling of an eye. Notice, too, that the two criteria of
imagination proposed by Aristotle at 427b16-24 are satisfied in the
relevant way in this case as in the one where imagining takes time.
Just because imagination is here employed as an aid to perception,
not in free fantasy, one's attitude to the appearance in question
is not likely to resemble much one's attitude to a picture; but
neither is it probable that someone to whom it merely looks as if
there is an enemy soldier in the distance will be immediately affected by the spontaneous emotion appropriate to perceiving an
enemy clearly - the caution, doubt or non-committal signalled by
φαίνεται will tend to act as a brake. Again, imagination remains
subject to the will in these cases, inasmuch as it makes perfect
sense to ask a person to exercise his imagination upon what he imperfectly sees.[43] The fact that he may have no psychological option but to see what he sees as a man no more counts against this
being an instance of imagination than the obsessive, haunting character which mental images may exhibit, pleasantly or unpleasantly,
debars them from being products of the imagination.

Aristotle in his argument at 428a12-15 alerts us to a use of
φαίνεται which is appropriate only in special perceptual circumstances. He takes it to show that men exercise φαντασία precisely
where sense perception fails them. It would be perverse to read
him as tacitly allowing[44] (indeed insisting) that nonetheless φαντασία has a broad Protagorean scope, and is in fact present in all
sense perception. If Aristotle had meant us to make this inference, he should have phrased his argument differently; and he should
have introduced the concept of φαντασία as an essential tool of his
analysis of sense perception, instead of omitting virtually all mention of it throughout Book II of De anima.

φαίνεται occurs, probably as an index of φαντασία, in the first
and fifth arguments of the set designed to show that it cannot be
identical with sense perception (428a6-8, 15-16). In the latter case
Aristotle has in mind a special phenomenon - after-images seem the
likely candidate;[45] this suggests a sceptical as much as a Protagorean use of the verb. The same is true of its use in his first argument, which is more general in scope: 'Perception is either a capacity (e.g. sight) or an activity (e.g. seeing); but something can

appear (φαίνεται) even if neither of these is in question[46] (e.g.
dreams).' I submit that we should be guided by the results of our
examination of the fourth argument, and take it that in both these
further arguments Aristotle means to point to φαντασία conceived
as a faculty for non-paradigmatic sensory experiences.

His other arguments at 428a5-16, in which φαίνεται does not occur, are best interpreted upon the same assumption. Certainly they
are hard to marry with a broad Protagorean conception of φαντασία.
Consider the rather opaque second argument (428a8-11). Aristotle
there claims (a10-11) that all animals have perception, but apparently not all φαντασία. But on a Protagorean or typically phenomenalist view of 'appearances', these are the raw materials of
which all perception, in however lowly an animal, is constructed.[47]
The third argument is likewise easy to square with the interpretation of φαντασία I am advancing, difficult with the broader interpretation. Aristotle says (428a11-12): 'Next, perceptions [sc. in
the strict sense, of proper objects] are always true, but most φαντασίαι turn out false.' Aristotle's point is perhaps best expanded
in terms of imagining: if someone has an image of an *F*-thing, or
sees *X* as *F*, what he imagines – an *F*-thing – may not and probably
will not exist (be a real contemporaneous *F*-thing) at all. *'Probably* will not?' Perhaps Aristotle had run his mind over some of
the main sorts of non-paradigmatic sensory experience – e.g. dreams,
memory-images, after-images, fantasy, hallucinations, the seeing of
aspects – and reckoned that correspondence to truth was on the whole
a rarity among these phenomena; perhaps his trust in common forms of
speech suggested to him that the scepticism or caution or non-committal implied by the use of φαίνεται he associated with φαντασία
was usually likely to be justified. In any event, the claim that
most φαντασίαι are false is not implausible, so construed. Yet if
φαντασίαι were here in effect a mere synonym for Protagorean φαινόμενα, it would surely be a highly improbable, if not indeed in the
end unintelligible, thesis.[48]

But if those who believe that Aristotle sometimes gives φαντασία
a broad Protagorean scope cannot sustain their interpretation relative to these arguments for the non-identity of sense perception
and φαντασία, they may yet turn for support to his attack on Plato's
view that φαντασία is a blend of perception and belief. Aristotle's

argument there (428a24-b9) has recently been well analysed by Lycos[49] (whose account is lucidly summarized in Hamlyn);[50] and since
I am concerned simply with the scope φαντασία is allowed by Aristotle to have, I refer the reader for a detailed treatment of the
reasoning to these authors.

Aristotle first expounds Plato's view of φαντασία, according to
which 'appearing (φαίνεσθαι) will be believing what one perceives
(and that not just coincidentally)' (428b1-2). He then offers a
counter-example to this thesis, a case where one experiences a
false 'appearance' about what is before one which conflicts with
the true belief one holds about it (428b2-4): 'But things also appear (φαίνεται) falsely, when one has at the same time a true supposition about them (e.g. the sun appears (φαίνεται) a foot across,
but is believed to be bigger than the inhabited world).' Now as
we have remarked, Plato, in the passage of the *Sophist* to which
Aristotle's discussion relates (264ab), holds that any belief which
is formed as a result of perception is a case of φαντασία and can
properly be expressed by a form of words which includes φαίνεται.
He seems to opt for a generously Protagorean range for φαντασία and
φαίνεται, even if he does not identify perception and φαντασία.
But in producing his single counter-example to Plato's thesis, Aristotle does not commit himself to accepting a similarly broad conception of φαντασία. All he needs to do is to produce a case which
he himself accepts as a case of φαντασία and which Plato too might
reasonably be expected to accept as such. So if the particular use
of φαίνεται involved in the statement of the counter-example is one
which is indicative of φαντασία for both Plato and himself, that is
sufficient for Aristotle.

I submit that Aristotle accepts the sun example as a case of
φαντασία just because it involves a use of φαίνεται which is naturally read ('appears ... but is believed') as implying scepticism.
This accords not only with the results of our examination of 428a5-
16, but also with the context in *De insomniis* in which this example
is used a second time. Aristotle argues at 460b3sqq. that we are
easily deceived with respect to our senses when we are in pathological conditions - in emotional states like love and fear or physiological disturbances like fevers. He points out that the coward in
his fear thinks on the basis of a slight resemblance that he sees

the enemy, the amorous man in his passion that he sees his beloved;
and he comments that the greater the sway of the emotional state,
the more tenuous the resemblance needed to make these things appear
so (φαίνεται: the word is used four more times of deceptive appearances in the next sixteen lines). This, then, is the context in
which Aristotle produces the sun example to show that in a normal
frame of mind we are well able to resist and contradict a false appearance, exercising another faculty besides φαντασία.[51] Notice
the company which φαίνεται, used of the sun's misleading appearance,
and in consequence φαντασία, are made to keep - sceptical employ-
ments of φαίνεται, non-paradigmatic sensory experiences which we
may think of as hallucinations, or as the seeing of unreal aspects.

The sun's looking a foot across would in truth be a rather un-
convincing example of a Protagorean φαινόμενον. Someone who pro-
nounces that the sun looks to him a foot across may be endeavouring
to offer a report of his perceptual field sufficiently cautious to
satisfy a sceptic or a phenomenalist that no illegitimate inferences from the perceived to the real are being made. But if so, he
is not going about his task in the most convincing way. It is one
thing to aver that the sun looks small in comparison with the other
items in one's perceptual field. It is quite another to make an
estimate of *how* small it appears to be. For judgements of size
take into account perspective, yet the very problem with the sun
is that one's normal procedures for coping with perspective break
down. So the assertion that the sun looks a foot across seems to
presuppose some tacit, and no doubt highly questionable, assumption
about how far the sun looks to be from the earth. It in fact em-
bodies an imaginative comparison such as : the sun looks like a
foot-wide beach ball kicked high in the air (but not *very* like -
for the sun looks much higher than that). Compare Austin's observation on 'The moon looks no bigger than a sixpence':[52] 'It doesn't
look as if it *is* no bigger than a sixpence, or as a sixpence would
look as if it were as far away as the moon; it looks, of course,
somewhat as a sixpence looks if you look at it at about arm's
length.' There is no sign in the text either of the *De anima* passage or of the *De insomniis* passage that Aristotle had reflected on
the oddity of his example or on its non-paradigmatic perceptual
circumstances. But it helps to make the texture of the analysis of

φαντασία in *De An*. III 3 the richer; and it does something to rein-
force the identity of φαντασία and imagination, albeit beneath the
surface of the argument.

A final passage in *De An*. III 3, at the end of the causal analysis of φαντασία, helped to persuade Ross that Aristotle in this
chapter construes the faculty in the broad manner I have been denying. He states that at 428b18-30 Aristotle

  'distinguishes between φαντασία with respect to the special sensibles, the incidentals, and the common sensibles, and points out
  that while in the first case φαντασία is infallible so long as
  the sensation is present, in the other two it is fallible even
  in the presence of the sensation. This amounts to throwing on
  to φαντασία the work of apprehending the incidentals and even
  the special sensibles as well as the common sensibles; and sensation would accordingly be reduced to the level of a mere passive affection which has to be interpreted by φαντασία before
  it can give any information or misinformation about objects.'[53]

Ross's statement of Aristotle's doctrine is seriously misleading,
and his gloss on it the product of oversight and faulty inference.
He omits to mention that in the first part of the passage to which
he refers, Aristotle has restated his view (cf. *De An*. II 6) that
there is sense perception not merely of special or proper objects
(e.g. white) but of incidentals (e.g. that this white thing is
Coriscus) and common objects (e.g. movement and magnitude). This
view of perception is offered in Book II of *De anima* as an adequate
account of the matter; and even if sense perception, αἴσθησις, is
there treated very much as a passive affection, in the present
chapter Aristotle is keen to stress that it is a capacity in virtue
of which we *judge*.[54] Nor does there appear to be a general need
for a special interpretative faculty performing the job Ross assigns
to it; for however bare Aristotle's conception of perception of
incidentals may be, it is (I take it)[55] an interpretative sort of
perception. It would therefore be surprising if in his causal analysis of φαντασία Aristotle meant to abandon the relatively self-
sufficient theory of perception reiterated in the course of his
argument at 428b18-25. The only evidence Ross appears to rely on
in believing that he is committed in the passage to a new theory
is that cited in his first sentence - the distinctions made between

sorts of φαντασία (428b25-30). Yet those remarks could suggest that
the work of apprehending sensibles is now assigned to φαντασία only
if what Aristotle has said in the immediately preceding lines about
perception is forgotten, as of course it is forgotten in Ross's description of the passage; as it is, we can only understand Aristotle's doctrine here about φαντασία by reference to his reasserted
doctrine about αἴσθησις.

Nonetheless, the account of φαντασία at 428b25-30 reported by
Ross does present an embarrassment for my own interpretation. If
φαντασία is imagination or non-paradigmatic sensory experience, it
is easy enough to see how it is possible to have φαντασία of incidentals or common sensibles while one is still engaged in the relevant sort of perception. Aristotle's examples of an indistinctly
perceived thing looking like a man and of the sun appearing a foot
across are respectively cases in point - and cases which illustrate
the fallibility of φαντασία.[56] But what of the notion that while
someone is perceiving a special object, e.g. seeing something white,
he may also enjoy an infallible kind of φαντασία of that selfsame
object? It will not do to suppose (for example) that the perception
in question is indistinct, leaving interpretative work for φαντασία to
do. For interpretation carries with it the possibility of error,
especially if one cannot clearly *see* what colour one is looking at;
it may look white, but be some other colour. I have no answer to
this puzzle. All I can suggest is that Aristotle has here been over-
whelmed by the scholasticism of this attempt to distinguish three
sorts of φαντασία corresponding to his three kinds of sense perception, which strikes most readers as a baroque extravagance. That
is, he is so intent on constructing parallel subdivisions that he
fails to notice that the idea of an infallible type of φαντασία cannot bear scrutiny.[57]

φαντασία AND φάντασμα

In *De An.* III 3 Aristotle specifies the faculty of φαντασία as 'that
in virtue of which we say that a φάντασμα occurs to us', and contrasts this usage with 'saying something with a metaphorical use
(*sc.* of φαντασία)'[58] (428a1-2). In the previous section we examined
some texts which have suggested to some (wrongly, in my view) that
φαντασία is sometimes given an extremely broad Protagorean scope by

Aristotle. Here, by contrast, is a considered statement prominently
placed in his official treatment of φαντασία which has often been
taken to restrict the faculty to experience of mental images (for
φάντασμα is standardly translated 'image'). If the text really does
mean this, it will require considerable ingenuity to explain on Aristotle's behalf why examples such as those of the sun appearing to
be a foot across or of an indistinctly perceived thing looking like
a man are pertinent to a discussion of φαντασία. In neither of
these examples does it seem plausible to suppose that the contemplation of mental images is involved; nor does Aristotle in presenting
them suggest that it is.

I hold that it is a mistake to interpret φάντασμα at 428a1 as
meaning 'mental image'.[59] 'Image' is not the root meaning of the
word, nor is it a very frequent meaning in Plato; and there are
strong contextual reasons, supported by a crucial piece of evidence
in the passage of De insomniis to which I have already alluded, for
taking it otherwise here. I do not deny that in many Aristotelian
contexts the φαντάσματα of which he speaks are what we would call
mental images, nor that the word φάντασμα may conveniently and aptly
be translated and understood as 'image' (as e.g. in De memoria);
only that that translation is inappropriate in De An. III 3.

φαντάζω, the verb from which φάντασμα derives, means 'make apparent', 'make show', 'present'. Only passive and middle forms (in
particular contexts it is often hard to tell which) occur in pre-
Hellenistic literature;[60] we find these used both absolutely and
with a complement or predicate. Thus in Herodotus Artabanus reminds
Xerxes that God smites with his thunderbolt not the small animals
but the 'excessive' ones, and does not allow them to 'make a show of
themeselves' (φαντάζεσθαι); the Scythians 'make themselves no longer
apparent' to Darius (οὐκέτι ἐφαντάζοντό σφι); a dream 'is presented'
to Xerxes (ὄνειρον φαντάζεταί μοι).[61] Plato supplies numerous examples of the verb with a complement. God is not a magician who
presents himself or makes himself appear in different guises on different occasions (φαντάζεσθαι ἄλλοτε ἐν ἄλλαις ἰδέαις);[62] the beautiful will not present itself to the philosophic lover as beautiful
in the way that a face is (οὐδ' αὖ φαντασθήσεται αὐτῷ τὸ καλὸν οἷον
πρόσωπόν τι);[63] some pleasures 'present themselves as great and numerous, but are in fact jumbled up with pains' (μεγάλας ... τινὰς

ἅμα καὶ πολλὰς φαντασθείσας, εἶναι δ' αὐτὰς συμπεφυρμένας ὁμοῦ
λύπαις);[64] and so on.[65] Notice how in these Platonic examples the
guises described by means of the verb are all deceptive guises,
guises which are at odds with reality.

We should consequently expect φάντασμα to mean 'appearance',
'apparition', 'guise', 'presentation', often with the strong implication of unreality. The pre-Aristotelian evidence in general bears
out this expectation, although the range of the noun is narrower
than that of the verb: I have not met with an instance of φάντασμα
as 'guise', and 'presentation' never seems a very apt translation.
In its earlier extant uses in the tragedians the word is used of
ghosts or apparitions in dreams; and both Plato and Aristotle so
use it on occasion.[66] Plato, however, more often employs φάντασμα
to talk of unreal appearances more generally; he treats it as the
abstract noun corresponding to φαίνεσθαι, 'appear' (which perhaps
helps to explain why in him, at least, the meanings 'guise' and
'presentation' available from φαντάζω are not exploited). Examples
of this usage are particularly frequent in contexts where Plato is
developing his metaphysics of copies and paradigms or where he is
concerned with artificial representations.[67] It certainly hardens
on occasion in such a way that φάντασμα can almost be said to *mean*
'image' or 'representation' in context. A notable psychological
instance, which is very like Aristotle's favourite usage, occurs in
the *Philebus*.[68] But Plato himself makes the basis of his own usage
quite plain in the *Sophist*. He there defines sophistry as a species
of image-making, viz. φανταστική, appearance-making (or as Cornford
translates, semblance-making); and he is naturally concerned with
φαντάσματα that are images. But his word for image is εἴδωλον, not
φάντασμα, and he explains why he calls one species of εἴδωλον φάντασμα - because there are some εἴδωλα which *appear* to be faithful
likenesses or copies (εἰκόνες) of an original, but are not really:
ἆρ' οὐκ, ἐπείπερ φαίνεται μέν, ἔοικε δὲ οὔ, φάντασμα;[69] And elsewhere (e.g. in the seventh deduction of the *Parmenides*) Plato uses
φάντασμα as the noun corresponding to φαίνεσθαι when he has no concern with images: if you approach nearer to *the others*, then contrary
to your first impression they appear many and different, and because
of this appearance of difference (τῷ τοῦ ἑτέρου φαντάσματι), different in character and unlike.[70] Again, in the *Cratylus* Socrates in-

sists against Protagoras and Euthydemus that things have a fixed
being of their own, and are 'not dragged up and down relative to us
or by us through private appearance (τῷ ἡμετέρῳ φαντάσματι)'.[71]

It is with these last two examples of φάντασμα in Plato that one
in our *De insomniis* passage (2,460b3sqq.) is most closely comparable.
In view of the Protagorean reference of the *Cratylus* text this might
suggest once again a broad Protagorean conception of φαντασία in
Aristotle. But what disposes Plato to use φάντασμα in these contexts
is the unreality or unreliability of the appearances in question; and
it is with just such appearances that Aristotle too is concerned at
460b3sqq., as my earlier references to the passage showed. After
giving his examples of the way in which persons in pathological conditions are liable to be deceived by false appearances, Aristotle
adds a qualification: if a man is not gravely ill (Aristotle is
thinking of fever), he can sometimes realize that what appears to
him is false; but if his affliction is greater, he may be so deceived that (for example) he actually recoils from the animals he
thinks he sees. Then comes the crucial couple of sentences (460b16-
20): 'The reason for these things happening is that the governing
element (τὸ κύριον) and that to which the φαντάσματα occur do not
judge in respect of the same faculty. An indication of this is
that the sun appears (φαίνεται) a foot across, but often something
else contradicts φαντασία.' Here φάντασμα is plainly used simply as
the noun corresponding to φαίνεσθαι, one of the verbs Aristotle employs in presenting and discussing his examples of false appearances
throughout the passage, as well as in the sun example. For the frequent employment of φαίνεται to indicate unreal appearances is the
only feature of the passage which adequately and naturally accounts
for the mention of a part of the soul concerned with φαντάσματα.
The most striking support for this reading of φαντάσματα is Aristotle's immediate employment of the sun example to illustrate and
justify his distinction between τὸ κύριον and 'that to which the
φαντάσματα occur'. But that distinction is, of course, introduced
to help explain how it is that false appearances deceive some but
not others - as we learn in chapter 3 of *De insomniis*, it is when
τὸ κύριον is enfeebled or incapacitated that deception is most
likely to take place. There is no hint, on the other hand, that
Aristotle is at all preoccupied with mental images in the passage.

The topic is 'being deceived with respect to our senses' (460b3-4).
And although the phenomena Aristotle mentions are pathological in
character, and might be dismissed as hallucinations, and so as mere
mental imagery, by a modern writer, that is not how he describes
them. In the sun example, there is even less room for imagery; the
same is true of the example known as 'Aristotle's experiment' which
follows it in the text.[72] Could Aristotle, however, be using φαντάσματα to mean '*sense*-images', what Hume would have called 'impressions'? That seems highly unlikely. Aristotle has a technical term,
αἴσθημα, which at least in some contexts seems to denote an image-
like sense-datum.[73] But I do not known any text where it is very
plausible to suppose that φάντασμα is used in this way; indeed, φάντασμα is sometimes contrasted with αἴσθημα, as being a term appropriate to occasions where there may be no actual perceiving going
on.[74]

The similarities between this *De insomniis* passage and *De anima*
III 3, 428a1-b9, make it hard to resist the conclusion that when
Aristotle specifies φαντασία as 'that in virtue of which we say that
a φάντασμα occurs to us' (428a1-2), φάντασμα again does duty simply
as the noun corresponding to cautious, sceptical, and non-committal
φαίνεται. Here, too, Aristotle illustrates his arguments with examples employing the verb, twice as an explicit pointer to the nature of φαντασία; he uses the same sun example, which we know from
De insomniis to constitute an instance of a φάντασμα in this sense
of 'appearance'. Moreover, to read φάντασμα in this way allows us
to see in the analyses which follow the fulfilment of a methodological promise held out by the formula at 428a1-2. For notice that
φαντασία is not stated to be the faculty in virtue of which φαντάσματα occur to us, but that in virtue of which *we say that* a φάντασμα occurs to us. I take Aristotle to be intending by this formula to distinguish cases of φαντασία by the linguistic behaviour
they prompt. Now the linguistic behaviour in question must surely
be the utterance of factual statements about what is perceived (or
as it were perceived) which include and rely significantly on φαίνεται, used in the cautious, disbelieving or non-committal way I
have attempted to specify. That, at least, is the one type of
locution which is prominent and is implied by Aristotle to be an
important clue to the character of φαντασία in the body of the

section of the chapter that begins with the formula about φάντασμα.

Aristotle's choice of this linguistic criterion as the working
guideline for his investigation of the connection or want of connection between φαντασία and other faculties of the soul, perception, belief, knowledge, etc., is one of the most impressive features of his treatment of the imagination. It provides a particularly clear and arresting testimony to his enthusiasm for philoso-
phizing on the basis of ἔνδοξα, of course.[75] But it is also evidence of deep insight into the problems of characterizing a psychological phenomenon such as imagination. For in attempting to say
what makes imagination different from sense perception or belief
Aristotle steers clear of two opposite but equally fruitless modes
of differentiation, with which he was nonetheless familiar. He
does not make the distinction between imagination and perception
in physical or physiological terms; he employs those terms in his
causal analysis, at 428b10sqq., but only after he has sought to
clarify in quite different terms what the two phenomena are that
he wants to relate in a causal connection. Nor, on the other
hand, does Aristotle adopt the procedure associated with Hume, of
reflecting on the presence of sensory features in imaging, and
then attempting to give an account, based on introspection, of the
difference in sensory quality between imaging and perception. He
had once defined φαντασία as a sort of weak perception, in the
early *Rhetoric*;[76] but that approach has been abandoned by the time
of *De anima*. Instead he opts firmly for behavioural criteria.
Thus at 427b16-24 he asks: is believing a voluntary activity like
imagining? are the emotional consequences of imagining the same
as those of belief?[77] And he divines that *linguistic* behaviour is
of fundamental importance. Not only does he advert to it as a
means of differentiating imagination from perception, as when he
notices that the language a man characteristically uses when imagining - 'appears' - is not what one would expect if he were re-
porting what he could see without difficulty (428a12-15). He also
hits on the propensity to say φαίνεται as giving a way of *identifying* instances of imagination or φαντασία. Imagining is not the
sort of thing one can in any interesting sense observe; and its intentional, thought-dependent aspects make language a peculiarly
appropriate vehicle for its realization, not only its communication.

It is true that within the section 428a1-b9, it is only at 428a
12-15, in the example of an indistinctly perceived thing looking
like a man, that Aristotle explicitly draws attention to the use of
the *word* φαίνεται. But it is hard to see any more immediate reason
for his taking the sun example to be a case of φαντασία than that
he has observed that people say: 'The sun looks a foot across', when
they believe its size to be very much larger (cf. 428b2-3). The
sceptical, cautious or non-committal implications of using the word
may, as I have suggested, have led him to assert that 'most φαντασίαι turn out false' (428a12). And when he remarks that things appear (e.g. dreams) although sense perception is not involved (428a7-
8), it may be the disposition people have to employ φαίνεται in
their dream reports which is again for Aristotle the most immediate
pointer to the presence of φαντασία - or at least what governs his
approach to φαντασία in dreaming.

This last point deserves elaboration. Dreaming is a particularly
interesting sort of φαντασία, not least because with dreaming neither
of the criteria for imagination laid down by Aristotle at 427b16-24
is satisfied: dreaming is not subject to the will, except in Freud-
ian ways which Aristotle shows no sign of anticipating; nor is one
always as emotionally detached from the horrors of a dream as from a
horrific picture - sometimes it is much more as if belief were involved, as Aristotle recognizes in *De insomniis*.[78] Consequently
dreaming presents a challenge to my thesis that there is a unity to
Aristotle's treatment of φαντασία which is compatible with identifying φαντασία with imagination.

One might perhaps suppose that, if a philosopher is going to as-
sociate dreams with imagination at all, he will do so on the basis
of the consideration that dreams involve mental imagery. That is at
any rate the sort of interpretation a reading of Ross's account of
Aristotle's treatment of φαντασία might suggest;[79] and certainly
Aristotle's use of φάντασμα with respect to dreams in e.g. the first
chapter of *De insomniis* is compatible with such an interpretation.
But in fact between dreams and cases of φαντασία which do satisfy
the criteria for imagination spelt out at 427b16-24 Aristotle forges
a different link. What he exploits in *De insomniis*, and indeed
makes central to his account of dreaming, is the appropriateness of
φαίνεται, 'appears', both to descriptions of the content of dreams

and to the seeing of aspects.

He takes as the starting point for his analysis of dreams the
phenomenon of pathological appearances – the way marks on the wall
look like animals to the sick man, or the way that, from the slight-
est resemblance, the amorous man takes a boy he sees in the distance
or with back turned to be his beloved (*Insomn.* 2, 460b3sqq.). This
is not just the point from which Aristotle happens to begin; in the
first chapter of *De insomniis*, after puzzling over the relation of
dreaming to sense perception and judgement, he seems to despair of
finding any other mode of attack on the problem of the nature of
dreaming (458b25-8): 'With respect to this whole matter, so much at
least is clear, that the very same thing which is responsible for
our being deceived while suffering from fever causes this phenomenon
(sc. being deceived) in sleep.' The similarity between the two
cases which leads Aristotle to suppose their causal analysis must
be the same is evidently that, as with the pathological seeing of
aspects, so in dreaming things appear to be what they are not, and
are often mistakenly taken to be what they appear. This is borne
out not only by his explicit concentration on the phenomenon of deception here and throughout much of the treatise, but by the thor-
oughgoing character of the parallelism he endeavours to establish
in chapter 3 between dreaming and pathological 'appearances'. He
goes so far as to construe the φαίνεται of dream reports as the
φαίνεται appropriate to the appearance of an aspect. What happens
in a dream, according to him, is that *something* looks, in virtue
of some small resemblance, like something else (*Insomn.* 3, 461b10-
21): it is not just that Coriscus appears to me, but that a trace
of my sense-datum of Coriscus appears to me as Coriscus (*ibid.* 461
b21-30). Coleridge was wittingly or unwittingly a pretty faithful
Aristotelian when he described dreams as devices 'by which the
blind fancy would fain interpret to the mind the painful sensations
of distempered sleep'.[80]

Now the pathological seeing of aspects shares with dreaming an
important difference from cases like seeing an indistinct object
as a man, or (to take an instance from *De insomniis*) seeing the
shifting shapes made by clouds now as a man, now as a centaur (461
b19-21). The difference in question is that very failure to satisfy
the criteria of imagination proposed at *De An.* III 3, 427b16-24,

which we noted with respect to dreams: the fevered man's appearances
are *not* subject to his will; and if his affliction is bad enough,
not only his emotions but his actions will resemble those appropriate
to belief (cf. *Insomn.* 2, 460b15-16). But Aristotle's own unitary
explanation of dreams and such pathological phenomena, on the one
hand, and the similarity between pathological and normal seeing of
aspects, on the other, put us in a position in which we can now exhibit the unity in Aristotle's conception of φαντασία while retain-
ing our characterization of it as imagination. For the causal explanation of dreaming and of pathological appearances accounts for
just those features of these phenomena which make them unlike cases
of φαντασία which satisfy the criteria of 427b16-24. It is evidently because sleep and fever impair the operation of our faculties
in general, leaving φαντασία alone efficacious, that the will has
no control over what appears to us in such conditions[81] - or to put
it in a more Aristotelian way, we cannot *act* when asleep.[82] And as
Aristotle himself labours to show, it is for the same reason that
the 'governing element', the faculty we have for making judgements
on the basis of what our senses tell us, is also stifled, so that
appearances are taken as veridical by default;[83] and consequently
φαίνεται can be employed to refer to the appearances in a sceptical
manner only by an observer (or the patient himself upon recovery,
the dreamer when he has woken). Should these differences incline
us to withhold the name 'imagination' from dreaming and the pathological seeing of aspects? The question has by this stage, I hope,
an artificial air. We could appeal to 427b16-24 and refuse the
name if we wished; but we could also agree to be impressed more by
the similarity between these phenomena and the central cases of
imagination, and rule that the criteria of 427b16-24 apply to *normal*
imagination, reflecting that in *De insomniis* Aristotle has provided
both a description and a causal explanation of the abnormality of
what we might call *abnormal* imagination.[84]

IN CONFINIO INTELLECTUS ET SENSUS

It is instructive to notice what occasions Aristotle's introduction
of the topic of φαντασία in *De An.* III 3. By the beginning of that
chapter he has completed his account of sense perception, and he
now turns to consider thinking, reminding us of what his investiga-

tion of the opinions of his philosophical predecessors in I 2 had
revealed; that soul in animals is defined by them in one of two
ways above all, by reference to the capacity for movement or to the
capacity for judgement (criteria accepted by Aristotle himself: III
9, 432a15-17; cf. I 2, 403b25-7 et passim, III 3, 427a17-21). The
fact that both in thought and in perception the soul judges and is
acquainted with things that are led the ancients, Aristotle tells
us, to identify the two faculties. And so in his attempt to determine the nature of thinking he takes for his first task the demonstration that this identification is a mistake. He observes that
all animals have sense perception, but not all think; and he moves
immediately to forestall a possible counter-argument based on the
idea that animals *do* think in a way, because they have φαντασία,
which is also a sort of perception.[85] The equation cannot be thus
circuitously reinstated. φαντασία (which Aristotle agrees, nearly
all animals[86] do have) is different both from sense perception and
from thinking, although sense perception is indispensable to it as
it is itself to ὑπόληψις (427b6-16). This thesis about φαντασία
evidently requires defence, a digression necessary for Aristotle's
justification of his treatment of thinking as a genuinely independent faculty in the chapters which follow (III 4-8). The first
sections of the discussion of φαντασία (427b16-428b9) show that it
cannot be the same as perception or thinking (at least in the sense
of νοεῖν which most interests Aristotle and which he studies at III
4-8). The final section (428b10-429a9) shows how sense perception
is indispensable to it (argument for the contention that thinking
requires φαντασία is reserved until III 8, 432a3-10).

Aristotle shows himself aware, then, of a real temptation to
assimilate φαντασία to perception on the one hand and thinking on
the other (cf. also III 9, 432a31-3). But he was intent on demonstrating why these temptations must be resisted rather than on ex-
ploring them. This preoccupation with refutation, as so often in
Aristotle, has unfortunate consequences. His combative instincts
give him a predilection for single short knockdown arguments which
can leave the hungry reader unsatisfied. In stressing non-identi-
ties he does not pause to reflect on the equally important affinities between φαντασία and the other faculties which incidentally
come to light in the course of his arguments. Nor does he appear

to have tried to formulate in his own mind a single statement about what φαντασία is like (as distinct from what it is not like), free from the inconsistencies which at least apparently result when we lay side by side observations he finds it natural to make in one contrast with opposed observations or ways of speaking which seem to come naturally to him in other contexts. For us these features of his treatment of φαντασία are as interesting as his avowed aims and intended achievements.

Although at 427b14-15 and in a number of other places Aristotle states or implies that φαντασία is not the same as thinking (διάνοια, νοεῖν), it is perhaps significant that in his official account of φαντασία in *De An*. III 3 he seems to waver on this point - as though when he came to consider φαντασία at length on its own account, not briefly in the course of comments on thinking, he had found it more like thinking than his usual characterization[87] of it as a *sine qua non* of thinking suggests. At any rate, he there states his favourite thesis about the indispensability of φαντασία to thinking in the more restricted formulation: 'there is no ὑπόληψις without φαντασία' (427b16); his argument for the non-identity of φαντασία and διάνοια is billed as proof that φαντασία and ὑπόληψις are not the same (427b 16-17), and actually confines itself to differences between φαντασία and δοξάζειν, believing (427b17-24); and he moves on to the next section of the chapter with the cautious observation 'thinking ... seems[88] to include on the one hand φαντασία and on the other ὑπόληψις' (427b27-8).

ὑπόληψις is 'taking something to be the case' or (in that sense) 'judgement', a general notion here including as its species ἐπιστήμη (knowledge), δόξα (belief), φρόνησις (practical understanding) and their opposites (427b24-6). The illustration of φαντασία Aristotle gives is of someone producing things before his eyes like the mnemonists (427b18-19). It might seem natural to infer that Aristotle here supposes the relation of ὑπόληψις and φαντασία as species of νοεῖν to be that of the disposition or act of judgement and the piece of thinking from which the disposition or act results.

But it would be rash to attribute to him the view that the activity of thinking is φαντασία on the basis of this evidence. He has not stated that φαντασία and ὑπόληψις are the only forms of thought; and elsewhere he shows himself ready to distinguish between φαντασία and the process of thinking. A passage from *De memoria* (1, 449b31-450a5) is particularly instructive, employing as it does language similar to that Aristotle uses when speaking of φαντασία at 427b16 sqq.:

'It is not possible to think without φάντασμα. For the same effect occurs in thinking as in drawing a diagram. For in the latter case, though we do not make any use of the fact that the size of the triangle is determinate, we none the less draw it with a determinate size. And similarly someone who is thinking, even if he is not thinking of something with a size, places something with a size before his eyes, but thinks of it not as having a size.'[89]

This passage makes it plain that not merely the ὑπόληψις which results from thinking, but the process of thinking itself is distinct from φαντασία, which it nevertheless requires. Aristotle, exploiting a point made by Plato in the *Republic* (510d-511a), recognizes that what one engages in thinking about and what one imagines in so thinking may be distinct in the sense he hints at.

It is perhaps not possible to demonstrate that the distinction between φαντασία and the activity of thinking adumbrated in this *De memoria* passage is presupposed in the treatment of thinking in *De anima* (although it is perfectly consistent with the doctrine of III 4-8).[90] But the fact that Aristotle in III 3 makes his distinction merely between φαντασία and ὑπόληψις is not enough to suggest that he has not yet seen that distinction between thinking and φαντασία. For we should recall that a principal concern of III 3 is to show that φαντασία is not any of the more familiar capacities in virtue of which we *judge* and are acquainted with what is. It is enough for him to demonstrate that φαντασία is not ὑπόληψις or any of its species. And if he guardedly allows that φαντασία may be reckoned a species of thinking, that may in part be due to this overriding concern with judgement: he may be prepared for the sake of argument to concede to the man who equates φαντασία and thinking *tout court* that φαντασία is a sort of thinking, so long as it is distinguished from thought in the sense of judgement, ὑπόληψις.

At the same time, Aristotle may have been the readier to make the concession because of a feature of the arguments by which he distinguishes φαντασία from ὑπόληψις. He notes that φαντασία, unlike be-

lief, is up to us when we wish; and that the emotional responses appropriate to belief and φαντασία are different - in the former case
'we are immediately affected', in the latter it is 'as if we were
looking at terrible or enheartening things in a picture' (427b17-24).
These criteria of φαντασία do not distinguish it from the activity
of thinking: that, too, is in our power when we wish (cf. 417b24);
nor does the thought of disaster or success automatically inspire
immediate gloom or cheer. Aristotle may well have been persuaded
by these features common to φαντασία and thinking to allow the claim
of φαντασία to be a sort of thinking at 427b28. Nor is that claim
without plausibility. A mnemonist instructing his pupil might well
ask him to *think* of a set of places in which mental images may be
put.

So Aristotle is tempted to view φαντασία as a form of thinking,
or at least as a thought-like component of thinking. But as we saw
earlier, he also speaks of φαντασία in ways which suggest that, if
pressed, he would have had to agree that the thought-like features
which he takes to be characteristic of φαντασία at 427b16-24 are
not invariable features of it. Thus it seems unlikely that he would
wish to allow that the persons in the grip of fevers or strong emotion described in *De insomniis* are able to engage in φαντασία or not
as and when they wish: what appears to them is patently not under
their control. And he obviously does not think such persons capable
of maintaining the emotional detachment from their φαντάσματα seen
as typical of φαντασία at 427b23-4: they, like dreamers, are often
helplessly deceived, even to the point of moving bodily towards or
away from what appears to them. Moreover, in just this context in
De insomniis Aristotle permits himself to speak of φαντασία as a
faculty in virtue of which we judge (460b16-18). Here, evidently,
φαντασία is much more like perception (one might think of it as
*mis*perception)[91] than thought.

So, too, in the remaining part of the discussion in *De An.* III
3, from 428a1 to the end of the chapter. It is, for example, striking that, for his causal analysis of φαντασία, Aristotle draws from
the considerations which have filled the preceding pages the single
idea that it is thought 'not to occur without sense perception, but
only in things which perceive and with respect to those things of
which there is perception' (428b11-13); and the chief conclusion of

the analysis is that the change resulting from actual sense perception which he argues is φαντασία 'must be like perception' (428b14).
When he goes on to infer that it, too, must be capable of truth and
falsehood, working out an elaborate comparison between the propensi-
ties of sense perception and φαντασία for the one or the other (428b
17-30), it looks as though, having begun by treating φαντασία as a
form of thinking, he ends by taking sense perception to be the key
to its nature.[92] In particular, in concentrating on its propensity
to give true or false views of facts, Aristotle seems clearly to
count φαντασία, like sense perception, as a faculty of judgement -
contrary to what the discussion at 427b16-24 might have led one to
expect. It is worth stressing this point, since some scholars,
adopting Ross's emendation at 428a3 (which turns the statement of
the MSS that φαντασία is a faculty or disposition for judgement
into a question), suppose that in rejecting at 428a5-b9 any identification of φαντασία with other faculties of judgement, Aristotle
means to deny that it is itself such a faculty.[93] As Rodier saw,[94]
emendation at this point is unnecessary; and the associated interpretation is impossible. For Aristotle glosses 'faculties in accordance with which we judge' by the words 'and take things truly
or falsely' (ἀληθεύομεν ἢ ψευδόμεθα, 428a4). And his strategy
throughout the section 428a5-b9 is not to argue that the dimension
of truth and falsehood is inhabited by sense perception, knowledge,
belief, etc., but not by φαντασία. It is rather to maintain that,
although φαντασία is properly to be assessed for truth and falsehood no less than perception or belief, the assessment has or can
have different results in the case of φαντασία from those obtained
in the other cases. This is the point of the sun example (428b2-
9); and besides remarking that perceptions are always true, but
some φαντασίαι false (428a11-12), Aristotle distinguishes φαντασία
from knowledge and understanding (νοῦς) on the very same ground
(428a16-18), and is prepared to concede an initial plausibility to
the identification of φαντασία and belief precisely because they
cannot be differentiated in this way (428a18-19).

So the unity of Aristotle's conception of φαντασία begins to
look somewhat fragile. One might argue on his behalf that in different parts of *De An.* III 3 Aristotle endows φαντασία with such
very different features just because he has different sorts of

exercise of the imagination in view. Seeing a distant object as a
man (cf. 428a12-15) *is* very like seeing, while imagining a set of
places for mnemonic purposes (cf. 427b18-20) *is* very like thinking;
and in the former case one does - albeit hesitantly - take something truly or falsely (viz. the distant object to be a man), but
not in the latter case. It would perhaps be possible to place Aristotle's examples and his remarks about them on a complex, but consistent and unified, conceptual map of the imagination, in the style
I have adopted in the two preceding sections of this paper. But
profitable and charitable though the exercise might be, it is time
to notice that Aristotle himself shows no sign of being aware of
the tensions within his account of φαντασία; nor, consequently, of
the importance and difficulty of the philosophical task of saying
just how thinking and sensing both contribute to the imagination.
Moreover, some of the inconsistencies of Aristotle's account seem
more than merely apparent. Doubtless the fact that in belief, unlike φαντασία, one *necessarily* takes something truly or falsely
(cf. 427b20-1)[95] does serve to differentiate φαντασία and belief.
Yet it does not follow (as he evidently thinks) that φαντασία is
not sometimes a sort of ὑπόληψις closer to belief than to knowledge
or practical understanding. As commentators have noticed,[96] it is
difficult to report or discuss such examples as the sun looking a
foot across without introducing words like 'suppose', 'conjecture',
etc., which connote precisely the sort of thinking involved in ὑπόληψις; and Aristotle himself, in an unguarded moment, once uses
δοκεῖ in presenting the example (*Insomn.* 1, 458b29).[97]

CONCLUSION

My intention, however, has been to show reason to celebrate Aristotle's pioneering treatment of the imagination. The great virtue of
his account is its recognition of the range of psychological phenomena which deserve to be associated in this familial concept. His
attempt to generalize from them about the logical peculiarities of
the imagination is not carried through with a clear and steady view
of the whole topic. But it remains seminal for anyone who seeks a
better understanding. For Aristotle reminds us of the variety of
the phenomena we need to consider, and compels us to find ways of
connecting them; he puts in our hands, even if he himself does not

exploit them very fully, many of the contrasts and comparisons which
seem fundamental for the conceptual mapping of imagination; and his
very inconsistencies suggest crucial problems in its comparative anatomy.[98]

NOTES

1 See in particular *Phlb*. 38a-40e, *Sph*. 263d-264b. In the former
passage, it seems hard to deny that Plato, in talking of the
work of the painter in the soul, is identifying imagination (so
e.g. Hackforth, *Plato's examination of pleasure* (Cambridge 1945),
72); the latter passage is too brief for very sure appraisal,
but its account of φαντασία is not dissimilar enough from that
of the painter's work in the *Philebus* nor from Aristotle's
treatment in *De An*. III 3 for one to be able to share Cornford's
brisk confidence in asserting that φαντασία is not here imagination (*Plato's theory of knowledge* (London 1935), 319). But
these are both late dialogues, which may owe something at this
point to discussions in the Academy to which Aristotle contri-
buted.

2 Useful surveys are offered by J.Freudenthal, *Ueber den Begriff
des Wortes* ΦΑΝΤΑΣΙΑ *bei Aristoteles* (Göttingen 1863); J.I.Beare,
Greek theories of elementary cognition (Oxford 1906), 290sqq.;
W.D.Ross, *Aristotle* (5th ed. London 1949), 142-5; D.A.Rees,
'Aristotle's treatment of φαντασία', in *Essays in Ancient Greek
philosophy*, ed. J.P.Anton with G.L.Kustas (Albany, N.Y. 1971),
491-504.

3 *Tht*. 152a-c.

4 *Sph*. 264a-b.

5 So at least he seems to say at 264a4-6; but no doubt he would
allow that 'because' (διά) requires elaboration and restriction.

6 L.Wittgenstein, *Zettel*, ed. G.E.M.Anscombe and G.H. von Wright,
trans. G.E.M.Anscombe (Oxford 1967), no.621.

7 So e.g. Beare (*op.cit. n.2*), 290; Ross (*op.cit. n.2*), 142-3; K.
Lycos, 'Aristotle and Plato on "Appearing"', *Mind* n.s. LXXIII
(1964), 496 and n.1; D.W.Hamlyn, *Aristotle's De Anima* Books II
and III (Oxford 1968), 129, 131, 133-4.

8 E.g. by Hamlyn and Lycos.

9 Ross, *loc.cit.*

10 See e.g. R.D.Hicks, *Aristotle. De Anima* (Cambridge 1907), *ad*
428a1; Hamlyn (*op.cit. n.7*), 129 (although it was Professor

Hamlyn who in discussion sowed the seeds of doubt in my mind
about this interpretation).

11 (*op.cit. n.2*), 143-4.

12 See e.g. H.Ishiguro, 'Imagination', *Proc. Arist. Soc.* Suppl. Vol.
41 (1967), 37-56; P.F.Strawson, 'Imagination and perception', in
Experience and theory, ed. L.Foster and J.W.Swanson (London
1970), 31-54; R.Scruton, *Art and imagination* (London 1974), 91-
120. The basic texts in Ryle and Wittgenstein are: *The concept
of mind* (London 1949), ch.VIII; *Philosophical investigations*,
trans. G.E.M.Anscombe (Oxford 1958), II xi (cf. also *op.cit. n.6*,
nos. 621sqq.).

13 See *Sense and sensibilia* (Oxford 1962), esp. chs.3 and 4: also
R.M.Chisholm, *Perceiving: a philosophical study* (Ithaca, N.Y.
1957), esp. ch.4.

14 Scruton (*op.cit. n.12*), 97.

15 φαντασία, like φάντασμα, derives from the verb φαντάζω (found
only in its middle and passive forms before the Hellenistic
period), which means 'to make apparent', 'to cause to φαίνεσθαι'.
Now nouns of the -σία type formed from -ζω verbs tend in the
first instance to connote the action signified by the verb; nouns
of the -σμα type so formed regularly connote the result of the
action, or what is done by doing the action. One might therefore
expect that φαντασία, in its primitive sense, would signify just
that action which consists in producing φαντάσματα: that if φαντάσματα are (say) 'presentations' (in the sense 'what is presented'), φαντασία will be 'presenting' (or 'presentation' in an
active sense) and likely to behave syntactically not unlike 'imagining' or 'imagination'. But this expectation is largely dis-
appointed in Greek before Aristotle; and the reason is not far
to seek. We have noted the absence of active forms of the verb
φαντάζω in pre-Hellenistic texts. What this means in practice
is that we read not of persons *making* things appear thus and so,
but of sights, dreams, etc. *being presented* or *presenting themselves* to persons. This fact no doubt explains both the relative rarity of φαντασία compared with φάντασμα (cf. LSJ s.vv.)
and the near absence of an active force in φαντασία when it does
occur in writers before Aristotle. If human agents do not φαντά-
ζειν, actively make apparent or present things, if φαντάσματα
are rather made to appear by the chances of life, then there will
not be much scope for the *nomen actionis* φαντασία as 'presenting',
'making apparent', although φάντασμα will find a place naturally
enough. Contrast other pairs of nouns similarly formed from -ζω
verbs whose active voices are, however, employed: διαδικασία,
διαδίκασμα; εἰκασία, εἴκασμα; σκευασία, σκεύασμα. Here it is
invariably the latter member of the pair which is the rarer.
When φαντασία does gain what one might call a natural toehold in
the language, it does so in a secondary sense, 'presentation' as
corresponding not to the active but the passive of the verb - a
frequent use in Aristotle (cf. Bonitz, *Index Aristotelicus* 811a
38-b11).
     Not only φάντασμα and φαντάζω, then, but φαντασία too has a

natural passive tendency in the language as we find it, at odds
with the active force of 'imagination'. This certainly leaves
its mark on Aristotle's treatment of the faculty of φαντασία in
De An. III 3 - notably in his predilection for φαίνεται, 'appears', as an index to the operation of φαντασία, a predilection
which suggests that he thinks of the mind in φαντασία as the
passive recipient of experiences, not as actively imagining.
Nonetheless, the very fact that Aristotle (like Plato before him)
presses φαντασία into service as the name for a mental disposition or act, comparable with thinking and perceiving, reveals a
philosophical impulse to force the word into a more active sense
(latent, of course, within it). Again, he occasionally refers
to φαντασία the faculty as τὸ φανταστικόν (De An. III 9, 432a31;
Insomn. 1, 458b30, 459a16), which must be either (following
Plato in the Sophist 236c) the capacity for producing φαντάσματα,
or the capacity for φαντάζεσθαι in the novel Aristotelian sense,
attested (though in the passive) in two places at least (Ph. I
9, 192a15, De An. III 10, 433b12), of 'making (something) appear
for oneself' - i.e. a middle usage predicable of persons, with
a force approximating to that of 'imagining'.

16 On this notion see further n.25 below.

17 Cf. e.g. Ryle, The concept of mind (Penguin edition, London
   1963), 233; Wittgenstein (op.cit. n.12), II 213; Zettel (op.cit.
   n.6), nos. 621, 626-8, etc.

18 Cf. Ryle's construction of imagining as a sort of pretending (op.
   cit. n.17), 244-57 (criticized by H.Ishiguro, 'Imagination', in
   British analytical philosophy, ed. B.Williams and A.Montefiore
   (London 1966), 161sqq.); Scruton (op.cit. n.12), 97, etc., who
   treats imagination as unasserted thought (and will, no doubt,
   come under fire for doing so). In mentioning Ryle and Scruton,
   I do not mean to subscribe to their views on imagination, only
   to point up parallels between Aristotle and some of the best
   contemporary work.

19 This is because Aristotle thinks of imagination first and foremost as visualizing, on which see B.Williams, Problems of the
   self (Cambridge 1973), ch.3; Scruton (op.cit. n.12), 100-6.

20 The principal ground for this claim is that the discussion of
   the relation of δόξα and φαντασία at 428a18-24 makes no reference to the arguments already offered at 427b14-24 (cf. Hicks
   (op.cit. n.10), 456). Freudenthal thought the passage 427b14-
   24 was not only hard to relate to what preceded and followed,
   but also in contradiction with Aristotle's usual views on the
   topics it discusses (op.cit. n.2), 9sqq.); but he received a
   magisterial (if not entirely convincing) rebuke from G.Rodier,
   Aristote: Traité de l'Ame (Paris 1900), II 408-13.

21 Notice the references to the chapter as Aristotle's official
   account at Mem. 1, 449b30-1 (where De An. III 7-8 is also in
   Aristotle's mind), Insomn. 1, 459a15 (possibly an editorial
   addition), MA 6, 700b21-2.

22 (*op.cit. n.2*), 143.

23 This objection I owe to Profs. D.J.Allan and D.J.Furley.

24 This point was put to me by Fr. E. de Strycker.

25 In a memorable intervention in the discussion of this paper at
   the Symposium (whose text she kindly showed me subsequently),
   Prof. C.J. de Vogel took my interpretation of φαντασία in *De An.*
   III 3 as *non-paradigmatic* sensory experience to be in conflict
   with the evident fact that Aristotle elsewhere treats φαντασία
   as indispensable to thinking and as playing a *normal* part in the
   acquisition of knowledge. But let us take the case where the
   φαντασία we are concerned with is a piece of visualizing: I do
   not mean to deny that, according to Aristotle, all thinking involves visualizing or that that is the norm; what I mean is
   rather that visualizing is not normal sensory experience (for
   normal sense experience requires, as it does not, that we keep
   our eyes and ears open, etc.), but is sufficiently like and
   sufficiently closely connected with normal sensory experience
   to be thought of as a non-standard form of it. Of course, one
   is not very often going to use sceptical, cautious, or non-
   committal φαίνεται in commenting on the visualization one does
   in the course of thinking, just because one is interested
   principally in the thought, not in its accompanying imagery.
   But (as Mr Sorabji pointed out in the discussion) if one did
   reflect on it one would certainly wish to report on it in terms
   which (as φαίνεται does) make it clear that one is not necessarily making a claim about how one sees the world. The same would
   not be true of animal imagination; but animal imagination is an
   obscure corner of Aristotelian doctrine (cf. nn.47, 57, 86 below).

26 *Contra* the interesting interpretation advanced by M.Nussbaum in
   her Harvard thesis 'Aristotle's De Motu Animalium' (1975; to be
   published by Princeton University Press); I am grateful to Prof.
   Nussbaum for allowing me to discuss a draft of her material on
   φαντασία with her.

27 *De An.* III 10, 433a9-12.

28 See especially *De An.* I 1, 403a8-9; III 7, 431a14-17; 8, 432a3-
   14; *Mem.* 1, 449b31-450a7.

29 Cf. *De An.* III 3, 429a4-8; 10, 433a10-12 (with 9, 433a1-8).
   φαίνεται bulks large in the discussion of pathological conditions
   in *Insomn.* 2, 460b3-16, used with its sensory connotation. The
   φαίνεται appropriate to mention of τὸ φαινόμενον ἀγαθόν (cf. *De
   An.* III 10, 433a26-30 with e.g. *EE* VII 2, 1235b25-9, *EN* III 5,
   1114a31sqq.) need not, of course, of itself suggest a *sensory* appearance; but no doubt Aristotle would say that any thought of
   the form: 'this *seems* a good plan' must involve visualization.
   (I owe an awareness of the importance of Aristotle's remarks
   about τὸ φαινόμενον ἀγαθόν in this connection to Prof. Furley's
   paper in this volume.)

30 *De An.* III 10, 433b28-9; *MA* 8, 702a17-19. As Prof. Nussbaum
   suggests, Aristotle may put such stress on φαντασία partly because it (unlike thinking) has a material basis which renders
   it an appropriate component in a physiological account of
   movement.

31 (*op.cit. n.2*), 142.

32 Translation adapted from C.Kirwan, *Aristotle's Metaphysics
   Books* Γ Δ Ε (Oxford 1971), whose version and interpretation
   (p.110) are, however, spoilt by the assumption that φαίνεται is
   to be rendered 'is imagined'.

33 On the interpretation of this premiss (and on its text), see
   the excellent discussion by Kirwan (*op.cit. n.32*), 110-11.

34 Cf. 1010b8-11.

35 Cf. 1010b4-8.

36 We should observe how *very* much wider the concept of αἴσθησις
   ascribed to Protagoras in the *Theaetetus* is than Aristotle's
   perception of proper objects. It includes feeling cold or hot,
   pleasures, pains, desires, fears (156b2sqq.).

37 With most editors and commentators I reject the words τότε ἢ
   ἀληθὴς ἢ ψευδής (428a15) as a gloss.

38 (*Op.cit. n.7*), 131.

39 W.Hazlitt, *Why distant objects please* (from *Table Talk*).

40 For discussion, after Wittgenstein, of the close relation between
   imagining and 'seeing as', see e.g. Strawson (*art.cit. n.12*), 44-
   52; Scruton (*op.cit. n.12*), ch.8.

41 On going beyond the evidence as a criterion of imagination, see
   Scruton (*op.cit. n.12*), ch.7.

42 For some remarks on this use of 'imagine', see Strawson (*art.cit.
   n.12*), 53-4; also Ryle (*op.cit. n.17*), 244-5.

43 For this interpretation of what it is for imagination to be subject to the will, see Scruton (*op.cit. n.12*), 94-5.

44 Perhaps in something resembling the manner of H.P.Grice, 'The
   causal theory of perception', *Proc. Arist. Soc.*, Suppl. Vol. 35
   (1961), 121-52.

45 Cf. Hicks (*op.cit. n.10*), *ad loc.*

46 ὑπάρχοντος is usually translated not 'in question', but 'present',
   which is perhaps an easier rendering of the Greek. But the idea
   that the faculty of perception is not present in sleep is not
   only not Aristotelian doctrine, but in direct contradiction with
   what Aristotle is most naturally taken as saying in the next

sentence (428a8-9), when he states: 'sense perception is always present'. My translation attempts to capture what Aristotle (as the Greek commentators saw) must have been meaning to say: see Rodier and Hicks *ad loc*. I suspect a similar use of the word at *PA* I 1, 642a5.

47 At the same time it is difficult to be confident of just what conception of φαντασία does lie behind Aristotle's denial of it to some animals. Is it that only more sophisticated organisms like the ant and the bee have the capacity for interpreting and misinterpreting the world, but not the worm or grub (I follow Torstrik's reading at 428a11-12)? Aristotle's whole treatment of φαντασία in the non-rational animals is puzzling. See further nn.57, 86 below.

48 Cf. J.Bennett, 'Substance, reality, and primary qualities', in *Locke and Berkeley: A collection of critical essays*, ed. C.B. Martin and D.M.Armstrong (London 1968), 104-18; *Locke, Berkeley, Hume* (Oxford 1971), 89-102.

49 (*Art.cit. n.7*), 496-508.

50 *Ad loc.*

51 Beare, the Oxford translator, takes the actual word φαντασία, used here at 460b19-20, to refer not to the faculty but to the presentation of the sun as a foot across. This may be right; but there is no doubt that the faculty to which Aristotle does refer is φαντασία, as is shown e.g. by the mention of τὸ φαντασ-τικόν as the faculty involved in cases of this sort at *Insomn.* 1, 458b30, and by *De An.* III 3, 429a7-8, where Aristotle says that men act in accordance with their φαντασίαι (again, the translation is doubtful) because their reason is sometimes clouded by emotion or sickness or sleep.

52 (*Op.cit. n.13*), 41; cf. now S.R.L.Clark, *Aristotle's man* (Oxford 1975), 75-6.

53 (*Op.cit. n.2*), 142-3.

54 Cf. D.W.Hamlyn, 'Aristotle's account of aesthesis in the *De Anima*', *CQ* n.s.9 (1959), 11-13.

55 Following Hamlyn in his commentary (*op.cit. n.7*), 107-8, 119; and see now the excellent discussion of S.Cashdollar, 'Aristotle's account of incidental perception', *Phronesis* 18 (1973), 156-75.

56 I take it that these count as cases of φαντασία just because the perception involved is non-paradigmatic: if in the first example one's perception was distinct, then it would be a straightforward instance of incidental αἴσθησις (which might still, of course, be mistaken in its apprehension of the object in question); if in the second example the distance of the sun from the earth were such as our normal perceptual adjustments for perspective could accommodate, we should be dealing with a normal case

of αἴσθησις of a common object. Notice Aristotle's observation
that φαντασία goes wrong especially when the perceived object is
a long way off (428b29-30).

57 Some members of the Symposium seemed in the discussion to feel
that the schematism involved in Aristotle's distinctions between
(for example) perception and φαντασία of incidentals was so
artificial that it might well break down in other contexts. We
might then find Aristotle using the terms αἴσθησις or φαντασία
indifferently to refer to any perception involving interpretation of the proper objects of perception, without any hint of
the unreliability of φαντασία. This would certainly suggest
one explanation of why he treats now αἴσθησις, now αἰσθητικὴ
φαντασία as the condition of movement in the lower animals. Cf.
e.g. *De An.* III 7, 431a8-10 (αἴσθησις); *MA* 7, 701a29-36 (αἴσθησις or φαντασία indifferently); *De An.* III 11, 433b31-434a7
(φαντασία).

58 I take the metaphorical use of φαντασία which Aristotle has in
mind to be what Simplicius thought: he wrote (*ad loc.*) that
Aristotle distinguished the use of φαντασία he was concerned
with from that derived metaphorically from it 'when we use (the
expression) φαντασία for τὸ φαινόμενον (what appears [to be the
case]), both in sense perception and in belief' (cf. the common
use of the word recorded by LSJ s.v.1, Bonitz, *Index* 811a38-b11).
In short, Aristotle is concerned with the employment of 'appears'
peculiarly appropriate to imagination or non-paradigmatic sensory experience, and treats its applications in ordinary perceptual reports or in statements of belief ('that seems to me a
dangerous course of action') as extensions of that usage. His
justification would presumably be that it is preeminently in
cases of non-paradigmatic sensory experience that φαίνεται (and
so φαντασία) has distinctive force: it is most especially in
these cases that one really needs an expression whereby one can
convey that it *looks* so; in ordinary perceptual reports one can
as well say: 'It's a dog' as: 'It appears to me to be a dog',
and in voicing one's beliefs: 'That is a dangerous course of
action.' Contrast the way Grice would handle the question of
basic sense and metaphor (*art.cit. n.44*), 121-68.

59 In addition to the considerations I adduce in the text, I might
add that it would be hard for anyone to maintain that the basic
sense of φαντασία had to do with mental images, when its common-
est meaning in Greek is 'presentation', in the sense of 'what is
presented'. If, on the other hand, Aristotle means to claim
that the word is used in its basic sense in connection with just
a particular sort of presentation, viz. non-paradigmatic sensory
presentations, then his position is a very much more plausible
one.

60 LSJ s.v. II say 'in early writers only in Pass.'; but this is
clearly wrong.

61 VII 10; IV 124; VII 15.

62 *R.* 380d.

63 *Smp.* 211a.

64 *Phlb.* 51a.

65 Cf. Ast, *Lexicon Platonicum*, s.v.

66 Cf. LSJ, s.v. Ia.

67 E.g. *R.* 510a, 532c, 598b, 599a; *Sph.* 234e, 236c, 240d.

68 *Phlb.* 40a.

69 *Sph.* 236b.

70 *Prm.* 165d (cf. 166a); see in general LSJ s.v. II.

71 *Cra.* 386e.

72 *Insomn.* 2, 460b20-2; cf. Ross's note on the passage in *Aristotle, Parva Naturalia* (Oxford 1955), 273-4.

73 For a good discussion of the evidence, see R.Sorabji, *Aristotle on memory* (London 1972), 82-3.

74 Cf. *De An.* III 7, 431a14-15; 8, 432a9-10; *Insomn.* 3, 462a29-30. In the second of these passages Aristotle says that 'φαντάσματα are as αἰσθήματα, except without matter'. 'Without matter' has caused difficulty. Rodier said (*ad loc.*): 'En réalité, les αἰσθήματα n'ont pas plus de matière que les φαντάσματα, puisque la sensation ne saisit que la forme sans la matière. Seulement la sensation se produit en présence d'un objet matériel, tandis que l'imagination peut avoir lieu même en l'absence de cet objet.' I take Aristotle to mean that in imagining it is as if one were actually perceiving, but of course the physical basis of the sense-image of actual perception, viz. the coloration of the κόρη is not present - or at least, if it *is* present (as in the case of genuinely perceptual appearances, like seeing an indistinct object as a man), it is not the physical basis of φαντασία: the matter of a φάντασμα even of a perceptual sort is a change or motion in the sense organ caused by the perception itself (cf. *De An.* III 3, 428b25-30; *Insomn.* 2, 460b22-5). On the matter of αἰσθήματα, see Sorabji (*op.cit. n.73*), 83; 'Body and soul in Aristotle', *Philosophy* 49 (1974), 72 n.30.

75 Cf. G.E.L.Owen, 'τιθέναι τὰ φαινόμενα', in *Aristote et les problèmes de méthode* (Louvain/Paris 1961), 83-92.

76 *Rh.* I 11, 1370a28.

77 At *Metaph.* Γ 5, 1010b9-11, he distinguishes between the action appropriate to perception and that appropriate to φαντασία, unfortunately too briefly and obscurely: cf. Kirwan (*op.cit. n.32*), 109-10.

78 See ch.3 *passim*.

79 (*op.cit. n.2*), 144.

80 *Biographia Literaria*, p.5 of the Everyman Edition.

81 See especially *Insomn.* 3, 460b28-461b5.

82 Cf. e.g. *EN* I 8, 1098b31-1099a3.

83 See *Insomn.* 2, 460b3-16; 3, 461b5-462a8.

84 Here I am attracted by the argument of Ryle (*op.cit. n.17*, 244-5): 'Make-believe is compatible with all degrees of scepticism and credulity, a fact which is relevant to the supposed problem, "How can a person fancy that he sees something, without realizing that he is not seeing it" ... The fact that people can fancy that they see things, are pursued by bears, or have a grumbling appendix, without realizing that it is nothing but fancy, is simply a part of the unsurprising general fact that not all people are, all the time, at all ages and in all conditions, as judicious or critical as could be wished.' Ryle has been criticized for 'lumping together', as conditions in which people are particularly prone to be uncritical of their fancies, 'dreams, delirium, extreme thirst, hypnosis, and conjuring-shows' (p.233): see Ishiguro (*art.cit. n.18*), 160-1, and more fully J.M.Shorter, 'Imagination', in *Ryle*, ed. O.P.Wood and G.Pitcher (London 1971), 138-9, 142-3. And no doubt it is indeed dangerous to suppose that, just because in all these conditions one can be said to have imagined things (no less than if one visualized Helvellyn knowing perfectly well that one was doing so), a genuinely unitary concept of imagination is applicable to all the different cases. But where we apply a single word without evident ambiguity to different phenomena, there is a case for assuming that there are important conceptual connections and affinities between them (why else should the same word be used? and how is one to be sure that in differentiating distinct senses of a word one is not merely extrapolating illegitimately from different contexts of its use?). At any rate, it is plain that Aristotle thought that a single faculty of imagination was involved in the very various phenomena he treats as cases of φαντασία; and I have endeavoured, in the manner of more recent students of the imagination such as Strawson, in *Experience and theory* (*art. cit. n.12*), and Scruton, in *Art and imagination* (*op.cit. n.12*), to trace the similarities between the different phenomena noticed by Aristotle which might have fortified him in this belief.

85 For this interpretation of the connection of 427b14-16 with what precedes, see Rodier *ad loc*.

86 'Nearly all animals': the doctrine of this chapter (cf. 428a9-11, 21, 23), and elsewhere (II 3, 415a10). At the end of the day he allows, notwithstanding his ἀπορία on the matter, that even 'incomplete' animals have an indeterminate sort of φαντασία (cf. II 3, 414b16, III 11, 433b31-434a5, with Rodier *ad* 413b22, 433b31, 434a4; Hicks *ad* 434a1); or at least, those of them that move: presumably the stationary animals (cf. I 5, 410b19-20, with Hicks *ad loc*.) do not.

87 Cf. I 1, 403a9; III 7, 431a17; *Mem.* 1, 449b31-450a1. Imagination seems to be regaining some of the credit as handmaid to thought which it lost in the heyday of Oxford philosophy: see e.g. Z.Vendler, *Res cogitans* (Ithaca, N.Y. 1972), 73-80; D. Kaplan, 'Quantifying In', in *Words and objections*, ed. D. Davidson and J.Hintikka (Dordrecht 1969), 225-31, with Quine's reply, 342-3.

88 Rodier (*ad loc.*) took δοκεῖ here to mark an 'opinion courante' (i.e. an ἔνδοξον), not a view of Aristotle's own. This may be right; but (as we shall see) there is reason to think Aristotle found something tempting in the opinion. I have not put any weight on 427b16-17 in this connection, since the text is doubtful and obscure. But emboldened by Prof.W.J.Verdenius, I would retain νόησις, and translate (with Prof. D.J.Allan): 'It is clear that φαντασία is not the same sort of thinking as ὑπόλη-ψις.'

89 Translation after Sorabji (*op.cit. n.73*); cf. his comments *ad loc.*, and pp.5-7 of his first chapter.

90 For in *De An.* Aristotle seems to be concerned with judgements, not with the process of thinking, in passages in which the relation of thought and φαντάσματα is in question.

91 An interpretation given further licence by *Insomn.* 1, 458b31-3. There, having referred in a general way to the φαντάσματα discussed at 460b3-27, Aristotle remarks that whether the faculties of sense perception and φαντασία are the same or different, it is clear that sense perception is a *sine qua non* of φαντασία: 'For mis-seeing and mis-hearing belong to the man who sees and hears something which is truly there, but not what he takes it to be.'

92 We need not suppose that the original association with thinking is abandoned. It is certainly significant that Aristotle relates φαντασία to perception rather than to thinking in his definition at 429a1-2. But the significance lies in the evidence his treatment of φαντασία affords of the consistency of his approach to psychology. The fact that Aristotle's definition is, a *causal* definition suggests that he is characteristically concerned, in his discussion at 428b10sqq., with the question what it is in our psychological nature which makes us able to exercise φαντασία in the way we do. And his answer 'prior perception' characteristically relates φαντασία first and foremost to the hierarchy of faculties distinguished in Book II. It does not greatly illuminate the specific psychological character of φαντασία. The definition is presumably supposed to be true equally of dreams and memory, where the prior perception must be a thing of the past, and of the 'seeing as' cases, phenomenologically quite distinct, in which the prior perception has to be contemporaneous (I take it that Aristotle insists on the priority here simply because it is a precondition of one's seeing *x* as *y* that one should see *x*). And the definition leaves it quite open what further conditions besides prior perception must be satisfied if the change that is φαντασία is to occur.

Do I have to activate φαντάσματα - and if so what governs my success? Or if φαντάσματα just happen to me, why those particular φαντάσματα at that precise moment? It is not even clear that the definition could not apply as well to Aristotle's conception of discursive thinking (διανοεῖσθαι) as to his notion of φαντασία (cf. III 8, 432a3-8; I 4, 408b1-29).

93 So e.g. Rees (*art.cit. n.2*), 498; Lycos (*art.cit. n.7*), 497.

94 (*op.cit. n.20*), II 412-13, 416; Hicks (*ad loc.*) shows no dissatisfaction with the received text.

95 'Takes something truly or falsely' is the sense ἢ ψεύδεσθαι ἢ ἀληθεύειν must have if this observation is to supply a reason for differentiating belief and φαντασία. It does not prove the difference Aristotle alleges, viz. that believing, unlike φαντασία, is not in our power. Hamlyn (*op.cit. n.7*), *ad loc.*, notes: 'The real point is that beliefs are determined at least by *our view of the facts*; this is not true of imagining something.' Cf. Scruton (*op.cit. n.12*), 94-7. This construction of the Greek is in agreement with Greek usage (cf. LSJ s.vv.); and it is supported by the fact that Aristotle at 428a4 glosses κρίνομεν, 'judge', by ἀληθεύομεν ἢ ψευδόμεθα.

96 E.g. Rees (*art.cit. n.2*), 499.

97 But although Aristotle does appear to be committed to an inconsistency here, it is perhaps not a very serious one. For he could simply withdraw his claim that φαντασία is quite distinct from ὑπόληψις, while insisting that it is to be differentiated from the particular sort of ὑπόληψις he has in mind at 427b17-24, viz. δόξα (belief).

98 In writing this essay I have incurred numerous debts of gratitude: to Prof. J.L.Ackrill, who proposed the topic to me; to the members of the Southern Association for Ancient Philosophy (and particularly Prof. D.W.Hamlyn), who heard and discussed an ancestor of the present paper at their meeting in Cambridge in 1973; and to Messrs. J.Barnes, M.F.Burnyeat and R.R.K. Sorabji, each of whom sent me valuable comments on a penultimate draft. I hope I have made profitable use of their generous help. The paper has been revised in the light of the discussion at the Symposium, and of comments made to me privately by its members.

5: THE INTELLECTION OF 'INDIVISIBLES' ACCORDING TO ARISTOTLE, DE ANIMA III 6[1]

Enrico Berti

THE PROBLEM

In chapter 6 of book III of the *De anima* Aristotle, as is well known, distinguishes two operations of the intellect (νοῦς), the intellection of 'indivisibles' (τῶν ἀδιαιρέτων νόησις) and the synthesis of notions produced by intellection (σύνθεσις ... τῶν νοημάτων), stating that the former is free from errors, i.e. is always true, while the second can either be true or false.[2] Concerning the 'indivisibles', which are the objects of the first operation, he adds that not only realities that are potentially indivisible, i.e. those which cannot be divided at all, can be regarded as such, but also realities that are indivisible only in actuality, i.e. those which in fact are not divided, even if they may undergo division. He then gives a series of instances of indivisible realities, among which there are length, said to be 'indivisible according to quantity'; the 'indivisible according to species', not otherwise identified; realities such as the point and such like, called 'divisions', i.e. limits; 'privations', such as evil and black; and finally realities which have no contrary, described as existing in actuality and separate, these being identified by the great majority of interpreters as the divine intelligences, or the unmoved movers.[3] Discussing this first operation, Aristotle also states that it takes place in an indivisible time, that is one not involving succession; that it has as its object 'the what it is according to the what it was to be' (τὸ τί ἐστι κατὰ τὸ τί ἦν εἶναι), in other words what we call the 'essence'; and finally that it concerns realities 'without matter' (ἄνευ ὕλης).[4]

This theory seems closely to tally with *Metaph.* Θ 10, where Aristotle, asking the question what truth and falsity are in the case of 'incomposite' realities (τὰ ἀσύνθετα), answers that truth lies in 'touching and saying them' (θιγεῖν καὶ φάναι), while falsity properly does not exist, because the alternative to truth is constituted only by not touching them, that is by ignoring them (τὸ δ' ἀγνοεῖν

μὴ θιγγάνειν).[5] The same, Aristotle continues, happens in the
case of 'incomposite substances' (αἱ μὴ συνθεταὶ οὐσίαι) which are
in actuality and are 'what it is to be something' (ὅπερ εἶναί ττ):
in their case, too, it is not possible to be mistaken, that is to
find oneself in falsity, but only either to have or not to have intellection of them (ἢ νοεῖν ἢ μή), so that one can say that truth is
having intellection of them, while falsity does not exist, but instead there is ignorance.[6]

The reference in *De An.* III 6 to the indivisibility of the time
in which intellection of indivisibles occurs, together with the
metaphor of touching, used in *Metaph.* Θ 10, and recurring elsewhere,[7] give the impression that Aristotle conceives the intellection of indivisibles as an immediate knowledge, i.e. as an intuition. If one adds to this the impression that the object of this
intuition is constituted also by immaterial substances, i.e. separated, divine ones, as many interpreters have maintained,[8] one
necessarily gets the conclusion, drawn by an interpreter such as
W.Jaeger, that Aristotle admits a direct intuition (i.e. one that
is not mediated by experience) of the pure forms, and that therefore this doctrine is an obvious remnant of Platonic intuitionism.[9]

Or else, if one prefers to think that the object of such an intuition is, more generally, being, one will make Aristotle a fore-
runner of Heidegger, as Heidegger himself would have liked to make
him, by ascribing to him a conception of truth as the original re-
velation of being, which precedes all discursive thinking,[10] and
by interpreting the νοεῖν which Aristotle talks about as a sort of
mystical contact with being.[11]

All this, however, clearly conflicts with what Aristotle states
in the immediately following chapters of the *De anima* itself, where
he declares that the soul never thinks without images, that is
without the mediation of experience,[12] and that a man who had no
sense perception would neither learn nor understand anything.[13]
Further, this view conflicts with the famous final chapter of the
Posterior analytics, where it is said that knowledge of the first
principles of the sciences - among which are included, as is well
known, definitions, that is essences - belongs indeed to the intellect (νοῦς) and is indeed always true,[14] but that this fact does
not exclude its deriving from experience, even from sense perception

(αἴσθησις) itself, through a laborious process called induction (ἐπαγωγή).[15] Finally, in the same chapter 10 of *Metaph.* Θ, precisely where he talks of a supposed intuition of incomposite substances, Aristotle mentions an 'enquiry' about their essences (τὸ τί ἐστι ζητεῖται περὶ αὐτῶν);[16] similarly when dealing with 'simple' realities, in *Metaph.* Z 17, he had talked of a search which, though being different from teaching, i.e. from demonstration, is not on that account any the less a search (ἕτερος τρόπος τῆς ζητήσεως);[17] and earlier still, in *Metaph.* E 1, when dealing with the essence and the existence of objects, he had spoken of a type of clarification (τρόπος τῆς δηλώσεως) different from demonstration proper and consisting, at least in some cases, in making them clear by means of sensation.[18] All of this leads us to rule out any form of intuitionism from Aristotle's thought and it raises the problem of whether *De anima* III 6, together with the related passage at *Metaph.* Θ 10, can also be interpreted in a manner different from that adopted by the scholars I have mentioned, namely in a non-intuitionist way.

THE 'INDIVISIBLES' OF *DE AN.* III 6

To solve this problem it is necessary to examine carefully what the 'indivisibles' are which are talked about in *De An.* III 6 and what the 'incomposite' realities are which are spoken of in *Metaph.* Θ 10, and then to see what type of knowledge the intellect has of them.

In the relevant chapter of *De anima*, Aristotle first characterizes them as things concerning which falsity is not possible, that is concerning which knowledge is necessarily truthful. This necessarily true knowledge, or intellection, is contrasted with the synthesis which the intellect makes between two notions 'as if they were only one' (ὥσπερ ἓν ὄντων), this latter being capable of being either true or false. The insistence with which Aristotle points out how, in this second case, unity is produced by the intellect (τὸ δὲ ἓν ποιοῦν ἕκαστον, τοῦτο ὁ νοῦς),[19] makes one think that the difference between the first and the second operation, and therefore the reason for the infallibility of the first and the fallibility of the second, lies in the fact that the first has to do with already given unities, which must simply be discovered, while in the case of the second the unity must be produced, and therefore can both either correspond or not correspond to a real unity. Hence the indivisibility of the objects of the first operation must be understood simply as unity; by indivisibles are understood all those objects of the intellect which possess a certain unity.

Aristotle does not provide, initially, any instance of these already given unities; instead he gives two examples of unities produced by the intellect, that is the statement that the diagonal is incommensurable (with the side of the square) and the statement that Cleon is white. In the first case the objects which are unified are mathematical entities, in the second they are physical ones. If one supposes that the same entities, when they are each the object of a separate intellection, instead of a synthesis, are 'indivisibles', i.e. already given unities, one can conclude that the indivisibles can be either mathematical or physical entities which possess a certain unity.

The fact that Aristotle calls the objects of synthesis 'notions' (νοήματα) does not mean that they are purely mental entities, such as those mentioned in the somewhat similar texts of the *Categories* and the *De interpretatione*. In these passages, in fact, he talks about things 'said' without connection among themselves, that is taken in separation,[20] or, in other words, of 'notions' or of 'sounds' taken independently of any connection, including that with being;[21] and he states that they are neither true nor false. The difference, then, between the 'notions' of the *De anima* and the notions or sounds talked about in the *Categories* and the *De interpretatione* lies in the fact that the former are considered as cognitions of real entities, that is provided with being, and therefore necessarily true, while the latter are considered in themselves, independently of the fact that the things to which they refer may be real or imaginary (indeed, among the examples of these Aristotle mentions the famous 'goat-stag'), and hence, since they are not proper cognitions, they are neither true nor false.

The indivisibles of the *De anima* are, in short, genuine entities, possessing unity and susceptible to intellectual knowledge. The term 'indivisibles' therefore should not be taken in the strict sense, as indicating things that *cannot* be divided, but simply as indicating things that *are not* divided.[22] Further, as objects of intellectual knowledge they cannot be individuals, but must be universals; hence the unity they possess is the one proper to universals.[23]

Their twofold character as unities *de facto* and not proper indivisibles, and as unities as universals and not as individuals, is confirmed by Aristotle's assertion that the indivisibles can be such – that is indivisible – only in actuality, while being divisible in potentiality; it is also confirmed by the two examples of indivisibility in actuality provided by Aristotle, that of length, called indivisible according to quantity, and that of the indivisible in species.[24] In the first example we meet mathematical entities again, while the second applies to entities of any kind, including physical ones, always taken universally.

Strictly these entities, according to Aristotle, are all divisible, more precisely a quantity is divisible into parts and the universal into individuals, but they are considered by the intellect '*qua* indivisible': 'for there is in these too something indivisible, although probably not separated (ἀλλ' ἴσως οὐ χωριστόν), which confers unity etc.'.[25] The language used here clearly alludes to Aristotelian universals, as contrasted with the Platonic ideas.

Two other types of indivisibles mentioned by Aristotle are 'divisions' and 'privations'; as an instance of the former he mentions the point, of the latter evil and black. A point is what divides a line, just as a line is what divides a surface and a surface is what divides a solid; these divisions, or limits, are mathematical entities well known in Aristotle's (and Plato's) times. Like privations, they have, as Aristotle says, the property of being known together with their contraries. In fact, just as the notion of evil is inseparable from that of its contrary, good, and the notion of black is inseparable from that of its contrary, white; so the notion of point is inseparable from that of which it is the limit, and to which it is in that sense the contrary, i.e. the line; point in fact cannot be defined otherwise than as a limit of line.

Here, then, the concept of indivisibility is enlarged still further; it includes not only universals that are known in themselves, like those already mentioned, but also universals that are known together with others, that is with their contraries or with those things of which they are limits. A pair of contraries, just as the pair formed by the limit and the limited, itself constitutes a unity, the object of a single intellection, which is necessarily true. It is, however, important to observe that, according to Aristotle, the two contraries do not behave in the same way, in that the negative term, as it were, such as limit or privation, cannot be thought of separately from the positive one, while on the other hand the reverse is not true: it is not ruled out that the positive term can be thought of independently of the negative one; indeed from other passages it appears that it can be thought of by itself.[26]

Immediately after having illustrated this type of indivisibility and having observed that - in the case of two contraries - the subject who knows one is in potentiality with respect to the other, and that in this way the other too is present to him, Aristotle says: 'but if there is something which has no contrary, the subject himself knows the object by itself and is in actuality [in relation to it] and separated [i.e. it is nothing else, not even in potentiality]'.[27] The great majority of interpreters translate the passage in a different way, as if Aristotle were alluding to a subject who knows himself, is pure actuality and is transcendent, i.e. the unmoved mover, thinking of thinking.[28] Hence the conviction that Aristotle also includes the divine substances among the indivisibles, and therefore admits a direct knowledge of them, falling thus into Platonic intuitionism. However nothing in the context authorizes this interpretation; on the contrary, everything suggests that Aristotle, having talked of the knowledge of contraries, which involves the presence of both of them in the knowing subject (one in actuality and the other in potentiality), simply wants to observe that nothing like this happens in the case of things that have no contrary, referring by this expression to any other reality that is the object of intellection, i.e. any other universal.[29]

At the end of the chapter Aristotle restates the distinction between the two operations of the intellect in the case of all the universals that he refers to as 'indivisibles'. He explains that the first consists in knowing, for each indivisible, 'what it is according to the what it was to be', i.e. its essence, and therefore is always true, while the second consists in attributing something, that is an indivisible, to something else, and therefore can be either true or false.[30] This removes any doubt about what we are to understand by intellection of the indivisibles: it is

knowledge of the essence of any universal. The universals concerned
must be real, not imaginary, but can be any type of reality, from
the first substance (if taken universally) down to the last accident.
As it is said in fact in a well known passage of the *Topics*, he who
signifies the 'what it is', i.e. the essence, sometimes means substance, sometimes quantity, sometimes quality, etc., i.e. any of the
categories.[31]

The fact that in the last line of the chapter Aristotle desig-
nates all these things, of which there is intellection, as things
'without matter' (ἄνευ ὕλης), does not mean that they are immaterial
substances, since all essences, whether of substances or of accidents, are immaterial, but, being universals, they can never be
separated substances, that is they cannot exist independently of
material realities, but are, rather, the immaterial essences of
material realities.[32] The examples previously given, that is length
and point, confirm this: it is well known that for Aristotle the
objects of mathematics are not immaterial substances, but aspects of
material realities considered as if separated from them.

THE 'INCOMPOSITE' REALITIES OF *METAPH.* Θ 10

One arrives at similar conclusions from an analysis of the 'incomposite' realities which Aristotle talks about in *Metaph*. Θ 10.
Here a preliminary observation must be made, namely that Aristotle
first makes certain remarks concerning incomposite realities in
general (τὰ ἀσύνθετα) and subsequently states that they hold also
for 'non-composite substances' (μὴ συνθεταὶ οὐσίαι), evidently intending by the latter expression to refer to objects that do not
wholly coincide with the former.

Aristotle does not give any instance of incomposite realities in
general, with relation to which truth and falsity do not have the
same meaning as they have in relation to composite realities. However, there is reason to suppose that the instances of entities
which combine among themselves can also serve to illustrate the incomposite realities, when they are considered apart from the composition itself. These are the terms of the propositions: 'wood is
white' and 'the diagonal is incommensurable'.[33] We are then confronted with the same types of entities that we met in *De An*. III
6, that is mathematical and physical entities, which can be

considered either in isolation from each other, as already given unities - and in such a case truth consists simply in 'touching and saying them', so that their intellection is always true - or else combined among themselves, so that unity is produced by the intellect by means of composition: in the latter case the composition can be either true or false, true when it reflects a really existing relation, false when it does not.

Hence there seems no doubt that the 'incomposite' realities of *Metaph.* Θ 10 coincide perfectly with the 'indivisibles' of *De An.* III 6. Whereas the term used in the *De anima* points out their unity, i.e. their universality, the term used in the *Metaphysics* tends, rather, to indicate their separateness, that is the condition of isolation in which they are considered by the cognitive act of the intellect. In any case they are universals, considered each by itself and not in connection with others, with the aim of knowing what each of them is, that is its distinctive essence.

The identification of the 'non-composite substances' is rather more complex. Aristotle says that they are all in actuality and not in potentiality, that they are not generated or destroyed because they are being itself (τὸ ὄν αὐτό) and 'what it is to be something' (ὅπερ εἶναί τι).[34] These characterizations led some interpreters to suppose that they are immaterial substances, that is forms existing separately from matter, endowed with pure actuality and eternity, in short the unmoved movers.[35]

But it has rightly been pointed out that the expressions in question (being in actuality, ungenerability and incorruptibility, being itself, what it is to be something) apply equally to the essences of material substances;[36] indeed I should say that the last one (what it is to be something) applies almost exclusively to this type of essence, since it seems to me to involve a certain distinction between the 'something' and what to be that 'something' consists in, a distinction that has to be understood as one between the composite of matter and form, and the form which constitutes its essence.

In this connection too, then, we meet the same objects referred to in *De An.* III 6, that is the immaterial essences of material realities. However, it is now no longer a question of all material realities, but only of some. In fact to understand the distinction

drawn by Aristotle between the 'incomposite' realities in general
and the 'non-composite substances' we must take the latter to refer,
within the wider realm of essences of realities belonging to all
the categories, to the essences of those realities which belong to
the category of substance, i.e. the essences of substances, the famous 'substantial forms'. However these essences too, like all the
others, are immaterial essences of material realities, because the
substances of which they are the essences are constituted, as we
have seen, by form and matter.

In connection with both the 'incomposite' realities in general
and the 'non-composite substances', Aristotle states, just as he
had done in the *De anima* concerning the 'indivisibles', that knowledge of them is necessarily true and that the only alternative to
it is ignorance. To explain this statement he declares that 'about
the what it is it is not possible to be mistaken, save accidentally'.[37] This means that, if one can have intellection of an essence, one will well understand the 'what it is', that is one cannot understand essence without knowing what it is, error being possible only in attributing that essence to one determinate subject
rather than to another. And further on he adds: 'about the things
which are what it is to be something [that is about essences], it
is not possible to be mistaken, but only either to have or not to
have intellection of them (ἀλλ' ἢ νοεῖν ἢ μή); but about them we
do enquire into their what it is, whether they are such and such
or not (ἀλλὰ τὸ τί ἐστιν ζητεῖται περὶ αὐτῶν, εἰ τοιαῦτά ἐστιν ἢ
μή)'.[38]

Since in the passage cited Aristotle had stated that it is not
possible to be mistaken about the 'what it is', one must suppose
that the 'what it is' is also the object of having intellection or
not having intellection (νοεῖν ἢ μή), which he now says is the only
possible alternative to being mistaken. Hence the statement that
follows - 'but about them we do enquire into their what it is' -
should be understood not as contrasted with 'having intellection or
not having it', but as qualifying it.[39] In the same way the final
clause, 'whether they are such and such or not', should, it seems
to me, be taken as nothing but an explanation of what the 'what it
is' consists in.[40]

All this is very important in relation to the problem raised at

the beginning of the present paper: from the passages we have now
examined it emerges in fact that the intellection of the incomposite realities consists in a search (ζητεῖται), which has as its
object the 'what it is', and this search, like all genuine enquir-
ies, is faced with two possible outcomes, of either succeeding or
failing. The infallibility of intellection, therefore, does not
exclude a certain process, such as a search must necessarily be,
nor does it exclude the risk of failure, since it is possible not
to find at all what one is looking for. The only difference between this type of search and others is that, while the latter,
for instance those concerning the connection between a subject and
an attribute, can result in establishing either a connection that
corresponds to reality and is true, or a connection that does not
correspond to reality and is false, the search concerning the
'what it is' on the other hand results either in getting effective
knowledge of this or in nothing at all. In any case it is a genuine search, that is a process, and the fact that it ends in an
infallible intellection does not mean that it is not a genuine
search, for it could equally end in nothing at all. Hence the
infallibility of intellection is not an *a priori* guarantee of the
success of the search, but a characteristic which belongs to the
intellection only when it actually takes place.

Indeed, as we have seen at the beginning, Aristotle talks of a
proper search, though one different from other kinds, in a context
wholly analogous to this one, namely in *Metaph.* Z 17. There he
declares that the search for the reason why a certain thing is what
it is, for instance the search for the reason why a certain matter
has a certain form, is 'another type of search' (ἕτερος τρόπος τῆς
ζητήσεως) than the search for the reason why a given subject possesses a given attribute.[41] Now, to enquire why a given matter has
a given form is nothing but - as Aristotle himself had previously
explained - to enquire into what that given thing is.[42]

Thus the intellection of incomposite realities is not necessarily an act that is easy, immediate, direct, but is the end point of
a search which, as we shall see better later on, in certain cases
can even be difficult and laborious. All of this seems to me to
rule out ascribing to Aristotle a position of an intuitionist type,
that is a faith in the intellect's capacity to intuit essences

immediately.

THE 'TIME' OF INTELLECTION IN *DE AN*. III 6 AND *METAPH*. Λ 9

However there is a passage in *De An*. III 6 that seems to attribute to the intellection of indivisibles a character of immediacy. This is the statement that it takes place in an indivisible time and by an indivisible act of the soul.[43] But this assertion, too, if examined with care, does not necessarily seem to imply a conception of intellection of an intuitionist or immediatistic sort. In fact it can be understood in relation to the distinction between indivisibles in potentiality and indivisibles in actuality, where Aristotle explains that one can also consider as indivisibles (in actuality) an object such as length — even though it is (potentially) divisible into parts; or what is indivisible according to species — even though it is (potentially) divisible into individuals. Now these indivisibles can be grasped by the intellect in a time that is itself indivisible, but indivisible in the same sense in which they are, that is in actuality, not in potentiality.[44] They are then not necessarily grasped all at once, because the time in which they are grasped can be divided into a series of successive moments; indeed, it is possible to think of each of the two halves into which a length can be divided, in two successive times: it is only if one thinks of the length as a whole, and not as divided into parts, that one thinks of it in a unitary time and not in successive times.[45] In short, the same indivisible can be thought either in its parts — and then this takes place in successive times — or as a whole, when it takes place in a unitary time.

This discussion becomes particularly interesting if applied to the indivisible according to species: in this case, in fact, the 'whole' is the universal and the 'parts' are the individuals of which it is predicated. Now, when one actually thinks of the universal, that is of the whole, one thinks of it in a unitary time, i.e. all at once. But this does not mean that one is not able, indeed that one is not obliged, first to consider the individuals that make it up: and this is something which happens in successive times, i.e. by a process which lasts in time, which precedes the total grasp of the universal strictly speaking.

This possibility, which is not ruled out in *De An*. III 6, appears to be, at least for the human intellect, a genuine necessity if one considers the famous passage of *Metaph.* Λ 9, where Aristotle compares the human intellect and the divine intellect precisely from the point of view of time. The problem there treated is whether the object of divine intellection is composite (συνθετόν) or not. Aristotle points out at once that, if it were such, that is if it were a whole divided into parts, the divine intellect would change in passing from one part to another, and therefore would no longer be unchangeable, which is what it must be.[46] Once this possibility is ruled out, then, it is necessarily the case that the object of the divine intellection is, on the contrary, incomposite or 'indivisible' (ἀδιαίρετον). This other possibility is, in any case, already confirmed by the fact that every immaterial reality is indivisible.[47]

This last statement can, however, have different meanings, as we have seen in connection with *De An.* III 6. It can refer to an indivisible that is such not only in actuality, but also in potentiality, or else to an indivisible that is such only in actuality and not in potentiality. In the first case it would be an essence that is not common to many individuals, but is itself an individual, and therefore cannot in any way be divided; such is the case with the divine essence, which, as is well known, is the unique object of the divine intellection. In the second case it will instead be an essence that is common to many individuals, that is a universal, which, though capable of being divided into many, also possesses a certain unity in actuality, a unity constituted precisely by its universality: this is the case with the essences of material entities, which are the objects of human intellection.

Apart from various differences between the two intellections, the divine and the human, there is also a certain affinity between them, and it is to this affinity that Aristotle calls attention at the end of the passage, to make us understand, *via analogiae*, the nature of divine intellection. He says in fact: 'Just as the human intellect, or rather the intellect which at any rate is intellection of composite things, is in a certain definite time – it in fact does not possess its good in this or that individual (ἐν τῳδὶ ἢ ἐν τῳδί), but possesses the best in the whole (ἐν ὅλῳ), which is something different – so that intellection which is intellection of itself is through all eternity.'[48]

The difference between the human intellect and the divine intellect, pointed out in this passage, is that the first finds itself
only at certain moments in the same condition in which the second
finds itself all the time. Which are these moments? Those in which
it grasps the whole, that is the universal. But why does this happen only at certain moments? Because, before grasping the universal, the human intellect must grasp the singular individuals, since
the essences it knows are the immaterial essences of material realities, and they cannot be known except by starting from realities
which are material, and therefore individual, and which are grasped
by means of sense experience. Before the intellection of the universal there is, then, a process, which is temporal as well; at the
end of this process, however, the intellect grasps the universal at
last, and at this moment there is no longer any process, but an immutable intellectual vision. Now, the divine intellect is always
in this condition of immutable vision, that is it does not have to
pass through a process to reach it, since its object is not the immaterial essences of material realities, but an immaterial essence
which is realized only in itself, is pure form, indivisible in actuality and in potentiality, that is individual, and is grasped directly, without needing any sense experience. It seems to me, then,
that this passage clarifies the 'time' of human intellection perfectly: this takes place, indeed, in a unitary time, inside which
there is no process, i.e. there is no succession, but which however
is the result of a previous process, which involves a temporal succession. In short, the oneness, or indivisibility, of the time in
which intellection takes place, does not involve its immediacy,
that is its direct accessibility. Only in God does intellection
have the character of immediacy, that is to say, it is a genuine
intellectual intuition, and therefore it is only in the case of God
that one can talk of an Aristotelian intuitionism.

The immobility of, and therefore the absence of any process in,
intellection, are also confirmed, as also is its resulting from a
previous process, by all those passages in which Aristotle compares
the intellection with a condition of quiet (ἠρεμία), as opposed to
movement, and at the same time considers this quiet as a halt (ἐπί-
στασις), a stopping, which thus happens at the end of a process.[49]
Nor do they conflict with the metaphor of touching, which indicates,

to be sure, a direct relation with the object, but not necessarily a
direct access to it: in fact, to touch a thing, it can be necessary
to come close to it, that is to *arrive* to touch it, and therefore to
accomplish a process of approaching, which precedes the act of touching itself.

THE 'SEARCH' FOR ESSENCES IN *METAPH*. E 1

Up to now we have seen that the intellection of indivisibles, or of
essences, is not immediate: it does not exclude an antecedent process of research and therefore mediation. This search, however, is
not always of the same type and does not present the same degree of
difficulty. For certain objects, such as those of the physical
sciences, it turns out to be rather complex and difficult, while
for others, such as those of the mathematical sciences, it can be
much simpler and easier, to the point of giving the impression that,
at least in these cases, intellection is an immediate knowledge.
Aristotle did not discuss this question adequately, but the few suggestions he does make on the topic, especially in *Metaph*. E 1, are
sufficient to make us understand his view.

At the beginning of *Metaph*. E, when he distinguishes first philosophy, that is the science of being *qua* being, from the other theoretical sciences, such as, precisely, physics and mathematics, he
proceeds, as is well known, as follows. First he remarks that first
philosophy, like the other sciences, must 'search' for the causes
and principles of its object. The example he gives makes clear that
he is thinking of physics, for he refers to the health and well-
being of the body, which is the object of medicine, which falls under
physics; mathematics is explicitly referred to.[50] All the objects
of the sciences have, then, principles and causes: among these he
certainly includes their essence, or formal cause, as is clear from
the following lines. Therefore the essences of all the objects are
not known immediately, but must be searched for, and this search
leads to a knowledge which, for some sciences - as Aristotle says,
probably alluding to mathematics - is more exact, while for others
- here he is alluding to the physical sciences - is more approximate.[51]

At this point Aristotle indicates what distinguishes philosophy
from the other theoretical sciences, that is first of all the exten-

sion of their objects (for philosophy this is being *qua* being – the
totality of being – while for the other sciences it is a particular
genus of being), and secondly – and it is this that interests us
more especially – the approach that is adopted concerning the essence and the existence of such objects, that is their principles.
In other words, according to Aristotle the other sciences 'do not
offer any discussion about the what it is', i.e. do not offer any
justification of the essence of their objects, 'but some make it
clear by means of sense perception (αἴσθησις), others assume the
what it is as an hypothesis (ὑπόθεσιν λαβοῦσαι τὸ τί ἐστι): starting from this they demonstrate (ἀποδεικνύουσιν) either more rigor-
ously or more weakly the properties which belong *per se* to the
genus with which they deal'.[52] It is evident that recourse to
sense perception concerns the objects of physics, while the assumption of hypotheses concerns the objects of mathematics. Now – Aristotle observes – 'it is obvious that such an induction (ἐκ τοιαύτης ἐπαγωγῆς)' [that is making clear by sense perception or assuming
as an hypothesis] ' does not yield any proper demonstration (ἀπόδει-
ξις) of the essence or of the what it is', that is a demonstration
of the same type as that which physics and mathematics give in the
case of the properties which belong *per se* to their objects, 'but is
another type of making clear (ἀλλά τις ἄλλος τρόπος τῆς δηλώσεως)'.[53]

In this passage we again meet the doctrine already expounded at
the end of the *Posterior analytics*, according to which knowledge of
the principles of the sciences, to which essence in fact belongs, is
not the work of the science itself, that is of demonstration, but of
the intellect, and takes place at the end of a process called 'induction' (ἐπαγωγή). The most interesting feature of this discussion is
the connection between this 'induction' and the use of sense perception and of hypothesis, which are proper to physics and to mathematics respectively, and consequently the distinction between an induction proper to physics, consisting in the process which leads
from sense perception to intellection, according to the illustration provided in *APo*. II 19, and an induction proper to mathematics,
consisting in assuming the essence as an hypothesis. Apart from
this it is interesting to notice that the knowledge of the essence
reached by mathematics is considered more exact than that reached
by physics, just as the successive demonstration of properties

carried out by mathematics is considered more rigorous than that
carried out by physics.

Thus Aristotle admits different types of induction, not only in
the sense that he talks of an induction generally understood as a
process from the particular to the universal - for instance to
establish the premises of dialectical syllogisms - or of an induction understood more technically as a type of syllogism - precisely
the inductive syllogism - or finally of an induction that leads to
knowledge of the principles of the particular sciences - defined by
some people as 'intuitive induction': [54] but also in the sense that,
within this last kind, he distinguishes the induction which leads
to the essence of the objects of mathematics, from that which leads
to the essence of the objects of physics, considering the former
induction as more exact than the latter. [55]

What is the difference in procedure between these two types of
induction? According to some interpreters it lies in the fact that,
in order to establish the essence of an object of mathematics, in
particular of geometry, by means of induction, it is sufficient to
start from only one particular instance provided by sense perception, while in order to establish the essence of an object of physics by means of induction it is necessary to start from many particular instances provided by sense perception. [56] Hence in the
case of the essence of physical objects repeated perception, i.e.
experience, plays a far more important role than it does in the
case of the essence of mathematical objects, and yet it is never
sufficient to give us that exact knowledge which can, on the other
hand, be had in the case of mathematical objects. Probably for
this reason it may seem very easy, even if not wholly legitimate,
to talk of intuition, i.e. of immediate intellection, in the case
of the essence of mathematical objects, and not in the case of the
essence of physical objects.

Perhaps however this is not the difference pointed out by Aristotle, [57] but rather one that derives from the use of hypothesis to
know the essence of mathematical objects. Elsewhere too, in fact,
Aristotle states that the geometrician knows certain objects only
by an hypothesis (ἐξ ὑποθέσεως). [58] To clarify this it would be
necessary to go more fully into the meaning of 'hypothesis', a task
beyond the limits of the present enquiry. In any case it would seem

that hypothesis involves an intervention of the knowing subject, who somehow modifies what is given by experience, possibly by isolating some data from others (as in fact geometric abstraction or ἀφαίρεσις does), or by supposing that what is given is presented with a greater degree of evidentness than it actually possesses. In short, the unity of mathematical universals seems to be rather something constructed than something given, and this fact explains why it is easier for the intellect to grasp and understand them wholly and adequately. In this way too, then, one can see how it may seem very easy to talk of intuition in the case of the objects of mathematics and not in the case of those of physics. In order to know the latter, in fact, we still need to pass through many experiences: we must become real 'experts' (ἔμπειροι) in an object, before we can succeed in understanding its essence; and indeed, not even in this case is it possible ever to grasp it adequately, so that even the demonstrations on the basis of this intellection will never be truly rigorous.

There is only one science, according to Aristotle, which seems to possess an intellection of its own principles just as exact and rigorous as that which can be had of the essence of mathematical objects, without however having recourse to hypotheses or to artificial interventions on its object. This is first philosophy, or the science of being *qua* being, which later was called metaphysics or philosophy *simpliciter*. This science, in fact, unlike the particular sciences, seems to be able to give an account - a justification - of the essence of its own object. In fact, to the question what the essence of such an object, i.e. of being *qua* being, is, it replies by distinguishing its many meanings, that is the categories, and showing the priority which, among them, substance enjoys; or else by distinguishing the many meanings of one, corresponding to those of being, and by illustrating its proper attributes, that is the identical, the similar, the equal, and their contraries; or finally by formulating the logical principles which are co-extensive with being and one, that is the principles of non-contradiction and excluded middle, and by defending them against any attempt to deny them.[59] Now, concerning objects such as being, the one, the categories, the identical, the principle of non-contradiction, etc., we have an intellection which is more rigorous than that of physical essences, since their objects are of the greatest universality – they are the most universal things that there are, and therefore relatively simple.[60]

In this case, however, it does not seem to be wholly legitimate to talk of an immediate intellection, or intellectual intuition, for there is no doubt that, according to Aristotle, even being, the one and similar objects are grasped only and exclusively inside experience, by means of an induction:[61] the only difference between this induction and that performed in the case of physical objects lies in the fact that its result is perfectly rigorous and adequate.

CONCLUSION

The problem we raised at the beginning was to see whether *De An.* III 6 and *Metaph.* Θ 10 can be interpreted in a non-intuitionist sense, that is in accordance with other passages in Aristotle like *De An.* III 7-8, *APo.* II 19, etc. The answer we have arrived at is a positive one. Our conclusion is that the intellection of indivisibles, or of incomposite realities, has as its object true essences, but that, though being infallible and taking place in a unitary time, that is one not involving succession or process or movement, it is not an intuition in the strict sense, that is a knowledge which is immediate, direct, and accessible at once. It is rather one that presupposes a process of research, which has as its point of departure experience, does have a temporal duration, and can be more or less difficult and laborious, according to whether it has as its objects mathematical, physical or metaphysical essences. On these grounds one cannot attribute to Aristotle, as various interpreters have done, an intuitionism of the Platonic sort, consisting in a direct knowledge of immaterial realities which does not pass through experience.

Aristotle's position is not to be sure an empiricism like that of Locke, of Hume, or of Kant himself, since it does not exclude an intellectual knowledge of essences understood as unities that are given and not simply produced by the intellect with an act of synthesis. However, this knowledge is possible only through experience and in most cases is approximate and incomplete, that is such as not to allow rigorous deductions. Only in the case of mathematical essences does it seem to reach an adequate degree of rigour, but at

the price of a loss of objectivity in favour of a certain synthetic
or constructive element. In the case of metaphysics, finally, such
a rigour is indeed achieved, but only because of the extreme universality of its object. For Aristotle only God has a genuine direct intuition of a specific, indeed absolutely individual, essence,
in that he thinks of himself.

Moreover the same intuitionist interpretation of Plato should itself be reconsidered to see whether he does indeed admit a direct
and adequate knowledge of immaterial essences. If we consider the
famous passage in the *Republic* on the knowledge of the Good, or of
the unhypothetical principle - to which the Aristotelian distinction
between mathematics, understood as a hypothetical procedure, and
philosophy, understood as a non-hypothetical procedure, owes so
much - this passage seems in fact to indicate that the intellectual
knowledge of the Good is always inadequate and anyhow is never direct, but is only reached by passing through questions, replies and
refutations of every kind, that is by means of a properly dialectical procedure.[62]

NOTES

1 The present paper is an entirely rewritten version of one with
  the same title which I submitted to the Symposium in Cambridge.
  Not only does it take into account the discussion which took
  place during the Symposium, with interventions by J.Moreau, A.
  Graeser, R.Sorabji, S.Mansion, C.J. de Vogel, P.Aubenque, C.
  Lefèvre and J.Brunschwig, but also some observations on the previous version made by W.Leszl and M.Mignucci and, further, a
  letter on the topic sent to me by R.Sorabji. In view of the
  radical transformation the text has undergone, many of the objections raised have no relation to it in its present form, and
  need not be mentioned here: for them however I warmly thank the
  colleagues I have named.

2 *De An*. III 6, 430a26-b6.

3 430b6-26.

4 430b26-30.

5 *Metaph*. Θ 10, 1051b17-26.

6 1051b26-1052a3.

7 Cf. *Metaph.* Λ 7, 1072b21. On the analogy between thought and
  touch see S.H.Rosen, 'Thought and touch. A note on Aristotle's
  De anima', *Phronesis* 6 (1961), 127-37.

8 J.Philoponus, *Commentaire sur le De anima d'Aristote*,trans. G. de
  Moerbeke, ed. G.Verbeke (Louvain-Paris 1966), 84-90; St Thomas
  Aquinas, *In Aristotelis librum De anima commentarius*, III, XI,
  758, and *In Metaphysicam Aristotelis commentarius*, IX, XI, 1901;
  A.Schwegler, *Die Metaphysik des Aristoteles* IV (Tübingen 1848),
  187; H.Maier, *Die Syllogistik des Aristoteles* I (2nd ed. Leipzig
  1936) (Tübingen 1896), 9; W.D.Ross, *Aristotle. Metaphysics* (Oxford 1924), II, 275-6; J.Owens, *The doctrine of being in the
  Aristotelian Metaphysics* (2nd ed. Toronto 1961) (1951), 413-14;
  P.Merlan, *From Platonism to Neoplatonism* (2nd ed. The Hague
  1960) (1953), 186; P.Aubenque, *Le problème de l'être chez Aristote* (2nd ed. Paris 1966) (1962), 374-5, and 'La pensée des
  simples dans la *Métaphysique* (Z 17 and Θ 10)', communication
  submitted to the VI Symposium Aristotelicum (Cérisy-la-Salle
  1972), typescript.

9 Cf. W.Jaeger, *Aristotle*, trans. R.Robinson (2nd ed. Oxford
  1948), 204-5, who says: 'The truth of metaphysical statements
  expressing a being that is not an object of experience rests,
  according to Aristotle, on a special intuitive form of apprehension, which ... is a sort of intellectual vision, a pure
  "contact and assertion". This is the only remnant of Plato's
  contemplation of the Ideas, that has survived in Aristotle's
  metaphysics.' Cf. also *Studien zur Entwicklungsgeschichte der
  Metaphysik des Aristoteles* (Berlin 1912), 51-2.

10 M.Heidegger, *Sein und Zeit* (4th ed. Tübingen 1972), 225-6.
   Cf. also *Platons Lehre von der Wahrheit* (Bern 1947), 44.

11 M.Heidegger, *Brief über den Humanismus* (6th ed. Frankfurt a.
   Main 1964), 20. Heidegger's interpretation influenced P.Prini,
   Verso una nuova ontologia (Rome 1957), 31, and D.Composta,
   'Intuizione ed essere in Aristotele', *Divus Thomas* (Piacenza
   1963), 66-79.

12 *De An.* III 7, 431a16-17.

13 *De An.* III 8, 432a7-8.

14 *APo.* II 19, 100b5-17.

15 99b20-100b5. Concerning the principles of the sciences, *Top.*
   I 2, 101a36-b4, states that dialectic, which certainly is a
   process, is useful for their discovery.

16 *Metaph.* Θ 10, 1051b32.

17 *Metaph.* Z 17, 1041b9-11.

18 *Metaph.* E 1, 1025b11-16.

19 *De An.* III 6, 430b5-6.

20 *Cat.* 4, 2a8-10.

21 *Int.* 1, 16a9-18.

22 Hence D.W.Hamlyn is right, in *Aristotle's De anima*, Books II and III (Oxford 1968), 142, in translating ἀδιαίρετον as 'undivided'.

23 Hence the translation of ἀδιαίρετα as 'individua', adopted by F.A.Trendelenburg, in *Aristotelis De anima* (2nd ed. Berlin 1877), 409, does not seem satisfactory to me.

24 *De An.* III 6, 430b14-15.

25 430b17-18.

26 Cf. e.g. *Metaph.* Λ 7, 1072a31-2: 'One of the two series of contraries is intelligible by itself.'

27 *De An.* III 6, 430b24-6. The text is probably corrupt, but from the readings given in the manuscripts it is not difficult to get the proposed translation.

28 Cf. Themistius, *Commentaire sur le Traité de l'âme d'Aristote* trans. G. de Moerbeke, ed. crit. G.Verbeke (Louvain-Paris 1957), 250-1; Philoponus (*op.cit. n.8*), 84-5; Thomas Aquinas, *In De an.* III, XI, 758-9; R.D.Hicks, *Aristotle. De Anima* (Cambridge 1907), *ad loc.*; W.Theiler, *Aristoteles, Über die Seele* (Munich 1968), *ad loc.*; P.Siwek, *Aristotelis Tractatus De anima graece et latine* (Rome 1965), *ad loc.*; Hamlyn (*op.cit. n.22*), 144-5.

29 This conclusion, which I put forward only orally to the Symposium, met general agreement, and indeed was corroborated with philological arguments by Professors Verdenius, de Strycker and Aubenque.

30 *De An.* III 6, 430b26-9.

31 *Top.* I 9, 103b27-39.

32 The expression 'without matter' also recurs in *De An.* III 4, 430a3-9, and in *Metaph.* Λ 9, 1075a3-5, where it equally means immaterial essences of material things. Cf. Hicks (*op.cit. n.28*), *ad* 430a3.

33 *Metaph.* Θ 10, 1051b20-1.

34 *Metaph.* 1051b26-31.

35 Cf. note 8. A different opinion is expressed by H.Bonitz, *Aristotelis Metaphysica* II (Bonn 1849, Hildesheim 1960), 409-10, according to whom they are substances without accidents.

36 K.Oehler, *Die Lehre vom noetischen und dianoetischen Denken bei Platon und Aristoteles* (Munich 1962), 221-34; cf. also H.Seidl, *Der Begriff des Intellekts* (νοῦς) *bei Aristoteles* (Meisenheim am Glan 1971), 183.

37 *Metaph.* Θ 10, 1051b25-6.

38 1051b30-2.

39 On this point I agree with the observations made, during the Symposium, by R.Sorabji, while I am not in agreement with P. Aubenque, according to whom the search for the 'what it is' comes after 'having intellection or not having it'. On this issue interventions were made also by S.Mansion, G.Verbeke, M.Woods, E. de Strycker, J.Moreau, J.Brunschwig.

40 This point was made, I believe, by J.Moreau.

41 *Metaph.* Z 17, 1041b9-11.

42 1041a32-b2.

43 *De An.* III 6, 430b14-15.

44 430b6-10.

45 430b10-14.

46 *Metaph.* Λ 9, 1075a5-6.

47 1075a6-7.

48 1075a7-10.

49 *De An.* I 3, 407a32-3; *APo.* II 19, 100a6, 15; *Metaph.* α 2, 994b 23-4; *Int.* 3, 16b20-1; *Ph.* VII 3, 247b29-30. To these passages one could add *Metaph.* Θ 6, 1048b18-35, where intellection is chosen by Aristotle as one of the paradigmatic instances to illustrate the difference between activity (ἐνέργεια), which does not involve any change, and movement (κίνησις), or change properly called so. On this passage see the different interpretations of J.L.Ackrill, 'Aristotle's distinction between *Energeia* and *Kinesis*', in *New essays on Plato and Aristotle*, ed. by R. Bambrough (London 1965), 121-41; M.M.Mulhern, 'Types of process according to Aristotle', *The Monist* 52 (1968), 237-51; and W. Leszl, 'Aristotele: un filosofo analista?', *Giornale di meta - fisica* 24 (1969), 286-91.

50 *Metaph.* E 1, 1025b3-5.

51 1025b5-7.

52 1025b10-13.

53 1025b14-16.

54 Cf. K. von Fritz, 'Die ἐπαγωγή bei Aristoteles', *Bay. Ak. d. Wiss.*, *Phil. - hist. Kl.*, SB 1964, Heft[3], rept. in *Grundprobleme der Geschichte der antiken Wissenschaft* (Berlin 1971), 623-76. This is, in my view, the best treatment to date of induction in Aristotle. It has the merit of having clearly distinguished the three types of induction I have mentioned.

55 This distinction, too, is pointed out by von Fritz (*art.cit.* *n.54*), 649-54, though he does so in a way that seems to me, for the reason indicated in the next note, to be inadequate.

56 Cf. von Fritz (*art.cit. n.54*), 675. Yet at pp.653-4, the same author states that one particular instance only is sufficient for the objects of physics also, since he thinks that *APo.* II 19, 100a15-16, can be interpreted in this sense. There Aristotle declares that the halt of one individual object of sense perception is sufficient for the soul to know the universal. In my view, however, the context of this passage shows that the object of sense perception comes to a halt and produces knowledge of the universal only because, as in a battle, there has first been a retreat, that is the passage of many things (cf. 100a11-12): and elsewhere Aristotle repeats that experience arises from many memories (100a3-5) and the universal from many experiences (*Metaph.* A 1, 981a5-6).

57 Contrary to what von Fritz claims, it does not follow from *APo.* I 18, where Aristotle talks of induction in the case of the objects of geometry, that for them one particular instance only is sufficient.

58 *Metaph.* Γ 2, 1005a11-13.

59 This, as is well known, is the task of the science of being *qua* being according to *Metaph.* Γ.

60 The intellection of these objects is well explained by Seidl (*op.cit. n.36*), 171-97, esp. 185, where it is shown that this is possible because everything, that is every essence, is immediately (εὐθύς) being and one (cf. *Metaph.* H 6, 1045a36-b9).

61 He probably alludes to this induction at *APo.* II 19, 100b2 where he talks of things 'without parts and universal' (τὰ ἀμερῆ καὶ τὰ καθόλου), where interpreters have recognized the categories.

62 Plato, *R.* VI, 505e-511e; cf. also VII, 531d-534c.

David J. Furley

Aristotle sometimes calls animals self movers. We must try to determine what exactly he means by this. In particular, we must look
at this thesis in the light of certain passages in the *Physics* which
appear to deny that there can be self movers. Is this apparent anomaly to be explained genetically? Are we to believe that Aristotle
criticized and rejected his earlier thesis that animals are self
movers? Or is his position as a whole consistent? How then are we
to explain away the apparent anomaly?

To anyone who reads *Physics* II a little incautiously, it might
appear that since nature is declared to be an internal source of
change and rest (ἀρχὴ κινήσεως καὶ στάσεως, 1, 192b13-33), anything
that has a nature must be a self mover.[2] For what else is a self
mover but a thing that has *in itself* a source of change and rest?
Thus all the things specified at the beginning of *Ph.* II 1 would be
self movers: living things and their parts, plants, and the simple
bodies, earth, water, air and fire.

But this turns out, of course, to be too generous. We are told
explicitly in *Ph.* VIII 4, 255a5-10 that the bodies that move by nature up or down cannot be said to move themselves. Three reasons
are given: (*a*) to move itself is a 'life property' (ζωτικόν) and
confined to things that have souls; (*b*) if they moved themselves,
they would be able to stop themselves, and if it is 'in its own
power' for fire to move upwards, it must likewise be in its power
to move downwards; (*c*) nothing that is homogeneous and continuous
can move itself.

Clearly, then, things with souls have an ἀρχὴ κινήσεως καὶ στάσεως in themselves in a stronger sense than lifeless natural bodies.
The refinement, according to *Ph.* VIII, is a difference in the voice
of the verb: the natural bodies, as opposed to things with souls,
have a source not of causing movement or of acting (κινεῖν, ποιεῖν)
but of being acted on (πάσχειν). In fact, this gives too little to
the natural bodies in Aristotle's theory. He should at least stress

that they have an internal source of being acted on *in a fully de-*
terminate way. But we do not need to pursue that subject here, and
we can also leave aside the difficult question of what is the *active*
mover of the natural bodies when they move according to their nature
- a question to which Aristotle offers no wholly satisfactory answer.

In ch. 5 of *Ph.* VIII Aristotle starts from the proposition that
we can distinguish chains of movers, such that *A* is moved by *B*, which
is moved by *C*, and so on. He produces a number of arguments to show
that such a series cannot be infinite: it must be stopped - or rather
started - by something that is not moved by another but by itself:
'If everything that is moved is moved by something, but the first
mover, although moved, is not moved by another, it must be that it
is moved by itself' (256a19-21).

Initially, Aristotle considers only the possibility that such a
series is started by a self mover, not the alternative that it is
started by an unmoved mover. It is something of a surprise that he
next (256b3sqq.) produces an argument from which he says 'these same
conclusions will follow', but from which he draws a conclusion in
the form of a disjunction: 'So either the first thing that is moved
will be moved by something at rest, or it will move itself' (257a
26-7).

The reason why Aristotle can regard this disjunctive conclusion
as the same as the other is clear from its context in chapters 4 and
5, in which the concept of a self mover is analysed. As a whole, a
thing may be said to move itself; but within the whole it must always
be possible to distinguish a mover and a moved. This is argued *a*
priori, on the grounds that one and the same thing cannot simultaneously be active and passive, or in a state of actuality and potentiality, in the same respect. The conclusion is expressed in these
words: 'Well, it is clear that the whole moves itself not by virtue
of having some part such as to move itself; it moves itself as a
whole, moving and being moved by virtue of part of it moving and
part of it being moved. It does not move as a whole and it is not
moved as a whole: *A* moves, and only *B* is moved' (258a22-7). This
conclusion is quite general: for *any* self mover, we can distinguish
a part (or aspect - the article with the genitive is as non-committal as possible) that moves without itself being moved, and a part
that is moved.

The same analysis is applied explicitly to living creatures in
ch. 4 (254b14-33). There is no doubt, says Aristotle, that there *is*
a distinction in this case between the mover and the moved, but it
is not obvious how to draw the distinction. 'For it seems that as
in boats and things that are not naturally constituted, so in living
beings also there is something that causes movement distinct from
what is moved, and thus the whole animal moves itself.' At first
sight, this explanatory sentence appears to support the statement
that there *is* a distinction, rather than the nearer statement that
there is some difficulty about how to draw it. But Simplicius' interpretation probably gets the right nuance (*Ph.* 1208, 30sqq.). It
is obvious, he says, that a living being is moved by its soul, but
it is not clear how this is to be distinguished from that which it
moves - whether it is altogether distinct in nature and place, or in
some other way. The movement of a living being looks like that of a
boat or a chariot, in which the cause of motion is the helmsman and
the driver [not, incidentally, the oarsmen or the horses]; and these
both have a distinct spatial individuality and their own nature.
But, he implies, there is doubt about whether the soul is such an
individual. Simplicius probably has an eye on *De anima* II 1, 413a8,
where Aristotle writes: 'On the other hand, it is still unclear
whether the soul is the ἐντελέχεια of the body as a boatman is of a
boat.'[3]

There is a qualification to be added to the conclusion that a
self mover includes an unmoved mover. What Aristotle has shown is
that the first mover in a series must cause motion in some way other
than *by* being moved itself. The first mover may be moved incidentally. This is true, of course, of living beings, which are moved by
their souls, and in turn carry their souls about with them (259b16-
20).

Aristotle now faces the suggestion that if animals can initiate
motion by themselves from a state of rest, without being moved by
anything outside themselves, perhaps the whole cosmos might have
initiated motion in itself in this way. He attempts to rebut this
argument by showing that after all animals do *not* start moving from
a state of rest without any external cause.

There are two passages where this point is made: *Ph.* VIII 2, 253a
11-21 (A) and *Ph.* VIII 6, 259b1-16 (B). Aristotle seems to think of

A as an outline sketch, the detail of which is to be filled in by B
(see 253a20-1). But in fact each passage contains some details omit-
ted from the other. There is some significance both in the differences, and in Aristotle's attitude to them; so we shall have to look
at them in detail. I number the points in A; B can be divided into
three sections, in the middle one of which I number the correspond-
ences with A.

A

But this (*sc*. that animals move, from a state of rest, having
been moved by nothing external to them) is false. (i) We always
see one of the con-natural parts of the animal in a state of motion, and (ii) it is not the animal itself that is the cause of
the motion of this, but perhaps (ἴσως) its environment. (iii) In
using this expression, that a thing moves itself, we speak not of
every [kind of] motion, but only of locomotion. (iv) So nothing
prevents - perhaps rather it is necessary - that many motions
come about in the body because of the environment, and some of
these move the mind [διάνοια] or desire [ὄρεξις], and the latter
then moves the whole animal - (v) as happens in sleep, for when
there is no perceptive motion present, but there is *some* motion,
animals wake up again.

B

(*a*) We see that there plainly are things that move themselves,
such as the class of things with souls, and animals; and these
suggested that it may be possible for motion[4] to arise in something from total non-existence, since we see this happening in
them (being immobile at some time, they are then put into motion,
as it seems).
(*b*) Well, we must note this, (iii) that they move themselves with
one motion, and this not strictly; for the cause is not in themselves, but (i) there are other natural motions in animals, (ii)
which they do not have because of themselves - for example,
growth, decay, respiration, which are motions undergone by every
animal while it is at rest and not moved with its own motion.
The cause of this is the environment, and many of the things that
enter [the animal], such as food; for (v) while it is being di-

gested they sleep, and while it is being distributed they wake up
and move themselves, the first cause being outside themselves.
(*c*) Hence they are not always being moved continuously by themselves. For the mover is another, which is itself moved and in
change with respect to every self mover.[5]

We shall return to discuss these two passages shortly. Before
doing so it may be as well to look around elsewhere in *Ph*. VIII to
see the extent of the disharmony in Aristotle's attitude to self
movers.

Aristotle does not *reject* the concept of self movers in *Ph*. VIII.
Chapters 4 and 5 are sometimes regarded as amounting to the rejection of the concept. Chapter 4 contains the sentence 'It is clear,
then, that none of these moves itself' (255b29), which has been
taken as a general rejection of *all* self movers.[6] But it is not.
The reference of the pronoun is to inanimate natural bodies only
– 'the light and the heavy' (255b14-15). Nothing is said or implied
about animals. Nor does the *analysis* of self movers into a moved
part and a moving part imply that there is no such thing as a self
mover. It is evidently quite legitimate, in Aristotle's view in
these chapters, to call the whole a self mover, provided that the
moving part is itself unmoved except accidentally.

But passages A and B seem to deny that proviso, and hence, taken
together with chs.4-5, to reject the possibility of self movers.
Yet Aristotle clearly does not want such a conclusion. Even at the
end of B, he continues to speak of self movers ('the cause of its
moving itself by itself' 259b17). Even in his final argument for
the existence of an eternal unmoved mover, he continues to allow the
possibility of non-eternal unmoved movers, and although he does not
say so, commentators generally take him to mean animal souls (258b
12, 20, 32). The *MA* summarizes the position reached in the *Physics*
thus: 'Now, that the ἀρχή of other motions is that which moves itself, and the ἀρχή of this is the unmoved, and that the first mover
must necessarily be unmoved, has been determined previously' (698a7-
9). Self movers here are still allowed the role of ἀρχή for other
movements: he still has in mind the distinction between inanimate
natural bodies which have an ἀρχή of *being* moved, and animate beings,
some of which have an ἀρχή of *causing* movement (*Ph*. VIII 4, 255a5-10).

He has neither rejected this distinction, nor provided different criteria for drawing it. In *EE* II 6 and *EN* III 5, he insists that a man is the ἀρχή of his actions. There is a class of actions that are voluntary, and one of the criteria for picking them out is that the ἀρχή is *in* the agent himself (*EN* III 1, 1111a22).

The tension in Aristotle's thinking about this subject is set up by a clash of motives. He clearly wants to preserve the common sense intuition that the movements of animals, and especially the actions of human beings, are not brought about by external agents in the same way that the movements of inanimate beings are. On the other hand, he sees a danger that *all* the movements in the cosmos might be thought explicable on this principle of the self movement of autonomous parts, and so insists that even this self movement presupposes some external changes that are independent of animal movements.

What is particularly striking about the argument of passages A and B is the way in which it assimilates intentional action to mere mechanical movements. What moves the animal is διάνοια or ὄρεξις, but what moves this is the physical metabolism that goes on all the time in the animals, and what moves this is in the first place food, etc., which enters from the environment. This is a pattern of explanation which one might think suitable, perhaps, for the movements of the periodical cicada of the eastern United States (*magicicada septemdecim*), which lies dormant in the earth until it emerges, noisily and with all its millions of congeners, every seventeen years (next in May 1987). It seems thoroughly inadequate for explaining the action of a man signing a contract or even of a bird building a nest.

Passage B does not even mention ὄρεξις. Passage A does (iv), but instead of treating it teleologically, as Aristotle does in *De anima* and *MA*, it reduces it to a simple mechanical response. Even food is not something the animal moves to get (an ὀρεκτόν), but only something that 'enters from the environment' and eventually causes the animal to move when it wakes up from its post-prandial sleep. The reason why Aristotle puts it this way is surely the nature of his argument. He has an *a priori* argument in *Ph.* VIII 1 to show that both time and motion have no starting point. Observation of animals suggests that they do function as starting points for motion.

All Aristotle needs to show is that their motions do not provide an
example of a beginning of motion in a system in which *no* motion took
place before, and that they could not be explained at all on the assumption that no motion took place before. It does not matter to his
argument *how* the previous motion is related to the alleged beginning of
motion, so long as it is a necessary condition for it. So he uses the
simplest possible mechanical model - *A* is pushed by *B*, *B* by *C*, and so on.

The same oversimplified model seems to be in his mind in *De anima*
III 10. 'There is good reason for the view that these two are the
causes of motion, ὄρεξις and practical intelligence; for the object
of ὄρεξις causes motion, and because of this the intelligence causes
motion, because its ἀρχή is the object of ὄρεξις' (433a17-20). The
pronouns are slightly ambiguous; but presumably the sense is that
the object in the external world that is desired stimulates the
practical intelligence to search for means to get it and thus to put
into practice the steps needed to get it.

'What causes motion would be one in form, the ὀρεκτικόν as such,
but the first of all would be the ὀρεκτόν, since this moves without
being moved, by being the object of thought or imagination [νοεῖν or
φαντάζειν], although the causes of motion would be many in number
[sc. because desires can oppose each other]' (433b10-13). Again,
the unmoved mover of animals in this is the *object* of desire.

If we distinguish three items in a case of motion: (a) that which
causes motion but not by virtue of being moved itself; (b) that
which causes motion by virtue of being moved by (a); and (c) that
which is moved by (b) without necessarily moving anything; then the
role of (a) is played by the external object of ὄρεξις, that of (b)
by the faculty of ὄρεξις in the soul, and that of (c) by the animal
(433b13-18).[7] Here again the unmoved mover is not the soul or any
'part' of the animal, but something external to it - the object of
ὄρεξις, here identified with the πρακτὸν ἀγαθόν. At the end of
this section, Aristotle sums up: 'In general, then, as has been
said, it is as appetitive (ὀρεκτικόν) that the animal is such as to
move itself (ἑαυτοῦ κινητικόν)' (433b27-8). As in the *Physics*, we
have both an account of an external mover, and a claim that the
animal is a self mover.

The picture is not essentially different on this point in the *MA*:
'The first cause of motion is the object of ὄρεξις and of διάνοια'

(700b23-4). 'ὄρεξις and the ὀρεκτικόν cause motion by being moved'
(701a1). 'According to the account which states the cause of motion,
ὄρεξις is the middle item, which causes motion by being moved'(703a
4-5).

This oversimplified model produces at first sight a very blatant
clash with De anima I 3-4, where it is explicitly denied that the
soul is moved. The ὀρεκτικόν is certainly part of the soul, or an
aspect of it; in III 10 it is described, deliberately, emphatically
and repeatedly, as a moved mover; yet in these early chapters of the
De anima Aristotle has claimed that the soul is not moved. In a
justly famous passage (408b1-18), he argues that the habit of saying
that the soul is pained, pleased, encouraged, terrified, or angered,
and that it perceives and thinks, might suggest that it is moved;
but this, he says, does not follow. It would be better - i.e. less
misleading - to say that the man is moved to pity, or to learn, or
to think, with or in his soul (the simple dative): 'and this, not in
the sense that the motion is in the soul, but in the sense that [sc.
the motion proceeds] sometimes as far as the soul, and at other times
from it'. The cryptic last clause is explained briefly in the next
sentence: 'Perception, from these [sc. objects in the perceptible
world]; recollection, from it [sc. the soul] to the movements or ces-
sations from movement in the sense organs.' We can ignore the second
part of this; but what does the first suggest? Perceptible objects,
it seems, cause the motion (cf. 417b19-21, 426b29-31), and the motion
proceeds 'as far as' [μέχρι] the soul, which is not, however, moved
by it.

In De anima II 5 Aristotle says something about the difficulty of
finding the right language to describe the relation between the soul
and the objects of perception. αἴσθησις consists in being moved and
in πάσχειν (416b33). We first proceed on the assumption that being
moved and πάσχειν are the same as ἐνεργεῖν (417a14-16). But we have
to distinguish different senses of πάσχειν and ἐνεργεῖν. A man who
is ignorant of letters πάσχει something when he learns his letters
from a teacher. His ignorance is destroyed, and his potentiality for
knowledge is actualized. But this degree of actualization is itself
a potentiality for further actualization, when the man actually has
in mind the letter A. In this latter move, the state of potentiality
is not destroyed but preserved: hence we ought not to say that the

man is changed (ἀλλοιοῦσθαι), or at least we ought to recognize a
different kind of ἀλλοίωσις (417b2-16). So with αἴσθησις. To have
an αἴσθησις is to pass from the first to the second state of actuality, and what causes the actualization is the object of perception.

So the soul is not *moved* by the objects in the external world in
any of the senses enumerated in I 3 (φορά, ἀλλοίωσις, φθίσις, αὔξησις), except that it experiences this highly specialized form of
ἀλλοίωσις.[8] Is this qualification sufficient to allow Aristotle to
maintain his distinction between the movements of animals and the
natural motions of inanimate bodies? It is certainly not sufficient
in itself, because he uses the same pattern in his explanation of
natural motion (*Ph.* VIII 4, 255a30-b13). In this case too we can
distinguish two stages: the change from (say) water, which is potentially air, into air, through an external agency; and then the full
actuality of the element in attaining its natural place. Here too
Aristotle uses the simile of the man first learning, and then exercising his skill. So if animals are self movers, but inanimate
natural bodies are not, the difference in the explanation of their
motions is not to be found in this point.[9]

The problem comes into particularly sharp focus in the *Ethics*.
In the *Physics* and the biological works, including *De anima*, Aristotle was concerned with fitting the movements of animals into certain
general patterns of explanation. In the *Ethics*, he has to find the
distinguishing characteristics of a sub-set of animal movements -
namely, human actions for which we hold the agent morally responsible. It now becomes crucial for him to decide whether a man is
really a self mover, and in what sense, and when. The notion that
the object of desire is what moves a man to action becomes a challenge to the whole concept of moral responsibility.[10]

'Suppose someone says that pleasant and good objects are compulsive, since they exercize force upon us and are external to us.
Then (1) everything would be compulsive on such a theory, since
these are the objects for which everyone does everything. Moreover (2) people who act because they are forced, involuntarily,
do so with pain, whereas those who act because of anything pleasant and good do so with pleasure. But (3) it is absurd to blame
external objects rather than oneself as being too easily caught
by such attractions, and to take the credit for one's good

behaviour but blame pleasant objects for one's bad behaviour.'
(*EN* III 1, 1110b9-15)

The third point in this passage is the only one which gives an idea
of *how* Aristotle proposes to rebut this challenge: the responsibility lies in the man's character, and cannot be shifted on to an external object of desire. 'A man is the source and originator of his
actions as he is of his children' (1113b17). We cannot go back to
ἀρχαί beyond those which are in us. Aristotle considers a possible
objection: perhaps our feeble moral character is itself given to us
by nature and is out of our control:

> 'But perhaps he is the kind of man *not* to take care. No; people
> are themselves responsible for having become men of this kind, by
> living in a slack way. They are responsible for being unjust or
> overindulgent, by cheating, or by spending their lives drinking
> and so on. In every field of action, actions of a certain kind
> make a corresponding kind of man. This is clear from the case of
> people who practise for any sort of contest or similar activity
> - they practise by continually repeating the action.' (*EN* III 5,
> 1114a3sqq.)

He raises a similar kind of objection a little later, this time in a
form more directly relevant to our present theme:

> 'Suppose someone were to say that everybody desires what *appears*
> good (φαινόμενον ἀγαθόν) but is not master of the appearance
> (φαντασία) --the goal appears to each man in accordance with the
> kind of man he is. But [against this] if each of us *is* somehow
> responsible for his disposition, he will be somehow responsible
> for this appearance; otherwise no one is himself responsible for
> acting badly, but does these things through ignorance of the
> goal, believing that he will achieve what is best for himself by
> these means. And the desire for the goal is not a matter of
> choice, but it is necessary to be born with a natural faculty of
> sight, as it were, by which one will judge well and choose what
> is really and truly good; in that case, to be born well will be
> to have a good natural faculty of this kind... Well, if this is
> true, how will virtue be any more voluntary than vice? To both
> alike, the good man and the bad man, the goal is presented and
> established by nature or however else it may be; and they both
> act in whatever way they do act by referring all the rest to

this. So, whether the goal is presented to each man in whatever
form it may be presented not by nature but with some dependence
on the man himself, or the goal is natural but virtue is voluntary because the good man performs the actions leading to the
goal voluntarily, in either case vice must be no less voluntary
than virtue.' (*EN* III 5, 1114a31sqq.)

This passage suggests - admittedly in a very sketchy way - an important modification of the theory of desire set out in the *Physics*. In
the ·latter, 'the object of desire' (ὀρεκτόν) was presented as if it
were simply an object in the external world. But people desire
things in the external world, and exert themselves to get them, *under
certain descriptions*, and their actions cannot be explained without
some notion of what each of their goals means *for them*. The ὀρεκτόν
cannot be identified as such independently of the ὀρεκτικόν, and in
this sense the ἀρχή of action produced by desire is 'inside' the
agent.[11]

Does Aristotle recognize that the ὀρεκτόν, as the unmoved mover
of human action, is always an intentional object? He does not say so
explicitly. At first sight he appears to hedge his answer somewhat
in the passage we have just quoted: 'whether the goal is presented ...
not by nature but with some dependence on the man himself, or the
goal is natural but virtue is voluntary because the good man performs
the actions leading to the goal voluntarily ...'. One might think
that Aristotle meant to suggest here that the goal, being natural,
moves a man to action in some way that does not involve how it appears to him, by the properties inherent in the nature of the external object that constitutes the goal. But clearly that is not what
he meant. He was still thinking rather of the nature of the *agent*.
The suggestion is just that one's *perception* of the goal may be in
some sense natural - the same suggestion that has just been rejected
in the preceding twelve lines. Probably he revives it again here to
forestall a possible objection, that *some* human goals do after all
have a claim to be called natural - εὐδαιμονία itself, for example.
Even in that case, he suggests, virtue and vice would be equally
voluntary, because the subordinate goals depend on moral character,
which is in our power.

The answer is given more clearly in *De anima* III 10. Aristotle
begins the chapter by observing that there are apparently two causes

of motion, either ὄρεξις or νοῦς, 'if one lays it down that φαντασία
is a kind of νόησις' (the latter proviso is to take care of the case
of animals which have no νοῦς). But these are not put forward as
alternative causes of motion, as it seems at first sight: ὄρεξις is
always involved, whether or not νοῦς or φαντασία is involved. Aristotle continues: 'Now νοῦς is always right, but ὄρεξις and φαντασία
are both right and wrong. Hence, although what causes motion is the
ὀρεκτόν, this may be the good or the seeming good' (φαινόμενον ἀγαθόν,
433a26-9). Does this suggest that νοῦς is an alternative to φαντασία
in this case, and that either one or the other apprehends the object
of desire? The same may be suggested by 433b12, where he says that
the object of desire moves either by νοηθῆναι or by φαντασθῆναι.
This would appear to be a consequence of Aristotle's regard for linguistic usage as a guide to the truth. When we are clear and in no
doubt about something, we do not say 'it appears so' (φαίνεται, 428a
14), and hence we do not want to say there is a φαντασία in this
case.¹² But it is awkward to use two different terms for what is evidently the same faculty according to whether it gets something right
or possibly wrong. At the end of the chapter, in his summary, Aristotle lets νοῦς drop out of the picture: 'In general, as has been said,
an animal moves itself in that it is capable of ὄρεξις; and it is not
capable of ὄρεξις without φαντασία. Every φαντασία is either rational
(λογιστική) or perceptual (αἰσθητική). Animals other than man have a
share of the latter too' (433b27-30). The discussion in *MA* repeats
this point: 'The organic parts are put into a suitable condition by
the πάθη, the πάθη by ὄρεξις, and ὄρεξις by φαντασία; the latter
comes about either through νόησις or through αἴσθησις' (702a17-19).¹³

     This line of thought will give Aristotle most of what he wants to
defend his distinctions in *Ph.* VIII and to make a consistent whole of
the theses announced there. Animals are clearly distinguished from
inanimate natural bodies in that although both require external
things to explain their movements, only animals require external
things perceived (or otherwise apprehended) as having significance
for them. Note that this is not just a difference in the complexity
of the response to a stimulus, but a difference in kind. Only a
being with a soul can move in this way. An animal is correctly described as a self mover, because when it moves, its soul moves its
body, and the external cause of its motion (the ὀρεκτόν) is a cause

of motion only because it is 'seen' as such by a faculty of the soul.[14] However, there must *be* an external object, and hence the movement of an animal does not provide an example of a totally autonomous beginning of motion – an example, which, as we saw, Aristotle thought of as a danger to his cosmology.[15]

The suggestion made in this paper is not that Aristotle was ready with an articulate theory of intentionality to defend his view of animals as self movers. It is that he was sufficiently aware of the intentionality of objects of desire to want to retain the notion that animals move themselves, in spite of finding that they are moved by the objects of desire. I think therefore that the apparent inconsistencies in his texts on this subject are not to be explained genetically, but rather as coming from two different approaches that he has not fully articulated. I think they could reasonably well have been made into a consistent theory that would have required him to do only a little rewriting.

Although he could plausibly retain the proposition that animals are self movers, I am not sure that it would be worth struggling to retain the concept of the animal soul as *unmoved* mover. The point is that external objects are not in themselves sufficient causes for the voluntary movements of animals. But they do have some effect on the soul, and it would be obstinate of Aristotle to deny that the effect can be called a movement.

There is one conspicuous loose end in the theory that the ἀρχή of human actions is 'in' the agent. Aristotle maintains that people are moved to act by what appears desirable to them; what appears desirable depends on their character; and their character in turn depends on their actions, and is *therefore* 'in their power'. His theory needs some explanation of these character-forming actions, and how it is that they are not caused by external pressures but proceed from an ἀρχή in the agent himself.

NOTES

1 During the preparation of this paper, I had the opportunity of studying two unpublished manuscripts: Dr Martha Nussbaum's

'Aristotle's *De Motu Animalium*' (Harvard University Doctoral Thesis, 1975; shortly to be published by the Princeton University Press); and Dr Edwin Hartman's 'Substance, body, and soul: Aristotelian investigations' (also to be published by the Princeton University Press). The problem investigated in this paper is one that has interested me for a long time; but the manner of treating it here is much influenced by these two works. I am also indebted to their authors for comments on the first draft of this paper.

I am especially indebted to Prof. D.J.Allan, Dr Malcolm Schofield and Dr Richard Sorabji for their comments, which have greatly assisted me in revising the paper for publication.

2 For a review of this subject, especially in its relations with Plato and the Presocratics, see F.Solmsen, *Aristotle's system of the physical world* (Ithaca, N.Y. 1960), 92-102.

3 This very controversial sentence is also discussed elsewhere in this volume by M. Lefèvre (see pp.23 sqq.). Although it is not strictly relevant to my argument, it may be worth mentioning one or two points on which I differ from him.

(*a*) Grammatically, this sentence beginning 'ἔτι δὲ ἄδηλον ...' is coordinate with a4 'ὅτι μὲν οὖν ... οὐκ ἄδηλον ...'. It is neither a new beginning, as M. Lefèvre thinks, nor coordinate with a6 'οὐ μὴν ἀλλὰ ...'. (On this point, see Mr John Easterling's article in *Phronesis* 11 (1966), 159.)

(*b*) The boatman-boat analogy is not inconsistent with the ἐντελέχεια theory of soul. The problem raised in this sentence is whether the activity that constitutes soul is *localized* (in the heart, although Aristotle does not mention the heart here); that is what is still unclear. That Aristotle would not have thought localization in itself to be inconsistent with the ἐντελέχεια theory (as Sir David Ross thought, among others) may perhaps be shown by considering the analogies with which he introduces the ἐντελέχεια theory - the analogies of the axe and the eye (412b10sqq.). The 'soul' of these is the ἐντελέχεια of the whole, but in both cases it is localized - the chopping power of the axe in its edge, and the seeing power of the eye in its pupil or wherever it may be.

4 Motion in general, not *a* motion, as in Apostle's translation.

5 For analysis of these two passages, see especially F.Solmsen, 'Plato's First Mover in the eighth book of Aristotle's *Physics*', in *Philomathes, Studies ... in Memory of Philip Merlan* (The Hague 1971), 171-82. I am not wholly convinced, however, either that these passages attack particularly the Platonic notion of a self moving soul, or that passage B interrupts the 'triumphant progress of the thought' in the rest of ch.6.

6 For example by G.A.Seeck, '"Nachträge" im achten Buch der Physik des Aristoteles' (*Abhandlungen der Geistes- und Sozialwissenschaftlichen Klasse, Akademie der Wissenschaften und der Literatur, Mainz*, 1965), 151; and by W.K.C.Guthrie, *Aristotle: on the Heavens* (Loeb ed., London-Cambridge (Mass.) 1953), xxix. Guthrie interprets the cross-reference at *De Caelo* 311a12 in the same sense.

7 See Prof. J.B.Skemp's paper in this book for more comments on this passage. I do not differ from his interpretation.

8 Aristotle nevertheless freely uses the term ἀλλοίωσις of sense perception in *MA* (701a5, b17-18) and elsewhere.

9 This is explored further by Henri Carteron, *La Notion de force dans le système d'Aristote* (Paris 1923), 142sqq.

10 I have examined Aristotle's theory about this at more length in my *Two studies in the Greek atomists* (Princeton 1967), Part II 'Aristotle and Epicurus on voluntary action'.

11 'Systems to whom action can be attributed have a special status, in that they are considered *loci* of responsibility, centres from which behaviour is directed. The notion "centre" seems very strongly rooted in our ordinary view of such systems, and it gives rise to a deep-seated and pervasive metaphor, that of the "inside". Beings who can act are thought of as having an inner core from which their overt action flows ... What is essential to this notion of an "inside", however, is the notion of consciousness in the sense of intentionality' (Charles Taylor, *The explanation of behaviour* (London 1964), 57-8). Taylor quotes (pp.68-9) Merleau-Ponty, *Structure du comportement* and *Phénoménologie de la perception* for an extension of this notion to include the goals of non-human animals.
   Stuart Hampshire explains Aristotle's position thus: 'The reason for an action has been given when the agent's conception of the end has been explained together with his calculation of the means to it. We then see the fusion of the thinking, which is an inhibited discussion of the desired end and the means to it, and the mere wanting. The reason for the action is a fusion of these two elements, because the representation to myself in words of an object desired modifies the direction, and sometimes the intensity, of the original, blind appetite' (*Thought and action* (London 1959), 167).

12 See M.Schofield's paper in this book.

13 There is an excellent discussion of φαντασία and its role in action in Martha Nussbaum's thesis (*op.cit. n.1*).

14 There is no reason to think it is an internal *image* of the object that moves the animal, rather than the object itself, perceived in a particular way. Dr Nussbaum (*op.cit. n.1*) has discussed this fully, and persuaded me that some of what I wrote in *Two studies in the Greek atomists*, Part II (*cit. n.10*), about 'mental pictures' was at least too hasty.

15 What about delusions, hallucinations, etc.? Aristotle could reply that although animals may on occasion move in pursuit of a purely imaginary goal, these cases are parasitic on genuine cases. They would not pursue the imaginary goal unless there were similar goals in reality.

J.B.Skemp

This paper is intended as an expansion of a paragraph in the paper I
read at Cérisy in 1972 and of some questions which arose there in
the subsequent discussion. It seeks to be aporetic, and in its latter part will simply raise and not attempt to answer the very wide
questions that a consideration of this chapter of the *De anima* necessarily suggests.[1] In my earlier paper clues were being sought in
other πραγματεῖαι to the precise sense in which the πρῶτος οὐρανός
is 'moved' by the unmoved first mover. An obvious parallel is the
discussion in *De anima* and the *De motu animalium* of the way in which
animate beings are led by ὄρεξις to initiate movement in space. This
requires study of the ninth, tenth and eleventh chapters of the third
book of *De An.*, but of the tenth especially, and attention may be
focused on 433b15-18. Here we encounter the triadic formula κινοῦν
ἀκίνητον, κινούμενον καὶ κινοῦν, κινούμενον. Unfortunately there
are obscurities and textual variations because there seems to be a
certain vacillation on Aristotle's part in identifying the three members of the triad in the case of animal ὄρεξις and κίνησις. At 433b
14 τὸ κινοῦν is said to be διττόν, one factor being unmoved the other
moved-and-moving. The second member of the triad is 'that wherewith
it effects movement' and the third 'the living creature set in motion'. Yet in 433b15 we find a different grouping of the factors.
We now have (a) τὸ πρακτὸν ἀγαθόν, (b) τὸ ὀρεκτικόν and (c) - as before - τὸ ζῷον. 'That wherewith it effects movement' is only brought
in after the triad at 433b18. It is described as an ὄργανον and it
is said to be ἤδη σωματικόν. This ὄργανον is distinct from the ὀρεκτικόν itself, which is therefore by implication regarded by Aristotle as ψυχικόν - as indeed has already been said at 432b2. In spite
of the difficulty there stated of recognizing 'parts' of the ψυχή,
τὸ ὀρεκτικόν is said to be καὶ λόγῳ καὶ δυνάμει ἕτερον πάντων, and
its status as a μέρος is confirmed at 433b3.

   The ὀρεκτικόν is then said to be κινούμενον καὶ κινοῦν, as it is
also said to be at *MA* 701a1 - a passage which supports our interpre-

tation of the present one. There seems no good reason to doubt that ὀρεκτικόν is the correct reading of the first word in 433b17 immediately before the parenthesis. This must govern our decisions about the disputed readings within the parenthesis. Here τὸ ὀρεγόμενον has some textual support as against τὸ κινούμενον, but it is most probably a gloss on τὸ κινούμενον which it has supplanted in these MSS. Philoponus' wish to substitute τὸ κινοῦν (meaning 'that which sets the animal in motion') for it cannot stand. Therefore we must accept that in this explanatory parenthesis Aristotle speaks of the ὀρεκτικόν, the psychical faculty of ὄρεξις, as being itself set in motion - in κίνησις - by the real or apparent good. When therefore desire is thus 'activated' this is in some sense a κίνησις (κίνησίς τις) or alternatively may be described as a faculty of the ψυχή in operation, and it is therefore an ἐνέργεια. Possibly ἤ is corrective in *nuance* and means 'or rather' (cf. *Top.* 159a11): certainly it is not an exclusive *aut...aut*. It could be *sive...sive*, as in the succession of ἤ at *MA* 701b20. Aristotle's use of ἤ is very flexible and there is no case for rejection of it here as conveying a wrong sense. Of the variants ἐνεργείᾳ, proposed by Torstrik and accepted by Ross, which they would regard as opposed to ἡ δυνάμει ὄρεξις, is not convincing. Such antithesis seems irrelevant at this point, and we shall see reason to question later how far Aristotle thinks of ὄρεξις as dormant (analogously to the senses, which are regarded as existing δυνάμει- in sleep at 417a12). Moreover in the phrase λόγῳ καὶ δυνάμει used of the ὀρεκτικόν at 432b3sqq. the word δυνάμει seems to mean something rather like 'function' and not to be expressing the usual contrast of potential to actual. (This is also the case at 433b1.) ἤ ἐνέργεια, preferred by Bekker and Trendelenburg, has some support from Simplicius' interpretation,[2] but it either implies that *any* ἐνέργεια is a kind of κίνησις or it forces the words into meaning that any ἐνέργεια is an ἀρχὴ κινήσεως. Neither of these variants is satisfactory, and the extra ι required is not in any of the MSS. The reading κίνησις ὄρεξις in EL is possible, but would presumably have to mean 'the setting in motion in this case (of the ὀρεκτικόν by the φαινόμενον ἀγαθόν) takes the form of a desire (τις becomes less meaningful) or a faculty of ψυχή'. This is needlessly obscure, and we do best to keep the text of most MSS.

Most commentators seem to accept our text and are therefore worried

by the apparent equation of κίνησις and ἐνέργεια here. κίνησίς τις
in fact makes it easier. For the τις compare the decision to regard
φαντασία as νόησίν τινα at 433a10. ὄρεξις as a faculty of ψυχή ought
not itself to be regarded as a κίνησις, since this is against Aristotle's principle, laid down in *De An.* I 3, ἀλλ' ἕν τι τῶν ἀδυνάτων τὸ
ὑπάρχειν αὐτῇ κίνησιν (406a2). This principle is not abrogated but
only modified by 408b1-18 where we are told that the emotions might
be thought to be κινήσεις, but we ought to say not ἡ ψυχὴ κινεῖται
but ὁ ἄνθρωπος τῇ ψυχῇ κινεῖται. It would seem that Alexander here
insisted that ψυχή is said to be moved with spatial motion, but only
κατὰ συμβεβηκός. Simplicius wavers between Alexander and Plutarch
of Athens, 'who expounds the passage by boldly asserting that the
desiring faculty itself has been called a κίνησις here after the
manner of Plato'. Whether Aristotle in this passage follows Plato's
use of κίνησις for psychic as well as for physical motions or not,
he seems not to have followed strictly his own rules and terminology.
Perhaps what has happened is not so much a return to Platonic usage
as the pressure on his language of the triad κινοῦν ἀκίνητον, κινούμενον κινοῦν and κινούμενον. ὄρεξις here is the second term, and
therefore is said κινεῖσθαι (ὑπὸ τοῦ ἀγαθοῦ) and κινεῖν (τὸ ζῷον) but
Aristotle does not see that this means transition from one kind of
'motion' to another; or rather, he sees it confusedly and therefore
brings in a parenthesis that ὄρεξις is after all κίνησίς τις.[3]

We have next to consider the ὄργανον ᾧ κινεῖ which is said to be
ἤδη σωματικόν at 433b19. We have a clear cross-reference to discussions elsewhere of 'functions common to body and soul'. The most
obvious reference is to *De motu animalium* where at least the means
of 'transmission' from psychic to physical motion are dealt with,
and we may note Siwek's observation that in most MSS *MA* follows the
Parva naturalia and not the biological works proper. There could, of
course, have been other works, or the reference could be to what we
call *Parva naturalia* together with *MA* and *IA*. It might seem at first
strange that the γιγγλυμός is taken at line 22 as the example of the
ὄργανον and there is reference to ὦσις and ἕλξις, but none to the
subtler changes in the region of the heart or to the heating and
cooling there caused by the πνεῦμα σύμφυτον as described in *MA*. But
Aristotle here mentions the γιγγλυμὸς ὡς ἐν κεφαλαίῳ εἰπεῖν and we
need not question Peck's detailed treatment in his appendix to his

Loeb edition of *GA* (pp. 576-8), the first section of which explains
this operation of the σύμφυτον πνεῦμα.[4] The discussion in *MA* ch. 8,
after ranging more widely over the changes shown in various πάθη,
returns specifically to animal locomotion and insists that what first
moves the animal organism must be a joint at the end of one limb and
the beginning of another – and yet just as when a man moves a stick
in his hand neither stick nor hand is the real ἀρχή, so the changes
in the central region are really prior even to the action of the
joint which initiates actual locomotion.

   This discussion of this passage in *De An.* III 10 leads to some
general observations on Aristotle's account of ὄρεξις which claim
only to be tentative and aporetic but nevertheless have a wide range
of significance because of the way ethics, psychology and biology
are here combined and the 'bridge-building' between the disciplines
seems quite intentional on Aristotle's part. I shall simply put
down these observations with some attempt at orderly sequence, but
I do not pretend to claim that this sequence presents more than my
own reactions to the various questions that arise, or that the questions here asked are all that ought to be asked.

(1) *Why does Aristotle here seem to assimilate animal movement in*
   response to desire and human response to the πρακτὸν ἀγαθόν?
I find a notable tendency in the account to run in opposite direc-
tions, to the intellectual (meaning of course the practical intellect) and to the almost unconscious biological. Animals rather than
man have memory but not recollection, and they do not have δόξα.[5]
Yet because they have φαντασία they are able to 'respond' by ὄρεξις
to a φαινόμενον ἀγαθόν, and when they do so seem to be regarded as
acting in a basically similar way to a man exercising βουλευτικὴ
ὄρεξις in a situation calling for critical moral decision. Aristotle
is clearly anxious to assign ὄρεξις to all animals, even to the zoo-
phytes and the ἀτελῆ ζῷα. The sense of touch implies pleasure and
pain: these imply ἐπιθυμία, a kind of ὄρεξις; and a dim and wavering
but real φαντασία αἰσθητική is therefore claimed for them at the
beginning of the eleventh chapter (433b31 – 434a5).[6] This attempt to
include all living creatures within the scope of ὄρεξις seems to
arise partly from Aristotle's basic teleology, his wish to deny what
is merely random and to insist that the movement of animals in space

is always ἕνεκά του (432b15). The basic desire to seek food and to
avoid harm conditions δίωξις and φυγή, and these reflect the basic
ἡδονή and λύπη. There is therefore an implicit purpose and a rudimentary 'debate' even in the movements of the parts of a worm cloven
by the ploughshare. There is discernment and decision, not mere
awareness, even in these cases.[7] The other motive in Aristotle's
account of ὄρεξις and local movement seems to be to find a basis in
psychology (in Aristotle's meaning of that word) for his account of
the practical syllogism, of προαίρεσις and of ἀκρασία in the ethical
works. As in the Ethics, the discussion in De An. III 9-11 shows
Aristotle wrestling with a Platonic psychology and deciding to reject it, but the psychology he himself wishes to substitute is not
at all clear.[8] Objecting to the tripartite account of Plato, Aristotle insists (at 432b6sq.) that if the parts of the soul are the
three Platonic divisions, ὄρεξις will be found in all three and it
is unreasonable to 'tear it apart'. Yet he himself acknowledges
ἐπιθυμία καὶ θυμὸς καὶ βούλησις as species of ὄρεξις in the preliminary survey at De An. II 3 (414b2sqq.) and he repeats this in the
present discussion, saying that βούλησις arises in the λογιστικόν
while ἐπιθυμία and θυμός arise in the ἄλογον, and of these the former clearly belongs to τὸ θυμικόν (τὸ θυμοειδές in Plato) and the
latter to the ἐπιθυμητικόν. But though he protests against tripartition or dichotomy of ὄρεξις on Platonic lines, we find him using
descriptions which suggest the alliance of ὄρεξις with the 'lower'
nature in man in his analyses of human conduct. The ἀκρατής resists
the commands of νοῦς in respect of pursuit and avoidance and initiates movement issuing in responsible action in obedience to ἐπιθυμία
alone. Conversely the ἐγκρατής refuses to initiate such motion, although 'motivated' by ὄρεξις, in obedience to the veto imposed by
νοῦς (433a8). Here we seem to have a direct contradiction of the
basic proposition that, except under compulsion, no living being
moves unless it is seeking or avoiding something (432b15) and the
statement (432b26) on which he enlarges immediately before that τὸ
λογιστικὸν καὶ ὁ καλούμενος νοῦς cannot of itself cause movement
(which in the case of the ἐγκρατής is a movement of avoidance). In
fact we have here the difficulty of combining a Platonic view of the
ψυχή as having a good 'higher' and an at least potentially bad
'lower' element with the more morally neutral and more strictly bio-

logical view that seems to be Aristotle's basic view of animal moti-
vation – namely that an inborn desiring faculty, moved by an apparent
good, decides, in some rudimentary sense of the word 'decide', to
impel the animal to move in space to attain it. The word φαινόμενον
in the term φαινόμενον ἀγαθόν has the usual *double entendre* that the
Greek language allows, and which Plato exploits in the parallel case
of δόξα. Now the human βουλευτικὴ ὄρεξις seeking the πρακτὸν ἀγαθόν
can be seen as a particular case of this orectic process, and Aristotle clearly intends us in *De An*. III 10 to see it as such. It is
interesting that he makes little use of his own classification of
βούλησις as a species of ὄρεξις either in the *De anima*[9] or in the
Ethics. In the *Ethics* this seems to arise from the importance attached to ἕξις as basic to moral conduct while in the *De anima* assimilation of human behaviour to that of living creatures in general
discourages the idea of inception of movement by βούλησις which has
to do with aims in a far more elevated sense. It has less relation
to decision made in πρᾶξις on an action here and now. Men can indeed calculate with the help of past experience and future expect-
ancy, but they are nevertheless concerned with particular response
to particular stimulus as are the animals. Therefore whereas attempts to bring symptoms of ἀκρασία within a general account of
ὄρεξις seem unsuccessful because of the Platonic 'hangover' in Aristotle's mind, the assimilation of ὄρεξις βουλευτικὴ to other ὄρεξις,
which can be understood amorally, is fairly successful.

(2) *What basic doctrine of* ὄρεξις *does this chapter (De An. III 10)*
    imply?
The chapter is essentially part of the discussion of animal locomotion. It lays down the triadic formula of (relatively) unmoved
mover, the moved and moving, and the moved. This is partly related
to the actual mechanism of animal motion, as shown in detail in the
De motu animalium, but the unmoved mover is not the fixed point like
a joint at the end of one limb and the beginning of another, but an
object external to the appetent creature which arouses in it the
orectic faculty which seems in any case to be always ready to act:
the desire precedes in time the presentation of the means of its
satisfaction.[10] Because the natural tendency is to regard the positive case of pursuit rather than the negative one of avoidance,

ὄρεξις tends to be used mainly of δίωξις, but the real position seems
to be that τὸ ὀρεκτικόν, and therefore ὄρεξις in its wider sense, cover δίωξις and φυγή alike. This is important when we turn to the
Ethics to see if further light can be found there. In Book VI ὄρεξις
is indeed said to include δίωξις and φυγή and to these correspond
κατάφασις and ἀπόφασις from which there is shown to exist ὄρεξις
ὀρθή, which is the activating force of προαίρεσις σπουδαία, and ὄρεξις οὐκ ὀρθή. But we really ought to go back from these adult manifestations to human ὄρεξις in infancy, and here we come up once again
against the Platonic antecedents, but this time it is the second book
of the *Laws* (653a sqq.) where the child's sense of pleasure and pain,
attractions and repulsions, are to be trained so that he is properly
habituated when he comes to an age of moral responsibility. This
Aristotle seems to accept in his account of habituation (*EN* 1104b11
sqq.). χαίρειν καὶ λυπεῖσθαι οἷς δεῖ is the basis of a right ἕξις.

When we turn to the *De anima*, we find in the seventh chapter of
the third book a close approximation of ὄρεξις and φυγή to αἴσθησις.
They represent discrimination by means of the αἰσθητικὴ μεσότης in
respect of what is to be sought and avoided. They are, as in *EN* VI,
κατάφασις and ἀπόφασις. But in the ninth chapter of the third book
the effort is made rather to distinguish ὄρεξις from αἴσθησις and to
claim for it a status of its own in the ψυχή (432b2,3). It is denied
that the sensitive faculty as such causes movement (432b19-28). This
distinguishing of ὄρεξις from other psychic activity seems to be Aristotle's real doctrine. Pursuit and avoidance guided by some discrimination and prompted by an external object - an object of desire
rather than simply an object of perception - explains for Aristotle
all animal locomotion.[11] Eventually it is νοῦς πρακτικός and ὄρεξις
that are recognized as causes, and though the discriminating and deciding element is intelligent (or based on φαντασία), the sheer 'mo-
tivation' comes from ὄρεξις. The conclusion of this rather tangled
argument would seem to be that there exists in man and animals a
basic appetency guided by reasoning or by what we should unscientifi-
cally call 'instinct' to acts of choice or avoidance based on outside
causes of stimulation. These impel it to purposeful movement tending
to its effective development: the basic case is that of the animal
seeking its proper food and so achieving its τέλος. We come therefore to a general view of pursuit of its own fulfilment biologically

or (in man's case) morally by the conditioning of basic desire either unconsciously or consciously. This brings Aristotle close to the later discussions and dissent on the question of the πρῶτα κατὰ φύσιν. For while his account of primitive ἡδονή and λύπη could be construed in one way by the Epicureans, the Stoics could also find a basis for the view that the inborn desire of each creature is to seek what preserves its life and reject what destroys it. Plato's conception of a universal δίωξις[12] of the ἀγαθόν at *Republic* VI 505de, though in a very different context, states something about ψυχή (ἄπασα ψυχή is notable at 505d11) which Aristotle in his account of ὄρεξις reasserts in his own language.

NOTES

1 One can only regret deeply that we no longer have Dr A.L.Peck with us. I think we could have prevailed upon him to deal far more completely with a subject he had made so much his own.

2 Simplicius (*An.* 303, 1sq.) knows the variant readings ἧ and ἤ and prefers the former but concedes the latter as possible, as ἐπίρρημα ἀντὶ τοῦ καθό.

3 Simplicius (*An.* 301, 11) gives a dramatic explanation here: τὸ ὀρεκτικὸν ... ὑπὸ τοῦ ὀρεκτοῦ διαναστὰν καὶ εἰς τὴν τάξιν αὐτοῦ ὁρμῆσαν καὶ διὰ τοῦτο κινεῖσθαι λεγόμενον, κατ᾽ αὐτὴν τὴν τοῦ ὀρεκτοῦ μεταδίωξιν κινεῖ τὸ ζῷον. This picture of the ὀρεκτικόν as aroused like a sleeping soldier and leaping into its appointed activity emphasizes dramatically the interpretation of κινεῖσθαι here as a psychic event, not in the first instance a physical one.

4 Peck's account is largely based on our passage, and he concludes that there are four factors not three at work: σύμφυτον πνεῦμα as well as τὸ ὀρεκτικόν can be said to κινεῖν κινούμενον and this can be said to happen according to Aristotle's canon for κίνησις, *in space* - i.e. in the region about the heart. This πνεῦμα excited by ὄρεξις and ultimately moving the limbs can be said to be ἤδη σωματικόν. Being capable of expanding and contracting, it can exert force and so cause movement operating *through* the γιγγλυμός. But this does not alter the fact that ὄρεξις itself is said κινεῖσθαι.

5 R.Sorabji, *Aristotle on Memory* (London 1972), 77-8.

6 Compare 413b23, 414b2.

7 The basic thought here is perhaps indicated by *MA* 700b19sqq.:

καὶ γὰρ ἡ φαντασία καὶ ἡ αἴσθησις τὴν αὐτὴν τῷ νῷ χώραν ἔχουσι.
κριτικὰ γὰρ πάντα.

8 Joachim in his commentary on the *Nicomachean Ethics* ·(Oxford
   1951, 66-8) dealing with ὄρεξις says 'In what follows I am only
   making suggestions, and with great hesitation.' Such caution
   is very necessary, but someone ought to venture, even if unsuc-
   cessfully.

9 There is the cryptic passage 434a12-15, where the reference to
   σφαῖραι seems to be a game (or even to boxing? see σφαῖρα sense
   4 in LSJ, 9th ed.). Here βούλησις seems to be the higher ὄρεξις
   overpowered, but not permanently, by the lower. But any view of
   πειθαρχεῖν attaching to ὄρεξις ἄλογος (as in *EE* VIII 1 and II
   1220a11 and *EN* I 1102b28) goes back to the Platonic account of
   moral conflict, as it appears in *Republic* IV 439a sqq.

10 The account of thirst in *MA* 701a32sqq. seems to imply a precedent
   ἐπιθυμία which prompts the immediate response to the desired object. ποτέον μοι ἡ ἐπιθυμία λέγει. τοδὶ τὸ ποτὸν ἡ αἴσθησις
   εἶπεν ἢ ἡ φαντασία ἢ ὁ νοῦς· εὐθὺς πίνει.

11 It is notable that there is no emphasis on or mention of ἔρως.
   The desire to reproduce, which is basic in Plato's *Symposium*,
   has no place here. This is presumably because reproduction belongs to τὸ θρεπτικόν for Aristotle, but ὄρεξις does not (432b
   8-10). Movement toward a desired object, if it is locomotive,
   could arise from ὄρεξις however.

12 Plato uses διώκειν or ὀρέγεσθαι but not ὄρεξις. At *Philebus*
   35cd he uses ἐπιθυμία in a wide general sense.

G.Verbeke

En plusieurs passages de son oeuvre, Aristote parle d'un pneuma congénital, qui semble jouer un rôle important dans la vie physiologique et psychique des êtres vivants.[1] Est-il possible de construire
une théorie cohérente à partir de ces données éparses? M. Düring
estime que non; à son avis on ne peut élaborer une doctrine systé-
matique concernant la chaleur innée et le pneuma congénital sur la
base des quelques renseignements dispersés qui se rencontrent dans
des contextes variés.[2] Il est vrai que le Stagirite ne propose
nulle part un exposé synthétique sur le pneuma: peut-on en conclure
que pour Aristote ce sujet ne mérite que des observations occasion-
nelles non-intégrées dans une vue d'ensemble? Pareille interprétation ne peut guère s'appliquer à Aristote: qu'il y a dans sa pensée
des hésitations, des progrès, des lacunes et des variations, on en
conviendra aisément. Mais il n'est pas facile de croire que le
maître grec, sur un thème aussi important que le pneuma, se soit
contenté d'une doctrine incohérente. On ne peut nier que le rôle
attribué au pneuma s'étende à des domaines très distincts. Dans
son livre *Greek theories of elementary cognition* J.I.Beare écrit:
'Si nous pouvons découvrir toutes les propriétés et les fonctions du
σύμφυτον πνεῦμα, nous aurions pénétré jusqu'aux secrets les plus
intimes de la perception sensible.'[3] Ce n'est pas seulement par
rapport à la connaissance sensible que le pneuma joue un rôle de
premier plan, il y a bien d'autres domaines où ce même élément intervient et prend une part essentielle au déroulement des fonctions
vitales.[4] Examinons de plus près la fonction spécifique attribuée
au pneuma congénital dans ces différents secteurs.[5]

    Aristote admet la génération spontanée: il est persuadé que les
testacés se forment spontanément et il mentionne quelques faits
d'observation pour appuyer son point de vue.[6] L'auteur se demande
comment des animaux et des végétaux peuvent naître de la terre ou
de l'eau, comment la vie peut se développer à partir d'une matière
apparemment inanimée. Il répond que la terre contient de l'eau,

•

que celle-ci à son tour est pénétrée de pneuma et que le pneuma est
animé tout entier de chaleur psychique: tout est donc rempli d'âme;[7]
la terre et l'eau ne sont pas des éléments purement inertes èt ina-
nimés, elles portent en elles une force vitale qui donne naissance à
des êtres vivants. Comment se produit ce phénomène? Un nouvel être
vivant ne pourra surgir que si la chaleur psychique se concentre à
un endroit déterminé et y est enfermée; c'est pourquoi cette génération spontanée ne peut se produire que dans un liquide qui renferme
des éléments solides; c'est le cas de la mer qui est riche en éléments terreux. De cette manière s'explique la formation des testacés: l'élément terreux se durcit et produit de la sorte une enveloppe épaisse qui sépare le nouvel être vivant de son milieu envi-
ronnant; à l'intérieur de cette enveloppe se trouve le corps qui
possède la vie.[8] Il reste cependant une difficulté à résoudre:
puisque dans le cas de la procréation s'unissent deux constituants,
celui qui est fourni par la femelle et celui qui vient du mâle et
donne l'impulsion au résidu plutôt passif procuré par la femelle,
Aristote se demande quel est le principe actif dans le cas de la
génération spontanée; à ses yeux, le processus de la procréation
normale fournit la réponse. Comment le principe actif de l'embryon,
c'est-à-dire la semence du mâle, est-il produit? Le Stagirite répond que le sperme est constitué à partir de la nourriture sous
l'action de la chaleur innée; l'auteur décrit cette action comme une
séparation et une coction. Dans le cas de la génération spontanée,
le rôle joué par la chaleur innée est attribué à la chaleur ambiante
qui agit sur l'eau de mer et sur la terre: elle y produit également
une certaine coction et une concentration, qui sont à l'origine d'un
nouvel être vivant. Et puisque tout est rempli d'âme, la parcelle
de force psychique, contenue dans le pneuma, produira l'embryon et
lui donnera le mouvement.[9] De même que l'action de la chaleur innée
produit le sperme à partir de la nourriture, ainsi la chaleur ambiante, par son action sur l'eau de mer et la terre, constitue la
semence qui est à l'origine d'un nouveau vivant.

Faisant allusion à une croyance très ancienne et très répandue,
Aristote se demande si les hommes et les quadrupèdes sont nés de la
nature. L'auteur envisage deux réponses possibles: il ne prétend
pas que la vie a commencé un jour; le temps et le mouvement n'ont
pas de commencement et n'auront jamais de fin. Il n'en résulte pas

cependant que la vie des hommes et des quadrupèdes n'ait pu avoir de
commencement. Si la vie de ces êtres a commencé, il faut que ce soit
par l'éclosion d'oeufs ou par la formation d'une larve.[10] La première solution est écartée comme étant moins vraisemblable: car la
génération spontanée ne se fait pas à partir de l'éclosion d'oeufs.
L'auteur retient l'autre alternative: si la vie des animaux a eu un
commencement, c'est par la formation d'une larve, car ainsi s'explique la génération spontanée de certains insectes et des testacés.[11]
Aristote ne s'arrête pas davantage à cette question qui ne présente
pour lui qu'un intérêt secondaire: puisque tout est rempli d'âme, la
génération spontanée s'explique sans difficulté. Dans le cas de
l'homme toutefois, il reste le problème de l'intellect: celui-ci
s'insère-t-il à son tour dans le processus de la génération? Aristote répond que l'intellect seul vient du dehors et qu'il est seul
divin: car les organes corporels ne contribuent en rien à l'activité
de ce principe intellectif.[12]

   Passons maintenant à la procréation et au développement de l'embryon. Selon Aristote le principe actif de la génération est le
sperme; il se joint à l'élément passif qui est fourni par la femelle.
D'où la question de savoir ce qui donne à la semence ce pouvoir
d'être féconde:[13] ceci n'est rien d'autre que la chaleur ou le chaud.
Cependant, il ne s'agit pas du feu, car celui-ci n'engendre aucun
vivant et il n'y a aucun être qui se constitue dans des matières qui
sont en feu, qu'elles soient humides ou sèches.[14] Ce qui donne à la
semence sa puissance génératrice, c'est un pneuma contenu dans le
sperme et dans la matière écumeuse, ou plutôt la nature qui est in-
hérente à ce pneuma et qui est semblable à l'élément astral; il
s'agit donc d'un principe qui se situe au-dessus des quatre éléments
à partir desquels le monde sensible a été formé. La chaleur dont
il est question ici doit être assimilée à la chaleur du soleil qui,
elle aussi, est vivifiante.[15] Parlant de la composition du sperme,
Aristote mentionne deux éléments: l'eau et le pneuma, celui-ci étant
de l'air chaud.[16] Cette déclaration n'est-elle pas en contradiction
avec ce qui vient d'être dit? Nous ne le croyons pas, car il importe
de préciser le caractère spécifique de cette chaleur. L'essentiel
pour Aristote est de savoir que le chaud en question ne coïncide pas
avec le feu.

   Comment peut-on décrire l'action du sperme? Aristote dit que le

sperme est animé d'un mouvement identique à celui qui se constate
dans la croissance du corps grâce à l'assimilation de la nourriture.[17]
Le mouvement dont il s'agit est donc un développement vital, il est
comme la croissance d'un organisme vivant qui sans cesse intègre dans
sa substance des éléments nouveaux. Quand le sperme pénètre dans
l'utérus, il coagule le résidu fourni par la femelle: il produit donc
une concentration et une condensation de cette matière qui provoque
graduellement la naissance d'un être distinct de son milieu. En
outre, il imprime à ce résidu le mouvement de croissance et de développement dont il est lui-même animé: en langage aristotélicien,
le résidu de la femelle est actualisé par l'élément issu du mâle, ce
qui ne veut pas dire que la structure de l'organisme qui résultera
de l'union des deux principes, provient uniquement du sperme. Au
contraire, la matière fournie par la femelle contient en puissance
toutes les parties de l'organisme, même les parties par lesquelles
la femelle se distingue du mâle.[18] Le rôle attribué au sperme et au
pneuma qui en constitue le principe actif, est donc d'introduire
dans cette matière passive un mouvement de croissance et d'en développer les possibilités latentes. Aux yeux d'Aristote, la formation
des différents organes peut se comparer au travail de l'artisan,
bien qu'il y ait par ailleurs une différence essentielle entre les
deux: dans le cas d'une oeuvre d'art, le principe et la forme ne
résident pas dans le produit, mais en dehors de lui, tandis que dans
les oeuvres réalisées par la nature le principe réside dans ce qui
est produit.[19] Il y a cependant une analogie frappante entre ces
deux phénomènes: ce n'est ni le chaud ni le froid qui produisent une
oeuvre d'art, mais l'artisan qui se servira de ses outils et aussi
de la chaleur et du froid pour travailler les matériaux qu'il utilise.
Il en est de même dans la formation des organes d'un être vivant:
que telle partie soit de la chair et que telle autre soit osseuse ne
dépend pas de propriétés matérielles comme le chaud et le froid, mais
du mouvement qui provient du générateur; celui-ci possède en acte ce
que l'élément passif contient en puissance: il est donc capable
d'actualiser les possibilités du principe matériel. En ce sens, le
rôle du générateur est comparable à celui de l'artisan.[20]

   Les parties de l'organisme sont-elles produites simultanément?
Aristote admet que tout être est engendré par un autre qui est semblable à lui: l'homme est engendré par l'homme; toutefois l'être

procréé se développe de l'intérieur et par lui-même, ce qui implique
qu'il possède en lui un principe de croissance.[21] On constate que
chez certains animaux le coeur se forme en premier lieu; chez les
animaux qui sont dépourvus de coeur, un organe correspondant est
constitué avant les autres.[22] C'est que, selon Aristote, le pneuma
congénital se forme à partir du sang qui est en même temps chaud et
humide: cette production se fait principalement dans le coeur par
une évaporation constante: nous savons que le pneuma interne contient en lui la chaleur vitale; il en résulte que ce pneuma remplit
le rôle d'instrument dans les activités de l'âme et tout d'abord
dans l'activité de l'âme nutritive.[23] Le coeur est donc vraiment
l'organe central de l'organisme vivant: c'est la raison pour laquelle
il est formé avant toutes les autres parties, même avant le cerveau.[24]

Aristote admet que l'âme nutritive est contenue en puissance dans
la semence et dans l'embryon aussi longtemps qu'il n'est pas encore
séparé. En est-il de même de l'âme sensitive et de l'âme pensante?
L'auteur estime que les êtres doivent posséder ces âmes en puissance
avant de les avoir en acte:[25] ceci ne veut pas dire cependant qu'elles préexistent ou qu'elles sont introduites du dehors, puisque leur
activité, et donc leur être, dépend directement de leur union à
l'organisme corporel. La seule exception prévue par Aristote, on l'a
dit ci-dessus, est celle de l'intellect.

La chaleur vitale qui réside dans le pneuma congénital est-elle
vraiment la cause de la croissance et de tout le développement de
l'être vivant? Aristote se pose la question dans le *De anima*[26] et il
répond que c'est l'âme qui est à l'origine de la croissance; la chaleur vitale est une cause concomitante (συναίτιον), elle est plutôt
l'instrument dont l'âme se sert en vue de préparer la nourriture qui
doit être assimilée par l'organisme. Elle est comme la main du
pilote maniant le gouvernail pour orienter le navire: la nourriture,
comme le gouvernail d'un bateau, est purement passive; elle est
transformée au cours de la digestion sous l'action de la chaleur vitale. Le rôle instrumental du pneuma se manifeste aussi dans le
battement du coeur et le mouvement des membres. Comment s'explique
la pulsation du coeur? Aux yeux de notre auteur ce phénomène est
comparable à une sorte de gonflement, produit par l'ébullition d'un
liquide. La pulsation du coeur provient, en effet, de l'évaporation
du sang causée par la chaleur. Le sang est élaboré dans le coeur;

il est formé et entretenu sans cesse à partir de la nourriture.
L'évaporation du sang produit un gonflement et donc une dilatation
des parois: la membrane extérieure se soulève, et comme l'afflux
de nourriture est régulier et continu, il en résulte une pulsation
qui se fait au même rythme et qui se transmet simultanément aux vaisseaux sanguins.[27] Cette pulsation du coeur est une des fonctions
essentielles de l'être vivant; on la constate dès l'éclosion d'une
nouvelle vie. Le coeur étant l'organe central de l'organisme, est
constitué en premier lieu, avant que les vaisseaux sanguins ne
soient formés distinctement.[28] Étant liée à l'assimilation de la
nourriture et à l'évaporation du sang, la pulsation est plus rapide
chez les animaux jeunes que chez les vieux: dès lors la production
de pneuma congénital est plus abondante chez les premiers que chez
les seconds.[29] Tout ceci nous amène véritablement à la source des
fonctions vitales: le sang est élaboré dans le coeur à partir de la
nourriture et le pneuma est formé sans cesse par l'évaporation du sang.

   Selon Aristote, le pneuma intervient aussi dans le mouvement des
membres corporels: d'après le *De motu animalium* tous les animaux
sont dotés de ce pneuma congénital et c'est grâce à lui qu'ils sont
capables d'exercer leurs activités. Son rôle est d'être une sorte
d'intermédiaire: vis-à-vis du principe immobile il est à la fois mû
et cause de mouvement; et comme l'origine du mouvement se trouve
dans le coeur, c'est là manifestement que le pneuma réside, c'est
là aussi qu'il exerce son influence.[30] Il y a deux manières de produire un mouvement: on peut le faire par l'action de pousser ou celle
de tirer. L'organe du mouvement doit donc pouvoir se dilater et se
contracter: ceci correspond à la nature du pneuma, qui tout naturellement se contracte et se dilate et qui, de ce fait, est capable
d'exercer une traction ou une poussée; comparé au feu le pneuma possède un certain poids, tandis qu'il est léger si on le compare aux
éléments opposés au feu. C'est ce qui est requis de la part d'un
principe qui est à l'origine du mouvement sans qu'intervienne un
changement qualitatif: ce qui est léger est poussé vers le bas par
un élément plus lourd, ce qui est lourd est soulevé par ce qui est
plus léger.[31] Étant plus léger que l'eau et la terre le pneuma est
donc apte à mettre en mouvement les membres de l'organisme sans
qu'un changement qualitatif n'intervienne.

   En quel sens peut-on dire du coeur qu'il est le principe du mouve-

ment? Notons tout d'abord que le coeur est aussi le centre de la
perception sensible: si un objet de pensée ou de sensation est saisi
comme utile ou nocif, bon ou mauvais, il en résultera spontanément
un sentiment de plaisir ou de douleur. Traduit en termes physiologiques cela signifie que, dans le cas du plaisir, le degré de chaleur s'accroît, tandis que dans le cas de la douleur, le froid devient plus intense. Il en résultera donc une dilatation ou une
contraction du coeur, ce qui aura comme conséquence que les membres
du corps seront ou étendus ou rétractés: si le coeur se dilate, ils
seront poussés, si le coeur se contracte, ils seront tirés. La sensation de plaisir en dilatant le coeur pousse donc les membres corporels à la poursuite de l'objet, tandis que la douleur en contrac-
tant notre organe central attire les membres et les éloigne de l'objet. L'interprétation qu'on vient de donner du mouvement est d'ordre
thermodynamique.[32] Aristote en donne aussi une autre qui, elle, est
mécanique et suivant laquelle le mouvement des membres est produit
avec l'aide des tendons qui émanent du ventricule le plus large du
coeur, et ce qu'on appelle l'aorte est une veine de nature tendi-
neuse, surtout dans sa partie terminale, car elle n'y est pas creuse
et elle s'étend à la manière des tendons, là où ils se terminent aux
joints des os.[33] Selon cette interprétation le mouvement des membres
ne dépend pas de la dilatation ou de la contraction du coeur, il est
produit directement par les tendons situés dans le coeur et qui s'é-
tendent jusqu'aux joints des os.[34]

Le coeur n'est pas seulement le principe qui est à l'origine du
mouvement des membres, il est aussi le centre de la connaissance
sensible: c'est dans le coeur que réside l'âme sensitive. Dans le
De sensu[35] Aristote traite du goût et du toucher: il considère le
coeur comme l'organe central de ces sensations. Dans le *De juventute*[36] il décrit le coeur comme le centre de toutes les sensations,
tandis que, dans le *De partibus animalium*,[37] l'auteur parle de la
région qui entoure le coeur. En somme, c'est dans le coeur que
toutes les sensations ont leur principe et leur fin;[38] ce dernier
point est important: le coeur n'est pas seulement à l'origine de la
vie sensitive, il est aussi le centre où les données sensibles sont
recueillies. Le Stagirite s'efforce de justifier cette fonction
prédominante attribuée au coeur: à ses yeux, il faut qu'il y ait un
principe unique partout où la chose est possible et il est raison-

nable que ce soit le coeur parce qu'il est situé au centre de l'organisme. Dans son *De generatione animalium* l'auteur déclare que le
coeur se développe le premier parce qu'il est le principe des sensations et de tout l'animal[39] et comme cet organe est particulièrement chaud, la nature a formé un organe homologue qui assure l'équi-
libre, à savoir le cerveau; celui-ci se trouve à l'endroit où, en
haut, se terminent les vaisseaux sanguins. Étant donné le rôle
modérateur qui est attribué à la tête, celle-ci se développe immédiatement après le coeur et elle est plus grosse que les autres
parties.[40]

Comment s'établit la liaison entre le coeur et les organes sensoriels? Parlant de l'organe de la vue, Aristote signale que celui-
ci, comme tous les organes sensoriels, est établi sur des conduits
(πόροι);[41] quant à l'odorat et l'ouïe ces organes sont des conduits
remplis de pneuma congénital: ils aboutissent aux petits vaisseaux
qui partent du coeur et entourent le cerveau.[42] Dans ce cas-ci
l'explication donnée par Aristote est tout à fait nette: la continuité entre les organes sensoriels et le coeur est assurée par des
canaux qui sont remplis de pneuma inné, qu'il s'agisse des conduits
ou des petits vaisseaux. Nous savons déjà que ce pneuma est produit
sans cesse dans le coeur, comme une évaporation du sang: il peut
donc se répandre à partir de ce centre à travers tout le corps et
assurer une liaison permanente entre le coeur et les organes sensitifs. De cette façon on peut comprendre que toute sensation a son
origine dans le coeur et que le résultat de la perception sensible
aboutit également au même organe. Ceci ne veut pas dire toutefois
que le coeur et le pneuma congénital sont les véritables causes de
la connaissance; le pneuma n'y a qu'une fonction instrumentale.[43]
En ce qui concerne le toucher et le goût, la situation est différente: leur organe est directement le corps ou une partie du corps:
Aristote écrit à ce sujet que le goût et le toucher sont manifestement reliés au coeur.[44]

Toute cette doctrine d'Aristote vise à montrer comment l'unité
de la vie sensitive se traduit dans la structure organique: elle se
manifeste dans le fait que l'on perçoit simultanément non seulement
des qualités du même genre, mais aussi des sensibles appartenant à
des genres différents. Dans son *De sensu*, le Stagirite situe l'explication de ce phénomène dans le *sensus communis*: il est nécessaire

qu'il y ait dans l'âme une faculté sensitive fondamentale par laquelle elle saisit tous les objets possibles, quels que soient leurs
caractères spécifiques.[45] La perception d'une couleur ne peut entièrement coïncider avec la sensation d'une odeur: dès lors Aristote
admet que le principe qui perçoit tous les sensibles, est numérique-
ment un et identique, mais que sa manière d'être est différente d'a-
près les objets dont il s'agit; tel sensible sera saisi par la vue,
tel autre par l'odorat. Ces deux facultés sont distinctes, et pourtant elles plongent leurs racines dans un principe qui est foncière-
ment un et qui est à l'origine de la perception des sensibles communs.[46] C'est d'ailleurs cette racine commune de toute la vie sensitive qui permet d'expliquer le sommeil et la perception du temps:
le sommeil se caractérise par l'inactivité de tous les sens, ce qui
doit se comprendre comme l'inactivité de la faculté sensitive centrale, dont les sens ne sont que des différentiations.[47] Quant à
la perception du temps, elle se rattache à la saisie du mouvement,
c'est-à-dire du devenir sous toutes ses formes, aussi variées qu'elles soient: c'est pourquoi elle relève de la faculté sensitive centrale.[48] Cette unité foncière s'exprime et s'incorpore dans les
conduits et les petits vaisseaux, qui sont remplis de pneuma congénital, celui-ci étant en quelque sorte un instrument universel inter-
venant dans l'activité sensitive.

Dans l'optique d'Aristote, le coeur n'est pas seulement le centre
des sensations, il joue aussi un rôle important dans la vie émotion-
nelle: toute émotion se rattache à une disposition determinée de
l'organe central qu'est le coeur. Dans son *De anima* Aristote se demande si on peut dire de l'âme qu'elle est en mouvement: en effet,
on dit qu'elle éprouve de la peine et de la joie, de la confiance
et de la peur, comme on prétend qu'elle se fâche, qu'elle perçoit
et qu'elle pense. Ne faut-il pas en conclure qu'elle n'est pas un
principe immobile, mais qu'elle est en mouvement? Le Stagirite répond que pareille conclusion ne se justifie pas: supposons que la
douleur, la joie et la pensée soient des mouvements et qu'elles aient
leur origine dans l'âme; supposons en outre que la colère et la peur
signifient un mouvement déterminé du coeur et que la pensée, elle
aussi, soit un mouvement de cette partie centrale ou d'une autre;
supposons enfin que certains de ces mouvements soient des déplace-
ments locaux, alors que d'autres sont des changements qualitatifs,

même alors on ne peut pas dire de l'âme qu'elle éprouve de la colère,
comme on ne peut pas déclarer qu'elle tisse ou construit un édifice.
Il est préférable de ne pas dire de l'âme qu'elle éprouve de la
pitié, qu'elle apprend ou qu'elle pense, mais d'attribuer ces activités à l'homme. En quel sens peut-on dire de l'âme qu'elle est en
mouvement? Sûrement pas dans le sens que le mouvement aurait lieu
dans l'âme, mais pour exprimer que dans certains cas le mouvement
aboutit à l'âme, alors que dans d'autres, il part de l'âme: la perception sensible prend son origine dans les objets particuliers,
tandis que le souvenir part de l'âme et s'oriente vers les mouvements
ou les traces de mouvements conservées dans les organes sensoriels.
Le sens de ce texte est de mettre en relief l'unité de l'être vivant:
c'est lui, et non un de ses composants pris séparément, qui est à
l'origine des différentes activités, même des activités intellectuelles; dans cette perspective il serait faux de vouloir réduire
les émotions à des mouvements déterminés du coeur.[49] Selon Aristote,
les émotions présentent un rapport étroit avec la vie corporelle et
spécialement avec le coeur: c'est le cas de la colère, de la douceur,
de la pitié, de la crainte, du courage, de la joie, de l'amour et de
la haine. Il arrive parfois que des causes très légères nous mettent
en état de colère ou de peur; cela se produit quand le corps est pré-
disposé à ces émotions. Parlant de la définition de la colère, le
Stagirite attire l'attention sur la différence qui existe entre le
point de vue du physicien et celui du philosophe: au sujet de la
colère, le philosophe dira qu'elle est un désir de revanche, alors
que le physicien la définira comme un bouillonnement du sang ou de
la chaleur qui se trouvent dans la région du coeur. Aristote fait
remarquer que l'un signale la matière et l'autre la forme.[50] Si le
coeur est le centre d'où naissent le sang et le pneuma congénital,
qui est produit sans cesse dans cet organe central et subsidiaire-
ment dans les artères, si d'autre part le coeur est le centre de la
vie sensitive, on comprend que le Stagirite y localise également les
différentes manifestations de la vie émotive: la colère, la crainte,
la joie, le courage, toutes ces émotions se rattachent à certaines
transformations qui se produisent dans la région du coeur et qui se
rapportent au sang et au pneuma interne.

   Qu'en est-il maintenant des fonctions supérieures de l'homme, la
pensée et la vie volitive? Ces activités sont-elles entièrement

indépendantes de l'organisme corporel ou bien doit-on les attribuer
elles aussi au composé d'âme et de corps qu'est l'homme? On sait
que le Stagirite pose formellement cette question au début de son
De anima, tout en étant conscient de sa complexité. Aux yeux du
maître grec la plupart des phénomènes psychiques sont étroitement
liés au corps: c'est le cas de la colère, du courage, du désir, en
un mot de toute la vie sensitive.[51] Reste la question de savoir si
la pensée n'est pas entièrement indépendante de l'organisme corporel.
La question est importante en rapport avec l'immortalité de l'âme:
si aucune des activités exercées par l'homme n'est indépendante de
la matière, l'âme ne peut exister séparément. La manière dont le
problème est formulé doit inévitablement amener le Stagirite à nier
l'immortalité de l'âme: toute activité de l'homme, même la pensée,
est dépendante du corps. La pensée s'appuie sur la sensation et
celle-ci est manifestement liée à l'organisme corporel.[52] Aristote
se demande si la constitution du sang et donc du pneuma interne qui
en est une évaporation, joue un rôle dans l'aptitude à penser ou
dans l'exercice de l'activité intellectuelle; il aborde cette question dans le *De partibus animalium* et sa réponse est affirmative.[53]
Il fait remarquer d'abord que tous les animaux ont ou bien du sang
ou bien une autre humeur qui y ressemble: un sang plus épais et plus
chaud donne plus de force, tandis qu'un sang plus léger et plus
froid favorise l'activité sensitive et intellectuelle;[54] la capacité
de percevoir et de penser est donc mise directement en rapport avec
la constitution du sang ou de l'humeur qui y correspond chez les
animaux non sanguins. Ainsi les abeilles et les autres animaux de
cette espèce sont plus intelligents (φρονιμώτερα) que beaucoup
d'animaux sanguins; la situation idéale toutefois est d'avoir du
sang qui soit à la fois chaud, léger et clair: l'être qui possède
du sang de cette qualité est doué à la fois pour le courage et l'intelligence. Parmi tous les êtres vivants l'homme est le plus intelligent grâce à la pureté de la chaleur vitale qu'il possède dans
son coeur.[55] Que la constitution du sang détermine en quelque sorte
le niveau plus ou moins élevé de l'activité sensitive, on le comprend. Il est plus difficile de voir ce qu'Aristote veut dire quand
il prétend que même la pensée dépend de la qualité du sang: il est
vrai que le terme 'intelligence' est pris ici dans un sens plutôt
large, puisqu'il est appliqué aux abeilles; d'autre part, l'activité

de la pensée s'exerce en liaison étroite avec la vie sensitive. Ce
qui est rendu intelligible par l'intellect actif, n'est rien d'autre
que les données sensibles: il en résultera que les objets de pensée
dépendront de la qualité des données d'expérience.

Dans ce qui précède il a été question du rôle joué par le pneuma
congénital dans le mouvement des membres corporels; dans ce domaine
comme dans les autres que nous avons examinés, la fonction du pneuma
est d'ordre instrumental: l'âme se sert de ce souffle pour produire
le mouvement du corps. La position du pneuma vis-à-vis de l'âme et
de l'objet du mouvement est donc intermédiaire; car ce souffle est
à la fois mû et cause de mouvement, il est comme le point dans un
joint.[56] Le centre de la vie psychique se trouve dans le coeur ou
dans un organe analogue à celui-ci chez les animaux non sanguins; on
comprend dès lors que le pneuma congénital soit établi lui aussi dans
cet organe central. Chez les animaux irrationnels le mouvement du
corps prend sa source dans le désir ou l'aversion: si un objet perçu
se présente comme bon et désirable, il sera poursuivi; s'il se présente comme mauvais, l'animal s'en écartera. Aristote le dit formellement dans le *De anima*: un être vivant n'est capable de se mouvoir lui-même que pour autant qu'il est doué d'une puissance appéti-
tive. Celle-ci toutefois ne peut exister sans imagination, qui,
elle, est ou bien rationnelle ou sensitive: l'homme seul parmi les
animaux est doué d'une faculté rationnelle qui permet de connaître
des objets intelligibles.[57] C'est à cela que se rattache chez
l'homme la capacité de délibérer et la responsabilité morale. L'homme
n'est pas entraîné invinciblement par les objets qui lui sont présentés comme désirables, car il détermine en quelque sorte lui-même
ce qui sera considéré par lui comme une valeur.[58] Dès que l'homme,
après délibération, décide qu'un objet est à poursuivre, le mouvement du corps sera déclenché à partir du coeur par l'intermédiaire
du pneuma congénital.

Au terme de cet aperçu synthétique, on constate que le pneuma
congénital joue un rôle capital dans les différentes fonctions vitales telles qu'elles sont décrites par Aristote: dans la génération
spontanée, dans la procréation et le développement de l'embryon,
dans la nutrition et la croissance, dans la pulsation du coeur et
le mouvement des membres corporels, dans la connaissance sensible
et la vie émotive, dans la pensée et l'activité volitive. L'inter-

vention du pneuma n'est pas dans tous ces domaines également importante: cependant dans la description de ces diverses activités, le
pneuma joue un rôle d'ordre instrumental, qui lui confère une fonction irremplaçable dans la doctrine psychologique du Stagirite.

Il nous reste à examiner maintenant si la doctrine du pneuma congénital telle qu'elle vient d'être exposée est compatible avec l'entéléchisme d'Aristote. Il est important d'insister sur cette dernière
précision: il ne s'agit pas de savoir si la doctrine en question est
compatible avec l'entéléchisme tel que nous le concevons, mais tel
qu'il a été présenté par le Stagirite, principalement dans son *De
anima*. Si notre auteur définit l'âme comme la première entéléchie
d'un corps organique qui possède la vie en puissance, comment peut-
il encore soutenir que le coeur est le centre des fonctions vitales
et que le pneuma interne est un instrument dont l'âme se sert dans
l'exercice de ses fonctions?

En ce qui concerne le rôle attribué au coeur, T.J.Tracy dans son ouvrage sur *Physiological theory and the doctrine of the mean in Plato
and Aristotle*, arrive à la conclusion que, même dans les écrits de
la dernière période, le Stagirite considère toujours le coeur comme
le centre des opérations vitales. Ainsi d'après le *De generatione
animalium*, l'âme exerce son activité grâce à la chaleur vitale, con-
centrée dans le coeur. C'est dire que le coeur occupe le premier
rang dans l'exercice des fonctions physiologiques et psychiques; cet
organe est le centre à partir duquel principalement l'âme agit dans
le domaine de la nutrition, de la croissance, de la vie sensitive et
de la motion.[59] L'auteur estime que la même conclusion se dégage
de l'étude du *De anima* d'Aristote: dans ce traité les références au
coeur ne sont pas tellement nombreuses; elles sont plutôt d'ordre
occasionnel; pourtant il en résulte que, là aussi, le Stagirite considère le coeur comme le centre de la nutrition et de la sensation,
la source de la vie émotive et du mouvement des autres membres de
l'organisme, l'organe dans lequel réside la chaleur vitale; celle-
ci est utilisée par l'âme comme un instrument dans l'exercice de
ces fonctions vitales.[60] Manifestement Aristote ne voit pas de
contradiction entre le rôle qu'il assigne au coeur et sa conception
de l'âme comme forme substantielle du corps. Il importe donc de
s'interroger sur l'entéléchisme du maître grec afin d'en dévoiler

les lignes essentielles.

Aux yeux d'Aristote l'âme est donc la première entéléchie d'un corps physique organique qui possède la vie en puissance.[61] Cette doctrine ouvre une perspective nouvelle; il n'y a pas d'opposition entre l'âme et le corps. Toute opposition est exclue, puisque le lien qui unit les composants est un rapport d'acte et de puissance. D'ailleurs l'âme n'est pas seulement l'acte du corps, elle en est la première entéléchie; si cette expression a un sens, elle doit signifier que le principe corporel tient toute sa perfection de l'âme, sans cela l'âme ne serait pas la 'première' entéléchie de l'organisme corporel, mais une perfection postérieure et surajoutée. On l'a vu déjà dans ce qui précède, aussi bien dans l'explication donnée de la génération spontanée que dans celle que le Stagirite présente de la procréation: la génération spontanée est possible parce que tout est rempli d'âme. Cette génération ne signifie donc pas que l'âme est produite grâce à une évolution à partir de la matière inanimée; au contraire, c'est l'âme qui est la source et l'origine des animaux qui naissent de cette façon. Cette génération se caractérise par conséquent par l'absence de fécondation. Dans le cas de la procréation, c'est l'âme nutritive qui est la cause de la croissance et du développement de l'embryon. Aristote constate que l'organe qui est formé en premier lieu est le coeur: il est le centre de la vie, il contient le sang et le pneuma congénital. Toutefois le coeur ne se constitue pas de lui-même, il est formé par l'âme qui est à l'origine de tout le développement de l'embryon.[62] D'où vient cette âme? Elle est contenue dans l'élément actif de la procréation, le sperme, sauf dans le cas de l'intellect. On peut donc dire que l'embryon et tout ce qu'il renferme, est formé par l'âme, ce qui vaut également pour le coeur et le pneuma congénital. La doctrine du pneuma congénital et le rôle qui lui est assigné dans le développement de l'embryon, ne sont donc pas incompatibles avec l'entéléchisme. Ils le seraient, si on attribuait au corps une perfection qui ne provient pas de l'âme: dans ce cas on aboutirait à une doctrine instrumentiste, qui reflète encore un certain degré de dualisme. Ce dualisme disparaît si l'instrument lui-même est constitué par le principe psychique.

L'entéléchisme d'Aristote est l'expression, en langage philosophique, de l'unité de l'être vivant, de l'unité aussi de l'être

humain. L'homme est un composé et les philosophes se sont posé la
question de savoir comment il fallait concevoir l'union des deux
éléments constitutifs: est-elle une union forcée, une juxtaposition,
un mélange, peut-être un mélange total, une certaine inclination des
composants l'un vis-à-vis de l'autre? Un grand nombre de solutions
ont été proposées: celle d'Aristote est supérieure aux autres en ce
qu'elle traduit en catégories métaphysiques l'unité de l'être vivant. Aux yeux du Stagirite l'âme et le corps ne sont pas deux
principes autonomes, deux composants capables d'exister séparément:
l'âme ne peut exister sans le corps, puisque toutes les activités
qu'elle exerce, sont dépendantes de l'organisme corporel; le corps
ne peut exister sans l'âme, car toute sa perfection provient du
principe psychique. S'il en est ainsi, Aristote peut-il admettre
un intermédiaire entre l'âme et le corps, un pneuma congénital dont
l'âme se sert dans l'exercice de ses fonctions vitales? La réponse
dépendra de ce qu'on entend par 'intermédiaire': il est vrai que
l'âme utilise le pneuma congénital dans beaucoup de ses fonctions.
En résulte-t-il que ce pneuma entrave l'unité de l'être vivant? Un
'intermédiaire' pourrait être un élément qui permettrait d'unir deux
composants hétérogènes. Il n'en est pas ainsi dans le cas du pneuma
congénital: l'âme et le corps sont dans le rapport de forme substantielle et de matière, d'acte et de puissance. Ils n'ont pas besoin
d'un lien qui unisse l'un à l'autre les composants. Le pneuma congénital appartient à l'organisation du corps: l'âme constitue le
corps de façon à ce que toutes les activités vitales puissent se développer; la formation du coeur, comme celle du sang et du pneuma,
font partie de cette organisation. On ne voit donc pas comment dans
l'optique d'Aristote le rôle joué par le pneuma interne serait contraire à l'unité substantielle du vivant.

On peut en dire autant de la fonction que le pneuma remplit dans
la vie sensitive et donc indirectement dans l'activité intellectuelle.
Le fait que le centre de la vie sensitive est établi dans le coeur
et qu'il y a une liaison continue entre lui et les organes sensitifs
grâce aux conduits et aux petits vaisseaux, n'empêche pas que l'âme
soit la forme substantielle de l'être humain. L'unité de l'homme se
manifeste d'ailleurs à tous les niveaux de la vie cognitive: la vie
sensitive n'est point la juxtaposition de différentes puissances qui
ne seraient pas reliées entre elles. Il y a une faculté sensitive

fondamentale, dont les différentes puissances ne sont que des différentiations: c'est ce qui nous permet de comparer des objets saisis par des puissances sensitives différentes, d'avoir le sens du
temps et de posséder une conscience inchoative du sujet connaissant.
Par ailleurs, il y a dans l'homme un rapport étroit entre la connaissance sensible et le savoir intellectuel: tout objet de pensée
prend son origine dans l'expérience sensible; il est même impossible
de penser un objet en dehors de tout lien avec la sensibilité.[63]
C'est que les objets de pensée sont empruntés aux données sensibles,
qui ont été rendues intelligibles grâce à l'intervention du principe
actif de l'intellection.

Le pneuma congénital n'est donc pas un instrument qui se situe à
mi-chemin entre l'âme et le corps et qui serait requis à cause du
caractère hétérogène de ces composants. Il est vrai qu'il est utilisé par l'âme dans beaucoup de fonctions vitales; mais ce n'est
jamais un instrument indépendant du principe psychique, mais un organe qui dans l'optique de l'entéléchisme a été formé par lui. Mais
s'il en est ainsi, l'âme ne pourrait-elle pas se passer de cet instrument? L'interprétation de l'entéléchisme ne serait-elle pas
plus adéquate, si le Stagirite n'introduisait pas cet instrument
privilégié? On ne peut nier qu'Aristote n'a pas tiré toutes les
conséquences de sa nouvelle conception de l'âme: si l'être humain
est véritablement un, c'est le composé d'âme et de corps qui est le
principe de la nutrition, de la croissance, du mouvement et de la
sensation, ce n'est pas l'âme qui se sert d'un instrument dans l'exercice de ces fonctions. Il faut le reconnaître, cette manière de
présenter l'activité de l'âme n'est pas adéquate: elle ne signifie
pas cependant que la doctrine du pneuma congénital serait incompatible avec l'entéléchisme; car, même en admettant que le coeur est
le centre des fonctions vitales et que le pneuma interne est l'instrument de l'âme, Aristote pourrait et devrait enseigner que c'est
le composé d'âme et de corps qui est à la source de la nutrition,
de la sensation et des autres activités vitales. Si le pneuma
était considéré comme un instrument ayant une existence indépendante, comparable aux outils dont l'artisan se sert dans son travail,
pareille conception ne pourrait s'accorder avec l'entéléchisme.
Mais il n'en est pas ainsi: le pneuma fait partie de l'organisation
du corps dont l'âme est le principe.

Il reste à reconnaître cependant que dans le *De anima* le pneuma
congénital n'est pas formellement mentionné: est-ce parce que cette
doctrine est incompatible avec l'entéléchisme? Nous ne le croyons
pas; cette absence s'explique plutôt par le point de vue que l'auteur adopte dans ce traité. La structure de l'organisme corporel a
été exposée longuement dans d'autres traités, surtout dans le *De
partibus animalium* et le *De generatione animalium*; dans le *De anima*,
il ne s'agit pas du corps, mais de l'âme qui est définie comme la
forme substantielle de l'organisme. Il en résulte que dans ce traité la fonction du coeur et de la chaleur vitale n'est mentionnée
qu' occasionnellement, mais elle n'est plus à l'avant-plan de l'exposé.

Quelques conclusions d'ordre général se dégagent de cette étude:

1. La doctrine d'Aristote sur le pneuma congénital ne coïncide pas
   simplement avec celle des auteurs médicaux qui ont vécu avant
   lui ou qui furent ses contemporains. Sans vouloir s'attarder à
   des différences de détail, il importe d'attirer l'attention sur
   une distinction essentielle: chez Aristote, la théorie du pneuma
   congénital est reprise dans le cadre d'une anthropologie philosophique, ce qui n'est pas le cas chez les auteurs medicaux.
   C'est le mérite incontestable du Stagirite d'avoir repensé la théorie du pneuma en fonction d'une conception générale de l'homme:
   étant l'instrument de l'âme, le pneuma congénital remplit des
   fonctions variées mais précises dans l'exercice des différentes
   activités de la vie.

2. Les Stoïciens ont identifié le pneuma avec la substance de l'âme
   et avec celle de la divinité immanente. A leurs yeux, l'âme in-
   dividuelle est une parcelle du Logos divin qui pénètre partout
   et qui est à l'origine de l'évolution cosmique. Le rôle attribué
   au pneuma congénital chez Aristote est bien plus réduit, puisque
   ce souffle est considéré comme un instrument dont l'âme se sert
   dans le déploiement de ses activités. D'où vient cette différence? Nous croyons qu'elle dépend de la nature des deux philo-
   sophies: celle des Stoïciens est matérialiste, celle d'Aristote
   reconnaît à l'homme une dimension spirituelle.[64]

3. La doctrine aristotélicienne du pneuma congénital n'est pas incohérente, elle n'est pas non plus un *asylum ignorantiae*. Il est

vrai que le pneuma intervient dans des activités vitales très diverses: la chose n'est guère étonnante puisque ce pneuma est por-
teur de la chaleur vitale, lié étroitement avec le sang, de nature subtile et circulant à travers tout l'organisme. Comment ne
serait-il pas un outil plurivalent, mis à la disposition de l'âme
en vue de ses multiples activités? Si l'on objecte que la théorie
du pneuma est incohérente parce que ce souffle intervient dans des
activités trop différentes, pareille objection devrait s'appliquer
aussi à l'âme, puisque celle-ci est en dernière analyse la source
et l'origine de toutes les fonctions vitales.

NOTES

1 Aristote n'est pas l'inventeur de la doctrine du pneuma: cette
notion se recontre dans des écrits antérieurs et contemporains
du Stagirite. On la trouve dans le *Traité sur la maladie sacrée*
(Περὶ ἱρῆς νούσου) du *Corpus Hippocraticum*: l'auteur y expose
que le pneuma est introduit du dehors par la respiration; sa fonction est d'abord de modérer la température de l'organisme. Mais
en outre il est principe de la connaissance intellectuelle (ξύνε-
σις) par l'intermédiaire du cerveau. Avec le sang, ce pneuma psychique circule dans les veines à travers l'organisme corporel: il
peut arriver toutefois qu'une obstruction se produise dans les
veines, causée par des humeurs froides provenant du cerveau. Dans
ce cas le sang est arrêté, il se condense, perd sa fluidité et
empêche le pneuma de se répandre. C'est l'explication de l'épi-
lepsie ou maladie sacrée. Dans le Περὶ φυσῶν du même *Corpus hippocratique* la nature de l'air inspiré est regardée comme la cause
de toutes les maladies. L'auteur admet que le pneuma circule
dans les veines avec le sang: si la circulation de ce souffle est
irrégulière, le sang en est affecté et toutes sortes de maladies
s'en suivent. (Cf. F.Rüsche, *Blut, Leben und Seele* (Paderborn
1930), 117-27.) Rappelons aussi que le philosophe sicilien Empédocle croit que l'âme s'identifie avec le sang, celui-ci étant
le mélange le plus parfait des éléments. Même les activités les
plus nobles de l'homme sont attribuées au sang: le principe de
la pensée n'est autre que le sang qui se trouve dans la région
du coeur. C'est pourquoi le coeur étant le siège de la chaleur
vitale (ἔμφυτον θερμόν) se développe dans l'embryon avant tous
les autres organes: parmi les éléments Empédocle attribue un rang
privilégié au feu, à la chaleur implantée ou innée (Théophraste,
De sensibus 10-11; *Dox.* p.502, 7-22). Quant à Dioclès de Carystos qui fut probablement un contemporain d'Aristote, il admet,
lui aussi, que le coeur est le centre de l'organisme corporel
et le point de départ du pneuma psychique, dont dépendent la
pensée, la sensation et le mouvement. Ce pneuma ne coïncide pas
avec l'air inspiré: Dioclès semble avoir enseigné plutôt que le

pneuma provient de l'évaporation du sang dans le coeur et que le
rôle de l'air inspiré est de régler et de tempérer ce processus
d'évaporation. Aux yeux de notre auteur, c'est la chaleur qui
est l'élément le plus actif dans le pneuma. (Cf. W.Jaeger, *Diokles von Karystos. Die griechische Medizin und die Schule des
Aristoteles* (2e éd. Berlin 1963).) Bien qu'Aristote ne soit pas
l'initiateur de la théorie du pneuma il est indéniable cependant,
qu'il a repensé cette doctrine en fonction des catégories de sa
propre philosophie.

2 *Aristoteles, Darstellung und Interpretation seines Denkens* (Heidelberg 1966), 343.

3 Oxford 1906, 336. Cf. *Aristotle, Generation of animals* (Loeb ed.
London-Cambridge (Mass.) 1943), 593.

4 En rapport avec les multiples fonctions attribuées par Aristote
au pneuma, M. Joseph Moreau (Bordeaux) a bien voulu souligner
l'intérêt d'un passage du *GA* (V 8, 789b7-12): 'Les causes qu'il
(Démocrite) cite ne sont causes qu'en tant que moteurs, instruments et matière, puisqu'aussi bien il est vraisemblable que la
plupart des choses sont faites avec le souffle (πνεῦμα) comme
instrument: de même que certains outils utilisés dans les métiers
ont plusieurs usages, comme le marteau et l'enclume dans le travail des métaux, de même le souffle (πνεῦμα)dans les organismes
naturels' (trad. P.Louis). Au sujet de ce texte M. Moreau écrit:
'En résumé, les causes matérielles, mécaniques, sont des instruments au service de la finalité; parmi ces instruments, celui
qui a les usages les plus divers est le pneuma. Est-ce à dire
que le biologiste a recours à lui comme à un expédient, quand il
ne trouve pas d'autre explication? Ce n'est pas tout à fait exact. Il y a, en effet, des cas où la fonction s'exerce sans organe spécifique au moyen d'une matière vivante diffuse, aux fonctions variées. C'est ainsi que le pneuma intervient d'abord
dans la génération spontanée. Puis, dans le développement embry-
ologique, dans la période qui s'étend entre la fécondation et les
premières différentiations, le pneuma joue un rôle primordial.
Enfin, quand les parties de l'organisme sont spécifiées, que chaque fonction a son organe propre, ce sont les fonctions les plus
complexes et les plus générales, par exemple celles du *sensus
communis*, qui ont besoin du pneuma comme instrument.' Je remercie M. Moreau de ses remarques intéressantes, avec lesquelles je
suis parfaitement d'accord.

5 Cf. Rüsche (*op.cit. n.1*), 188-250; *Das Seelenpneuma, Seine Entwicklung von der Hauchseele zur Geistseele* (Paderborn 1933), 4-6.

6 *GA* III 11, 763a24.

7 *GA* III 11, 762a18-21; *De An.* I 5, 411a7-11; *PA* I 5, 645a20-3.

8 *GA* III 11, 762a27-32.

9 *GA* III 11, 762b12-18.

10 *GA* III 11, 762b28sqq.

11 *GA* III 11, 763a3-10.

12 *GA* II 3, 736b27-9. Diverses interprétations ont été suggérées
concernant ce texte énigmatique. Ch. Lefèvre (*Sur l'évolution
d'Aristote en psychologie* (Louvain 1972), 274sqq.) rejette les
explications de M. De Corte et de P. Moraux; rattachant le *GA*
II 3 au *De anima* III 5 il écrit: 'Il est impossible d'attribuer
à l'acte générateur la transmission de l'intellect lui-même,
considéré en son essence' (p.276). Il n'en est pas de même toutefois de l'âme sensitive: celle-ci est introduite dans l'embryon par le sperme et donc par l'intervention active de l'homme
(*GA* II 5, 741b6-7; II 4, 738b25-7). A l'appui de cette interprétation on peut se référer aussi à un passage plutôt difficile du *GA* (II 3, 737a7-12). Aristote écrit: 'Quant à la matière du liquide séminal, qui sert de véhicule à la portion du
principe psychique (une portion de ce principe est indépendante
de la matière chez tous les êtres où se trouve inclus un élément
divin - tel est le caractère de ce qu'on appelle intellect -
tandis que l'autre en est inséparable), cette matière de la semence se dissout et s'évapore, du fait qu'elle possède une nature humide et aqueuse' (trad. P.Louis). Dans son édition M.
Louis a laissé tomber les mots τὸ σπέρμα (τὸ σπέρμα τὸ τῆς ψυχικῆς ἀρχῆς) qui se lisent dans les manuscrits S Y Z. Prof.
Drossaart Lulofs marque les termes d'une croix et fait remarquer
qu'ils se rencontrent aussi bien dans la version arabe que dans
celle de Guillaume de Moerbeke. La correction proposée par
Platt (lire τὸ πνεῦμα au lieu de σπέρμα) n'apporte pas de solution à la difficulté et n'est donc pas à retenir. Si on garde
la leçon τὸ σπέρμα il faudrait comprendre ce terme dans le sens
général de 'germe': la signification du passage n'en serait
point changée; Aristote voudrait dire que le liquide séminal
sert de véhicule au germe du principe psychique, pour autant que
celui-ci s'insère dans le processus de la génération.

13 *GA* II 3, 736b33-5.

14 *GA* II 3, 737a1-3.

15 *GA* II 3, 736b35-737a7. F. Solmsen a souligné l'importance et le
caractère exceptionnel de ce passage: 'Nowhere else in the body
of his preserved work does Aristotle establish this close connection between the vital heat, the *pneuma* and the element of the
stars, the so called aether' ('The vital heat, the inborn pneuma
and the aether', *JHS* 77 (1957), 119).

16 *GA* II 2, 735b37-736a2.

17 *GA* II 3, 737a18-20.

18 *GA* II 3, 737a22-5; I 20, 729a9-11; I 21, 729b1-9; 730a14-15, 22-3,
25-8; II 1, 735a12-13; II 4, 738b11-15; IV 1, 765b11-13; IV 3,
767b8-20; *Metaph.* H 4, 1044a34-5; Λ 5, 1071a13-17; Λ 6, 1071b29-
31.

19 *GA* V 8, 789b8-12.

20 *GA* II 1, 734b30-6; l'action du chaud et du froid est indéter-
minée alors que dans la procréation ce qui est en cause c'est la
production d'un être vivant déterminé.

21 *GA* II 1, 735a20-1.

22 *GA* II 1, 735a23-6.

23 *GA* V 8, 789b8.

24 Au cours de la discussion certains participants (M.M. Verdenius
et Brunschwig) ont soulevé la question de savoir quel est le
sens précis du terme σύμφυτον dans l'expression σύμφυτον πνεῦμα.
Dans l'esprit d'Aristote, ce terme désigne un élément constitutif de l'être vivant, un composant qui se développe dans l'organisme corporel et avec lui dès le début de sa constitution et
jusqu'à la fin de la vie, un instrument qui n'est pas emprunté
de l'extérieur, mais qui étant présent dans le sperme se développe avec la croissance du vivant et s'entretient en permanence
grâce à l'évaporation du sang dans le coeur. Le pneuma est dit
σύμφυτον parce qu'il n'est pas introduit du dehors, mais qu'il
appartient déjà à la constitution initiale du vivant et se développe avec lui. Dans le *PA* (II 16, 659b17-19) Aristote explique comment les animaux qui ne respirent pas reçoivent les
odeurs; dans ce contexte il fait remarquer que tous ces animaux
sont mus pour ainsi dire par le pneuma congénital (τῷ συμφύτῳ
πνεύματι); 'Ce souffle appartient par nature à tous et n'est pas
introduit du dehors' (trad. P.Louis). Dans ce passage le contraste entre φύσει et θύραθεν est particulièrement éclairant.
Au troisième livre du même traité (III 6, 668b33-669a2) l'auteur
parle des animaux sanguins qui possèdent un poumon parce qu'ils
vivent sur terre et ont besoin d'un refroidissement qui leur
provient du dehors: quant aux animaux privés de sang, ils peuvent se refroidir rien que par le pneuma congénital (τῷ συμφύτῳ
πνεύματι). La même opposition se lit aussi dans un passage du
GA (II 6, 744a3) où le Stagirite traite de l'odorat et de l'ouïe:
ces organes, écrit-il, 'sont des conduits en liaison avec l'air
extérieur, qui sont remplis d'un souffle d'origine interne (πλή-
ρεις συμφύτου πνεύματος) et qui aboutissent aux petits vaisseaux
qui, du coeur, s'étendent autour du cerveau' (trad. P.Louis).
Dans tous ces passages on retrouve le même contraste entre l'extérieur et l'intérieur, entre l'air inspiré du dehors et le pneuma qui appartient à l'équipement naturel du vivant et se développe avec lui. Dans son étude intitulée *Das Pneuma im Lykeion*,
W.Jaeger fait remarquer que le Stagirite est pour nous le repré-
sentant le plus ancien de la théorie du pneuma congénital *(Scrip-
ta minora* I (Rome 1960), 71).

25 *GA* II 3, 736b14.

26 *De An.* II 4, 416a13.

27 *De Resp.* 20, 479b30-480a7.

28 *Juv.* 4, 468b23-30; *PA* III 4, 666a10-11; *GA* II 4, 740a15-18. Ainsi
que nous l'avons mentionné ci-dessus, Dioclès de Carystos admet, '

lui aussi, que le pneuma est établi dans le coeur; dans l'élaboration de sa doctrine médicale il semble avoir fait appel au
pneuma psychique et à la chaleur vitale. Quant à Chrysippe il
s'appuie sur l'autorité de Praxagoras de Cos pour soutenir que
le coeur est le siège du souffle psychique. Entretemps on avait
découvert déjà l'existence des nerfs qui furent considérés comme
les conduits du pneuma (Solmsen (*art.cit. n.15*), 122).

29 *Resp.* 20, 480a7-15.

30 *MA* 10, 703a9-16.

31 *MA* 10, 703a19-28.

32 T.J.Tracy, *Physiological theory and the doctrine of the mean in
Plato and Aristotle* (The Hague - Paris 1969), 355.

33 *HA* III 5, 515a27sqq.

34 *PA* III 4, 666b13sqq.

35 *Sens.* 2, 439a1.

36 *Juv.* 3, 469a5sqq.

37 *PA* II 10, 656a27-33; III 4, 666a34-b1; *GA* V 2, 781a20-2; *Juv.* 3,
469a5-14.

38 *PA* III 4, 666a12-13.

39 *GA* II 6, 743b25; cf. *De An.* III 1, 425a6.

40 *GA* II 6, 743b29-32. Aux yeux du Stagirite le centre de la vie
sensitive ne se situe pas au cerveau (*PA* II 10, 656a17-18): celui-
ci ne contient pas de sang; il n'est donc pas capable de percevoir, ce qui peut s'établir de façon expérimentale (*HA* III 4, 514
a18; III 19, 520b16-17; *PA* II 10, 656a23-4; II 7, 652b4-5).

41 *GA* II 6, 743b35-7.

42 *GA* II 6, 744a2. Aristote enseigne que même les sens qui sont éta-
blis dans la tête et qui sont reliés au cerveau par des canaux,
se rattachent finalement au coeur par des veines qui partent de
la méninge vers le coeur (*Juv.* 3, 469a12-14; *PA* III 4, 666a11-13;
GA II 6, 744a2-5; V 2, 781a20-1). Alors que le cerveau est dépourvu de sang, la méninge contient un grand nombre de veines
très minces (*PA* II 7, 652b29-33).

43 *PA* II 10, 656b16.

44 *PA* II 10 656a29; *Sens.* 2, 439a1.

45 *Sens.* 7, 449a8-20.

46 La perception des sensibles communs semble être à l'origine de
l'évolution qui a conduit le Stagirite à la doctrine du *sensus*

communis. Les problèmes posés dans le *De anima* III 2 par la perception de soi et par le 'jugement' sensible ont amené Aristote à développer dans les *Parva naturalia* sa doctrine d'une sensibilité fondamentale, qui non seulement accompagne et synthétise les sensations particulières, perçoit les sensibles communs, mais qui est le fondement permanent de toute l'activité sensitive.

47 *De somno* 2, 455a12-26.

48 *Mem*. 1, 450a9-10; 451a16-17; 2, 452b7-13; *De An*. III 10, 433b7.

49 *De An*. I 4, 408b1-19.

50 *De An*. I 1, 403a16-403b1.

51 *De An*. I 1, 403a3sqq.

52 *De An*. III 7, 431a16-17; 8, 432a7-9.

53 *PA* II 1, 647b29-35.

54 *PA* II 2, 648a2sqq. Cf. F. Solmsen, 'Tissues and the soul', *Philos. Rev.* 59 (1950), 464.

55 *GA* II 6, 744a29sqq. Au sujet de cette question, M. Brunschwig a bien voulu me communiquer une note que je reprends bien volontiers à mon compte: 'A propos des différences de température et de tempérament entre les animaux, on peut noter qu'Aristote conjugue le couple chaud-froid avec le couple courage-intelligence, aussi bien chez les animaux que chez les hommes. D'après un texte des *Problèmes* (XIV 15, 910a26sqq.), les habitants des pays chauds sont froids (par compensation), sobres, craintifs et intelligents: car la peur développe l'esprit de recherche et d'investigation; les habitants des pays froids, au contraire, sont chauds, énergiques et courageux, mais peu intelligents. Un texte célèbre de la *Politique* (VII 6, 1327b23sqq.) reprend cette antithèse en l'appliquant aux peuples d'Asie et d'Europe, et en développant ses aspects politiques; les Grecs y sont présentés comme la synthèse de la thèse et de l'antithèse (courageux et intelligents, libres et organisés).' Bien que ces textes se rapportent directement à l'influence du climat et de la température sur les dispositions intellectuelles et morales des peuples, ils confirment cependant la relation établie par le Stagirite entre la constitution du sang (d'où le pneuma congénital émane) et les aptitudes psychiques.

56 *MA* 10, 703a11-14; *De An*. III 10, 433b25.

57 *De An*. III 10, 433b27; III 7, 431a15-16.

58 *EN* III 5, 1114b1-3.

59 Tracy (*op.cit. n.32*), 352-3.

60 Tracy (*op.cit. n.32*), 352.

61 *De An.* II 1, 412a19-b6.

62 Dans le *GA* (II 1, 735a4-9; II 3, 736a35-b1; b8-12) l'auteur se demande si la semence possède une âme ou non; la réponse du Stagirite est nettement affirmative: il ne fait pas de doute pour lui que la semence possède une âme et que celle-ci est en puissance. (Cf. F.Nuyens, *L'Évolution de la psychologie d'Aristote* (Louvain-Hague-Paris 1948), 259.)

63 *De An.* III 8, 432a7-9.

64 A propos de certains fragments du *De philosophia* d'Aristote (surtout le fragment 27 dans l'édition de R.Walzer) on s'est demandé si le Stagirite, à un stade déterminé de son évolution, n'a pas considéré le cinquième élément comme la substance de l'âme. Certains auteurs se sont prononcés en faveur de cette thèse, d'autres l'ont rejetée catégoriquement comme incompatible avec la pensée authentique du Stagirite. Il faut le reconnaître, la base sur laquelle cette interprétation matérialiste s'appuie n'est pas particulièrement solide (cf. P.Moraux, art. 'Quinta essentia', *RE* XXIV (1963), col. 1171-1266; J.Pépin, 'Interprétation du *De Philosophia* d'Aristote d'après quelques travaux récents', *Rev. des Études grecques* 77 (1964), 473-88).

9: THE EMPIRICAL BASIS OF THE PHYSIOLOGY OF THE *PARVA NATURALIA*

G.E.R.Lloyd

Aristotle's fame as a biologist is as firmly entrenched as any aspect
of his reputation. When he is acclaimed for his work in this field,
it is not only, and often not primarily, as a theorist - for example,
for his acute discussion of the problems of generation and heredity
in *GA* - but also, and perhaps more especially, as an observer, for
his detailed zoological descriptions. The zoological treatises show
a familiarity with a quite impressive range of animal species; the
exactness of many of his descriptions of the external and internal
parts of animals and of aspects of animal behaviour has often rightly
been praised,[1] and in many cases his accounts refer to or presuppose
the use of dissection, whether undertaken by Aristotle himself or by
his associates. Meanwhile the famous fifth chapter of *PA* I leaves
us in no doubt that he recognized the importance of detailed research
in zoology and the opportunities it presented for his enquiry into
causes, while he remained realistic both about the difficulties of
such research and about the repugnance that some of his contemporar-
ies would feel at the investigation of the less honourable animals
and of internal anatomy.[2]

The *PN*, whose subject is certain activities that are 'common to
soul and body', presupposes the study of the soul itself,[3] and the
opening sentences of *Sens.* not only look back to *De An.* but also forward to the study of living beings in general.[4] This poses, as a topic for investigation, the extent to which Aristotle's practice in *PN*
corresponds to the ideals enunciated in *PA* I 5, or, more generally,
the relation between empirical data and theories in *PN*. How far are
the theories advanced in those treatises suggested or supported by,
or checked against, empirical observations? To what extent does Aristotle appear to have engaged in deliberate research relevant to the
issues explored in *PN*? These are complex questions that have not received the attention they deserve.[5] In this paper I wish to consider
certain aspects of these problems not so much from the point of view
of the chronological question of the relative date of *PN*, as from

that of the methodological one of the role of observation in Aristotle's natural philosophy.

Given the recommendations of *PA* I 5, our initial presumption might
well be to expect fairly frequent references, in *PN*, to the findings
of empirical investigations, whether anatomical, physiological or
zoological, in the discussion of such topics as the individual senses,
sleep, respiration, life and death. Our first task, however, is to
review such passages in these treatises as bear directly on the question of the relevance of such researches. Although *PN* contains no
methodological programme such as we have in *PA* I, several texts allude to that question.

Thus one passage issues an explicit warning concerning the extent
to which it is appropriate to enter into detail on a point of anatomy.
This is *Somn.* 458a20sq. where Aristotle has been discussing the causes of sleep. He notes at 458a10sqq. that waking occurs when (1) digestion has been completed, (2) the heat once more prevails and (3)
the more corporeal, and the purer, blood have been separated. The
heart, he continues, is the ἀρχή of all the blood: the middle chamber
is common to each of the other two, each of which draws from its own
vessel (the great vessel and the aorta), and the separation takes
place in the middle chamber.[6] But, he goes on, τὸ μὲν διορίζειν περὶ
τούτων ἑτέρων ἐστὶ λόγων οἰκειότερον. What he draws back from, here,
is a detailed anatomical description of the heart and its vessels.
He has noted the one point that is of immediate importance for his
account of sleep, namely that there is a separation of blood in the
middle chamber of the heart. This passage neither states nor implies
that anatomy as such is irrelevant, only that detailed consideration
of the heart's anatomy is. We may compare occasions when he simply
refers to other treatises, or to the results of dissection, for a
more detailed or exact account on a particular point. He does this,
for instance, at *Resp.* 478a26sqq. on the question of the connections
between the heart and the lung. Here too we may distinguish between,
on the one hand, the bare fact that there is a connection (a fact
that is presupposed in his explanation of the role of breath in
cooling the heart) and, on the other, the detailed description of
those connections. Similarly at *Resp.* 478a35sqq.[7] he refers both to
'the *dissections*' and to 'the *Histories*' on the relation between the
heart and the gills in fish, although he gives a summary description

of that relation here.

While it is obviously not to Aristotle's purposes, in *PN*, to present detailed records of dissections (whether his own or other people's), he cites their results, or what he claims as their results, not infrequently. At *Somn.* 456b2, for example, he does so for the point that the heart is the ἀρχή of the φλέβες.[8] At *Juv.* 468b29sqq., after remarking that in sanguineous animals the heart comes to be first, he says 'this is clear from what we have observed in those cases where it is possible to see them as they come to be', and there is no need to emphasize the importance of this purported observation as support for his account of the role of the heart.[9] The passage continues: 'so necessarily in bloodless animals also what is analogous to the heart comes to be first'. Here, then, he claims that a point is established by observation in certain classes of sanguineous animals, generalizes from this to all sanguineous animals, and then extends the doctrine by analogy to the bloodless animals as well.

As in the zoological treatises proper, so too in *PN*, his careful noting that certain points have not yet been observed should be interpreted against the background of his evident readiness to extrapolate from those data that he believed had been established by observation. Thus at *Somn.* 454b21sqq. he calls in λόγος where αἴσθησις fails. Having remarked that almost all animals are clearly seen to sleep, and mentioned that the sleep of 'hard-eyed' creatures and insects is of short duration, he says of the testacea that κατὰ τὴν αἴσθησιν it is not yet clear whether they sleep, but if the λόγος given is trustworthy, it will be believed that they do so.[10] At *Juv.* 469a23sqq., in a difficult passage to which I shall return, he states that it is established both κατὰ τὰ φαινόμενα and κατὰ τὸν λόγον that the ἀρχή of both the perceptive and the nutritive soul is in the heart and in the middle of the three main divisions of the body.[11] The λόγος he mentions is that 'we see nature bringing about what is best in all cases so far as possible'. But what counts as φαινόμενα has to be judged from the immediately preceding discussion, where he says that two of the senses evidently stretch to the heart 'so the others necessarily do so also'.[12] Yet the clearest evidence in *PN* for Aristotle recognizing that it is important to take account of the data obtained by dissection comes at *Resp.* 470b8sqq. and 471b23sqq. where he criticizes his predecessors for their lack of familiarity with the facts and particularly with the internal organs of animals. In the latter passage he ascribes their mistaken belief that all animals breathe first to their lack of knowledge of internal anatomy (he has been talking about insects and fish particularly) and then to their non-acceptance of the final cause in nature.

But whilst it is not hard to cite texts in *PN*, as in his other works, that acknowledge the value of sensation in general and of dissection in particular, it is now time to consider some examples where we can test the extent to which in practice he appears to have attempted to bring the findings of empirical investigations to bear on the problems discussed in these treatises. Four topics in particular offer opportunities to do so, his accounts of the structure and function of the eye (*Sens.* 2), of the connections between the senses and the common sensorium (in *Juv.* especially), of the nature and function of the brain (*Sens.*, *Somn.*) and of the relations between the lung and the heart and the structure of the latter (*Somn.*, *Resp.*).

In *Sens.* ch.2 he engages in a general account of the sense-organs, especially the eye. The main ἀπορίαι he mentions for consideration are (1) how the five senses are to be correlated with the four elements (437a19sqq.) and (2) why the eye does not see itself (437a26 sqq.). During the course of his discussion he has occasion to refer to each of the three main parts he usually identifies in the eye, namely the pupil (κόρη, 438a16, b16), the 'so-called black' (τὸ καλ-ούμενον μέλαν i.e. the iris)[13] and 'the white' (438a20, i.e. the visible white surrounding to the iris). There is a brief reference to a, or rather the, membrane (μῆνιγξ) of the eye at 438b2, and to its passages (πόροι) which he says are cut off when a man is wounded on the temple (438b12sqq.). He mentions also that water or fluid (ὕδωρ) flows from decomposing eyes (438a17sq.), notes that in the case of embryos this fluid is exceptionally cold and glistening (a18sq.) and remarks that the eyes of bloodless creatures are σκληρόδερμοι (438a 24).

The impression this list of references may give is that Aristotle has been to some pains to collect and take into account relevant anatomical and other data. An analysis of the texts in question reveals, however, how selective and restricted his use of evidence is. Take first the reference to the membrane of the eye at 438b2. Here

he is objecting to various versions of the thesis that vision consists of a coalescence (συμφύεσθαι) of light with light and he asks
in particular how the internal light (i.e. within the eye) can co-
alesce with the external, since the membrane is in between. What is
the membrane he is speaking of? In fact *we* should say that light[14]
has to pass through (1) the transparent cornea, (2) the anterior
chamber of the eye and (3) the lens, before it enters (4) the bulb
of the eye, which is filled with vitreous humour, at the back of
which lie the retina and the optic nerve. Although we have to wait
until the Hellenistic biologists for what became the canonical Greek
theory of the four main membranes of the eye,[15] we can trace the
growth of knowledge of these membranes in earlier writers.[16] Now it
is true that if Aristotle's objection to the doctrine of 'coalescence' is, as it appears to be, that it ignores the presence of a
solid (even if transparent) barrier, then reference to *any such* barrier will serve his purpose. It is notable, however, that his reference is quite vague. If by 'the membrane' he means the *set of*
membranes that envelop the vitreous humour, he does not make this
clear. But even if - as is perhaps more likely - he means the outer-
most membrane (the cornea) alone, to speak of this as 'the' membrane
is, to say the least, elliptical.[17]

Precisely similar remarks apply also to the references to the πόροι
of the eye at 438b14, where he supports the claim that the perceptive
faculty of the soul is not located at the outer extremity of the eye
by referring to the case of men wounded on the temple who are blinded
when the πόροι of the eye are severed. An interest in the connections between the eye and the brain can be traced back to Alcmaeon[18]
and continues in some of the later Presocratics and Hippocratic writers, including some who did not endorse Alcmaeon's view that the
brain is the ἡγεμονικόν.[19] In Aristotle there are several general
references to the πόροι of the eye in the zoological works,[20] and at
HA 495a11sqq. three such pairs are distinguished by their sizes, and
their courses described. Thus the smallest pair is situated nearest
the nostril, they go to the ἐγκέφαλον, are the most widely separated
and do not meet: both the other pairs go to the παρεγκεφαλίς, the
largest 'run side by side and do not meet', whilst the medium-sized
ones meet 'and this is particularly clear in fishes'. The precise
interpretation of the details of this text is disputed,[21] but it is

at least possible that by the medium-sized πόροι which meet Aristotle is referring to the optic nerves and their chiasma, although he
had, of course, no knowledge of their function *as nerves*,[22] and indeed when he refers to all three pairs of πόροι behind the eye indifferently as πόροι there is nothing to suggest that he differentiated
their various functions.

The πόροι referred to at *Sens*. 438b14 might be any of a number of
different passages, channels or connections behind the eye.[23] Clearly the text can be taken to refer to what we call the optic nerves
(though not, let us repeat, to them understood *as* nerves). But the
πόροι might equally well refer to other structures behind the eye,
such as the opthalmic arteries or veins. Whether or not *HA* 495a11
sqq. was written before *Sens*. 438b14, the account of three separate
pairs of πόροι behind the eye provides a clear warning of the dangers
of assuming that those mentioned at *Sens*. 438b14 must be identified
with the optic nerves. That reference, like the mention of the membrane of the eye at 438b2, is quite vague: once he has given evidence,
or what he believes to be evidence, for his immediate point - that
the faculty of sensation cannot be located at the outer extremity of
the eye - we hear no more of the πόροι.

The main topic around which much of the discussion in *Sens*. ch.2
centres is what the eye is made of. Aristotle takes some trouble to
refute the theory - found in Empedocles and the *Timaeus* - that the
eye is fire, and adopts, or rather adapts, Democritus' view that the
eye is water, correcting it by adding that vision belongs to the eye
not because it is water but because it is transparent (438a12sqq).
Again there is an appeal to facts (here ἔργα a17) to support his theory, chiefly the evidence of decomposing eyes and that of the eyes
of embryos. Yet no attempt is made to describe the structure of the
eye as a whole, although this is, of course, complex. The three
main parts Aristotle identifies quite incidentally in the course of
this chapter, pupil, iris and white, relate primarily to the superficial appearance of the eye. Apart from the one reference to the
membrane of the eye and the one reference to certain πόροι, already
mentioned, his remarks on the internal structure of the eye are confined to the point that the pupil, κόρη, consists of water. We may
take it that this refers to the vitreous humour that occupies most
of the bulb of the eye and which, in certain lesions, might produce

a watery discharge. But there is no mention of the membranes envel-
oping the vitreous humour (retina, chorioid, sclera), nor of the
lens, nor of the anterior chamber between the cornea and the lens.
There is, in fact, no mention of most of the parts that seem difficult to identify straightforwardly as water,[24] and no systematic
description of the internal structure of the eye as such at all.
Whilst evidence is cited for his conclusion, the thesis that the eye
is water is clinched by an argument from exhaustion: the eye must
admit light and so be transparent; but if transparent, then either
water or air; but not air;[25] so water.[26]

The adequacy, or otherwise, of Aristotle's discussion must, to be
sure, be judged in relation to his particular, explicit, concerns.
The problem he poses at the outset of the chapter and returns to
deal with at some length at 438b16 - 439a1 is how the five senses
are to be correlated with the four simple bodies. For these purposes identifying water as the main constituent in the eye enables
some sort of answer to be given so far as that sense-organ is concerned. Even so, the impression of confidence Aristotle gives in
moving to his conclusion that the eye is water is only possible because of the superficiality of his account.

To recapitulate: no attempt is made to describe the internal
structure and relations of the eye, nor to investigate its functioning;[27] explicit appeals to evidence are made on a number of occasions, but references to anatomical points are generally vague to
the point of serious obscurity. So far as this chapter of *Sens.* is
concerned, there is no direct evidence that Aristotle had investigated the eye by dissection. Speculation about πόροι behind the eye
antedates Aristotle, and his reference to them comes in a passage
where he is discussing wounds sustained in battle; the evidence of
water flowing from the eye also comes from observation of lesions;
and even the reference to the coldness of the fluid from the eyes of
embryos could again come from observation of a lesion, rather than
from deliberate dissection. Such empirical evidence as is used in
Sens. ch.2 could have been collected without recourse to deliberate
research. We have, then, three possibilities: either (a) at this
stage Aristotle had not attempted to dissect the eye; or if he had,
then either (b) his dissection was confined to the confirmation of
the presence of water in the eye, or (c) he ignored such other find-

ings as complicated the answer to the question of the nature of its
constitution.

My second main example concerns Aristotle's doctrine that the heart
is the common sensorium. In a passage that has already been mentioned, *Juv.* 469a10sqq., he argues that 'what is responsible for the
senses in all the sanguineous animals is in this [the heart]; for the
common sense-organ of all the sense-organs is necessarily in it. We
see two [of the senses], taste and touch, evidently extending there,[28]
so the others necessarily do so too. For it is possible for the
other sense-organs to cause movement in it, but these [taste and
touch] do not extend to the upper region [of the body] at all. And
apart from these considerations, if life is located in this part for
all animals, clearly the sensitive principle necessarily is also.'
He goes on to acknowledge (469a21sq.) that the organs of sight,
hearing and smell are located in the brain,[29] but he emphasizes both
at *Juv.* 469a12sq. and elsewhere that taste and touch 'extend to' the
heart, which is, as he repeatedly states, the ἀρχή of all sensation.[30]

Passages in the zoological treatises help to clarify some of the
details of Aristotle's views on the transmission of sensation. In
GA 743b35sqq., especially, he says that the sense-organ of the eye is
'like the other sense-organs, set upon πόροι. Whereas the organ of
touch and of taste is directly the body or some part of the body of
animals,[31] smell and hearing are πόροι connecting with the outer air
and full of connate pneuma, and ending in the φλέβια that, coming
from the heart, stretch out round the brain.'[32] Again in a difficult
and probably corrupt passage at *GA* 781a20sqq. he appears to say that
the πόροι of all the sense-organs extend to the heart and to suggest
that those of hearing end at the part where the connate pneuma causes
either pulsation or respiration.[33] Finally at *PA* 656b16sqq. he
speaks more directly of the πόροι from the eyes going to the φλέβες
around the brain and of a πόρος from the ears going to 'the back
part'.[34] Although there are inconsistencies between these texts, and
a good deal remains uncertain, Aristotle's view of sight, hearing and
smell is that all three have πόροι of some sort, and from *GA* 743b35
sqq. it appears to be certain φλέβια (all of which originate in the
heart) that provide the connection he needs between the sense-organs
in the head and the common sensorium. The reference to the connate

pneuma in that passage suggests that it acts as the vehicle by which
the movements in the sense-organs are transmitted to the heart, although, to be sure, Aristotle does not commit himself to an explicit
statement to that effect.[35]

   Yet if the main outlines of his doctrine are tolerably clear, the
difficulties it presents are formidable. This is not one of those
occasions when he was simply not aware of another, alternative view,
at least on the question of the common sensorium. On the contrary,
he refers to the doctrine – which goes back to Alcmaeon and was en-
dorsed by Plato – that the brain is the seat of sensation both briefly in our passage at *Juv.* 469a21sq. and at some length elsewhere,
for example *PA* II 10, 656a15sqq.[36] But so far as his own doctrine
goes, the confidence with which he claims that touch and taste evidently support it is striking. Taste is included presumably on the
assumption that it is a modification of touch.[37] But as for touch
itself, in so far as flesh is either the organ or the medium of this
sense, there is, we might think, no more reason for saying that touch
extends to the heart than to any other part of the body. His only
anatomical grounds for specifying the heart is that it is the source
of all the blood-vessels, and this same point provides his main
counter to the apparent difficulty that the organs of sight, hearing
and smell are located in the head. Once again his scattered anatomical references are vague. Matching his remarks about the πόροι of
the senses against possible structures is – beyond a certain, rather
superficial, point – impossible.[38] We have already noted (pp.219sq.)
the difficulty of identifying the πόροι of the eye. Similarly when
he speaks of a πόρος leading back from the ear (*PA* 656b18sq.) and
ending in the φλέβια round the brain (*GA* 744a1sqq.) it is not at all
clear precisely what he may be referring to. The external acoustic
meatus continues behind and below the tympanic membrane[39] into the
pharyngo-tympanic or Eustachian tube, leading, of course, not to the
back of the brain but down into the pharynx.[40] Nor is it easy to
identify an obvious candidate for this πόρος from among the structures behind the middle or inner ear.[41] As to the sense of smell,
while the passages connecting with the external air (*GA* 744a1sqq.)
are obviously the nostrils, it is again in no way clear what precise
structure (if any) he had in mind when he implied that these πόροι
too end in φλέβια round the brain.

Although the question of the common sensorium and its connections
with the sense-organs had been much discussed before Aristotle, and
it was certainly open to him to investigate aspects of this problem
by dissection, there is little enough evidence, in *Juv.*[42] or in the
zoological treatises, of his attempting to do so. In this case his
own doctrine was principally based on the argument that the ἀρχή of
sensation must be identified with that of life itself. As he puts
it at *Juv.* 469a17sq., 'if life is located in this part for all animals, clearly the sensitive principle necessarily is also', and
elsewhere he often claims that there must be a single principle of
life, motion, sensation, nutrition and growth.[43] Now the view that
the heart is the principle of life is, as we noted, given empirical
support in the supposed observation that it is the first part of
the embryo to develop,[44] and that it is the first part to contain
blood is cited as evidence that it is the seat of sensation, for
example at *PA* 666a10 - b1.[45] But given first that he believed there
was an overwhelming theoretical reason for holding that the heart is
the seat of sensation, and secondly that *some* connection between
each of the sense-organs and the heart could be found, we may suspect that even quite detailed knowledge of the structures associated
with the sense-organs would not have shaken his conviction in the
correctness of his doctrine.

My next example relates to Aristotle's views on the nature and function of the brain.[46] The opposition between brain and heart is one
of the corner-stones of his physiology. Thus according to *Sens.* 438
b29sq.[47] the brain is the 'most fluid' and the coldest part of the
body (it is proportionately larger in man than in any other animal,
and particularly cold),[48] and the heart, as the hottest part of the
body, is said at *Sens.* 439a2sqq. to balance the brain. The first
problem here is the account of the brain itself. Whilst in passages
in *HA* especially he distinguishes two membranes, ὑμένες, that envelop
the brain[49] and identifies the 'so-called παρεγκεφαλίς' (i.e. cere-
bellum),[50] he adopts the view that the back of the head is empty and
hollow in all animals.[51] Although various conjectures have been
made as to the empirical basis of this doctrine,[52] it may be that
his adopting it owes more to the fact that a similar view appears in
some of the medical writers[53] than to any observations he had carried

out himself. Another puzzle is his claim that the brain is bloodless and has no φλέψ in it.[54] Finally there is the doctrine of the
special coldness of the brain. Even when we bear in mind the complexity of Aristotle's use of 'hot' and 'cold', and his careful distinctions between acquired and innate, accidental and essential, potential and actual, heat and cold,[55] his clear statement that the
brain is cold 'to the touch' is not one that can have been based on,
or checked by, an examination of a recently dead subject.[56] Yet the
doctrine of the coldness of the brain is fundamental to his conception of its function, which he describes as being to preserve the
whole body by counteracting the heat of the heart.[57]

One of the many contexts in which this theory is applied is in
the account of sleep and waking, which he explains in terms of an
interplay of hot and cold, specifically in terms of a concentration
(σύνοδος) or recoil (ἀντιπερίστασις) of the hot when matter from the
lower region is carried up to the brain and cooled there. While the
core of his theory is not in doubt, some of its details are hazy.
Thus there is some fluctuation (though perhaps no conflict) in the
terms in which he describes the material cause of sleep. Sometimes
he speaks of the evaporation from the food,[58] or, more loosely, of
the food itself;[59] he distinguishes the liquid[60] and the bodily[61]
parts of the evaporation, and from 458a2sqq. he introduces a further
distinction between two kinds of evaporation, the περιττωματική (responsible for catarrhs) and the τρόφιμος (responsible for sleep).[62]
More importantly, although he often speaks of the φλέβες or πόροι
which act as communicating links between heart and brain, these references are, with one exception, all quite unspecific. The exception is 455b6sqq., which mentions the φλέβες in the neck which, when
pressed, cause loss of sensation.[63] Elsewhere his references are
indeterminate, and this is, perhaps, all the more surprising in view
of the fact that he several times adduces the 'thinness' and 'narrowness' of the φλέβες round the brain (along with its coldness) as a
contributory factor in causing sleep.[64] Yet as with his remarks on
the channels of sensation, so too here Aristotle appears satisfied
with the fact that links of some sort can be found between heart and
brain and attempts no detailed account of their anatomy.

My final example concerns Aristotle's views on the relations between

the lung and the heart and on the structure of the latter. An impressive range of anatomical and zoological data is cited in the
course of his account of respiration. He takes his examples from a
wide variety of animal species, noting, for instance, that 'no animal has yet been seen' that has both lung and gills,[65] and observing
a contrast between tortoises and frogs on the one hand and fish on
the other in that the former discharge air when forcibly suffocated
in water, while in the latter no such discharge occurs.[66] He distinguishes inspiration through the nostrils and through the windpipe (ἀρτηρία), knows that only the latter is essential for life,
and specifies that in the former too the air passes through the
channel beside the uvula at the back of the roof of the mouth.[67] At
Resp. 476a31sqq. he gives a clear, if brief, account of the function
of the epiglottis and notes that in birds and oviparous quadrupeds,
where the epiglottis is absent, this function is performed by the
contraction of the windpipe.[68] We have seen that both in the context of the structure of the heart, and in that of the relation between heart and lung or gills, Aristotle deliberately draws back
from a detailed anatomical description.[69] On the other hand it is
in connection with the organs of respiration that he particularly
criticizes earlier writers for their ignorance of internal anatomy,
and these passages suggest that he is confident enough of the ac-
curacy of his own views on this topic even if he does not feel it
necessary to go into them at length.[70] Since he believes that the
function of respiration is to cool the vital heat,[71] his theory requires some connection between heart and lung or gills. So far as
his account of fish goes, where he speaks of an αὐλὸς φλεβονευρώδης
running from the heart to the middle 'where the gills join' (Resp.
478b7sqq.), this can be vindicated in the main.[72] Yet when we follow up what he has to say on the links between heart and lung[73] in
other sanguineous animals, we encounter problems.[74] Both at HA 496
a22sqq. and at 513a35sqq. we are told that there are connections
between all three cavities of the heart and the lung. Yet in animals with lungs, the lungs are directly connected with - at most -
two vessels of the heart. Thus in man the pulmonary artery (divided into right and left branches) and the pulmonary veins (divided
into right and left pairs) are connected with the right ventricle
and the left atrium respectively. It is true that in both passages

Aristotle notes that the connection is distinct in only one case –
which suggests that his theory of three connections is partly based
on inference. Yet the reference to the distinctness of only one
πόρος is itself strange since in most large vivipara the pulmonary
veins are not much less prominent structures than the pulmonary arteries.

This takes us to the vexed question of his account of the heart
itself.[75] Apart from *Somn.* 458a15sqq., the three main texts that
contain descriptions of the heart are *HA* I 17, *HA* III 3 and *PA* III
4. In each of these texts he speaks of three cavities, a right, a
middle and a left, although at *HA* 513a27sqq. and *PA* 666b21sq. he
suggests that in some smaller animals the heart has only two cavities, and in others only one.[76] Moreover the *HA* and *PA* passages
agree in identifying the right hand cavity as the largest, the left
as the smallest and the middle as intermediate in size.[77] Since at
HA 513b1-5 (cf. 496a25sqq.) the aorta is clearly stated to be attached to the middle cavity, and the great blood-vessel (i.e. Vena
Cava) to the largest, right cavity, this has been taken to establish that the middle cavity there is what we term the left ventricle (the right atrium being either deemed to belong to this cavity,
or considered as the dilated junction of the superior and inferior
Vena Cava).

There can be little doubt that, as D'Arcy Thompson put it,[78] the
account of the vascular system 'is so far true to nature that it is
clear evidence of minute inquiry'.[79] At the same time, as Thompson
also recognized, obscurities and inconsistencies remain,[80] and one
apparent inconsistency between *Somn.* and the zoological treatises
particularly concerns us. This relates to the identification of
the three cavities themselves, for whereas *HA* 513b1sqq. clearly
states that the aorta is attached to the middle cavity, *Somn.* 458a
16-19 no less clearly implies that the aorta is connected to the
left cavity. Yet what *Somn.* has in common with the accounts in the
zoological works is as revealing as what it does not. The role of
the heart as ἀρχή of the blood-vessels is fundamental and maintained
consistently throughout.[81] But when the heart has several cavities
(and in Aristotle's view it is better to have more than one) the
problem of the location of the ἀρχή arises. Now despite the evident divergence between *Somn.* and *HA* III 3 on the identity of the

cavities, *Somn.* agrees with *PA* that the middle cavity is 'common to'
the other two. At *PA* 666b32sqq., having argued that it is better
to have two cavities than one on the grounds that the main blood-
vessels, the great blood-vessel and the aorta, are two, he goes on
to say that it is better still to have three cavities, so that the
middle and odd one can be the common ἀρχή for the other two. Again
in *Somn.* 458a16sq. the middle cavity is said to be common to the
other two, and the place where the separation of the purer and less
pure blood occurs – despite the fact that the middle cavity is not
the same cavity as that called by that name in *HA* III 3. While
there is, as we said, ample evidence of close observation, using
dissection, in Aristotle's accounts of the heart, he is also concerned, especially but by no means exclusively in *PA*, with questions
of value, pointing out, for instance, that the heart, as the noblest
organ, occupies the noblest position in the body.[82] His doctrine of
the middle cavity as common to the other two reflects this preoccupation,[83] and if, as seems likely in view of the agreement on the
relative dimensions of the three cavities, the account of them in
PA III 4 is to be equated with that in *HA* III 3, it would appear
that the doctrine of the middle cavity as ἀρχή persisted even when
his views on the identity of the cavities changed. In this case,
what we have is not, or not only, the result of direct observation,[84]
but the application of preconceived ideas concerning the superiority
of the middle and its fitness to be ἀρχή.[85] Indeed one might even
conjecture that concern with the question of identifying the common
ἀρχή in the multi-cavitied heart was one factor that prevented Aristotle from seeing the heart as a two-sided, four-vesseled organ.[86]

The weakness of the work of Aristotle's predecessors in anatomy is
apparent both from his reports and from the Hippocratic writers. We
can be reasonably certain both that dissection had been practised
before Aristotle, and that its use was very far from extensive.[87]
Thus his comments on earlier views of the blood-vessels in *HA* III 2,
511b13sqq., make it clear first that some of his predecessors had
dissected animals in this connection, and secondly that this was not
the only method they had used, since some investigators relied on
what would be observed externally by examining emaciated living men.
The accounts he goes on to ascribe to Syennesis of Cyprus, Diogenes

of Apollonia and Polybus in particular bear out his general stric-
tures on their work.[88]

Aristotle's own use of dissection, and the range of his zoological
researches, were undoubtedly far wider than those of any earlier writer. Nevertheless the evidence we have considered concerning some
problems tackled in *PN* provides grounds for caution. Although a
fair body of zoological data is deployed in *PN*, and some of his anatomical references are accurate enough, some others are extremely
vague. In part this can be said to be because he deliberately omits
detail that is irrelevant to his immediate concerns: but in part the
vagueness of some of his accounts reflects the imprecision of his
ideas or the limitations of his knowledge. Although in one case (the
account of the three chambers of the heart) there is an apparent conflict between passages in *Somn.* and the zoological works, and it is
possible that these texts correspond to different stages in his investigation of that problem, there are several instances where the
supplementary material on anatomical points that is provided by the
zoological treatises is far from removing all the obscurities or
difficulties in Aristotle's views. Thus all his references to com-
munications between the heart and the sense-organs, and between the
heart and the brain, suffer from a greater or lesser degree of imprecision. In such cases a developmental hypothesis does not resolve
our problem, though that is not to deny that such hypotheses may
have a bearing on the issue.

PA I 5, whenever it was composed, suggests an open-ended programme
of research in zoology. Yet the difficulties of implementing any
such programme were immense. It is all too easy for us to assume
that once the method of dissection[89] had begun to be employed on
particular topics, it would rapidly be applied systematically and on
a large scale. Yet not only were the practical difficulties severe,[90]
but dissection had always to be guided by an idea of what to look for
and what there was to find. So far as the evidence we have taken
from *PN* goes, this shows the overriding importance of theoretical
considerations, both in determining the problems to be investigated
(as when he deals with the question of the constitution of the eye
very largely in terms of the problem of correlating five senses with
four elements) and in interpreting the findings of those investigations (as in the interpretation of the role of the chambers of the

heart, or that of the function of the various ducts he saw as the
links between different parts or organs in the body). In the *PN*
Aristotle cites anatomical and zoological data quite freely, and in
places quite effectively, both to disprove his opponents' theories
and to support his own. Yet in the latter connection the role of
observation is rather to corroborate, than to test, his theories –
let alone to attempt to falsify them. While some of his remarks may
create the superficial appearance that he was drawing on a considerable body of fairly detailed and thorough research, an examination
of how anatomical evidence is used in the cases we have discussed
shows that this appearance can, on occasion, be misleading. On
certain physiological problems – such as the temperature of the
brain – he seems not to have attempted to check his theory directly;
and on others his investigations were sometimes quite restricted,
being indeed, in some cases, confined to providing the barest anatomical grounds to justify his theories.

NOTES

1 Many of the finest descriptions occur in the later books of *HA*
  (e.g. VI and IX) whose authenticity is doubtful. The general
  point can, however, be established well enough from *PA* and *GA*.

2 See especially *PA* 644b28-31, 645a1-4, 7-36 and cf. *PA* I 1, 640b
  17sqq. At 645a6sq. and 21-3 he recommends the study of every
  kind of animal, so far as possible, without exception. That this
  enquiry is directed to the formal and final causes especially is
  made clear in both ch.5 and ch.1.

3 This study itself is, of course, seen as of primary importance
  for the study of nature, *De An.* 402a4-6.

4 See *Sens.* 436a1-11.

5 Much relevant material is, however, collected in W.Ogle, *Aristotle on youth and old age, life and death and respiration* (London
  1897).

6 On the discrepancies between this and Aristotle's other accounts
  of the heart, see pp.227sq.

7 I am most grateful to J.Brunschwig for raising the question of
  the precise sense of the contrast at *Resp.* 478a35sq. πρὸς μὲν
  τὴν ὄψιν ἐκ τῶν ἀνατομῶν δεῖ θεωρεῖν, πρὸς δ' ἀκρίβειαν ἐκ τῶν
  ἱστοριῶν, and distinguishing the two possibilities, (*a*) that

Aristotle is inviting his audience to practise dissection to
confirm his account, and (b) that he is inviting them to consult
anatomical diagrams. As has been noted, e.g. by E.Heitz (who
conveniently collected the relevant passages, *Die verlorenen
Schriften des Aristoteles* (Leipzig 1865), 70sqq.), when Aristotle refers to ἀνατομαί elsewhere, this is sometimes to actual
dissection (e.g. *PA* 677a9, *GA* 746a22, 764a35, 771b32, 779a8),
but sometimes to a work, now lost, which evidently contained,
and may even have consisted in, diagrams (cf. διαγραφή at *HA*
497a32, 525a8sq., cf. τὰ ἐν ταῖς ἀνατομαῖς διαγεγραμμένα at *HA*
566a14sq. and *GA* 746a14sq. which refers to ἔκ τε τῶν παραδειγ-
μάτων τῶν ἐν ταῖς ἀνατομαῖς καὶ τῶν ἐν ταῖς ἱστορίαις γεγραμ-
μένων; the fact that at *PA* 684b4 he refers to ἀνατομαί where he
has just been describing the *external* parts of the Crustacea
suggests that the work contained diagrams based on external observation as well as on dissection). Although the reference to
τὰ ἀνατεμνόμενα at *Resp.* 478a27 has been taken, e.g. by W.D.
Ross, to relate to dissection, I agree with J.Brunschwig that
at 478a35sq. it seems more likely that what is being opposed to
the exact account of the 'histories' is not the practice of
dissecting, but rather anatomical diagrams: what is implied is
not that dissection is inexact, but that diagrammatic representations are. One may compare *PA* 680a1sqq. where Aristotle contrasts what can be made clear better by a verbal account with
what can to sight (τὰ μὲν γὰρ τῷ λόγῳ τὰ δὲ πρὸς τὴν ὄψιν αὐτῶν
σαφηνίζειν δεῖ μᾶλλον) although elsewhere he is content enough
to refer to ἀνατομαί (with or without the 'histories') for an
exact (or more exact) account on an anatomical point (*HA* 511a13
sq., *PA* 668b28sqq., 696b14sqq., cf. *HA* 509b22sqq.).

8 Cf. also *Juv.* 468b31sqq.

9 Cf. especially *PA* 665a33sqq. and *HA* VI 3, the latter recording
sustained observations of the development of a hen's egg including the heart's first appearance as a blood spot that palpita-
tes and moves as though endowed with life (the so-called 'punc-
tum saliens'). Cf. Ogle (*op.cit. n.5*), 110 n.24: 'the heart is
not actually the first structure that appears in the embryo,
but it is the first part to enter actively into its functions'.

10 Reading τοῦτο at 454b23, with Bywater, W.D.Ross and others. The
argument is that sleep is a necessary affection of the perceptive faculty (which every animal must have).

11 These are (1) the part by which food is taken in, (2) that by
which residues are discharged and (3) what is intermediate between them, see *Juv.* 468a13sqq. That the ἀρχή of the nutritive
soul is in the centre of the body is said to be established both
κατὰ τὴν αἴσθησιν and κατὰ τὸν λόγον at 468a20sqq.

12 *Juv.* 469a12sqq., see pp.222sqq.

13 437b1, to be taken, with W.D.Ross, as the iris, not (with Beare,
for example, taking καί as epexegetic) as 'the central part'.
The main parts of the eye are identified at *HA* 491b21sq. as τὸ
μὲν ὑγρόν, ᾧ βλέπει, κόρη, τὸ δὲ περὶ τοῦτο μέλαν, τὸ δ' ἐκτὸς
τούτου λευκόν. Cf. also 492a1sqq.

14 Aristotle himself denies both that light, which is an ἐνέργεια,
   travels (De An. 418b9sqq., 20sqq., Sens. 446b27sq.) and that
   vision takes place because of something issuing from the eye
   (Sens. 438a25sqq., cf. 437b12sqq., Top. 105b6sq.: rather, according to Sens. 438b3sqq., it is a process, κίνησις, in the medium
   that causes sight). Yet dealing especially with the phenomena
   of reflection he often speaks of sight (ὄψις, that is the visual
   ray) reaching or not reaching its object (e.g. Cael. 290a17sqq.,
   Mete. III 374b13sqq., 378a4sqq., cf. 373b2sqq.).

15 That is (1) κερατοειδής (corresponding to the cornea and sclera),
   (2) χοριοειδής or ῥαγοειδής (the chorioid), (3) ἀραχνοειδής or
   ἀμφιβληστροειδής (the retina) and (4) κρυσταλλοειδής (the capsu-
   lar sheath of the lens), see, e.g. Rufus, Onom. 154, ps.-Rufus,
   Anat. 170sqq., Celsus, De medicina VII 7 13, where in each case
   the work of Herophilus in particular is referred to.

16 The first fairly detailed account of the various membranes in the
   eye is probably that in Loc. Hom. ch.2 (VI 280 2sqq., Littré)
   which identifies three such membranes (μήνιγγες), a thick outer
   one, a thinner middle one and a third inner one 'which guards the
   moist part' (cf. also Carn. ch.17, VIII 604 21sqq.). The exact
   date of Loc. Hom. cannot be determined, nor is it certain that
   Aristotle knew it. But some interest in the structure of the eye
   goes right back to Empedocles, to the very fragment quoted by
   Aristotle at Sens. 437b26sqq., even though Empedocles does not
   describe the 'membranes' (μήνιγγες) and 'tissues' (ὀθοναί) he refers to in the eye at all precisely; and later Democritus too not
   only identified the contents of the eye as water (as Aristotle
   tells us) but also (according to Theophrastus, Sens. para 50)
   distinguished between the dense, thin, 'outer membrane', and the
   porous inner parts.

17 Cf. De An. 420a14sq. and GA 780a26 (where the term is δέρμα) and
   GA 781a20.

18 Chalcidius, In Ti. ch.246, 256 16sqq., Waszink (on which see
   G.E.R.Lloyd, 'Alcmaeon and the early history of dissection', Sud-
   hoffs Archiv 59 (1975), 115sqq. and J.Mansfeld, 'Alcmaeon: 'Phy-
   sikos' or physician?', in Kephalaion, Studies in Greek philosophy
   and its continuation offered to C.J. de Vogel, ed. J.Mansfeld and
   L.M. de Rijk (Assen 1975), 26sqq.), and Theophrastus, Sens. 25sq.

19 References to connections of some sort between eye and brain (generally φλέβια or φλέβες) are found in, for example, Theophrastus'
   accounts of Diogenes of Apollonia (Sens. 40sqq.) and Democritus
   (Sens. 50), in Loc. Hom. ch.2 (VI 278 21sqq.) and Carn. ch.17
   (VIII 604 21sqq.).

20 See especially PA 656b16sqq., GA 743b35sqq. At GA 744a6sqq. he
   shows some knowledge of the fact that the eyes change position
   in relation to the brain during the course of the embryo's development (cf. Sens. 438b28sqq. on the eye being formed from the
   brain).

21 See, e.g., H.Magnus, Die Anatomie des Auges bei den Griechen und

Römern (Leipzig 1878), 25sq., W.Ogle, *Aristotle on the parts of animals* (London 1882), 176sq., and note to *PA* 656b17 in *The works of Aristotle translated into English*, ed. J.A.Smith and W.D.Ross, Vol. V *De partibus animalium* (Oxford 1912), F.Solmsen, 'Greek philosophy and the discovery of the nerves', *Museum Helveticum* 18 (1961), 173 and E.Clarke, 'Aristotelian concepts of the form and function of the brain', *Bulletin of the History of Medicine* 37 (1963), 3.

22 Knowledge of the nervous system as such does not antedate the Hellenistic biologists, see Solmsen (*art.cit. n.21*), 150sqq.

23 Cf. G.R.T.Ross, *Aristotle De sensu and De memoria* (Cambridge 1906), 143.

24 The 'white' is, however, said to be fat and oily at 438a20sq. when he speaks of its role as protection for the fluid of the eye.

25 Air is rejected partly on the grounds that water is εὐφυλακτότερον and εὐπιλητότερον, 438a15sq.

26 See 438a15sqq. and b6sqq.: ἀνάγκη ἄρα ὕδωρ εἶναι, ἐπειδὴ οὐκ ἀήρ (W.D.Ross: other editors read καὶ ἀνάγκη κτλ.).

27 Yet elsewhere Aristotle quite often refers to the effects of maiming on an animal's vital functions (e.g. *Juv.* 468b15, *IA* 708 b4sqq., *GA* 774b31sqq., *HA* 519a27sqq., and many passages referring to insects living when cut up), and although many of his observations may well have been carried out on animals that had become mutilated naturally, the frequency of the references may suggest some deliberate human intervention.

28 δύο δὲ φανερῶς ἐνταῦθα συντεινούσας ὁρῶμεν, 469a12sq., cf. a20sq. αἱ μὲν τῶν αἰσθήσεων φανερῶς συντείνουσι πρὸς τὴν καρδίαν.

29 Cf. *Sens.* 438b25sqq.: the organ of smell has its proper place near the brain, a cold organ, since cold matter is potentially hot (and smell belongs to fire, b20sq.), and 444a8sqq.: the ability to perceive odours that are fragrant *per se* (which he believes man alone to possess) is a safeguard to health, for man's brain is particularly cold and so particularly in need of the compensatory heat from such smells. Cf. a similar argument on the eye, *Sens.* 438b27sqq. and *PA* 656a37sqq.

30 Cf. also *Sens.* 439a1sq. and, e.g., *PA* 656a27sqq. (which refers to a discussion ἐν τοῖς περὶ αἰσθήσεως).

31 Aristotle sometimes says that the sense-organ of touch is flesh or what is analogous to it (e.g. *PA* 647a19sqq.), though he sometimes describes flesh as the medium, not the organ, of touch (*PA* 656b34sqq., *De An.* 423b22sqq., cf. *PA* 653b24-30, where both suggestions are made, and see Ogle, *The works of Aristotle* (*op.cit. n.21*), note *ad loc*).

32 *HA* 514a21sq. also speaks of φλέβες ending in the sense-organs.

33 The difficulties of the passage are fully discussed by A.L.Peck,
   Aristotle, Generation of animals (Loeb ed. London and Cambridge
   (Mass.) 1943), 563sq. The reference to the part where the pneuma
   causes either pulsation or respiration is, as A.Platt (*The works
   of Aristotle translated into English*, ed. J.A.Smith and W.D.Ross,
   Vol. V *De generatione animalium* (Oxford 1912), note *ad loc.*)
   pointed out, unintelligible, since no animal that respires lacks
   a heart. The doctrine concerning the pores of hearing here evidently contradicts both *GA* 743b35sqq. and *PA* 656b16sqq.

34 Cf. E.Clarke and J.Stannard, 'Aristotle on the anatomy of the
   brain', *Journal of the History of Medicine* 18 (1963), 134sqq.

35 The alternative would be to consider that the blood itself trans-
   mits the movements from the sense-organs (as might be thought to be
   suggested at *Insomn.* 461b11sq., 462a8sqq.). But blood itself lacks
   sensation (as he often says, e.g. *PA* 666a16sq.) although sensation is
   confined to those parts that have blood (e.g. *PA* 656b20sq.).

36 Among the objections he raises to this view are (1) that the
   brain itself is devoid of sense (*PA* 652b4sq., 656a23sq.) and
   (2) that it has no continuity with the organs of sense (*PA* 652b
   sqq.) and he was no doubt influenced also by his view that the
   brain is cold and bloodless (its function being to counteract
   the heat of the heart, see pp.224sq.) and by his observation
   that not all animals have a brain or analogous organ (see
   Ogle, *Aristotle on the parts of animals* (*op.cit. n.21*), 172sq.
   and *The works of Aristotle* (*op.cit. n.21*), note to 656a24).

37 Elsewhere, however, he recognizes the tongue as the organ of
   taste, for example in his discussion of the dual nature of the
   sense-organs, *PA* 656b36sq.

38 One major complication is that the term πόρος is so general and
   can refer to structures as diverse as the nostrils and infra-
   sensible apertures in the skin.

39 Cf. the reference to the μῆνιγξ at *De An.* 420a14.

40 As indeed is recognized by Aristotle at *HA* 492a19sq. That he
   has some idea of the internal structure of the ear is clear
   from his comparing it with a trumpet shell (*HA* 492a16sq., cf.
   also the reference to ἕλικες at *De An.* 420a13) and at *HA* 492a20
   (cf. 514a15sqq.) he speaks of a φλέψ from the brain to the ear.

41 Clarke and Stannard (*art.cit. n.34*), 146sqq., however, suggest
   that the idea may have originated from observations of the endo-
   lymphatic duct and sacs of a turtle or similar reptile.

42 *Juv.* ch.3 ends with a reference to another discussion of why some
   senses clearly extend to the heart, while others are located in
   the head. This is taken by Ogle and W.D.Ross, for example, to refer to *PA* II 10, 656a27 - 657a12. Yet 656a27sqq. begins with a
   reference to 'the works on sensation' (see above, n.30) and 656b
   16sqq. is, as we have seen (p.222), not much fuller or clearer
   than *Juv.* on points of anatomy.

43 E.g. *Somn.* 455b34sqq., *PA* 647a21sqq., 665a10sqq., 666b13sqq.
   Feelings of pleasure and pain and so on, as well as sense-percep-
   tions, are located in the heart, e.g. at *PA* 666a11sqq., 669a19
   sqq.

44 Cf. above p.217. At *GA* 743b25sqq. he reverses the usual argument: because the heart is the seat of sensation, it comes to be
   first.

45 Other factors that weighed with Aristotle are that the heart or
   an analogous organ is present in all animals, and that it is in
   the central position in the body, in the place appropriate to
   the controlling part.

46 Cf. Clarke and Stannard (*art.cit. n.34*), 130sqq. I am grateful
   to Professor P.Moraux for drawing attention to the important
   criticisms already mounted by Galen (e.g. *De Usu Partium* VIII 3)
   of Aristotle's views on the function of the brain (see P.Moraux,
   'Galien et Aristote', *Images of man in ancient and medieval
   thought. Studia G.Verbeke ... dicata* (Louvain 1976), 127-46).

47 Cf. *Somn.* 457b29sq. and many other passages, e.g. *GA* 782b17.

48 *Sens.* 444a8sqq., 28sqq. (see above, n.29) and cf. *HA* 494b27sqq.
   The doctrine of a cold brain appears also in the Hippocratic
   works *Liqu.* ch.2, VI 122 3sqq., and *Carn.* ch.4, VIII 588 14sqq.

49 *HA* 494b29sqq. At *PA* 652b30 and *GA* 744a10, however, he speaks of
   a single μῆνιγξ round the brain.

50 E.g. *HA* 494b31sq., 495a12.

51 *HA* 491a34sq., 494b33sqq., *PA* 656b12sq.

52 D'Arcy W. Thompson, *The works of Aristotle translated into English*,
   ed. J.A.Smith and W.D.Ross, Vol. IV *Historia animalium* (Oxford
   1910), note to *HA* 491b1, suggested that the view may have arisen
   from an association of hearing with air and a recognition of the
   fact that the auditory region of the skull contains air-spaces.
   Ogle, *Aristotle on the parts of animals* (*op.cit. n.21*), 174sqq.
   and *The works of Aristotle* (*op.cit. n.21*), note to *PA* 656b13,
   noted that a similar view is found in the Hippocratic writers but
   added that it may have derived support from an examination of the
   brain of cold-blooded animals (fish and reptiles) and remarked
   that the observation, in *GA* 744a17, that the volume of the brain
   changes as the embryo develops suggests that Aristotle had seen
   this in embryonic fish.

53 E.g. *Morb.* II ch.8, VII 16 11sqq., cf. *VC* ch.2, III 188 11sq.,
   190 12sq., 192 10sqq.

54 E.g. *HA* 495a4sqq., 514a18sq., *PA* 652a35sq. There are, however,
   φλέβια in the membrane round the brain from both the 'great
   blood-vessel' (i.e. Vena Cava) and the aorta, e.g. *PA* 652b27sqq.
   Cf. *Sens.* 444a10sqq. which speaks of the blood in the φλέβια
   round the brain as 'thin', 'pure' and 'easily cooled'.

55 See especially *PA* II 2.

56 κατὰ τὴν θίξιν *PA* 652a34sq., cf. *HA* 495a6. As J.F.Payne, *Harvey and Galen* (London 1897), 39 n.1, and Ogle, *The works of Aristotle* (*op.cit. n.21*), note *ad loc.*, remark, the doctrine of the coldness of the brain continued to be taught by Harvey in his *Prelectiones anatomiae universalis, Lectures on the whole of anatomy* (1616), ed. C.D.O'Malley, F.N.L.Poynter, K.F.Russell (Berkeley 1961) even though some thirty years previously Piccolomini (whose *Anatomicae praelectiones* (Rome 1586) was well known to Harvey) had recorded an experiment on a dog (whether living or dead he does not say) in which he found that the heart and the brain felt almost equally hot to the touch (*op.cit.* 275).

57 E.g. *PA* 652b6sq., 653a32sqq., cf. *Sens.* 439a2sqq.

58 *Somn.* 456b19sq., 33sq., 457a25, 29, b14, cf. πνεῦμα at 457a12.

59 *Somn.* 457a5.

60 *Somn.* 456b25, reading τὸ τε, cf. 457a19, 24. At *PA* 653a12sq. he speaks of the ἐπίρρυσις of the blood from the food.

61 *Somn.* 456b25, cf. 457b20, 458a26.

62 'The hot' is sometimes what is carried up to the brain (*Somn.* 458 a1, cf. 456b21sq., 457b1), sometimes what causes (other) substances to rise (*Somn.* 458a27 of the connate heat).

63 Cf. *HA* 514a2sqq. where the φλέβες in question are named σφαγίτιδες.

64 General references to the φλέβες occur at *Somn.* 457a13 (where he is comparing epilepsy with sleep) and b21. At 457a21sqq. he explains why the ἀδηλόφλεβοι sleep a lot in terms of the narrowness of their φλέβες – while the φλεβώδεις do not because of the εὔροια of their φλέβες (W.D.Ross reads πόροι). Again at 458a5sqq. he cites the thinness and narrowness of the φλέβες round the brain as contributing to its being kept cool and its not receiving the evaporation easily. Cf. 457b13sqq. referring to the cooling of the πόροι and places in the brain.

65 *Resp.* 476a6sq. Ogle (*op.cit. n.5*), 125 n.106, pointed out that there are exceptions to this general rule.

66 *Resp.* 471a31sqq. This was one of the points that led him to conclude that fish do not respire, but effect the necessary cooling of their vital heat directly by the intake of water, e.g. *Resp.* 476a1sq.

67 *Resp.* 473a17sqq., 474a7sqq., 17sqq., criticizing Empedocles.

68 Cf. *HA* 495b17sqq., where he rejects the view (found in some Hippocratic writers as well as in Plato, *Ti.* 70c, 91a) that drink goes to the lungs via the windpipe.

69 See above p.216 on *Somn.* 458a20sq., *Resp.* 478a26sqq., 35sqq.

70 See above pp.217sq. on *Resp.* 470b8sqq., 471b23sqq.

71 He cites as evidence for this (1) that exhaled breath is hotter than inhaled, e.g. *Resp.* 472b33sqq., and (2) that we breathe more frequently in hot weather, 472a31sqq.

72 See Ogle (*op.cit. n.5*), 131 nn.135 and 136. Cf. also *HA* 507a5sqq.

73 A minor difficulty is his statement that the lung is single: he remarks, however, that the lung has a tendency to be double, even if he goes on to say that this is least discernible in man (*HA* 495a32sqq., cf. *PA* 669b23sqq. and *HA* 513b16sqq.).

74 *HA* 495b14sqq. appears to suggest that when the windpipe is distended with air, the air can actually be seen entering the heart (if αὐτήν at b16 refers, as is generally thought, to the heart). *HA* 496a27sqq. notes more exactly, however, that there is no common πόρος between the ducts from the heart and those from the windpipe, although the former receive air from the latter διὰ τὴν σύναψιν.

75 The problem has been extensively discussed by, for example, T.H. Huxley, 'On certain errors respecting the structure of the heart attributed to Aristotle', *Nature* 21 (1880), 1sqq., Ogle, *Aristotle on the parts of animals* (*op.cit. n.21*), 197sqq., D'Arcy Thompson (*op.cit. n.52*), note to *HA* 513a35, A.Platt, 'Aristotle on the heart', in *Studies in the history and method of science*, ed. C.Singer, Vol. 2 (Oxford 1921), 521sqq., S.Byl, 'Note sur la place du coeur et la valorisation de la ΜΕΣΟΤΗΣ dans la biologie d'Aristote', *L'Antiquité Classique* 37 (1968), 467sqq., J.R.Shaw, 'Models for cardiac structure and function in Aristotle', *Journal of the History of Biology* 5 (1972), 355sqq. and C.R.S.Harris, *The heart and the vascular system in ancient Greek medicine from Alcmaeon to Galen* (Oxford 1973), 121sqq.

76 The number of cavities in the heart is indeed less than four in some reptiles and fish, though the number does not depend on the size of the animal, see Ogle, *Aristotle on the parts of animals* (*op.cit. n.21*), 199.

77 *HA* 496a20sqq., 513a32sqq., *PA* 666b35sqq. *Somn.* is silent on the relative sizes of the three cavities.

78 (*op.cit. n.52*), note to *HA* 513a35.

79 Apart from his clear account of many particular blood-vessels, he draws a general distinction between the textures of the Vena Cava and aorta, describing the former as ὑμενώδης and δερματώδης, and the latter as narrower and σφόδρα νευρώδης, *HA* 513b7sqq. He speaks of the sinews (νεῦρα) within the heart (though he does not identify its valves) at *HA* 496a13, 515a28sqq., *PA* 666b13sq.; and he knows that the heart in man is inclined to the left side of the body, e.g. *HA* 496a15sq., *PA* 666b6sqq.

80 The chief difficulty in the fullest account, *HA* III 3 relates to
the two sentences 513b2sqq. and b7, in which he appears to say
first that the great blood-vessel passes διὰ τοῦ κοίλου τοῦ μέσου,
i.e. through the middle cavity (not, as Ogle translated, 'through
the centre of the cavity') and then that it stretches to or towards (εἰς) the aorta from the heart. The only way to begin to
square these statements with anatomical fact is to suppose that
in both cases he is describing the foetal heart. Thus 513b2sqq.
might be taken to refer to the foramen ovale (by which blood
passes direct from the right to the left atrium) and b7 to the
ductus arteriosus (by which the pulmonary artery communicates
with the aorta), both structures present in the foetus which close
up after birth. Although it has been argued, most recently by
Shaw, that Aristotle had investigated the foetal heart, what we
have in these passages seems more likely to be either a mistake,
or more probably, a corrupt text. Most modern editors take 513
b7 at least as corrupt, and the transposition or deletion of
μέσου at b3 would allow the φλέψ mentioned there to be taken to
refer either, as Ogle wanted, to the pulmonary artery, or to the
superior Vena Cava.

81 E.g. *Somn*. 458a15sq., *HA* 513a21sq., *PA* 665b14sqq., 666a6sqq.,
31sqq. *PA* 666b24sq. states that the blood comes to be first in
the heart, though *Somn*. 458a17sq. seems to envisage the possibility of the right and left cavities drawing from (δέχεσθαι)
the great blood-vessel and aorta respectively.

82 E.g. *PA* 665b20sqq. and cf. 666b6sqq. for the explanation he gives
for the heart being on the (inferior) left side in man.

83 He also says that the blood in the middle cavity is purer than in
the other two, and of intermediate heat, *PA* 667a4sqq.

84 Whether we take the middle cavity as (*a*) the left ventricle (as
suggested by *HA* 513b4sqq.) or (*b*) the left atrium (when, as in
Somn. 458a17sqq., the aorta is deemed to be connected with the
left cavity, i.e. left ventricle), the idea that the middle cavity is common to the other two faces the major difficulty that
the septum of the heart acts as a solid barrier between the two
sides - although the difficulty for (*b*) would be mitigated if we
are prepared to believe that he may have observed the foramen
ovale in the foetal heart (see above, n.80 on *HA* 513b2sq.).

85 See especially Byl (*art.cit. n.75*), 467sqq.

86 The question arises whether the divergence between *Somn*. 458a16
sqq. and *HA* III 3 is of such a kind as to support a particular
hypothesis about their relative chronology. Firm conclusions are,
no doubt, impossible, especially since the account in *Somn*. is so
brief. But it might be argued that the connection between the
middle cavity and the aorta in *HA* III 3 is an embarrassment for
the doctrine of the middle cavity as common to the other two,
since it associates that cavity with one of the two main blood-
vessels (and indeed in contrast to *PA* III 4, that doctrine is
not actually stated in *HA* III 3). If so, it might be thought more
likely that the simple schema of *Somn*. represents the earlier view,

later modified in the more complex account of *HA* III 3, rather
than that the latter account was earlier and was later simpli-
fied to fit his preconceptions concerning the middle cavity as
ἀρχή, cf. Platt (*art.cit. n.75*), 522.

87 See Lloyd (*art.cit. n.18*), 128sqq.

88 On pre-Aristotelian accounts of the blood-vessels, see Harris
   (*op.cit. n.75*), chh. 1-3.

89 That is animal dissection: human dissection, where other inhibiting factors were at work, does not antedate the Alexandrian
   biologists, Herophilus and Erasistratus.

90 Thus Aristotle mentions the difficulty of observing the courses
   of the blood-vessels when the blood has drained from them in dead
   specimens, *HA* 511b14sqq.

Jürgen Wiesner

PREVIOUS VIEWS OF THE CHRONOLOGICAL RELATIONSHIP OF *DE SOMNO* TO THE REST OF THE *PARVA NATURALIA*

If we disregard the rare attempts to construe the *Parva naturalia* as
having been composed in their entirety as a single piece of work over
a relatively short period of time,[1] we find that the opening and final treatises, at least, are generally agreed to be associated with
certain works. *De sensu* and *De memoria* are placed near *De anima*,
while *De juventute* and *De respiratione* are put rather closer to
the biological treatises. This view has remained constant since
Brandis,[2] but differing opinions on the order of Aristotle's writings
have led to modifications in hypotheses concerning their relative dating. That *De sensu* and *De memoria* were composed before *De juventute*
followed from Brandis' placing of *De anima* before the biological
writings, and subsequently Jaeger[3] too, who arrived at a similar view
of those treatises in the *PN*, supported this order. Conversely, *De
juventute* had to be placed before *De sensu* and *De memoria* once it appeared to have been established that *De anima* had been composed late.
Nuyens, led by his investigation into the relationship of body and
soul to adopt his well-known thesis of three stages in the development of Aristotle's psychology – the dualism of the *Eudemus*, the instrumentalism of a long transitional period, and the hylomorphism of
his last years – placed *De juventute* in the middle, predominantly
biological, period, and *De sensu* and *De memoria* in the final phase
together with *De anima*.[4] Düring[5] and Ross[6] diverge on points of detail – such as Ross's distinction that *De sensu* and *De memoria* were
probably composed at the same time as the earlier sections of *De
anima*, but certainly earlier than *De anima* B, the last work to deal
with psychology – but in the main they differ little from Nuyens.
However, even Lefèvre affirms the relative earliness of *De juventute*
as compared to *De sensu* and *De memoria*, although the innovations in
his overall view of Aristotle's psychological development strongly
call into question the whole basis of the chronology, for all its

previous air of solidity. By demonstrating that, in a good number
of cases, instrumentalist and hylomorphic conceptions occur in juxtaposition with each other in texts which were previously regarded
as evidence for one or other of the approaches, he makes it necessary to place the biological writings nearer to *De anima* and sev-
erely restrict a separate, purely instrumentalist phase.[7] Nevertheless the *De juventute* is held to be early because of the strange
conception of the ψυχὴ ἐμπεπυρευμένη found there. As Lefèvre argues, the soul is not presented here, as it is elsewhere, as the
form bestowing unity upon a living creature. Rather it is simply a
corporeal substance conditioned by fire, a view that has parallels
in Hippocrates' περὶ διαίτης and that was later apparently criticized by Aristotle himself.[8]

It may be regarded as fairly certain that the opening treatises
of the *Parva naturalia* belong to a different period from the final
sections, since scholars who hold quite divergent views about Aristotle's production in general are unanimous on this. The question
arises of the position of the middle set of works on sleep, dreams
and divination through dreaming. Until Nuyens[9] and Düring[10] they
were regarded as belonging to the final phase, hence linked with *De
sensu* and *De memoria*. Then, however, Drossaart Lulofs[11] was led by
the identification of separate periods in Nuyens' book to propound
the view that two originally separate tracts, written at different
times, had been-combined in both *De somno* (*Somn.*) and in *De insomniis* (*Insomn.*). According to this view, a predominantly physiological early section follows a psychologically biased later section.
A whole series of discrepancies and overlaps which can be observed
in these short pieces can then be explained by contamination. Reaction to Drossaart varied. Diano[12] and Untersteiner[13] wrote fa-
vourable reviews, and von Ivanka considered his thesis possible for
De somno though not for *De insomniis*.[14] Ross was entirely opposed
on the grounds that the texts are too short to make such a division
into two at all probable; at the same time he took account of the
many features which Drossaart showed to be shared by the biological
writings, and accordingly supposed that *De somno* and *De insomniis*
belong to an earlier 'biological' period,[15] unlike earlier scholars,
who placed them, with *De sensu* and *De memoria*, in Aristotle's late
period. Düring[16] too now supports the view that Aristotle composed

the pieces without interruption, although Düring does not commit himself on the details of the chronology, taking the view that efforts
in that particular direction are unlikely to be fruitful.[17] In view
of the assessments briefly reviewed so far, it is perfectly legitimate for Lefèvre to assert that Drossaart's view has never been properly refuted and to rate it as a 'thèse plausible'.[18] At the same
time, it is precisely Lefèvre's conception of the matter that has unfortunate implications for Drossaart,[19] whose work was partly based
on that of Nuyens; for if, instead of being successive phases of development in Aristotle's psychology, instrumentalism and hylomorphism
can always be found juxtaposed to each other, there is no longer any
chronological criterion available on the basis of which *Somn.* and
Insomn. can be subdivided. Now Nuyens' view forms such a subsidiary
part of the structure of Drossaart's demonstration that the matter
should be decided on the basis of how far his other arguments with-
stand analysis. My intention is to take *De somno* as an example and
to subject it to such an analysis.

DROSSAART LULOFS' THESIS AND THE UNITY OF *DE SOMNO*

Drossaart divides the text of *De somno* into two basically on the
grounds that the development of the argument appears to he interrup-
ted after 455b13. The first section (453b11 - 455b13) is held to
start with a general introduction to the three treatises *Somn.*, *Insomn.*, *Div. Somn.*, and to move on to logical-psychological investigations. Thus sleep and waking always affect the same part of the
animal, and are a phenomenon of the body and soul together (453b24 -
454a11); they are dependent on perception and hence only occur in
living creatures, alternating in these creatures (454a11 - b14);
further, Aristotle discusses which living creatures are affected by
sleep and waking (454b14 - 455a3), and finally he also discusses
which sense or senses they should be regarded as appertaining to
(455a4 - b13). In this last section Aristotle explains that sleep
and waking hold and release, and are consequently affections of,
the common or central sense. He says that the central sense is especially closely related to the sense of touch, since this can be
separated from the other senses, whereas the others cannot be separated from it (455a22-6). Drossaart finds it most strange that the
sense of touch is not mentioned at all in what follows. It would be

reasonable to expect an account of how the central sense and the
sense of touch related to it are affected, so as to cause the phenomenon of sleep. Instead of this a new section is felt to begin
at 455b13 on the cause (δι' ἣν αἰτίαν) that leads to sleep and on
what sort of affection (πάθος) it is.[20] This fresh beginning from
δι' ἣν δ' αἰτίαν συμβαίνει τὸ καθεύδειν seems difficult to reconcile with the beginning of the previous section on sleep as an affection of the central sense and of the sense of touch; for there
already it was said: διὰ τί δὲ καθεύδει καὶ ἐγρήγορε (455a4).[21]
Drossaart further points out that several references to *De anima*
can be found before 455b13 (454a12, 455a8, a25), and that these are
entirely absent from the following section, in which points of close
affinity with *De juventute* and *De partibus animalium* II-III are no-
ticeable.[22]

All the features which have been mentioned (the breaking off in
the argument with no further mention of the sense of touch, the re-
sumption with a formula which is seemingly a duplicate of what had
come before, and finally a striking change in the cross-references
to other works) suggest that 455b13 marks a division in the treatise
in its present form. Drossaart assumes that *Somn.* A ends here, that
the rest of it is incomplete or lost, and that what is missing was
replaced by *Somn.* B.[23] He points out that this second part of the
present text represents a self-contained whole, for it contains precisely the discussion of the causes of sleep; it begins with a
sketch of the doctrine of causes and ends with a summary, the last
lines of which refer to the final cause (458a31-32) and hence back
to the start of this - originally separate - discussion which had
begun precisely with a consideration of this cause (455b16sqq.).[24]
It is argued that what *Somn.* B has to say on the efficient and material causes of sleep, on how it affects the heart and the central
sense residing within it and paralyses their activity, was applied,
in an essentially similar approach, to the sense of touch later in
the now missing part of *Somn.* A, and Drossaart tries to show this
to be plausible as an attempted reconstruction.[25]

The argument concerning the central sense and the sense of touch
The observation that the explanation of sleep at the end of *Somn.* A
is essentially linked with the central sense and the sense of touch

but that there is no subsequent mention of the sense of touch forms
the nucleus of Drossaart's thesis. It is true that there are grounds
for believing that the sense of touch is in fact mentioned again in
Somn. B since Michael of Ephesus, the earliest extant commentator on
the *Parva naturalia* as a whole (eleventh century) says at *PN* 52, 27-9
(*CAG* XXII, 1) on *Somn.* 456b6-10: ὅτι δὲ ὁ ὕπνος οὐκ ἔστιν ἡ τυχοῦσα
τῶν αἰσθήσεων ἀδυναμία, ἀλλ' ὅταν περὶ τὴν ἁφὴν τὸ τοιοῦτον πάθος
γένηται, καὶ πρότερον εἴρηται καὶ νῦν πάλιν ἀναμιμνῄσκει. But in
Aristotle the text referred to has only: θεωρήσωμεν ... τί πάσχοντος
τοῦ μορίου τοῦ αἰσθητικοῦ συμβαίνει ἡ ἐγρήγορσις καὶ ὁ ὕπνος ...
The question is how Michael comes to make his remark. In *PN* 48, 4
sqq. on *Somn.* 455a22sqq., to which his πρότερον εἴρηται refers back,
he considers Aristotle's remark that the central sense, of which
sleep is an affection, occurs especially in conjunction with the
sense of touch which all living creatures have in common, and interprets it in the sense that κοινὴ αἴσθησις and ἁπτικόν are identical:
'To tell the truth', he writes in *PN* 48, 7-8, 'the sense of touch and
the general sense are the same', going on to assert in 48, 9-10:
'hence sleep too is an affection of the sense of touch and of no
other' (ὥστε καὶ ὁ ὕπνος τῆς ἁφῆς ἐστι πάθος καὶ οὐδεμιᾶς ἄλλης).
After this identification Michael attempts to demonstrate that Aristotle's subsequent words at 455a27sqq. are an attempt to prove that
sleep is precisely not an affection of all the senses, but only of
the sense of touch. This interpretation is therefore the basis for
the later renewed mention of the sense of touch in Michael (*PN* 52,
27-9), which the original does not parallel. Compared with this,
Drossaart's remarks are much more cautious, since he only ever speaks
of the sense of touch as linked with the central sense;[26] but he
would also expect the sense of touch to be mentioned again in *Somn.* B.
The question is whether the passage 455a4 - b13 justifies this assumption.

In his exposition Aristotle points out that sleep must affect all
the senses in so far as they are present in the living creature concerned and that accordingly all the senses undergo the same affection
in sleep (455a5-12). Now each sense has a specific element, like
seeing for the sense of vision, and a general element, by which the
occurrence of sight is confirmed and one can judge, for example, the
differences between an object affecting vision, and one affecting

the sense of taste. Concerning this κοινὴ δύναμις (455a16), which
corresponds to a κοινὸν μόριον τῶν αἰσθητηρίων ἀπάντων (a19-20) or
κύριον αἰσθητήριον (a21), it is further stated: τ ο ῦ τ ο δ᾽ ἅμα
τῷ ἁπτικῷ μάλιστα ὑπάρχει (τ ο ῦ τ ο μὲν γὰρ χωρίζεται τῶν ἄλλων
αἰσθητηρίων, τὰ δ᾽ ἄλλα τ ο ύ τ ο υ ἀχώριστα ...), φανερὸν τοίνυν
ὅτι τ ο ύ τ ο υ ἐστὶ πάθος ἡ ἐγρήγορσις καὶ ὁ ὕπνος (455a22-6). The
question is whether the last τούτου (455a26) refers solely to the
first τοῦτο, which means the central sense (a22), or, in view of the
second τοῦτο and the τούτου, used of the sense of touch, whether it
refers to this as well. The immediately following text causes one
to hesitate, as the sense of touch is again introduced in the statement that therefore sleep affects all living beings: διὸ καὶ πᾶσιν
ὑπάρχει τοῖς ζῴοις· καὶ γὰρ ἡ ἁφὴ μόνη πᾶσιν (455a26-7). What follows, however, makes the situation clear: Aristotle says that it
would be absurd to assume that all the senses are inactive simultaneously, if these senses do not have to be, or even are unable to
be, active simultaneously. But according to what we say, he continues, this does not present any great difficulty: for when the
main one of all the senses, to which all the others are related, is
affected in some way, the others too are necessarily affected; but
when one of the latter is incapacitated, the former is not necessarily put out of action (455a27-b2). The contrast in this text is
obviously not one between the sense of touch and the other senses,
nor one between the sense of touch and the central sense as opposed
to all the other senses, but rather one between the central sense
on the one hand and all the other senses on the other. For the last
sentence (455a33-b2) implies that the central sense and the sense of
touch cannot be identical; for the sense of touch is included in
'the others related to the central sense' (πρὸς ὃ̀ σ υ ν τ ε ί ν ε ι
τἆλλα). This is also apparent from a text in *De juventute* (469a12-
15): δύο [sc. αἰσθήσεις] δὲ φανερῶς ἐνταῦθα σ υ ν τ ε ί ν ο υ σ α ς
ὁρῶμεν, τήν τε γεῦσιν καὶ τὴν ἁφήν (!), ὥστε καὶ τὰς ἄλλας ἀναγκαῖον.
ἐν τούτῳ μὲν γὰρ τοῖς ἄλλοις αἰσθητηρίοις ἐνδέχεται ποιεῖσθαι τὴν
κίνησιν...[27] So among the τἆλλα or τὰ λοιπὰ πάντα connected with the
central sense (*Somn.* 455b1), the sense of touch is to be included:
it is affected, too, when the central sense is affected; 'but when
one of the former', i.e. the τἆλλα or τὰ λοιπὰ πάντα, 'is put out of
action' - and this would apply to the sense of touch, too - 'the

central sense does not necessarily cease to function'.

This shows that Drossaart's attempted reconstruction of the missing part of *Somn*. A, which he supposes to have explained sleep by means of an affection of the sense of touch, is not entirely cogent; for Aristotle's own words show that an affection of the sense of touch does not imply a similar affection of the central sense. This would only be the case if the central sense and the sense of touch were identical as is argued by Michael of Ephesus but is at variance with Aristotle's text. In 455a22-7 the mention of ἁπτικόν can after all only be taken to mean that the sense of touch – in contrast to the others which are not found in all living creatures – is invariably found together with the central sense. In other words, all living creatures have a sense of touch as they have a central sense; hence we have an association which does not mean, however, an identity. The important conclusion that follows from this for Drossaart's thesis is that it is not at all strange that in the subsequent parts of *De somno* there is no further talk of the sense of touch, but only of the central sense. It can no longer be argued on this basis that the second part of the text, *Somn*. B, originally existed on its own.

Is the second part of De somno a self-contained whole?
We now turn to the other arguments in Drossaart's thesis. As he correctly pointed out, the final lines 458a31-2 refer back to the final cause dealt with at the beginning of *Somn*. B (455b16-28).[28] They are the component parts of a summary mentioning in a lapidary manner the four causes of sleep (458a25-32). Here, however, a problem arises. According to Ross, only three of these four causes appear to have previously been the subject of a thorough discussion. In a short comment on 455b13-16 he indicates the limits of the text's discussion of the causes. After the final cause (455b16-28) Aristotle talks about the efficient cause (455b28-458a25), at the same time clarifying the material cause. 'Finally', he goes on, 'in 458a 28-32 he states the formal cause, or definition (which includes a reference to the final cause), by saying that sleep is τοῦ πρώτου αἰσθητηρίου κατάληψις πρὸς τὸ μὴ δύνασθαι ἐνεργεῖν, ἐξ ἀνάγκης μὲν γινόμενος κτλ.'.[29] Ross, therefore, shares Drossaart's opinion that the consideration of causes is confined precisely to the part which the latter had separated as *Somn*. B from what preceded. The final

summary, according to this, would first of all (458a25-8) refer back
to the efficient and material causes previously dealt with at some
length, then in one and a half lines touch on the formal cause which
has not previously been treated, before immediately going on to the
final cause (ἐξ ἀνάγκης μὲν γινόμενος κτλ. corresponds to the ideas
expressed previously in 455b25-8).

If one considers only 455b13 - 458a25, i.e. Drossaart's *Somn*. B,
it has to be conceded that the only treatment of the formal cause is
to be found in the final recapitulation, and unlike the other causes
it has not been gone into in detail previously. Now if, however,
Somn. A and B can be considered as a unity, the picture is changed:
the mention of the formal cause can then quite easily refer back to
the end of *Somn*. A. We already know the discussion in this text about
which of the senses is affected by sleep and waking and it leads up,
in its last paragraph, to a similar definition. There it is stated
that it is clear for many reasons that sleep does not consist in the
inactivity and non-use of the senses, nor in the inability to perceive, which also happens in fainting, unconsciousness and constric-
tion of the throat; rather it is a question of the inability of the
primary organ of perception to function (455b2-10). The ἀδυναμία
τῆς χρήσεως and the ἀδυνατεῖν of the general sense, which are being
discussed here (455b8,b11), are naturally identical with the μὴ δύνασθαι ἐνεργεῖν in the final recapitulation (458a29), and μὴ ἐνεργεῖν
or ἀργεῖν are used by the commentators on the text.[30]

It seems even more legitimate to argue that the final recapitulation of *Somn*., therefore, refers back to 455b2-13, i.e. the final
section of Drossaart's *Somn*. A, in so far as yet another part of
Somn. B makes reference to it. At the beginning of his physiological
discussions in chapter 3, Aristotle attempts to investigate what affection of the part capable of perception accompanies the onset of
sleep and waking: 'for sleep is not a random incapacitation of the
faculty of perception, as has been said (καθάπερ εἴρηται); for unconsciousness, too, one type of suffocation, and fainting cause such
an incapacitation' (456b9-11). ἔκνοια, πνιγμός, λειποψυχία: these
are precisely the three phenomena that were specified in the earlier
definition of sleep (455b3-8), in order to justify his negative definition 'not an inability to perceive'. In view of the fact that
two separate places in *Somn*. B refer in the same way to the end of

Somn. A, it seems wrong to expunge as a later interpolation the explicit back-reference in 456b10 καθάπερ εἴρηται as Drossaart has
done.[31]

Now if the discussion of the formal cause is to be placed before
455b13, it becomes possible to explain why there is something of a
fresh start with the two expressions, διὰ τί on the one hand and δι'
ἣν δ' αἰτίαν on the other (455a4 and b13), especially as the καί
which follows in each case is explicative.[32] διὰ τί δὲ καθεύδει ...
κ α ὶ διὰ ποίαν αἴσθησιν (455a4-5) introduces the discussion which
ends by considering sleep as an incapacity of the central sense;
equally δι' ἣν δ' αἰτίαν συμβαίνει τὸ καθεύδειν κ α ὶ ποῖόν τι τὸ
πάθος ἐστί (455b13-14) appears as a broader question before the
discussion of the further causes. Within this text, other evidence
too can be pointed out, which makes it completely safe to bracket
Somn. A and B together. In 455b28 Aristotle begins with a discussion of the efficient cause; in 455b34 - 456a29 he explains how,
like perception, the movement characteristic of waking has its origin in the heart. From time to time however this movement occurs
in sleep as well (456a24sqq.). The essence of the argument is a
demonstration of the fact that primarily sleep and waking too derive
from the πρῶτον αἰσθητήριον located in the heart (456a21-4). Bonitz
has made a separate analysis of this passage[33] and correctly observes
that, in this proof, in the first part of the antecedent clause (456
a15) 'the movement' is 'ascribed to the heart', and in the second part
(a20) 'being moved or moving oneself are ascribed to the activity of
sensual perception and thereby to the heart as the central organ';
after these two parts of the protasis, the apodosis begins (456a21)
with a subordinate antecedent clause 'now if, as is recognized (δή),
sleep and waking are affections of the primary and central organ of
sensory perception', and this leads to the actual conclusion that
the heart is the place and the part of the body in which sleep and
waking first originate. Bonitz writes that the subordinate antecedent clause εἰ δή ... refers back to the earlier statement in 455b
8-10,[34] according to which sleep affects the primary organ of perception; 455a26 seems to me to be even closer in its formulation.
In any event, there is here yet another reference back to Drossaart's
Somn. A, making the third reference altogether in the second part to
the first.

Terminological evidence

Finally we must assess the evidence from terminology. In the text
we have just outlined, the words in 456a22 that sleep and waking are
πάθη τοῦ μορίου τούτου refer to the πρῶτον αἰσθητήριον (456a21) which
in 455a19-20 was characterized as κοινὸν μόριον τῶν αἰσθητηρίων. At
the start of the physiological chapter, Aristotle asks τί πάσχοντος
τοῦ μορίου τοῦ αἰσθητικοῦ συμβαίνει ἡ ἐγρήγορσις καὶ ὁ ὕπνος (456b7-
9) and says in justification that sleep is certainly not just a random ἀδυναμία τοῦ αἰσθητικοῦ (456b9-10, repeated b18). Now Drossaart
used as an argument concerning De insomniis that there were differences of terminology between the older and the more recent parts.
He points out that terms like τὸ αἰσθητικόν or φανταστικόν which are
normal in De anima only recur in later sections of Insomn. (A = 458
a33-459a22), not in the earlier part (B = 459a23-462b11); rather
other formulations are encountered there, for example in 460b17 τό
τε κύριον καὶ ᾧ τὰ φαντάσματα γίνεται as an equivalent for τὸ φανταστικόν in the discussion of De anima and Insomn. A (458b30, 459a16-
17, a22).[35] But τὸ αἰσθητικόν, claimed to be typical of the later
writings, reappears several times in the 'older' Somn. B (456b8, b9-
10, b18), to which, according to Drossaart, Insomn. B was appended.[36]
Moreover the formulation τί πάσχοντος τοῦ μορίου τοῦ αἰσθητικοῦ ...
refers back to the previous declaration in 454b9-12 that sleep is a
πάθος τοῦ αἰσθητικοῦ μορίου, on account of which, moreover, everything that sleeps has the αἰσθητικὸν μόριον. This suggests that the
supposedly earlier and the later part of Somn. are linked in their
choice of terminology; accordingly if, as Drossaart assumes, Somn. B
is to be placed in the same chronological layer as Insomn. B, choice
of terminology can no longer be used as an argument for the latter
text. Even the formulation τό τε κύριον καὶ ᾧ τὰ φαντάσματα γίνεται
can hardly be regarded as indicative of an older stage, since the
reverse is also found: instead of πρῶτον αἰσθητήριον (456a21 and
passim) Aristotle also writes τὸ πρῶτον ᾧ αἰσθάνεται πάντων, this
time in the 'later' part (455b10).[37] The conclusions to be drawn
from this for Somn. must also be valid for Insomn. This is precisely
because Drossaart emphasizes how on the one hand Somn. A and Insomn.
A and on the other Somn. B and Insomn. B belong together.[38]

If the foregoing is correct, the following holds good: (1) There
is no need to assume a break in the argument of Somn. on the grounds

that the sense of touch is no longer mentioned in the second part.
(2) *Somn.* B, originally regarded as a second and separate part, is
not a self-contained whole, but is linked in many respects with the
first part (e.g. the discussion of the formal cause already before
455b13); in view of the fact that the two parts are in many respects
interwoven one cannot hold that the back-references are interpolated.
(3) Terminological discrepancies, corresponding to an earlier or
later stage in the composition of the parts of the text, cannot be
shown to exist with any consistency. According to all these considerations *Somn.* A and B belong together.

Now Drossaart imagined *Somn.* A to be a late text on account of
its psychological character and the three references to *De anima*.[39]
Ross, it is true, calls this argument 'less conclusive' and refers
to the way such references are often later additions;[40] one of them,
however, (454a12) seems firmly rooted in the context, as Lefèvre has
now also pointed out in his paper.[41] The unity of the text having
been demonstrated, B must accordingly be given the same date as A.
But is there evidence in this physiological part that indicates
this period? Drossaart raises the point that *Somn.* B shows affinities to *De partibus animalium* II – III and particularly close ones to
De juventute.[42] Now as was said in the introduction to this paper,
Lefèvre places *PA*, like the other biological writings, close to the
time when *De anima* was written, seeing on the other hand an earlier
stage of Aristotle's teachings in *De juventute*. If this is true,
it raises the question of whether there are, among the parallels between *De juventute* and *Somn.* B, any of a type that would be valid
for *Juv.*, but not also at the same time for the later biological
writings. In other words, one can ask whether there is any evidence
in *Somn.* B to suggest that there was ever an earlier version of the
text on sleep not identical with B - as Drossaart thought - on which
Aristotle could draw in writing the psychological-physiological
treatise in the form we know it today. We must keep this question
in mind in considering now the physiological explanation of sleep.

THE PHYSIOLOGICAL EXPLANATION OF SLEEP
Warm or cold as the cause of sleep?
In our consideration of Drossaart's thesis we briefly mentioned his
attempted reconstruction of the assumed missing or lost part coming

after *Somn.* A. The justification for this in principle no longer
concerns us, but rather one aspect of the content of his thesis. In
the course of his account of the idea that sleep is an affection of
the central sense which is closely linked with the sense of touch,
Drossaart refers to the fact that the organ which is the source of
the sense of touch is actively warm and potentially cold, in so far
as it resides near the heart, which is the warmest organ (*Sens.* 438b
30sqq.). Sleep comes about since, when the warmth of the heart is
diminished, the organ of touch is cooled as well and consequently
the activity of the central sense is paralysed. According to Drossaart, this reconstructed argument was not dissimilar to that found
in *Somn.* B in the way it explains the cause of sleep; sleep is seen,
then, as coming about when the heart cools down.[43] However, the
question of the actual physiological cause is a thoroughly controversial one.

On the one hand, Drossaart was anticipated already by Zeller,[44]
Siebeck[45] and Wellmann[46] in his view that sleep is essentially a
matter of the cooling down of the heart. Zeller writes that the
nutritive exhalations rise to the brain and cool down there, then
move downwards causing 'a cooling down of the heart as a consequence
of which the activity of this most general organ of perception is,
to some degree, inhibited'. Wellmann stresses that, in attributing
sleep to the cooling of innate warmth, Aristotle follows an Empedo-
clean tradition. The doctrine derived from the Sicilian-Athenian
school that the heart is the original centre of perception is, in
him, pushed to its logical conclusion in the idea that it is the
heart itself which cools down. On the other hand Hicks,[47] Enders,[48]
and Mugnier[49] believe that the chief cause of sleep is a concentration of warmth in the heart. An objection made by Enders to the
views of Siebeck is that in *De somno* there is nowhere any mention
of the heart cooling down or of its activity being reduced.[50] There
is no mention of this disagreement on the explanation of sleep in
recent specialized studies like Drossaart's work on *De somno*, or
even in recent general surveys like Düring's book on Aristotle. This
is even more surprising when, as we shall see shortly, opinions dif-
fered also among the ancient and Byzantine commentators on Aristotle.
Is what Aristotle actually said so unclear? We would do well, first
of all, to undertake a brief examination of the text.

In the third chapter of *Somn.* the physiological explanation begins with a brief survey of how food makes its way in the body.
Food enters the δεκτικοὶ τόποι and thence the veins where it is
transformed into blood (μεταβάλλουσα ἐξαιματοῦται) moving ἐπὶ τὴν
ἀρχήν or in other words to the heart.   It is stated that this has
been discussed in περὶ τροφῆς, but that the matter is to be taken
up again in order to investigate the beginnings of the movement and
the affection of the μόριον αἰσθητικόν whereby sleep and waking
come about (456b2-9).   In 456b20sqq. this is portrayed as follows:
warmth rises quite naturally in each living being (b21-2) so that
the various moist and corporeal (b25) exhalations from the food are
thrust on to a certain point at which they all reverse direction
like the tide-race in a narrow strait (b20-1, 23); when they become
stationary, they cause heaviness and sleepiness, but when they have
inclined downwards and by their return have pushed back the warmth,
sleep comes about and the creature sleeps (456b26-8).   In what follows, Aristotle discusses factors conducive to sleep: apart from
food and intoxicants which make the head heavy (456b29), these are
states of exhaustion (b34) and certain diseases (457a1) which cause
excess warmth and moistness, and in addition early childhood (457a3),
a time at which all the food consumed rises upwards (a4-5, 17sqq.).
By a process of association the author makes a transition to heavy
and light sleepers (457a21sqq.): those with thin veins, whose narrow
veins make it difficult for the moist exhalation to flow downwards,
dwarfs and those with large heads, in whom the exhalation is considerable, as it is in children, are fond of sleep, whereas it comes
much harder to those with pronounced veins and to melancholics with
cold inner regions.   In 457a33-b6, then, he concludes for the first
time: sleep is clearly due to warmth running back and gathering
within the body, which also explains why considerable movement is
observed in sleeping people; but those parts from which warmth es-
capes cool down as a consequence.   Hence the eyelids close, the
upper and outer parts are cold and the inner and lower parts, like
the feet and the stomach, are warm.
    At 457b6 a discussion begins on the causes of cooling; it might
seem illogical to explain sleep as a cooling down while its causes
are warm (457b9-10).   Aristotle mentions three possible reasons all
of which may be able to explain the cooling down: (1) the filling

up of the passages and places in the head because of the movement
accompanying it, (2) a concentration of cold as a reaction to the
rise of warmth, so that the cold impairs the function of the natural
warmth and causes its withdrawal, (3) the considerable accumulation
of food, the effect of which is compared to that of more wooden logs
placed on a fire (457b10–19). All this is accepted as possible, but
it is the brain, the coldest point in the body, which is regarded as
crucial (457b26–31). This is because the narrow, thin veins cool
the nutritive exhalation despite its excessive warmth (458a5–10), a
process comparable to the condensation of vapour to rain in the atmosphere (457b31sqq.). The discussion concludes by saying that
awakening occurs, however, when the concoction has been completed,
and the warmth concentrated from the surrounding parts in a small
space has gained the upper hand (458a10–11). We shall be considering at a later point a section which is appended on the heart and
the separation of the blood.

The interpretations of the commentators

Let us now consider how the early exegetes differ from each other on
the subject of this treatment of sleep, and in respect of which sections of the text. For *De somno*, in the first place we have available the running commentaries, paraphrases and summaries from the
time of the Byzantine revival of Aristotelian studies in the eleventh
century when Michael of Ephesus wrote his commentary to *Parva naturalia*.[51] Drossaart[52] holds (albeit not entirely correctly, cf. below)
that all later texts are derived from Michael: they are those of
Georgios Pachymeres, Sophonias and Theodoros Metochites, who are all
to be dated around 1300; the last was the source of the summary of
the *PN* by Georgios Scholarios at the beginning of the fifteenth century, preserved in the autograph Vaticanus 115. But even earlier
exegetes, such as Alexander, Simplicius or Priscian, the pupil of
Dexippus, make occasional comments on sleep, and in doing so touch
on its physiological causes.

Byzantine exegetes. First of all we should consider briefly the
later interpreters who deal with the whole work. Michael of Ephesus
supports the view that a cooling of the heart brings about sleep.
In *PN* 53, 23sqq. (*CAG* XXII 1) he considers *Somn.* 456b20sqq., saying

the nutritive exhalation reaches the head, condenses because of the
coldness of the brain, and moves back down to the heart, reducing its
normal warmth so that the creature falls asleep (53,27-8: καταφέρεται
... ἐπὶ τὴν καρδίαν καὶ καταψύχει τὸ ἐν αὐτῇ θερμόν. οὗ ψυχθέντος
καθεύδει τὸ ζῷον). There is however also a later remark about this
which is somewhat different: after his discussion in *PN* 56, 15sqq. of
Somn. 457a33-b6 concerning the concentration of warmth in the inner
parts and the cooling of the upper parts which is responsible for the
closing of the eyelids (he adds by way of explanation, in 56,30, that
warmth is the element holding all parts together), he writes similarly, in *PN* 58, 4-5 on 457b23-5, that men fall asleep when warmth is
removed from the upper parts and runs downwards. It is true that
here too sleep is due to cooling, but not to cooling of the heart.

Whereas Sophonias (*CAG* V 6) mostly follows Michael closely,[53] Theodoros Metochites merits greater attention since he is concerned to
interpret the phenomena. In his view the exhalation cools the heart
in order to protect or strengthen (καταφράττει, 19, 2-4 ed. Drossaart
on 456b20sqq.) the warmth of the heart and the source of perception;
the anathymiasis makes heavy and, so to speak, encloses the heart,
thereby cooling it (21, 13-16 on 457b22-6). In principle, the cooling of the warmth of the heart remains the essential cause of sleep.
In this, Metochites goes beyond Michael, deriving his idea not only
from *Somn.* 456b20-8, but also from 458a4-5. Georgios Scholarios[54]
repeats all these statements - partly verbatim - and that he is dependent on Metochites - as Drossaart claims - is as evident as is the
close relationship of Sophonias to Michael, which has long been known.

The case of Georgios Pachymeres is different. Drossaart believes
that he too derives his views from Michael, but Drossaart only had
available the Latin translation of Philippus Becchius[55] because of
the constraints prevailing in 1943, the year in which his dissertation appeared. It is clear, however, from an examination of the
Greek original - I have consulted the autograph Berolinensis Hamil-
tonianus 512[56] - that arguments which are typical of Michael and his
successors do not recur in Pachymeres: (1) the attribution of sleep
to the sense of touch which is identified with the central sense
(Mich. Eph. *PN* 47,9-11; 48,4-14; Soph. *PN* 20,23-21,4; Metoch.
15,37-16,5; Schol. 458,13-14) is not found in him; Pachymeres makes
absolutely no mention of ἀφή, which he therefore takes to be

mentioned only incidentally in the course of Aristotle's argument.
(2) When the path taken by the food that is converted to blood in
the body is described, the liver is not included as an intermediary
between the δεκτικοὶ τόποι and the heart, as in Michael and his
successors (Mich. PN 52,12-26; Soph. PN 23,27-24,3; Metoch. 18,19-
26; Schol. 459,25-32) following Alexander (De An. 94,24sqq.).[57]
Equally, the stereotyped refutation of the view of Galen, who attributed an important role in the process of concoction to this organ,
is missing. (3) Finally Pachymeres also says nothing about any
cooling of the heart in his summary of Somn., mentioning only the
departure of the warmth from the upper parts and the concentration
of warmth within. He takes little account of cold as the actual
cause of sleep coming on, as is clear from the fact that he completely passes over Aristotle's discussion of the way cooling comes
about (457b6 - 458a10) - in other words he proceeds immediately from
a discussion of the concentration of warmth to the separation of the
blood in the heart (458a12sqq.). These texts make it necessary to
abandon Drossaart's assumption that he was dependent on Michael.

Exegetes of the second to sixth centuries. The two ideas that a
concentration of warmth in the heart, or that a cooling down of this
warmth, cause the onset of sleep, are, however, themes found also in
much earlier authors. In one of the earliest, the 'Anonymus Londinensis' from the second century, there is a line missing in the papy-
rus precisely at the point in question (Suppl. Arist. III 1, p.43
col. XXIV);[58] but the text, after first discussing the movement of
the cooled anathymiasis back to the heart, continues after the gap:
καὶ τῇ μίξει τὸ θερμόν. ὧδε τὸν ὕπνον γίνεσθαι. It is then certainly correct to assume that here the cause of sleep is a cooling
down reducing the warmth by admixture.

Various texts offer us both answers to the problem in Alexander's
name. It is true that we cannot be quite sure of the authenticity
of the first passage, Metaph. 558, 27sqq. (CAG I). This is because
the commentary refers to H 4, 1044b15-20: Alexander's original text
from E onwards is lost and it has been replaced by Michael of Ephesus, who, it is true, frequently bases himself on Alexander, and
perhaps here too represents his view. In Metaph. 558, 27sqq. the
question dealt with is what is first affected by sleep. Is the part

of the body first affected the brain, as Plato held, or the heart,
which Aristotle called the principle of the living creature? In
Metaph. 558, 32-8, there follow the familiar comparison with atmospheric processes and the explanation that the exhalation is cooled,
then moves downwards to the heart, where it extinguishes the warmth
- though not completely - and thus brings about sleep in the living
creature until the vapours are dissipated (σβεννυμένου τοῦ ἐν αὐτῇ
οὐ παντελῶς δὲ θερμοῦ ὑπνώττειν τὸ ζῷον ...). The problem is whether Michael or Alexander is speaking here. At any rate, in the
Quaestiones XX, 33, 26sqq. (*Suppl. Arist.* II 2) Alexander quite un-
ambiguously establishes the concentration of warmth as the cause.
He asks why we are sleepier in summer if sleep is caused by the
ἀντιπερίστασις, the withdrawal of innate warmth within. Alexander
attacks this problem by dealing first of all with the way sleep
comes about. This he describes as being due to the exhalation
which constrains the innate warmth of the body as it is borne down
from the head to the breast. It is because the warmth is contracted
in this part that perceptions cease (ἡ γὰρ τούτου (*sc.* θερμοῦ) αὐτό-
θι συστολὴ αἰτία τῆς ἀργίας ταῖς αἰσθήσεσιν, 34, 2-3). This κατοχή
of the warmth by the exhalation lasts until the latter is overcome
by the warmth (33, 28 - 34, 6). The expression ἀργία ταῖς αἰσθήσεσιν
apparently stands here for the affection of the central sense, without which the individual senses cannot function. Alexander can now
explain the different length of sleep in summer and winter. In winter the accumulated warmth can resist the cold exhalation longer;
consequently it is clearly not so easy to compress, and it can con-
coct the cold more quickly. In summer the warmth is more diffuse,
and hence more easily constrained; it can dissipate the cold less
easily, so that sleep is longer (34, 7-20).

There is a third text in Alexander, this time in the commentary
on *De sensu*, and because of the contradictions in our other information one might well have high hopes of it, particularly since
Alexander has the *PN* in front of him here. But *Sens.* 7,25 - 8,2
(*CAG* III) does not attribute sleep to anything that has to do with
warmth but only to the heaviness of the moisture present in the
exhalation which burdens the faculty of perception and makes it
less effective. It is true that the cooling of the exhalations by
the brain is mentioned, but this is not brought into a direct rela-

tionship with the cause of sleep. In exactly the same way Simplicius, too, in *Ph.* 1258, 20sqq. (*CAG* X) makes the heaviness of the
moisture in the exhalation responsible for inhibiting the organs of
perception.

None of the many differing interpretations we have reviewed
clearly sets out the alternatives and consciously attempts to decide
for one of them. Hence one final text that does formulate the problem explicitly is bound to be of particular interest in this respect. This is the *Solutiones* of Priscianus Lydus which are preserved in a Latin version (*Suppl. Arist.* I 2). Chapter 2 deals with
sleep and its nature, in particular whether it is a function of a
single or a dual soul and whether it is warm or cold (52,25 - 53,1).
De somno is adduced for its characterization of sleep as an affection of body and soul together (55,12-14) and for its full physiological explanation of the way sleep comes about (55,22sqq.). Bywater has made an almost complete record of references in his apparatus criticus (the only addition to be made is that of 57,8-9 corresponding to *Somn.* 457b9-10), so that we can easily see, by a comparison, how the author understood the text. For Priscian, sleep is
due to the cooling down of the warmth in the heart, and this he repeats several times (56,4-5 from *Somn.* 456b20sqq.; 56,9-15 from 457b
17-24; 57,5-7); before it is cooled, the warmth has been driven directly back into the heart by the moist nutritive exhalations (56,
8-9). In what follows a second theme is mentioned, namely the com-
pression of the primary faculty of perception by the anathymiasis so
that it is weakened and cannot function to the extent it would nor-
mally according to its own warmth (56,19-23). It is clear how this
statement has come about; the term ἀντιπερίστασις (458a27) in the
text referred to is not conceived of as a change of position (Michael
PN 56,15: παλίρροια; cf. *Insomn.* 461a5-6 εἰς τὸ ἐντὸς ... τοῦ θερμοῦ
παλίρροιαν and Alex. *Quaest.* XX, 33, 26-7 τοῦ ... θερμοῦ εἰς τὸ ἐντὸς
ἀντιπερίστασιν or εἰς τὸ ἐκτός), but as a 'compressura', that is to
say it is taken in a sense that is characteristic of the way in
which, in the doctrines based on warmth, the conflict of cold and
warmth is expressed.[59] This recurs, moreover, in the synopsis, which
is made up from *Somn.* 457b9-10 and b1-2: 'dormire igitur est refri-
geratio; causalia autem dormiendi calida, quia synodus quaedam est
somnus intus calidi et compressura naturalis' (57,8-10).

The account in De somno 456b17 - 458a25
The review of the early commentators shows that they disagree just
as much as some recent authors mentioned above about whether it is
actually cooling or warmth that causes sleep. Is it possible to
come to a decision on this controversial point by a precise interpretation of the passages adduced from the original text? Let us
first consider the passages in support of the 'cooling theory'.

Does sleep come about through the cooling of the heart? The first
text to be repeatedly adduced by the commentators was the passage
from 456b20-8, according to which sleep comes about when the nutritive exhalation, which rises and sinks, has shifted downwards and
by its return has pushed away the warmth (ἀπώσῃ τὸ θερμόν). Assuming it is this which leads Michael and his followers, as also Priscian, to assert that the descending current cools the warmth in the
heart, one might attribute this to the fact that 456b17sqq. is connected with the introductory lines 456b7-9 (separated by an excursus
in 456b9-17, after which b17 refers back to b9) - and according to
that passage it is important to recognize that the onset of sleep is
accompanied by an affection of the faculty of perception, which in
physiological terms is the heart. But since Michael here continues:
οὗ [sc. τοῦ ἐν τῇ καρδίᾳ θερμοῦ] ψυχθέντος καθεύδει τὸ ζῷον ἕως ἂν
πεφθῇ καὶ κρατηθῇ ὑπὸ τοῦ θερμοῦ (53,29-30) although nothing is said
until much later (458a10-11) about the concoction and overcoming of
the cold by the warm, it is clear that, either he is concerned with
giving a general explanation of sleep which is not based on 456b20-
8, or he is simply accepting the attitude of some tradition towards
the text, a tradition also followed by Priscian. At any rate all
that can be deduced from Aristotle's ὅταν δὲ ῥέψῃ κάτω καὶ ἀντιστρέψαν ἀπώσῃ τὸ θερμόν is that after the current turns back, i.e. in the
upper parts (456b23), the warmth is driven away; and this corresponds
exactly to *PA* II 7, 653a15-16 in which cooling by the brain κάτω
ποιεῖ τὸ θερμὸν ὑποφεύγειν μετὰ τοῦ αἵματος.
     The second text that is frequently invoked in support of the
cooling of the heart follows the comparison with the condensation of
rain in the atmosphere (457b31sqq.). As the warmth rises to the
brain, the excess anathymiasis collects into phlegm (which is why
catarrhs are seen to arise from the head). That part which is

nutritive and not sickly is condensed and carried down and cools the
warmth (καταψύχει τὸ θερμόν) (458a1-5). Does this refer to the warmth in the heart, or the warmth in the upper parts? The term τὸ
θερμόν itself does not allow us to decide because of its indeterminate nature as a πολλαχῶς λεγόμενον.[60] This becomes evident from an
analysis of a short text: in 457b15, it is certain that ἀνιόντος τοῦ
θερμοῦ refers to the warmth of the exhalation, but in 457b16-17 τὸ
κατὰ φύσιν θερμόν (otherwise referred to by such terms[61] as φυσικὸν
θερμόν, θερμότης φυσική) refers to natural body warmth (Juv. 469b6-8)
- in this case that of the upper parts. The expression τροφῆς ἣν
ἀνάγει τὸ θερμόν might suggest equally strongly the warmth residing
within the food as it moves to the upper parts of the body, or that
in the inner parts which causes things to rise. The latter is certainly referred to subsequently in 457b21 (ἀναφερομένου ὑπὸ τοῦ
θερμοῦ = 458a27 ἀναφερομένου ὑπὸ τοῦ συμφύτου θερμοῦ) whereas in
457b24 ὑποσπωμένου τοῦ θερμοῦ τοῦ ἀνάγοντος refers to the withdrawal
of the warmth that makes things upright or in other words the warmth
in the upper parts. What καταψύχει τὸ θερμόν is intended to mean in
458a5 can, therefore, only be determined on the basis of the context.

The comparison within which the statement occurs admits of both
interpretations. If one takes the formation of rain, at 457b33-458a1
one reads συστὰν καταφέρεται γενόμενον πάλιν ὕδωρ (in PA II 7, which
contains the same comparison, we have at 653a7-8 συνίσταται πάλιν εἰς
ὕδωρ διὰ τὴν ψύξιν καὶ ῥεῖ κάτω πρὸς τὴν γῆν), so that what is being
dealt with is the final point reached by the rain in falling: it
would correspond to this if καταφέρεται συνισταμένη καὶ καταψύχει τὸ
θερμόν referred to the warmth of the heart as the final point to
which the anathymiasis leads. On the other hand, if 458a4-5 is juxtaposed with the preceding 458a2-4, what is dealt with there is the
flow of residues from the head; so that a5 could also mean the warmth in the head and the upper parts. The latter assumption seems to
accord better with the spirit of the paragraph as a whole from 457b6
-458a10, which sets out to present sleep as a cooling down, despite
its having causes that are hot (457b9-10). This is because all the
preceding suggestions refer to the upper parts: (a) in the first
suggestion, that cooling could be due to the movement of the anathymiasis, the ἐν τῇ κεφαλῇ πόροι καὶ τόποι (457b13) are explicitly
named as what undergoes cooling. (b) In the second suggestion, ac-

cording to which the cold reacts to the warmth in such a way as to
come together and put out of action the τὸ κατὰ φύσιν θερμόν and
force it to retreat (ποιεῖ ... ὑποχωρεῖν 457b15-17) the reference
is no less clear (cf. *PA* II 7, 653a15 κάτω ποιεῖ τὸ θερμὸν ὑποφεύγειν). (*c*) With the third possibility too, according to which the
mass of food arriving causes cooling, as wood cools a fire when it
is placed on it, the expression τροφῆς ἣν ἀνάγει τὸ θερμόν suggests
that Aristotle refers to the possibility that the nutrient evaporation carried onwards to the head produces cooling there. All three
suggestions refer to the upper parts of the body, as also does the
discussion of the actual cause of cooling, from 457b26 onwards.

Until now, then, we can only be sure that in 458a5 καταψύχει τὸ
θερμόν refers to the cooling of the warmth in the upper parts. In
458a8-10 Aristotle himself makes it clear that the preceding discussion about cooling deals with the causes of the cooling down of
the anathymiasis despite its excessive warmth. So far we have not
found any clear indication that the anathymiasis also cools the
heart and, therefore, paralyses the central sense. But it may be
that Aristotle's comments on the role of warmth in sleep can take
us a little further.

Does sleep arise through the concentration of warmth in the heart?
So far two passages have been considered which were adduced for the
'cooling theory'. The second rounds off a lengthy discussion of
how it is that the exhalations are cooled down once they have risen
to the upper parts. Aristotle has said that, despite having causes
that are warm, sleep is a κατάψυξις (457b9-10) while he had previously specified the upper and outer parts as areas of cooling
(457b4-5). Yet, in the same place, sleep is held to be a function
of warmth flowing together and withdrawing to the inner parts (b1-2),
and the inner and lower parts are held to be warm (b5-6). It appears that, after all, the idea that the heart is cooled by the anathymiasis must be given up in the face of this statement.

A closer look at the phrasing, however, shows that the passage
does not say explicitly that the warmth puts the primary faculty out
of action. The references to the flow of warmth to the inner parts
are quite general, the only more detailed comments being to the
effect that the stomach and feet are warm (457b6). The heart and

the central sense are not mentioned here; neither are they explicitly referred to in the rest of the section 456b20-458a10. This is
all the more surprising in view of the fact that previously, in
456b7-9, there had been an explicit promise to investigate how the
μόριον αἰσθητικόν is affected when sleep and waking occur. The
statements which follow this (456b20sqq.) are quite precise on the
processes involved in the flow of the food to the upper parts and
its change of direction. We are told exactly how καρηβαρία is caused (456b26, 29-32), and we hear several times that the intensity
of sleep is directly related to the amount of exhalation that has
been borne upwards (456b33-4, 457a4-5, a24-5, 457b22-6); finally
the reasons why cooling in the head should take place are considered
in detail (457b10-458a10). Yet the information on the downward flow
of the anathymiasis is somewhat vague and indefinite, despite the
promise contained in 456b7-9; καταφέρεται (456b24), ὅταν ... ῥέψῃ
κάτω (456b27), κατιόν (457a24), κάτω ῥεῖ (457b23), καταφέρεται
(458a5) are all used in this connection, but no expression such as
καταφέρεται εἰς τὴν καρδίαν which appears in the commentators (who
are evidently influenced by the preceding introductory comment);
correspondingly there is no indication of what exactly happens in
the heart when the flow has arrived there. All this accords well
with the fact that the conclusions in 457a33-b6 ὥστε φανερὸν ἐκ τῶν
εἰρημένων speak only of σύνοδός τις τοῦ θερμοῦ εἴσω and of the warmth
in τὰ ἐντὸς καὶ τὰ κάτω ... οἷον τὰ περὶ τοὺς πόδας καὶ τὰ εἴσω.
The same holds good, then, of the warmth as was said above of the
cold: there is no definite statement to the effect that the warmth
affects the heart or central sense and causes sleep by so doing.

Now, similar observations can be made on *PA* II 7, a chapter about
the nature and function of the brain. Aristotle explains in 653a10
sqq. how the brain causes sleep, for it cools the blood which flows
to it from food or other similar sources, makes heavy the region of
the head and causes the warmth to escape downwards (κάτω) with the
blood. He goes on to say that by accumulating 'in the lower region'
it causes sleep; I take the words διὸ πλεῖον ἀθροιζόμενον ἐπὶ τὸν
κάτω τόπον ἀπεργάζεται τὸν ὕπνον (653a16-17) to refer to the warmth
because the πλεῖον ἀθροιζόμενον ἐπὶ τὸν κάτω τόπον accords with the
σύνοδος τοῦ θερμοῦ εἴσω and the localization of warmth in τὰ ἐντὸς
καὶ τὰ κάτω (*Somn.* 457b1 and b5-6). In this text of *PA*, too, there

is not an explicit statement about warmth paralysing the primary
faculty in the heart. It is the accumulation of warmth 'in the
lower region' that causes sleep. One aspect of the downward (κάτω)
flow of warmth which is particularly stressed is the loss of balance: it is no longer possible to stand upright or hold the head
erect (653a17-19); for, according to what we are told soon after,
the upright posture is a function of the upward tendency of warmth
(653a30-2). These themes, too, recur in *Somn*. 456b20-458a10: the
sections on καρηβαρία were mentioned above; loss of balance and
falling when the warmth with its raising force is withdrawn are referred to in 457b24-5 (πίπτουσί γε ὑποσπωμένου τοῦ θερμοῦ τοῦ ἀνάγοντος οἱ ἄνθρωποι).

The most important point about *Somn*. 456b20-458a10 is that despite the question in 456b7-9 as to how exactly the μόριον αἰσθητικόν is affected, the heart is not explicitly mentioned in the subsequent section although the processes described there must in any
case affect that organ too; there is no suggestion that warmth in
the heart or the central faculty is the cause of sleep (but only of
the individual senses being inhibited by cooling). As in *PA*,
warmth appears in the context of argumentation concerning the loss
of equilibrium (cold in the upper parts after the downflow of the
warmth which accumulates below). ·What actually happens in the
heart is not stated explicitly. When this organ comes to be discussed in *Somn*. 458a10-25 in the concluding section of the physiological explanation, Aristotle seems to turn to a theme not previously
introduced into his account of sleep.

*Does the explanation of sleep in Somn. represent a development from
that in PA?* It is one's impression on reading *Somn*. 458a10-12 that
the discussion has been concluded: 'one awakens when concoction is
complete and the warmth which was concentrated from the surrounding
parts in large quantity in a small space has gained the upper hand,
and when the more corporeal blood has been separated from the purer'.
The explanation that the blood in the head is thinner and purer,
while the blood in the lower parts of the body is thicker and more
turbid (458a13-15) leads into an outline treatment of the source of
the blood, the heart; but the brief anatomical statements are immediately broken off again with the remark that the subject-matter is

more appropriately dealt with in the context of other discussions.[62]
But there follows the somewhat surprising comment that it is because,
after the absorption of food, the blood is too mixed (or comes to be in
too mixed a state: διὰ δὲ τὸ γίγνεσθαι ἀδιακριτώτερον τὸ αἷμα) that
sleep comes about, until the purer blood has been separated upwards,
and the more turbid downwards; after this process awakening occurs
when the heaviness imposed by the food has been lifted (458a21-5).
The surprising thing about this remark is that it gives yet another
cause for sleep despite the fact that how sleep occurs has already been
discussed several times (γίγνεται ὁ ὕπνος in 456b27-8, 457b20), and the
account had seemingly been concluded with the mention of awakening.
It is true that the exhalation being of a moist and corporeal nature
had already been mentioned several times (456b25, 457a14, a24, 457b20),
but it is only now that we are told for the first time that it is the
mixed nature of the blood which is the cause. It is further remark-
able that this theme is introduced in connection with the heart, which
had previously not been mentioned explicitly; up to this point we had
only been told of the cooling down in the upper parts, the accumulation of warmth in the inner and lower parts and the loss of equilibrium.

Now a question arises concerning the two accounts that follow
one another in Somn. Is it legitimate to speak of two aspects of
the explanation of sleep which are separate in the sense that they
were not connected from the outset? We have already noted some
disproportion in the two accounts as they are given in the text.
The introductory comment in 456b7-9, θεωρήσωμεν ... τί πάσχοντος
τοῦ μορίου τοῦ αἰσθητικοῦ, is followed by a long exposition, in
which the processes taking place in the head (cooling down etc.),
and the question of balance, are stressed (456b20-458a10). But
although the processes dealt with affect the heart anyway, too,
this organ is not mentioned at all. It is only the last short
section that takes the heart into account explicitly (458a10-25)
but simultaneously introduces a new idea about the cause of sleep.
The argumentation concerning the head and about balance was shown
to have close affinities with PA II 7. If it can be shown that PA
takes no account of the idea of the mixed nature of the blood, this
would lend support to the idea that a development has taken place
and aspects which were not connected from the outset follow one
another in Somn., as suggested by the structure of the text. In

other words: the explanation of sleep, as we read it now as a unity
in *Somn.*, would be more elaborate and would contain one factor which
has been added in the course of a development of this explanation.

Ross already pointed out in a remark made in passing on *PA* II 7,
653a10 that sleep here is seen as related especially closely to the
brain and not to the heart in the usual way.[63] Against this, Drossaart objected that since this chapter is especially concerned with
the function of the brain, it is its role alone that Aristotle
stresses, and that there need be no more to it than that.[64] A similar objection could be made about the fact that the mixed condition
of the blood is not mentioned in *PA* II 7: the description in this
chapter is surely too short, and equally, the fact that the brain
is being discussed ought to lead one to expect the emphasis to be
laid only on those factors relating to warmth that are relevant to
its function. At the same time, however, we have available some
more general information concerning the causes of sleep, apart from
the special chapter devoted to the brain. In *PA* II 2, 648a21sqq.
there begins an investigation into 'warm' and 'cold', since these
basic powers underlie the nature of many things, although their
meaning or conceptual application in specific cases is subject to
dispute. The reason for this is that θερμότερον is a πολλαχῶς λεγόμενον, and Aristotle continues, 'Therefore we must be clear about
the extent to which one may call some things that are naturally
constituted warm, others cold, some things dry, others moist, since
it seems to be obvious that these are more or less the causes of
life and death, and also of sleep and waking, youth and old age and
sickness and health (ἐπεὶ ὅτι γ' αἴτια ταῦτα σχεδὸν καὶ θανάτου καὶ
ζωῆς ἔοικεν εἶναι φανερόν, ἔτι δ' ὕπνου καὶ ἐγρηγόρσεως ...); on the
other hand neither roughness and smoothness, nor heaviness and light-
ness, nor, so to speak, anything of that type [is a cause] (ἀλλ' οὐ
τραχύτητες καὶ λειότητες οὐδὲ βαρύτητες καὶ κουφότητες οὐδ' ἄλλο τῶν
τοιούτων οὐδὲν ὡς εἰπεῖν)' (648b2-8). So Aristotle distinguishes between two groups: warm and cold, dry and moist on the one hand, rough
and smooth, heavy and light on the other. The αἴτια for sleep and
waking are to be found in the first not the second group. In treating warmth and cold as the essential causes of sleep, *PA* II 7 exactly
mirrors the view expressed in the preceding section, II 2; if in
Somn. 458a21, however, the mixed state of the blood is introduced as

a cause, it is indeed the case that importance is now attached to
factors which one would otherwise have thought to be related to the
properties of the second group.

In *Somn.* the account of the causes of sleep is, therefore, apparently a more complex one. To the argumentation concerning equilibrium, in which the displacement of warmth is the most important consideration, the section dealing explicitly with the heart adds the
theme of the mixed condition of the blood. At this point for the
first time the text seems directly to answer the original question as
to what the μόριον αἰσθητικόν undergoes in sleep (456b7-9), and the
condition of the blood is supposed to explain this affection. Here
Aristotle seems to be, in essence, drawing on doctrines that belong
to the Sicilian tradition. Solmsen has dealt with these views,[65]
so that it is only necessary to recall the most important points
briefly here. As described several times in *PA*, there is a relationship between, on the one hand, the composition of the blood, and, on
the other, feeling and thought. Comparatively thin and cool blood
favours perception and thought, and thicker and warmer blood in-
creases strength (II 2, 648a2sqq.). However, the essential thing is
seen to be not so much the temperature, as the thinness and purity,
of the blood, as is clear from II 4, 650b18sqq.: it is not because
of the coldness of the blood, but because of its thinness and purity
that some living creatures have a more acute perception. In II 10,
656b3sqq. Aristotle says that it is for similar reasons that certain
organs of sense are placed in the head: the more precise sense-
perceptions are located in parts with comparatively pure blood, where
the activity of the senses is not impaired by the movement of the
warmth of the blood. To this group of doctrines belongs the explanation found in *Somn.* 458a21-2 according to which sleep is caused by
the mixed nature of the blood, the effect of which on the central
sense, however, is not discussed here in any greater detail. The
brevity with which this new theme is introduced is particularly striking (especially after the much broader treatment of the topic of
equilibrium etc.).

It may be surprising that in *PA* II there are found, in general,
some theories about the relationship between the composition of the
blood and the degree of ability to perceive, but that at the same
time in II 2, 648b2-8 factors like roughness, heaviness etc. are de-

nied to be causes of sleeping. But we have to pay regard to this
explicit statement of Aristotle and cannot but say, then, that in
Somn. he introduces an additional cause, the mixed state of the
blood, in his explanation of sleep. Perhaps it was his intention
thereby to stress the role of the heart more strongly than had been
the case in the less developed explanation of sleep which *PA* II 2
and 7 seem to contain. Although one must in any case suppose the
heart to be affected there, too, it is by introducing the new cause
that its crucial role is emphasized. We shall return later to the
relationship of *Somn.* and *PA* and to the possible existence of an
older work on sleep but now we have to resume and settle the problem
of warmth and cold as causes of sleeping.

Warmth and cold as causes of sleep (concluded). The idea that Aristotle dealt with rather briefly in *Somn.*, namely the effect of the
mixed nature of the blood on the central sense, is taken up more
fully in *De insomniis*, since it plays a part in causing us to dream
while we are asleep. Dreams are due to the fact that movements
arise from the actual sensations which leave after-impressions in
the individual organs (*Insomn.* 460b28sqq.). During the night, when
the warmth flows back and the greatest part of the blood flows down
from the head, these movements reach the heart (461a3-7, 461b11sqq.).
As long as there is considerable turbulence caused by food, fever
etc., there are no dreams (461a11-25); it is only after the blood
has ceased to move and is separated (καθισταμένου ... καὶ διακρι-
νομένου τοῦ αἵματος, 461a25) that the movements sent out from the
organs are preserved and are perceived through the medium of the
first faculty. In this connection Aristotle uses the interesting
formulation that the κύριον καὶ ἐπικρῖνον is moved by the movements
of the organs of perception as when it actually perceives, if it is
not completely repressed by the blood (ἐὰν μὴ παντελῶς κατέχηται
ὑπὸ τοῦ αἵματος 461b26-7, cf. 461b6-7). The mixture of the blood,
and its turbulent movement, are the factors affecting the primary
faculty, and are responsible, according to their intensity, for the
phases or stages called ἔκνοια and φαντασία in *Somn.* 457b25-6.

Now it is appropriate to ask what is said here about the part
played by warmth in these processes. It seems that the same holds
true as in *Somn.*: in *Insomn.* ch. 3, where the argument deals with

the principle of perception in the context of an explanation of
dreams, Aristotle does not say explicitly that it is warmth which
paralyses the central faculty. In 461a4-6 the flow of warmth back
from the outer parts to the inner, whereby the movements that remain from the former sensory impressions reach the heart, is only
mentioned in connection with the fact that the individual senses
cannot be active (cf. *Somn.* 457b4). Nevertheless, the statements
in *Insomn.* regarding the flow back of warmth are less general than
in *Somn.* (cf. 457b1, 5-6). In 461b11-12 it is said that the movements reach the heart with the mass of blood going there in sleep;
we may conclude from this passage that in 461a4-8 the causal clause
διὰ τὸ ἐκ τῶν ἔξω εἰς τὸ ἐντὸς γίνεσθαι τὴν τοῦ θερμοῦ παλίρροιαν
refers not only to the preceding words (the inactivity of the individual senses in consequence of the flowing back of warmth: this
statement is supported by comparison with *Somn.* 457b4) but also to
the subsequent ones: it is because of the reflux of the warmth within that the movements come to the heart. When we read, then, that
a reflux of warmth and of most of the blood to the heart takes place
in sleep (461a5-6, b11-12) and that the activity of the κύριον καὶ
ἐπικρῖνον can be inhibited completely by the blood (461b26-7), it
seems to follow that it is the warmth which puts the central faculty
out of action. Why does Aristotle not make any definite statement
to this effect?

Now the question is how the process of flowing down should be
imagined. The anathymiasis cooled by the brain seems to be an entity separate from the warmth in the upper parts as might be suggested by the formulation in *Somn.* 456b26-7 ὅταν δὲ ῥέψῃ κάτω καὶ
ἀντιστρέψαν ἀπώσῃ τὸ θερμόν. Is the warmth carried by the blood
- such as that of the sensory organs which flows downwards - and
should one distinguish between warm blood and the cold anathymiasis
that follows it? Such a distinction which the passages of *Insomn.*
cited above could suggest would accord with the statement found
elsewhere that sleep is a σύνοδός τις τοῦ θερμοῦ εἴσω καὶ ἀντιπερίστασις φυσική (*Somn.* 457b1-2) and that the warmth is forced together from the surrounding parts in considerable mass within a
small area (458a10-11). On the other hand, Aristotle lays so much
stress on the cooling of the anathymiasis that it may be legitimate
to think that the cooled anathymiasis does cause the warmth not

only to flow back but to cool down in some degree, too.[66] (In *PA*
II 7, 653a15-16 Aristotle seems to point to this when he says that
the cooling function of the brain causes τὸ θερμὸν ὑποφεύγειν μετὰ
τοῦ αἵματος; as αἷμα here is nothing other than the anathymiasis
previously called ἡ ἀπὸ τῆς τροφῆς τοῦ αἵματος ἐπίρρυσις one would
think that the chilled blood affects the warmth in some degree.)
In this case, the current arriving at the heart, the original source
of warmth, could be conceived as still warm and yet 'cold' in comparison to the warmth of the heart; its effect on the central faculty would then be to cool and paralyse it.

This last assumption could be supported by the fact that, as
previously mentioned, Aristotle owes certain of his opinions concerning the blood to the Sicilian tradition, which however attributes sleep to the cooling of the blood.[67] Yet on the other hand,
Aristotle is also indebted to the Hippocratic conception whereby
warm blood flows back to the inner parts (*Epid.* VI 5,15 = L. V 320:
τὸ αἷμα ἐν ὕπνῳ εἴσω μᾶλλον φεύγει. *Epid.* VI 4,12 = L. V 310: ἐμφα-
νέως ἐγρηγορὼς θερμότερος τὰ ἔξω, τὰ ἔσω δὲ ψυχρότερος, καθεύδων
τἀναντία). It may be that he never clearly specifies warmth or
cold as causes in conjunction with the central faculty for the reason that he had difficulties in this respect in arriving at a definite conception of their role in ϙonnection with his doctrine of
the heart as the principle of both perception and nutrition. To
understand those difficulties better, let us compare a text from
Problemata physica (XXXIII 15, 963a28-32): 'Since it is fire that
sets the parts of our body in motion but this is forced inwards
during sleep and leaves the region of the head, where the centre
of perception is located, our organs of perception would then be
most at rest and that would be the cause of sleep.'[68] Here in Ps.-
Aristotle the central faculty in the head and the individual organs are put out of action by the cold, whereas in Aristotle this
applies only to the individual organs. The heart is a principle
with a variety of functions, so that difficulties were bound to
arise in connection with it, since, although it was traditional to
relate the cessation of perception to cooling-down processes, the
preparation of nutriment, which is also located there, is tradi-
tionally related to warmth. Perhaps this could explain why Aristotle seems to speak both of a cooling of the warmth, which has its

effect on the heart, and of a flowing back of the warmth, and this
cooling down and flowing back of warmth may represent elements from
Sicilian and Hippocratic theories of sleep.

To recapitulate: in the preceding sections we have tried to deal
with two topics: (1) the problem of warmth and cold as causes of
sleep, (2) the question of a development in the explanation of sleep.
As regards the latter question we found it plausible to accept such
a development for two reasons: (a) From a comparison with *PA* II 2
and 7 it follows that in *Somn.* a new factor is introduced as a cause
of sleep, namely the mixed state of the blood. We may be sure about
this because *PA* II 2, 648b2-8 clearly states that factors like roughness, heaviness etc. do not play a role as causes of sleep. It
accords with this that *PA* II 7, 653a10-18 only mentions other factors as for example loss of equilibrium by accumulation of warmth
within. By introducing the new factor, Aristotle would have stressed the role of the heart in the concluding section of his physiological explanation in order to confirm the theory advanced earlier
in *Somn.* (456a21-4) that it is the heart in which sleep and waking
originate. (b) A development of this kind would have the further
advantage that it could account for some disproportion in the physiological explanation of *Somn.* as a whole. It could explain why
it is that after the introductory question 456b7-9 τί πάσχοντος ...
τοῦ μορίου τοῦ αἰσθητικοῦ there is a long discussion starting at b20
which makes no explicit mention of the heart. It describes only in
general terms the accumulation of warmth in the inner and lower
parts of the body but is quite vague as to what precisely happens
in the heart. There are several statements about how sleep comes
about which do not refer, however, to the heart but are more general.
It is clear that a definition like ὁ ὕπνος ἐστὶ σύνοδός τις τοῦ
θερμοῦ εἴσω concerns the heart anyway, too, but this organ does not
seem to play a part according to earlier statements such as 456a21-
4. The heart is discussed for the first time only in the concluding
section which, with its introduction of a new factor as cause of
sleep (the mixed nature of the blood), has almost the character of
an appendix after the remarks on waking. The brevity with which
the new factor is dealt with is particularly striking (especially
after the much broader treatment of the topic of equilibrium etc.)
as it is precisely the answer to the question how the faculty of

perception is affected.

If there is a development in the explanation of sleep this gives rise to the question whether there are other indications that the less developed explanation in *PA* II is earlier. Another question is whether evidence can be advanced for the existence of an older work on sleep; if one was available for Aristotle to draw on in his physiological discussions in *Somn.* this could perhaps explain the disproportion observed there. The end of the paper deals with these questions.

On the chronology of Somn. and the possible existence of an older work on sleep

We must now examine the chronological relationship between the phys-iological description of sleep given in *PA* II 7 and that given in *Somn.* Both texts contain references to each other: *PA* II 7, 653a 19-20 is rounded off with: περὶ ὧν εἴρηται καθ' αὑτὰ ἔν τε τοῖς περὶ αἰσθήσεως καὶ περὶ ὕπνου διωρισμένοις. On the other hand in *Somn.* 457b29, after the *aporiai*, a discussion of the brain begins - to the effect that it is crucial for the cooling process - and this discussion is linked with the reference ὥσπερ ἐν ἄλλοις εἴρη-ται, which the statements that follow show can only be to *PA* II 7.[69] Lefèvre, however, has once again pointed out recently[70] that such references are often little more than pointers to what Aristotle intended by way of a systematic ordering of his writings. Do the similarities in content offer a chronological criterion?

In *PA* the comparable points[71] occur in the context of a more ex-haustive and detailed discussion. Having dealt with the nature of the brain Aristotle goes on to discuss its function from 652b16. Its task is to balance the warmth of the heart by means of its cold. There are veins to bring warmth to the upper regions, as we read in 652b27sqq.; but in order to prevent injury they are thin and narrow veins with thin pure blood. The cold that prevails there is also responsible for the fluxes that flow from the head and are formed in a similar manner to rain; further discussion of them, however, is reserved for an investigation of the causes of disease. There follows a consideration of sleep: ποιεῖ δὲ καὶ τὸν ὕπνον ... (653a 10sqq.). The text of *Somn.* diverges in so far as the comparison with atmospheric precipitation, made in *PA* only in respect of phlegm,

is there extended to the anathymiasis which causes sleep. *PA* makes
only one of two possible points of comparison, in contrast to *Somn.*,
which both compresses and yet broadens the comparison. It is rather
surprising to find a reference to the residue associated with disease in this context, as this component of the anathymiasis had not
previously been mentioned. This seems in fact to indicate that
Somn. follows *PA* here in confirmation of our previous observations.

Everything points, then, to the fact that *Somn.* is later than *De
An.* and *PA*: (1) in the first part of *Somn.* we find passages that presuppose the doctrine of *De anima* II, as we have indicated above;[72]
one of the cross-references (454a12) cannot be separated from its
context. What we are told there, with reference to the θρεπτικόν,
about the hierarchy and separability of the various parts or faculties of the soul corresponds to the same stage of development as
that represented by 455a23-5 (cf. a6-7) in its remarks on the sense
of touch. (2) In the second part of *Somn.* the section of text just
considered in the passage on the brain would be written later than
PA, which agrees with *De anima* in its overall concept as Lefèvre
has shown.[73] That the order is *PA* - *Somn.* at this point agrees
with our argument above that *Somn.* represents a more complex explanation of sleep than *PA*. In *PA* II 7, the mixed nature of the blood
is not one of the themes represented, and previously, in II 2, such
a cause had been explicitly excluded for sleep as well as for other
phenomena.[74]

Now Drossaart stressed that the physiological part of *Somn.* was
especially closely related to *De juventute*, and since *Juv.* is unani-
mously considered to come before *PA*, this could constitute a possible
objection to the order proposed. However, if one considers the references to *Juv.*[75] in Drossaart, it immediately becomes clear that
many of them relate to views found also in *PA* and *GA* - as for example those on the division of the body into three, the heart as the
seat of the central organ and the disposition of the veins as they
leave the heart.[76] The most interesting of the texts compared by
Drossaart, in so far as it sheds particular light on the problem of
dating, is *Somn.* 455b34-456a1. Here it is established that the
principle of perception and the principle of movement both emanate
from the same part of the body; the same assertion is made concerning perception, movement and nutrition in *PA* II 1, 647a24-6 and,

similarly, in III 3,665a10-15, but for perception and nutrition only
in *Juv.* 469a5-7 and 474a25 - b3. This means that the reference to
movement in *PA* and *Somn.* is missing in *Juv.*, and this accords with
Lefèvre's finding - in support of which he refers to texts such as
479a4-6 -[77] that in *Juv.* the heart does not appear to be indispensable for movement. This gives us a firmer basis on which to say
that *Somn.* 455b34 -456a1 represents, with its parallels in *PA*, a
later stage in the development of the doctrine than does *Juv.*

This means that on the one hand there are aspects both of the
psychological and of the physiological sections of *Somn.* which seem
indicative of the time of *De anima* and *PA* or later, and hence corroborate the unity of the treatise. On the other hand, within the
physiological section (456b20sqq.) we found some disproportion as
sketched above, and this gives rise to the question of whether Aristotle might have been following some earlier work. But is there
positive evidence of its existence? What does strike one is that
sleep and waking are mentioned repeatedly in conjunction with the
phenomena which form the subject matter of the last, and obviously
the oldest, treatise of the *Parva naturalia*, namely *De juventute*.
According to *PA* I 1, 639a19-21 the characteristics shared by many
types of living creature which are otherwise different from each
other are sleep, respiration, growth, old age and death. In *PA* II
2, 648a36-b8, as we noted before, we are told that the same causes
- namely warmth and cold, dryness and moisture - underlie life and
death, sleeping and waking, youth and old age and illness and
health. It is important, however, to pay special attention to the
introduction to *De sensu*, which tells us in advance what the individual parts of *PN* are to be. Aristotle specifies two groups of
psychosomatic phenomena which are to be the subject of investigation: (1) τὰ μέγιστα which are common to ζῷα and characteristic of
them: αἴσθησις, μνήμη, θυμός, ἐπιθυμία, ὄρεξις and also ἡδονή and
λύπη, for these too are found in nearly all living creatures (*Sens.*
436a6-11). (2) A second group is then identified with πρὸς δὲ τούτοις, and this consists on the one hand of what is common to everything living (πάντων ... τῶν μετεχόντων ζωῆς), that is to say both
animals and plants, and on the other hand of what belongs to certain
living creatures (τῶν ζῴων ἐνίοις). It is stated that the most important of these phenomena form four pairs: ἐγρήγορσις καὶ ὕπνος,

καὶ νεότης καὶ γῆρας, καὶ ἀναπνοὴ καὶ ἐκπνοή, καὶ ζωὴ καὶ θάνατος
(*Sens*. 436a11-15).[78] Within the two groups, therefore, sleep and
waking once again make their appearance in close association with
phenomena which correspond exactly to the subject-matter and title
of the final treatise of the *Parva naturalia*.

But on closer examination such an association is difficult to
reconcile with what is said later in *De somno* regarding sleep. In
the introductory remark at *Sens*. 436a12, it is maintained that
sleep belongs only to τῶν ζῴων ἐ ν ί ο ι ς, since the other heading
mentioned ('everything living') has to be ruled out. This is because *De somno* is concerned purely with the physiology of animals,
in so far as plants cannot perceive and hence cannot sleep (cf.
Somn. 454a15-17; *GA* V 1, 778b32-779a4). But the treatise itself
contains entirely different pronouncements: *Somn*. 454b14-15 τὰ μὲν
οὖν ἄλλα σ χ ε δ ὸ ν ἄ π α ν τ α δῆλα κοινωνοῦνθ' ὕπνου, καὶ πλωτὰ
καὶ πτηνὰ καὶ πεζά ... 454b23-4 ὅτι μὲν οὖν ὕπνου κοινωνεῖ τ ὰ ζ ῷ α
π ά ν τ α, φανερόν ... 455a26-7 διὸ καὶ π ᾶ σ ι ν ὑπάρχει [sc. ἐγρήγορσις καὶ ὕπνος] τ ο ῖ ς ζ ῴ ο ι ς. According to what we are told
here, therefore, sleep and waking would belong rather in the first
group of phenomena, which are found in all, or nearly all, living
creatures. The question arises of why in the introductory remark in
Sens. Aristotle combined them with *Juv.-Respir.*, despite the discrepancies which arise. The psychosomatic phenomena concerned tend
to be of a more biological nature so that the affections dealt with
are linked thematically as well as in respect of their causes.
Hence there could be something to be said for the view that they
were dealt with together and that an older work existed for sleep,
which is often mentioned in connection with some of the subject-
matter of *Juv*.

When Aristotle edited the *Parva naturalia*, he wrote a new set of
prefatory comments for *De longitudine* so that we now have two parallel introductions.[79] If, similarly, he had used an older work in
his physiological explanation of sleep, this could explain, perhaps,
why we find some disproportion in *Somn*. 456b20sqq. For one would
think that the older work contained a less developed explanation
of sleep similar to *PA* which we have concluded to be earlier than
Somn., too. Now we have seen that in the physiological discussion
of *Somn*. the introductory question concerning how the central faculty

is affected is dealt with very briefly and only in the concluding
section; in the preceding section, although it is very extensive and
the definitions given there affect the heart anyway, too, this organ
is not mentioned explicitly. The contents of this broader section
offer several points of similarity to the earlier *PA* II and, as we
may suppose, to the earlier work on sleep. If Aristotle had this
to draw on in the physiological discussion of *Somn.*, the disproportion observed in the text could be more easily understood: the section 456b20-458a10 drawing on earlier expositions would be broader
than the brief concluding section introducing a new factor in the
explanation of sleep.

To sum up: *Somn.* was composed as a unity which cannot be divided
into a psychological and a physiological part. We have tried to
show that the arguments advanced for such a division are not convincing. Two topics have formed the nucleus of the subsequent exposition: firstly, a problem which has been thoroughly debated
among the early commentators as well as by recent authors, namely
whether it is warmth or cold that causes sleep by affecting the
central sense. Secondly, the question of a development in the explanation of sleep: whether or not an older work on sleep existed,
it seems sure to me, at least, that the explanation of *Somn.* is
more developed because the mixed state of the blood is introduced
as a cause of sleep whereas in *PA* II 2 and 7 factors of this kind
do not play a role and are expressly denied.[80]

NOTES

1 Apparent in remarks by W.Theiler, *Aristoteles Über die Seele*
 (2nd ed. Darmstadt-Berlin 1966), 75-6, and by P.Siwek, *Aristoteles, Parva naturalia* (Rome 1963), xiii-xv, and *Aristoteles,
 Tractatus De anima gr. et lat.* (Rome 1965), 14sqq. as previously
 indicated by C.Lefèvre, *Sur l'évolution d'Aristote en psychologie* (Louvain 1972), 182-3 n.4.

2 C.A.Brandis, 'Aristoteles und seine akademischen Zeitgenossen',
 Handbuch der Geschichte der griechisch-römischen Philosophie
 II 2 (Berlin 1857), 1193sq.

3 W.Jaeger, 'Das Pneuma im Lykeion', *Hermes* 48 (1913), 29-74, esp. 42, and *Aristoteles, Grundlegung einer Geschichte seiner Entwicklung* (2nd ed. Berlin 1955), 354.

4 F.Nuyens, *L'évolution de la psychologie d'Aristote* (Louvain 1948), 163-70 and 250-6.

5 I.Düring, *Aristotle's De partibus animalium, Critical and literary commentaries* (Göteborg 1943), 27-30 and 131.

6 W.D.Ross, *Aristotle. Parva naturalia* (Oxford 1955), 3-18.

7 Lefèvre (*op.cit. n.1*), 156-214 *passim*.

8 Lefèvre (*op.cit. n.1*), 189sqq. and cf. above, pp.42sqq.

9 Nuyens (*op.cit. n.4*), 255.

10 Düring (*op.cit. n.5*), 30, 131, 132.

11 H.J.Drossaart Lulofs, *Aristotelis De insomniis et De divinatione per somnum* (Philosophia Antiqua II, Leyden 1947), xvsqq.

12 C.Diano in *Doxa* 2 (1949), 280-2.

13 M.Untersteiner in *Paideia* 5 (1950), 391.

14 E. von Ivanka in *Anzeiger für die Altertumswissenschaft* 3 (1950), col.121.

15 Ross (*op.cit. n.6*), 12-13.

16 I.Düring, *Aristoteles. Darstellung und Interpretation seines Denkens* (Heidelberg 1966), 566.

17 Düring (*op.cit. n.16*), 560 and 561.

18 Lefèvre (*op.cit. n.1*), 154 n.19.

19 Compare C.Lefèvre, above p.62 n.93.

20 Drossaart Lulofs (*op.cit. n.11*), xvi.

21 Drossaart, xx.

22 Drossaart, xvi-xviii, xxisqq.

23 Drossaart, xix.

24 Drossaart, xix-xx.

25 Drossaart, xviii-xix.

26 Drossaart, xvi and xviii-xix.

27 Similarly *PA* II 10, 656a29-37 (compare Ross (*op.cit. n.6*), 300,

Lefèvre (op.cit. n.1), 186 n.18).

28 Drossaart (op.cit. n.11), xx.

29 Ross (op.cit. n.6), 260.

30 Georgios Pachymeres (see below note 56) defines sleep as ἐν τῷ πρώτῳ αἰσθητηρίῳ ἀργία; Theodoros Metochites, Somn., 16, 27 ed. Drossaart, Aristotelis De somno et vigilia liber adiectis veteribus translationibus et Theodori Metochitae commentario (Templum Salomonis 1943) writes in his commentary on 455b12-13 of the ἀδυνατεῖν καὶ μὴ ἐνεργεῖν of this primary faculty. Previously Aristotle himself had accompanied his negative description in Somn. 455b3 with the remark that sleep does not consist in an ἀργεῖν καὶ μὴ χρῆσθαι of the senses.

31 Drossaart (op.cit. n.11), xxv.

32 See H.Bonitz, Index Aristotelicus 357b13sqq.

33 H.Bonitz, Aristotelische Studien (Hildesheim 1969), 151-4 (reprinted from Sitzungsberichte der Akademie der Wissenschaften Wien, philosophisch-historische Klasse XLI 2 (1863), 431-4).

34 Bonitz (op.cit. n.33), 153 (= 433).

35 Drossaart (op.cit. n.11), xxviii-xxix.

36 Drossaart, xxvii.

37 Similarly τὸ κύριον ... αἰσθητήριον in 455a33.

38 For the sake of completeness, one final argument on this work should be mentioned briefly. Ross (op.cit. n.6), 13, already referred to the fact that the contradiction suggested by Drossaart (op.cit. n.11, xxxii-xxxiii) between Insomn. 460a1-2 and Sens. 437b10-23 on the question of whether the light leaving the eye is in any way responsible for causing sight, is more apparent than real; accordingly there is no discrepancy in content between an earlier (Insomn. B) and a later (Sens.) view.

39 Drossaart (op.cit. n.11), xvi-xvii and xx.

40 Ross (op.cit. n.6), 12.

41 C.Lefèvre, cf. above, p. 39.

42 Drossaart (op.cit. n.11), xxisqq.

43 Drossaart, xviii-xix.

44 E.Zeller, Die Philosophie der Griechen in ihrer geschichtlichen Entwicklung II 2 (4th ed. Leipzig 1921), 551.

45 H.Siebeck, Geschichte der Psychologie I 2 (Gotha 1880), 82-3.

46 M.Wellmann, *Fragmentsammlung der griechischen Ärzte* I: *Die Frag-mente der sikelischen Ärzte Akron, Philistion und des Diokles von Karystos* (Berlin 1901), 23.

47 R.D.Hicks, *Aristotle. De anima* (1907, reprinted Amsterdam 1965), liv.

48 H.Enders, *Schlaf und Traum bei Aristoteles* (Würzburg dissertation 1924), 29 n.2, 108.

49 R.Mugnier, *Aristote, Petits traités d'histoire naturelle* (Paris 1953), 73 n.1.

50 H.Enders (*op.cit. n.48*), 29 n.2.

51 The commentary on the treatises in *PN*, beginning with *Somn.*, in Monac. gr. 91 (from f. 101), which A.Wartelle (*Inventaire des manuscrits grecs d'Aristote et de ses commentateurs* (Paris 1963), no. 1110) attributes to the eleventh-century Michael Psellos, is the work of Michael of Ephesus.

52 Drossaart, *De somno* (*op.cit. n.30*), xxvii.

53 Compare Mich. *PN* 53, 27-8 ≈ Soph. *PN* 24,25-6. Mich. 56,30 ≈ 26, 23-4 etc. (all in Wendland's apparatus criticus in *CAG* V 6).

54 Metoch. 18,39 - 19,6 ≈ Schol. 458,31-8 (*Oeuvres complètes* VII ed. Petit-Sideridès-Jugie, Paris 1936), compare Drossaart (*op.cit. n.30*), 32. Metoch. 21, 29-30 ≈ Schol. 459,13-15 and 21,32-5 ≈ 459,15-19, the last in Drossaart (*op.cit. n.30*), 35.

55 Drossaart (*op.cit. n.30*), ix and n.9.

56 The text is in Ham. 512 at ff. 139-40. There are specimens of this MS in D.Harlfinger, *Die Textgeschichte der ps.-aristoteli-schen Schrift* περὶ ἀτόμων γραμμῶν (Amsterdam 1971), plates 25-6; for the identification see 357sq.

57 On this see Drossaart (*op.cit. n.30*), 31 (to 18,19-26).

58 In the most recent edition by W.H.S.Jones, *The medical writings of Anonymus Londinensis* (Cambridge 1947) the text is on 92.

59 See H.Flashar, *Aristoteles Problemata Physica* (Berlin 1962), 328-9.

60 See G.E.R.Lloyd above p.225 and n.55.

61 See Ross (*op.cit. n.6*), 41 n.1.

62 On this see G.E.R.Lloyd above p.216.

63 W.D.Ross, *Aristotle. Metaphysics* II (Oxford 1924), 235 (on H 4, 1044b17).

64 Drossaart (*op.cit. n.11*), xxiii.

65 F.Solmsen, 'Tissues and the soul. Philosophical contributions to
   physiology', *Philos. Rev.* 59 (1950) 435-68, particularly 464sqq.
   (reprinted in *Kleine Schriften* I (Hildesheim 1968), 502-35, here
   particularly 531sqq.), and also: 'Greek philosophy and the discovery of the nerves', *Museum Helveticum* 18 (1961), 150-97, particularly 171sqq. (reprinted in *Kl. Schriften* I, 536-82, here
   particularly 556sqq.).

66 Compare Solmsen, 'Greek philosophy ...' (*art.cit. n.65*), 161
   (*Kl. Schr.* I 547) 'the brain, being colder than the region of
   the heart, is in a position to quiet the latter by sending down
   currents of cooling matter', with supporting references in note
   13 to *Somn.* 457b29-458a10 and *PA* II 7, 652b16-653a10.

67 Empedocles in Aet. V 24,2 (*Dox.* 435,17-19) and V 25,4 (*Dox.* 438,
   2-3). Ps.-Hippocr., περὶ φυσῶν ch. 14, 28,4sqq. in A.Nelson,
   Die hippokratische Schrift περὶ φυσῶν, *Text und Studien* (Uppsala
   dissertation 1909). See Wellmann (*op.cit. n.46*), 23 and F.
   Rüsche, *Blut, Leben und Seele* (Paderborn 1930), 126 n.2, 130sqq.,
   135.

68 Based on the German translation of H.Flashar (*op.cit. n.59*), 278.

69 Ross (*op.cit. n.6*), 265.

70 Lefèvre (*op.cit. n.1*), 151.

71 These are: the brain or its analogue as the coldest part of the
   body (*Somn.* 457b29-31 ≈ *PA* 652a27-8, compare 652b23-5, 653a10-
   12); the comparison of the cooling of the anathymiasis with the
   condensation of rain (457b31-458a5 ≈ *PA* 652b33-653a8); the fine-
   ness and narrowness of the veins round the brain (458a7-8 ≈ *PA*
   652b31-2); the thinness and purity of the blood in the head (458
   a13-14 ≈ *PA* 652b33).

72 See above p.251.

73 C.Lefèvre (*op.cit. n.1*), 174-82.

74 See above pp.264-7. If this is correct, it would be possible
   here in the case of *PA-Somn.* to establish the 'discovery of ideas',
   and not only, as in the preceding case of *De An.-Somn.*, the time
   of the 'composition' and when it was 'put into final form'.
   C.H.Kahn ('Sensation and consciousness in Aristotle's psychology', *Archiv Gesch. Philos.* 48 (1966), 43-81, esp. 51 and 68
   n.59) quite correctly stressed the need to distinguish between
   these two aspects in order to avoid false chronological conclusions. Against I.Block ('The order of Aristotle's psychological
   writings', *AJP* 82 (1961), 50-77), who placed *PN* after *De anima*
   on the grounds of the more detailed treatment of the general faculty, Kahn affirms that the treatment concerned does not necessarily imply a more advanced stage of thought but is dealt with
   in more detail in *PN* simply because it corresponds more closely
   to the subject-matter of this type of treatise.

75 Drossaart (*op.cit. n.11*), xxi-xxii.

76 See the list in Lefèvre (*op.cit. n.1*), 184-5 notes 9-11.

77 Lefèvre (*op.cit. n.1*), 188 and n.25.

78 After mention of the two groups (436a6-11 and 436a11-17) there is still (436a17-b1) the note that the physicist has also to deal with the causes of illness and health (compare *Juv.* 480b 21-30). E.Rolfes, *Aristoteles' kleine naturwissenschaftliche Schriften* (Leipzig 1924), v and Nuyens (*op.cit. n.4*), 255-6 seem to make the surprising assumption that details of the contents of *PN* do not start to be given until 436a12.

79 On the double version, established by J.Cook Wilson, *Philol. Rundschau* 1 (1881), 1240, see now Drossaart (*op.cit. n.11*), xl; Ross (*op.cit. n.6*), 284-5; Düring (*op.cit. n.16*), 560.

80 I should like to express my thanks for advice and criticism to my teacher Paul Moraux and to all the participants in the seventh Symposium Aristotelicum and in particular Dr Lefèvre, Dr Lloyd, Dr Sorabji, Professor Verbeke and Professor Verdenius. Professor H.-J. Drossaart Lulofs could not attend the Symposium himself but has read this article with kind attention. I am grateful to him for providing a number of useful references. Only a short reference can be made to the thesis of H.Wijsenbeek-Wijler, *Aristotle's concept of soul, sleep and dreams* (Amsterdam 1976). It appeared after this paper had gone to press; the author has made use of my original German draft but unfortunately misunderstood several points.

11: LE *DE ANIMA* DANS LA TRADITION GRECQUE. QUELQUES ASPECTS DE L'INTERPRÉTATION DU TRAITÉ, DE THÉOPHRASTE À THÉMISTIUS

Paul Moraux

Bien qu'il ait été commenté moins souvent que d'autres traités - les *Catégories*, par exemple - le *De anima* d'Aristote a marqué la réflexion philosophique et la pensée scientifique des siècles suivants. Cette influence ne se limite pas aux seuls penseurs qui ont accueilli et parfois tenté d'approfondir le message d'Aristote; elle s'étend aussi à tous ceux qui, sans se réclamer de l'aristotélisme, se sont attachés à résoudre les problèmes sur lesquels l'ouvrage avait attiré l'attention; elle se manifeste aussi par les réactions et l'opposition plus ou moins ouvertement déclarée qu'ont provoquées certaines thèses d'Aristote. Il suffit de citer, parmi d'autres, le nom de Plotin, pour faire mesurer l'intérêt qu'ont suscité, en dehors de l'École, les idées qu'Aristote avait émises au sujet de l'âme.

On ne saurait énumérer ici toutes les questions et tous les thèmes du *De anima* qui, d'une manière ou d'une autre, ont alimenté la discussion philosophique et fécondé la réflexion, jusqu'à la fin de l'Antiquité grecque et bien au-delà, tant en Orient qu'en Occident. Parmi les plus importants, citons la conception de l'âme comme entéléchie du corps, avec le problème connexe de l'interdépendance du psychique et du somatique; cette conception, si opposée au dualisme platonicien, à ses présupposés et à ses implications, ne pouvait manquer de faire naître bien des débats. L'élargissement des recherches sur l'âme à la totalité du vivant a, par ailleurs, conféré une dimension nouvelle aux investigations des siècles postérieurs. L'intérêt s'est porté aussi sur la théorie des facultés de l'âme, que l'on a mise en regard de la théorie platonicienne des trois parties de l'âme, soit pour défendre l'une et rejeter l'autre, soit pour essayer de les harmoniser et de les combiner. Même chose à propos de la motricité de l'âme: si l'âme est bien cause de mouvement, faut-il, avec Platon, la considérer comme un être qui se meut lui-même, ou, avec Aristote, lui dénier tout mouvement qui lui soit propre? D'autres discussions portèrent

sur la sensation, son mécanisme en général, sa valeur en tant que
critérium, la localisation et les fonctions du sensorium commun,
etc. Les thèses d'Aristote sur la vision, la lumière et le diaphane
retinrent l'attention des spécialistes de l'optique scientifique.
Pour les sensations par contact direct, goût et toucher, les avis se
partagèrent sur le point de savoir si la chair en est l'organe ou ne
joue qu'un rôle de médium. Au problème de l'imagination et de la
mémoire était naturellement lié celui de la genèse des concepts, à
propos duquel on vit s'affronter des théories très différentes.
Enfin et surtout, les chapitres consacrés à l'intellect furent la
source d'interminables discussions; la difficulté du sujet et l'obscurité des déclarations d'Aristote semblent avoir incité les interprètes à rivaliser de sagacité, d'ingéniosité et d'imagination.
L'abondante floraison des théories que firent éclore ces quelques
pages suffirait, à elle seule, à montrer quelle fut l'importance du
De anima dans la pensée grecque tardive.

   De longues recherches seraient nécessaires pour mettre au jour
toutes les traces de l'influence du traité et tenter de les situer
historiquement, et il faudrait sans doute un gros livre pour présenter les résultats d'une telle enquête. Mon propos actuel, beaucoup plus modeste, est sensiblement différent. Je voudrais surtout
examiner les efforts qui ont été faits, après Aristote, pour comprendre et expliquer le texte du traité, efforts qui, bien souvent,
ont été au point de départ de la réflexion philosophique sur le
contenu du traité: ce sont donc avant tout les commentaires, les
résumés, les paraphrases, etc., qui retiendront mon attention,
qu'ils portent sur la totalité du texte ou ne soient consacrés qu'à
quelques morceaux choisis. Plotin, qui a pris position par rapport
à diverses thèses d'Aristote sans toutefois commenter le texte
phrase par phrase, m'intéresse donc ici moins que Porphyre, qui
semble être parti de l'explication du texte pour distribuer éloges
et critiques. Forcé d'être assez bref, je me limiterai dans le
temps, en ne descendant pas au-delà du quatrième siècle. Après
cette date s'ouvre l'âge des grands commentateurs néoplatoniciens;
les documents conservés deviennent très abondants; ils sont assez
bien connus et facilement accessibles. Je me limiterai aussi dans
la matière: l'exégèse du *De anima* touche à tant de questions
diverses qu'il faut bien faire un choix. En principe, je m'en

tiendrai donc à deux groupes de problèmes qui sont parmi les plus
importants et les plus souvent abordés: ceux des rapports entre
l'âme et le corps, soulevés par l'entéléchisme, et ceux qui ont trait
à la nature, au développement et au fonctionnement de l'intellect
humain. De nombreux autres problèmes ne seront évoqués que de manière
incidente, ou laissés tout à fait de côté. Il va sans dire que
je ne les considère pas pour autant comme dénués d'intérêt.

Les discussions relatives au *De anima* et à la psychologie d'Aristote s'ouvrent avec Théophraste. Dans les livres 4 et 5 de ses
Φυσικά, qui étaient consacrés à la doctrine de l'âme,[1] il soulevait
une foule de difficultés, formulait des observations, proposait des
solutions, et cela en peu de mots, la concision du style allant de
pair avec la richesse du contenu.[2] C'est bien en se référant à
l'exposé d'Aristote que Théophraste énonçait ses propres réflexions.
Pour autant que nous puissions en juger par la *Métaphrase* de Priscien, l'ordre des matières était, en gros, celui qu'avait adopté
Aristote: la sensation en général; les diverses sensations en particulier, vue, ouïe, goût, toucher; le nombre des sensations; la
perception des sensibles communs; la perception de la sensation;
l'imagination; l'intellect. Toutefois, Théophraste ne suivait pas
le texte d'Aristote pas à pas, comme l'eût fait un commentateur ou
l'auteur d'un abrégé. Concentrant son attention sur quelques problèmes choisis, il rapprochait des indications ou des thèses prises
à divers endroits de l'ouvrage ou même à des ouvrages différents,
soit pour en tirer une difficulté, soit pour les éclairer l'une par
l'autre. Dans quelle mesure a-t-il voulu être et a-t-il été en
fait un interprète fidèle de la pensée d'Aristote? La question est
controversée et, du moins en ce qui concerne la psychologie, mal-
aisée à trancher. La forme même des fragments est celle d'aide-
mémoire plutôt que de véritables exposés; sans doute avons-nous
affaire au simple canevas de considérations que Théophraste déve-
loppait dans son enseignement oral. Les théories d'Aristote, peut-
être aussi les discussions auxquelles leur présentation avait donné
lieu au sein de l'École, en constituent le point de départ, mais
il est manifeste que Théophraste a voulu éclairer, préciser, prolonger et compléter ce qu'avait fait Aristote.

En dépit de leur petit nombre et de leur concision, ces fragments nous montrent, du reste, qu'il a, le premier, attiré

l'attention sur plusieurs problèmes qui, pendant des siècles, allaient
occuper les commentateurs du *De anima*. Je n'en veux citer ici que
quelques-uns. Faut-il admettre pour toutes les sensations, y compris le goût et le toucher, l'existence d'un milieu intermédiaire
entre l'objet sensible et le siège de la faculté sensitive? Quelle
est la nature du diaphane, et à quel facteur doit-il son origine?
La lumière est-elle incorporelle, si elle naît de la présence de
corps déterminés? Comment les phénomènes de réflexion de la lumière peuvent-ils s'expliquer dans la perspective aristotélicienne,
selon laquelle la lumière est 'l'entéléchie du diaphane' et non une
sorte de 'projection' effectuant un certain trajet à partir de la
source lumineuse? Plusieurs des problèmes relatifs à la théorie de
l'intellect étaient appelés à connaître un avenir plus remarquable
encore.[3] Quelle est l'origine de l'intellect humain? Fait-il partie de notre nature, s'il est venu en nous 'du dehors'?[4] La potentialité totale de l'intellect ne force-t-elle pas à le tenir pour
identique à la matière? Comment et sous quelles causes l'intellect
en puissance passe-t-il à l'*habitus*? Quels sont les rapports entre
l'intellect en puissance et l'intellect actif? En outre, c'est
chez Théophraste qu'apparaissent les expressions δυνάμει νοῦς, ἐνεργείᾳ νοῦς, ποιητικὸς νοῦς et d'autres analogues, qui allaient rester en usage pendant de nombreux siècles.

Dans les deux siècles qui suivirent la mort de Théophraste, les
maigres restes de la littérature philosophique péripatéticienne ne
présentent aucune trace de l'utilisation du *De anima*, et on peut
supposer que l'ouvrage ne fut guère lu avant la renaissance de l'aristotélisme sous Andronicus. Le peu que nous sachions des doctrines
psychologiques d'un Straton ou d'un Critolaus montre, en tout cas,
qu'ils ne se fondaient pas sur le traité d'Aristote. Chez les
Stoïciens, pourtant, nous voyons Posidonius rejeter la thèse de
Chrysippe selon laquelle le seul *logos* serait à l'origine de toutes
les activités psychiques, et adopter au contraire une tripartition
de l'âme d'allure toute platonicienne; mais, comme Aristote, Posidonius se refuse à admettre qu'il existe des *parties* de l'âme; il
préfère parler des *facultés* d'une seule et même âme, dont il situe
le siège dans le coeur.[5] La sympathie de Posidonius pour l'aristotélisme est bien connue. Cependant, il serait osé de voir dans sa
théorie des facultés de l'âme le fruit d'une étude personnelle du *De*

anima.

La situation change radicalement au premier siècle avant J.-C.
Sans doute grâce aux travaux d'Andronicus, les traités scolaires
retiennent à nouveau l'attention; ils vont faire, désormais, l'objet d'études et de commentaires nombreux. Les rares renseignements que nous possédons sur l'oeuvre exégétique d'Andronicus lui-
même font voir qu'il n'hésitait pas à marquer ses réserves par rapport à certains points de la doctrine d'Aristote. En ce qui concerne notamment les rapports de l'âme et du corps, il interprétait
l'entéléchisme dans une perspective assez voisine de celle qu'avait
adoptée la médecine hippocratique pour expliquer la santé. Ce qui
compte avant tout, c'est, d'après lui, la juste relation entre les
divers éléments constitutifs du corps: l'âme, disait-il, n'est rien
autre que le mélange (κρᾶσις) des constituants du corps, ou qu'une
faculté (δύναμις) procédant de ce mélange. Dans ses remarques sur
la critique qu'avait faite Aristote de la définition de l'âme proposée par Xénocrate, il insistait également sur l'importance des
rapports numériques entre les éléments dont est formé le corps.
Ainsi, Andronicus ouvre la lignée des Péripatéticiens qui, contre
le dualisme platonicien, souligneront l'interdépendance de l'âme
et du corps au point de voir dans la constitution du corps organisé,
sinon la cause même de l'âme, du moins la condition indispensable
à son existence et à l'exercice de ses activités. Galien et Alexandre d'Aphrodise, pour ne citer que deux noms célèbres, illustre-
ront la même tendance.[6]

A la génération suivante, Boéthus de Sidon nous est présenté par
Simplicius comme un commentateur de très haut niveau, égal ou même
supérieur à Alexandre d'Aphrodise. Mais, alors que nous sommes
bien renseignés sur son commentaire aux *Catégories*, nous ne savons
rien de sa psychologie, le *Contre Boéthus* de Porphyre[7] visant, à
mon sens, un Stoïcien et non le Péripatéticien disciple d'Andronicus.[8] En revanche, nous avons deux indications sur celle de Xénarque de Séleucie, dont on connaît la féroce polémique contre la
doctrine aristotélicienne du cinquième élément. Ainsi que quelques
autres Péripatéticiens, il définissait l'âme comme 'la perfection
selon la forme, l'entéléchie qui, simultanément, existe en elle-
même et est unie au corps'.[9] Il semble que Xénarque ait voulu souligner par là que l'âme n'est pas identique au corps, mais n'existe

pourtant qu'en liaison avec lui. Plus curieux est un témoignage
d'Alexandre d'Aphrodise rapporté par Philopon[10] et relatif à l'intellect. Si, comme le dit Aristote, l'intellect n'est rien en acte
avant de penser et se réduit à une simple potentialité, et si l'âme
est bien 'le lieu des formes', l'intellect potentiel, disait Xénarque, est identique à la matière première. Plutôt qu'une véritable
interprétation, cette remarque de Xénarque n'est sans doute qu'une
difficulté soulevée contre Aristote et comparable aux multiples
objections dont était fait le traité *Contre la cinquième essence*.[11]
On se rappellera que Théophraste, déjà, avait prévu et écarté cette
objection[12] et que, plus tard, Alexandre qualifiera l'intellect potentiel de νοῦς ὑλικός, tout en soulignant qu'il n'est pas identique à la matière.[13]

De la grande compilation d'Arius Didymus sur la philosophie
péripatéticienne, on connaît surtout l'exposé de l'éthique conservé
par Stobée. L'exposé de la philosophie naturelle a laissé des
traces moins importantes,[14] se rapportant pour la plupart à la physique et à la météorologie. Une trentaine de lignes à peine[15] ont
trait à la théorie de l'âme; Arius y combine des éléments pris au
De anima et au *De sensu*, sans d'ordinaire s'écarter beaucoup d'Aristote;[16] on notera pourtant la phrase suivante, qui suit la mention
des cinq sensations: 'Il existe aussi une sensation composée, dans
laquelle naissent la faculté de représentation tout entière, celle
de la mémoire et celle de l'opinion, et qui, en conséquence, n'est
pas sans participer à l'intelligence.' Arius entend coordonner et
systématiser en ces quatre lignes, du reste assez obscures, diverses indications prises aux deux premiers chapitres du *De anima* III
et aux *Parva naturalia*.[17] La difficile question de la κοινὴ αἴσθησις est également évoquée par Aetius,[18] et elle retiendra longuement l'attention d'autres commentateurs, notamment d'Alexandre.[19]
Arius connaît également le problème, débattu par Aristote et repris
par Théophraste, de l'intermédiaire entre l'objet et l'organe dans
le cas du goût et du toucher; toutefois, la solution qu'il en donne
montre qu'il n'a pas travaillé sur le texte original du *De anima*,
mais plutôt sur un résumé assez maladroit, qu'il a mal compris.[20]
Dans les siècles suivants, et jusque chez Averroès, la question du
μέσον des diverses sensations restera controversée.

Nicholas de Damas, qui fut à la fois historien, diplomate et

philosophe, conseiller d'Hérode et familier d'Auguste, avait composé
un vaste compendium de la philosophie aristotélicienne, dans lequel
la psychologie occupait sans doute les livres X et XI. D'après le
témoignage de Porphyre,[21] il estimait que l'expression 'parties de
l'âme' ne désigne pas des parties quantitatives, mais plutôt les diverses facultés de l'être animé; c'est celui-ci, poursuivait-il,
qui vit, perçoit, se meut, pense (νοεῖ), désire; bien qu'à proprement parler dépourvue de parties, l'âme, qui est principe et cause
de ces diverses activités, peut être qualifiée de 'divisible' eu
égard à la multiplicité de ces activités. Nicolas s'oppose par là
à ceux des Platoniciens qui répartissaient les 'parties' de l'âme
entre diverses parties du corps, opérant ainsi une division κατὰ τὸ
ποσόν. Trouvant à maintes reprises chez Aristote l'expression 'parties de l'âme', il précisait comment il convient de la comprendre.
Il est remarquable, par ailleurs, que Nicolas cite le νοεῖν, au même
titre que l'αἰσθάνεσθαι, parmi les activités propres à l'ἔμψυχον.
Peut-être se refusait-il à accorder au νοῦς un statut particulier
et à le séparer des autres facultés dépendant du corps, à moins que,
comme d'autres le feront plus tard, il n'ait admis, à côté de l'intellect proprement dit, une sorte de κοινὸς νοῦς dont l'activité est
liée au corps. Par ailleurs, nous apprenons[22] que, comme Théophraste, Thémistius et d'autres représentants du Péripatos, il avait
mieux saisi qu'Alexandre la nature de l'intellect possible; il se
refusait donc à admettre que cet intellect n'ait d'autre nature que
son universelle potentialité; celle-ci ne définit point son statut
ontologique, mais seulement sa relation aux objets de connaissance.
Nous savons enfin que Nicolas avait écrit une *Réfutation de ceux
qui prétendent que l'intellect est identique à l'intelligible*, mais
nous n'avons jusqu'ici aucun renseignement sur le contenu de cet
ouvrage perdu.[23]

    Dans les deux premiers siècles de l'ère chrétienne, on peut ob-
server que certaines écoles se sont approprié divers éléments empruntés à l'aristotélisme. Le phénomène est particulièrement évident chez les néopythagoriciens et surtout dans le platonisme
moyen. Pour l'histoire de l'aristotélisme, ces emprunts présentent
un intérêt tout particulier, non seulement parce qu'ils montrent la
puissance du rayonnement de la pensée aristotélicienne, mais aussi
parce que leur forme même permet d'apercevoir dans quelle direction

s'était engagée, à l'époque, l'interprétation des ouvrages du Stagirite.

Philon d'Alexandrie n'a certes pas la prétention d'expliquer les
écrits d'Aristote ou d'exposer son système. Néanmoins, dans le
cadre de son interprétation des Écritures, il aborde certains thèmes
qui ne manquent pas d'intérêt pour notre propos. Je pense notamment
à ce qu'il dit du νοῦς. Philon distingue deux intellects: l'un est
propre à l'homme, et l'autre, celui de l'univers, est identique à
Dieu;[24] l'intellect humain est en soi de nature terrestre et corruptible,[25] mais il reçoit la puissance de vie que lui insuffle Dieu;[26]
ainsi constitué par Dieu, il devient plus immatériel, plus pur; il
cesse d'être en liaison avec la matière corruptible;[27] de terrestre
qu'elle était, sa nature devient céleste;[28] on peut donc se demander
si le νοῦς qui habite notre corps est humain, ou divin, ou fait du
mélange de ces deux qualités.[29] Il faut souligner, bien sûr, que
la noétique de Philon, dont nous venons d'évoquer quelques traits,
est loin d'être cohérente[30] et, en outre, que les textes sur lesquels il s'appuie sont des textes mosaïques.[31] Pourtant, son interprétation offre des traces évidentes d'idées tantôt platoniciennes,
tantôt aristotéliciennes, tantôt stoïciennes; il n'ignorait manifestement pas les thèses des philosophes sur la nature de l'intellect,
son origine, son immortalité, sa place dans le corps.[32] Sans pécher
par excès d'audace, on peut donc admettre qu'il n'a pas été sans subir
l'influence des discussions consacrées aux problèmes des rapports
entre un intellect humain, qui prolonge et couronne les facultés
inférieures de l'âme, et un intellect divin, venu en l'homme 'du
dehors' et promis à l'incorruptibilité. Ouvertes par Théophraste,
ces discussions ont dû connaître un regain d'actualité dès le premier siècle avant J.-C., encore qu'elles n'aient laissé alors que
peu de traces. Le témoignage de Philon montre qu'elles avaient dé-
bordé le cadre étroit de l'École.

On peut s'en convaincre en jetant un coup d'oeil sur le *Didaska-
likos* d'Albinus, qui se donne pour un exposé de la philosophie de
Platon. Dans son chapitre sur Dieu, Albinus écrit:

'Meilleur que l'âme est l'intellect; meilleur que l'intellect
en puissance est l'intellect en acte, qui pense toutes choses,
simultanément et toujours; plus beau que l'intellect en acte est
celui qui en est la cause, comme aussi tout ce qui pourrait leur

être supérieur. Dès lors, celui-là est véritablement le premier
Dieu, qui est cause d'activité ininterrompue pour l'intellect du
ciel entier; il agit sur celui-ci (l'intellect du ciel) sans être
mû lui-même ... de la manière dont le désirable meut le désir
tout en restant lui-même immobile: c'est donc de cette manière
que cet intellect va mettre en mouvement l'intellect du ciel entier. Et puisque le premier intellect est le plus beau de tous,
il faut que lui appartienne l'intelligible le plus beau; or rien
n'est plus beau que lui; c'est donc lui-même et ses propres pensées qu'il pense toujours, et cette activité constitue son essence, etc.'[33]

Peu nous importe ici qu'Albinus ait cru ou voulu exposer par là des
thèses de Platon: ce qu'il dit et la manière dont il le dit rappellent clairement Aristote. Au sommet, il y a le premier intellect,
immobile, mouvant comme objet de désir et se pensant lui-même éter-
nellement: c'est le premier moteur de *Métaphysique* Λ. Il meut un
intellect cosmique, le νοῦς κατ' ἐνέργειαν, lequel est qualifié de
πάντα νοῶν καὶ ἅμα καὶ ἀεί et, à son tour, administre la nature
entière.[34] En troisième lieu vient le νοῦς ἐν δυνάμει, dont nous
ne savons s'il faut le situer sur le plan cosmique ou sur le plan
humain individuel. De toute façon, derrière l'exposé d'Albinus,
nous entrevoyons les éléments d'une noétique proprement aristotélicienne, dans laquelle étaient rapprochés *Metaph.* Λ et *De An.* III
4-5. L'intellect agent n'y était pas identifié au 'premier Dieu',[35]
mais il était néanmoins considéré comme unique.[36] En ce qui concerne les intelligibles, Albinus, en platonicien qu'il est, pro-
clame l'existence d'intelligibles simples, premiers, indépendants
de la matière; ce sont les idées,[37] les pensées du premier Dieu;[38]
mais il admet aussi, influencé par l'aristotélisme, que les formes,
se combinant à la matière, donnent naissance aux corps:[39] les
'seconds intelligibles' sont les formes inséparables de la matière.[40]
L'homme, imbibé de sensation, ne peut penser l'intelligible sans que
s'y mêle une représentation sensible; souvent grandeur, configuration et couleur accompagnent chez lui la notion intelligible.[41] La
manière dont l'acte d'intellection de l'âme et les objets de pensée
dépendent du premier Dieu est comparée à l'action du soleil, lequel,
sans être lui-même acte de vision, nous donne la possibilité de
voir et confère aux objets la visibilité, du fait qu'il les éclaire:

ainsi le premier Dieu nous donne la pensée, et aux intelligibles,
la possibilité d'être pensés; principe de vérité comme le soleil
est principe de lumière, il illumine la vérité des intelligibles.[42]
Cette conception s'inspire directement de la *République*,[43] mais elle
apparaît en même temps comme l'explication de la phrase fameuse où
Aristote compare l'action de l'intellect agent à celle de la lumière,[44]
et on la retrouvera plus tard dans divers exposés de la noétique péripatéticienne, notamment chez Alexandre. On notera enfin qu'Albinus
connaît et utilise la distinction entre δυνάμει, καθ' ἕξιν (ou ἐν ἕξει)
et κατ' ἐνέργειαν,[45] distinction qui est d'origine aristotélicienne
et apparaît comme fondamentale dans les doctrines de l'intellect.[46]

Nous ne pouvons aborder ici le problème des sources d'Albinus.
Il est difficile de préciser d'où lui viennent les éléments aristotéliciens de son exposé. On peut se demander également s'il a cru,
à tort ou à raison, que certains aspects de l'aristotélisme étaient
déjà chez Platon et pouvaient, dès lors, être présentés en termes
aristotéliciens, ou si, plutôt, il a voulu compléter et parfaire le
platonisme en y intégrant, avec plus ou moins d'adresse, telle ou
telle 'découverte' d'Aristote.[47] Mais ces questions dépassent le
cadre du présent rapport. L'essentiel est pour nous de voir en
Albinus le témoin d'un certain état du développement de l'exégèse
d'Aristote. A cet égard, Albinus nous est précieux, du fait qu'il
permet de soupçonner que son époque et la précédente s'étaient
penchées avec intérêt sur le *De anima*; malgré sa brièveté, son témoignage jette ainsi quelque lumière sur les tentatives exégétiques
qui ont précédé les grands débats sur la doctrine de l'intelligence
tels que nous les connaissons à partir d'Alexandre.

A côté des Platoniciens qui, comme Albinus, faisaient appel à
Aristote pour interpréter et enrichir le platonisme, nous en trouvons d'autres, au second siècle, qui combattaient ouvertement l'aristotélisme et en dénonçaient les erreurs. Atticus appartenait à ce
second groupe. Parmi les critiques qu'il adresse au Stagirite, re-
levons celles qui se rapportent au *De anima*: Aristote a privé l'âme
de son immortalité; il a contesté qu'elle puisse se mouvoir; il a
poussé l'audace jusqu'à retirer à l'âme les mouvements qui lui sont
propres, pour attribuer à l'être humain tout entier des opérations
telles que la délibération, la pensée discursive, la prévision du
futur, le souvenir, le calcul. Dicéarque procède directement de lui

quand il dénie à l'âme toute espèce de subsistance. Bien sûr, Aristote continue de croire, avec Platon, à l'immortalité de l'intellect. Mais qu'a-t-il enseigné sur la nature de l'intelligence, son
origine, la source à partir de laquelle elle s'est introduite en
l'homme, sa destinée future? On le saurait sans doute si l'on pouvait tirer au clair ce qu'il a dit de l'intellect. Mais il est
comme la seiche qui se soustrait au chasseur en projetant autour
d'elle un liquide opaque: l'obscurité de son discours lui sert à
masquer l'insurmontable difficulté du sujet; en outre, il commet
l'erreur de séparer l'intellect du reste de l'âme.[48]

Dans l'histoire de l'aristotélisme de l'époque impériale, le
médecin Galien mérite d'occuper une place de choix. Il se trouve,
en effet, qu'il avait reçu une solide formation philosophique et
que son intérêt pour les grands systèmes de l'époque, platonisme,
aristotélisme et stoïcisme, ne s'est pas affaibli au cours des années. Plutôt platonicien de coeur, Galien connaît fort bien Aristote; il avait, dans ses jeunes années, commenté presque tout
l'*Organon*; l'examen de ses ouvrages médicaux montre que les traités
de psychologie, de biologie et de zoologie du Stagirite lui étaient
familiers. Dans plusieurs de ses ouvrages, nous le voyons confron-
ter les résultats de ses observations sur l'homme avec les thèses
des philosophes. En ce qui concerne plus particulièrement l'aristotélisme, on relève chez lui plusieurs interprétations qui pré-
figurent ou annoncent celles d'Alexandre et permettent ainsi de
situer ce dernier dans un courant d'idées qui, sans le témoignage
de Galien, nous échapperait presque complètement.[49]

Soucieux de ne rien avancer qu'il ne puisse démontrer scientifiquement, Galien répète à de multiples réprises qu'il ignore quelle
est la substance de l'âme (ψυχῆς οὐσία) et qu'il n'a découvert aucun
argument permettant d'établir si elle est mortelle ou immortelle, si
elle est de nature corporelle ou incorporelle.[50] En revanche, il
tient pour scientifiquement indubitable le fait que le mélange particulier des éléments qui entrent dans la constitution du corps et
des divers organes conditionne le fonctionnement des facultés psychiques et même la vie ou la mort. La thèse d'après laquelle l'âme
se trouve sous la dépendance du corps, nous apprend-il, a été souvent énoncée; il s'en est entretenu lui-même avec ses maîtres, puis
avec les meilleurs philosophes du temps, et il est convaincu qu'elle

est vraie.[51] C'est dans ce sens qu'il interprète l'hylémorphisme
et la définition aristotélicienne de l'âme. Quand Aristote dit
que l'âme est la forme du corps, il n'entend point parler de la
configuration extérieure, mais bien du second principe qui, avec
la matière, constitue les corps naturels. Ceux-ci remontent, en
définitive, à l'union d'une matière privée de qualités et connais-
sable seulement par une opération de l'esprit, avec les quatre
qualités fondamentales, chaud, froid, sec et humide. L'εῖδος
propre d'un corps naturel peut donc être ramené à la manière dont
sont combinées, chez lui, les quatre qualités fondamentales, ou,
si l'on préfère, les quatre éléments porteurs de ces qualités.
Voilà ce qu'est, pour Aristote, la substance de l'âme; de cette
substance doivent dépendre les facultés, puisque c'est elle qui
conditionne les activités psychiques.[52] Pour prouver qu'Aristote
a bien cru à l'influence déterminante du mélange corporel sur les
facultés de l'âme, Galien cite textuellement plusieurs extraits
des ouvrages zoologiques.[53] Mais, s'il croit trouver chez Aristote une notion de l'âme très voisine de la sienne propre, Galien
se refuse à suivre le Stagirite sur un autre point. A Chrysippe,
qui faisait dériver toutes les activités psychiques de la seule
raison, il oppose comme la seule légitime l'opinion de ceux qui
admettent une certaine pluralité dans l'âme: Platon, Aristote et
Posidonius ont eu raison d'admettre cette pluralité.[54] Pourtant,
avec Platon et contre Aristote et Posidonius, Galien estime qu'il
faut parler de trois genres d'âme ou des trois parties de l'âme
plutôt que de facultés, et que chacune de ces parties a son siège
en un organe différent du corps: le cerveau commande à la sensation et aux mouvements volontaires; le coeur assure les mouvements
involontaires, notamment la pulsation du sang dans les artères;
il est le principe de la chaleur innée; le foie détermine la formation du sang et est le siège de la vie nutritive et végétative.[55]
Aristote a eu tort de croire qu'il s'agissait là des fonctions
d'une substance unique, qu'il situait dans la région du coeur.[56]
Galien, quant à lui, place l' 'hégémonique' dans le cerveau, parce
que ses recherches anatomiques et physiologiques l'ont convaincu
de l'exactitude des vues hippocratiques et platoniciennes. Après
la publication des six premiers livres consacrés aux opinions
d'Hippocrate et de Platon, il écrit, non sans fierté, qu'après les

démonstrations qu'il a fournies, 'plus un philosophe stoïcien,
plus un péripatéticien, plus un médecin ne gardera la même audace;
certains se sont même déjà ralliés ouvertement à ce qui est l'expression de la vérité, les médecins en convenant que la faculté
sensitive et motrice rayonne du cerveau vers tous les membres de
l'animal, les philosophes en accordant que la partie raisonnante de
l'âme a son siège dans le cerveau.'[57] Un peu plus bas, il signale
que ces six livres, terminés depuis plusieurs années, ont été soumis
à l'examen critique des meilleurs représentants du Péripatos et du
Portique.[58] On pourrait donc s'attendre à ce qu'un Alexandre
d'Aphrodise, si proche de Galien en ce qui regarde la nature de
l'âme, se soit laissé convaincre par l'argumentation relative au
rôle du cerveau; mais il n'en est rien: Alexandre reste envers et
contre tout fidèle à la thèse d'Aristote faisant du coeur le siège
de la vie psychique, et l'on est assez déçu de constater la maigreur
des arguments qu'il avance contre celle de Galien.

Nous avons déjà dit un mot de la prudence avec laquelle Galien
évite de se prononcer sur l'immortalité de l'âme: la question se
soustrait, d'après lui, à tout examen scientifique. Il ne veut
pas prendre position dans un débat qui opposait les Platoniciens
entre eux, certains considérant la partie supérieure de l'âme comme
seule immortelle, d'autres accordant l'immortalité aux deux parties
inférieures également et disant que, si Platon les a déclarées mortelles, c'est uniquement pour marquer qu'elles sont inférieures au
λογιστικόν et n'agissent qu'en union avec un corps mortel.[59] Il
ignore si l'âme, mélangée aux substances corporelles qu'elle administre, est immortelle en soi ou si, en soi, elle n'est pas une
substance.[60] Pourtant, c'est la thèse de la mortalité de l'âme
que semble exiger la lògique de son système; si l'âme est forme du
corps et si le λογιζόμενον lui-même est bien le 'mélange' du cerveau de la même manière que toutes les facultés procèdent du mélange corporel, le λογιζόμενον ne peut être que mortel; si, comme
Platon, on le déclare immortel, il faut alors expliquer pourquoi
un déséquilibre dans la constitution du corps le sépare de ce corps;
cela, ni Platon ni aucun des maîtres platoniciens de Galien n'en a
donné la raison. Peut-être pourrait-on suggérer que ce n'est pas
dans n'importe quel corps que l'âme rationnelle peut s'établir et
demeurer, mais cela ne peut être démontré scientifiquement.[61]

La lecture de Galien révèle que, sur beaucoup d'autres questions, il a connu et discuté, pour les approuver, les modifier ou les corriger, les positions d'Aristote dans le *De anima*. Il y aurait beaucoup à dire sur la sensation en général, la vision, le sens commun, le mouvement de l'animal, la nutrition, etc., mais cela nous conduirait trop loin. L'essentiel était de rappeler ici comment, malgré ses sympathies marquées pour le platonisme, le grand médecin de Pergame a souligné avec vigueur l'étroite connexion de l'âme et du corps et interprété dans ce sens l'entéléchisme d'Aristote. L'influence de la constitution physique sur les activités psychiques lui a paru si forte qu'il s'est cru autorisé à regarder le mélange des qualités corporelles comme étant à l'origine même des facultés et des opérations de l'âme. Nous verrons qu'Alexandre s'est engagé dans la même direction, soit qu'il ait subi l'influence de Galien lui-même, soit que la tendance illustrée par Galien et Alexandre ait été celle de médecins et de philosophes influents de l'époque.[62]

Il va de soi que les Péripatéticiens du premier et du second siècle après J.-C. n'ont dû négliger ni le *De anima* ni les doctrines psychologiques d'Aristote, mais leurs travaux n'ont presque pas laissé de traces dans la littérature postérieure. Nous savons qu'Aspasius avait commenté le *De sensu*,[63] et cela permet de supposer qu'il s'était intéressé également au *De anima*. Le *De sensu* doit, du reste, avoir été commenté à plusieurs reprises avant Alexandre,[64] mais nous n'avons aucun renseignement précis à ce sujet. Un des maîtres d'Alexandre, Sosigène, avait abordé, dans un περὶ ὄψεως en au moins huit livres, le problème des corps phosphorescents soulevé par Aristote dans le *De anima* II 7, 419a1-7,[65] et il s'était occupé aussi du problème de la réfraction de la lumière,[66] problème qui devait embarrasser les adeptes de la théorie de la vision exposée dans le *De anima*.

C'est à un autre maître d'Alexandre et à Alexandre lui-même que nous devons les indications les plus intéressantes sur les discussions relatives à l'intellect à l'époque qui nous occupe. Alexandre rapporte en effet comment son maître Aristote – il s'agit probablement d'un Péripatéticien originaire de Mytilène – présentait et tentait de résoudre les problèmes posés par la théorie de l'intellect 'venu du dehors' (νοῦς θύραθεν).[67] Aristote de Mytilène expliquait tout d'abord pour quelles raisons le Stagirite avait été amené à

concevoir la nécessité d'un νοῦς θύραθεν. L'intellect humain est,
à l'origine, en puissance. Or son acte propre est de tirer des
sensibles les intelligibles qu'ils renferment, de les rendre intelligibles en acte. Pour que l'intellect potentiel devienne capable
d'accomplir cette opération, il faut qu'agisse sur lui un intellect
actif, qui soit lui-même et de par soi en acte; tel est le rôle de
l'intellect qui s'introduit en nous 'du dehors'. Il ne crée pas
notre intellect, mais collabore avec lui, en mettant en lui l'*habitus* qui lui permettra de penser les intelligibles potentiels, il le
parfait, le conduit à ses objets propres. Comment cet intellect
'du dehors' et immortel s'introduit-il en nous? Comment s'opère
son action sur l'intellect potentiel? La solution du problème est
assez curieuse. Du fait qu'il est, de par soi, intelligible en acte,
cet intellect actif peut être saisi par l'intellect potentiel dès
que celui-ci a atteint un certain développement naturel. Nous voilà
bien loin de la manière dont Aristote avait posé le problème dans
le *De generatione animalium* II 3! Par ailleurs, les choses qui ne
sont intelligibles qu'en puissance n'auraient point cette qualité
s'il n'existait un intelligible qui est tel de par sa propre nature. Ainsi, l'intellect suprême, qui est également l'intelligible
suprême, est à la fois pour l'intellect humain la source de la capacité d'abstraire et de connaître, et pour les objets sensibles la
cause de leur intelligibilité. Alexandre ne signale pas explicitement que son maître l'ait identifié à Dieu, mais il est clair pourtant que cet intellect suprême ne peut être autre que la νοήσεως
νόησις de *Metaph.* Λ.

Ces explications données par Aristote de Mytilène ont bien l'air
de représenter la *communis opinio* des Péripatéticiens de son temps,
car aussitôt après les avoir rapportées, Alexandre signale comment
son maître tentait κατ' ἰδίαν ἐπίνοιαν, selon une théorie qui lui
était propre, de démontrer l'immortalité de l'intellect et d'échapper à certaines difficultés que d'aucuns soulevaient contre la doctrine du νοῦς θύραθεν. Pour venir 'du dehors', disait-on, l'intellect doit changer de lieu; or s'il est incorporel, il ne peut être
dans un lieu ni passer d'un lieu dans un autre.[68] Le Mytilénien
résolvait le problème dans le cadre d'une théologie immanentiste
très voisine de celle des Stoïciens. L'intellect suprême, expli-
quait-il, est présent dans toute matière mortelle; il y agit sans

cesse de son activité propre. Mais, quand un mélange donné des
corps lui fournit une faculté adéquate – et c'est cette δύναμις même
qu'Aristote appelle intellect potentiel – il s'en empare et l'utilise comme instrument. L'intellect humain est donc composé de
notre faculté utilisée comme instrument et de l'intellect divin
immanent qui l'utilise. L'omniprésence de l'intellect divin n'exige
aucun changement de lieu pour que puisse s'effectuer sa réunion avec
notre faculté intellectuelle, et il n'y a pas non plus changement de
lieu quand il la délaisse et s'en sépare. C'est ainsi, ajoute Alexandre, qu'il comprenait la divinité et l'incorruptibilité de l'intellect proclamées par Aristote, et c'est à l'intellect divin omni-
présent qu'il rapportait les déclarations du troisième livre du *De
anima* sur la ἕξις et la lumière. Alexandre, quant à lui, rejette
catégoriquement la thèse stoïcienne de l'immanence divine, et il
se refuse aussi à voir dans la pensée une activité qui ne soit pas
notre activité propre, mais celle de Dieu lui-même. Sur d'autres
points, pourtant, il reste d'accord avec son maître et avec l'interprétation courante exposée par celui-ci; nous retrouverons chez lui
la thèse, rencontrée déjà chez Galien, que l'âme et les puissances
de l'âme résultent du mélange adéquat des qualités fondamentales
des éléments dont est fait le corps, la thèse de la divinité et de
l'unicité de l'intellect agent, lequel vient en nous du dehors, est
cause de toute intelligibilité du fait qu'il est lui-même l'intelligible suprême et est toujours en acte de par sa propre nature.

Dans les dernières années, les théories psychologiques d'Alexandre d'Aphrodise ont suscité diverses études qui ne manquent pas
d'intérêt. Sans entrer dans le détail, signalons ici quelques-uns
des problèmes abordés dans ces recherches. Plusieurs savants ont
souligné qu'Alexandre doit être étudié non seulement comme l'exégète d'Aristote, mais aussi – d'un point de vue dit 'prospectif' –
dans ses rapports avec Plotin, lequel l'aurait utilisé à plusieurs
reprises et n'aurait pas été sans subir son influence. Par ailleurs, la volonté d'orthodoxie aristotélicienne de l'Exégète a été
contestée; son interprétation d'Aristote plongerait ses racines
dans le moyen-platonisme de l'époque; cela se traduirait notamment
par le fait qu'à côté des formes engagées dans la matière, il aurait
admis, dans une perspective toute platonisante, l'existence d'une
classe d'intelligibles en acte et séparés. Enfin, la question des

rapports entre le *De anima* d'Alexandre et son *De intellectu* reste
posée. Voici plus de trente ans, j'avais souligné avec insistance
les divergences séparant la noétique du *De anima* d'Alexandre et
celle du *De intellectu*, et j'en avais conclu, avec l'audace de mes
vingt ans, que le *De intellectu*, quoique issu de l'école d'Alexandre, ne pouvait être regardé comme authentique. Dans l'entretemps,
le bien-fondé de mes observations a été contesté; il n'existerait
pas de divergences profondes entre les deux traités; le *De intellectu*, précisant certains détails restés obscurs ou négligés dans
le *De anima*, apparaîtrait comme un ouvrage plus mûr, plus évolué,
mais incontestablement authentique.[69] Une discussion approfondie
de ces problèmes dépasserait évidemment le cadre de ce rapport.
Je me bornerai donc à quelques observations générales.[70]

  Alexandre avait écrit un commentaire au *De anima* d'Aristote.
L'ouvrage est perdu, mais nous en possédons des fragments assez
nombreux, conservés surtout par Philopon, Simplicius (ou plutôt le
pseudo-Simplicius, puisque le commentaire au *De anima* conservé
sous son nom pourrait bien être de Priscien de Lydie) et le pseudo-
Philopon (le commentaire grec attribué à Philopon sur le troisième
livre du *De anima* étant sans doute d'Étienne d'Alexandrie). Le
De anima d'Alexandre doit être postérieur à ce commentaire perdu,
dont il résume les principaux résultats.[71] Plutôt que de nous attarder à l'étude des fragments du commentaire, jetons un rapide
coup d'oeil sur quelques aspects caractéristiques du *De anima*. Re-
levons tout d'abord la profession de foi d'Alexandre: dans tous les
domaines, il révère la philosophie d'Aristote comme étant plus
vraie que toute autre; pour exposer sa propre doctrine de l'âme, il
lui suffira donc de présenter aussi clairement que possible l'enseignement d'Aristote, en y ajoutant ses propres considérations sur
l'excellence des thèses qu'il soutient.[72] Les remarques d'Alexandre
sur la méthode à suivre dans l'étude de l'âme méritent également de
retenir l'attention. Il faut tout d'abord apprendre ce qu'est la
nature et se convaincre que ses oeuvres sont de loin plus étonnantes
que n'importe quelle merveille réalisée par l'art. Pour ne pas se
laisser mettre en difficulté par ce que les facultés et les opérations de l'âme semblent présenter de divin et de supérieur à toute
puissance corporelle, on doit prendre pour point de départ la constitution du corps animé, l'économie de ses parties internes,

l'accord bien réglé des objets extérieurs avec ces parties; alors
sachant que l'âme appartient à un corps doué d'une organisation si
remarquable, si merveilleuse, on ne trouvera plus rien d'extraordi-
naire à ce qu'elle ait en elle des principes de mouvements si
nombreux.[73] Bien qu'il ne réalise pas exactement tout ce programme,
c'est dans cet esprit qu'Alexandre présente l'hylémorphisme d'Aristote
et l'applique à l'âme. Un corps simple est ce qu'il est en vertu des
qualités naturelles qui le caractérisent. La forme du feu, par
exemple, est faite de sa chaleur, de sa sécheresse et de la légèreté qui en résulte; cette légèreté ne subsiste pas par elle-même,
elle n'est pas séparable, mais elle est cause du mouvement sans
être mue elle-même. Dans les corps composés, la matière prochaine
est complexe; elle apporte au composé la multiplicité et la variété
des formes propres aux divers corps qui la constituent; dès lors,
plus un mélange sera complexe, et plus sa forme elle-même sera complexe et riche de puissances diverses de mouvement. Ainsi en va-
t-il du vivant, où la complexité de la forme (l'âme) répond parfaitement à celle du corps animé. Les activités dont l'âme est le principe sont des activités non de l'âme, mais du vivant lui-même. Dès
lors, 'puisqu'il est impossible de concevoir aucune activité de l'âme
indépendamment d'un mouvement corporel, il est évident que l'âme est
quelque chose du corps et qu'elle est inséparable de lui; une âme
séparée existerait en vain, puisqu'elle ne pourrait exercer en
elle-même aucune des activités qui la caractérisent.'[74] Découle-
t-il de là que l'âme n'est rien d'autre que le mélange des corps qui
constituent le vivant, et qu'il faut adopter les vues de ceux qui
ont considéré l'âme comme l'harmonie du corps? Nullement. Si l'âme
dérive du mélange en question, elle ne se réduit pas à ce mélange.
Ainsi, dans un produit pharmaceutique complexe, la proportion du mélange est une chose, et les propriétés thérapeutiques qui en résultent en sont une autre. 'L'âme n'est donc pas tel mélange des corps
(comme c'est le cas de l'harmonie), mais la puissance engendrée sur
la base d'un tel mélange.'[75] Ces développements rappellent de très
près certaines pages du petit traité de Galien *Quod animi mores corporis temperamenta sequantur* dont il a été question plus haut. Pour
Alexandre comme pour Galien, la proportion des qualités propres aux
constituants corporels du vivant exerce une influence déterminante
sur la nature et les facultés de l'âme. Mais, alors que Galien

déclarait que, selon Aristote, la substance de l'âme, c'est, en
quelque sorte, le mélange des quatre qualités ou des quatre corps
premiers, Alexandre met les choses au point en précisant qu'il s'agit,
en réalité, d'une puissance engendrée sur la base de ce mélange. Il
est intéressant de noter que certains commentateurs avaient remarqué
l'étroite parenté des vues d'Alexandre sur l'âme avec celle que
Galien émet dans son petit traité.[76]

Dans cette âme étroitement dépendante du corps quant à l'exercice
de ses activités et quant à son existence même, l'intellect n'aura
point de statut privilégié. Bien sûr, il est la faculté la plus
haute, la plus parfaite, et, à ce titre, il apparaît en dernier lieu
dans le développement de l'être humain. A la naissance, nous ne
possédons ni l'intellect pratique ni l'intellect théorique, mais une
simple disposition à les recevoir. Cette disposition, naturelle
chez tous les êtres humains normaux, est appelée intellect potentiel
ou intellect matériel. Elle ne se développe naturellement pour devenir une véritable faculté que dans la mesure où la nature elle-
même nous guide vers la saisie de l'universel et la connaissance
par voie de rassemblement. A ce stade, elle est appelée intellect
commun, κοινὸς νοῦς. Pour le reste, c'est l'enseignement, l'étude,
l'exercice qui vont nous permettre d'acquérir la faculté qui est
forme, *habitus*, perfection, entéléchie de cette disposition innée
qu'est l'intellect potentiel. L'aptitude à saisir l'universel s'acquiert graduellement: les sensations répétées laissent en nous des
traces que garde la mémoire et, empiriquement, nous en arrivons à
dépasser le 'ceci' et le particulier pour atteindre le 'tel' et
l'universel. Ainsi se développe peu à peu l'*habitus* qui, comme une
sorte de faculté visuelle, va nous permettre de saisir les formes
intelligibles indépendamment de leur support sensible. Enfin, une
fois en possession de cette aptitude, l'intellect pourra agir; en
saisissant la forme intelligible, il deviendra intellect en acte;
comme, dans son acte, il s'identifie à son objet, l'intellect en
acte se pensera lui-même.[77]

Les formes engagées dans la matière sont-elles les seuls objets
que connaisse l'intellect humain? Alexandre s'est posé la question.
S'il existe des intelligibles au sens propre, écrit-il, c'est-à-dire
des intelligibles en acte de par leur propre nature et non engagés
dans la matière, notre intellect, je veux dire l'intellect en *habitus*,

s'assimile à elles quand il les pense: telles elles sont selon leur
propre subsistance et indépendamment du fait d'être pensées, telles
aussi elles sont dans l'intellect qui les pense, si bien que l'intellect qui les pense devient, quand il les pense, le même qu'elles.[78]
Cela signifie-t-il qu'Alexandre a bel et bien admis une classe
d'êtres intelligibles subsistant par eux-mêmes, analogue au monde
platonicien des idées? Cela signifie-t-il qu'en dépit de son anti-
platonisme notoire, il s'est laissé influencer par la plus fameuse
des doctrines platoniciennes?[79] J'ai peine à le croire. Le pluriel
dont il use - dans une phrase conditionnelle - ne doit pas nous
abuser: tout le passage ne vise, en fait, que la forme immatérielle
qui est en même temps l'intellect suprême, l'intellect en acte par
nature, l'intellect véritable,[80] c'est-à-dire la cause suprême, le
νοῦς du Λ de la *Métaphysique*, l'intellect divin auquel, on le verra,
l'intellect humain peut arriver à s'assimiler.[81]

Pour tous les êtres de nature où la matière reçoit une détermination, il existe une cause à l'origine de cette détermination. Comme
l'intellect matériel reçoit une ἕξις, il doit exister un intellect
agent (ποιητικὸς νοῦς), qui est cause de la ἕξις de l'intellect matériel.[82] Comment, selon Alexandre, s'exerce cette causalité de
l'intellect agent? La question est controversée. Elle a été tranchée différemment selon qu'on s'en tenait aux seules indications du
De anima ou qu'on tentait d'éclairer ce traité à la lumière de données prises au *De intellectu*. Dans le *De anima*, l'Exégète se borne
à dire que cet intellect agent est la forme intelligible suprême et
indépendante de la matière. A ce titre, il est la cause d'intelligibilité pour tous les êtres intelligibles, comme la lumière, visible
suprême, est cause de la visibilité des objets visibles.[83] Si nous
comprenons bien, le νοῦς ποιητικός n'agit donc pas directement sur
le νοῦς ὑλικός humain pour assurer son développement, pas plus que
la lumière n'assure le développement de la faculté visuelle; il est
au contraire la cause qui fait que les sensibles sont intelligibles
en puissance et peuvent ainsi être saisis par l'intellect humain, au
terme des opérations qui le mènent du particulier à l'universel. On
a tenté d'expliquer, pourtant, que, comme dans le *De intellectu*,
l'intellect agent, intelligible suprême, s'impose à l'intellect humain
avant tout autre intelligible, l'actualise, lui confère une lumière
grâce à laquelle les autres formes pourront devenir intelligibles si

l'intellect humain les lui rapporte.[84]

Cela nous conduit à l'examen des déclarations sur le νοῦς θύραθεν.
A diverses reprises, Alexandre souligne que l'intellect humain peut
appréhender l'intelligible pur et ainsi s'assimiler à lui.[85] Mais
est-ce cette saisie de l'intelligible suprême qui confère sa ἕξις à
l'intellect matériel? Diverses raisons nous interdisent de le
croire. Tout d'abord, l'intellect humain capable de saisir l'intelligible en soi, c'est, Alexandre le dit explicitement, l'intellect
καθ' ἕξιν,[86] donc l'intellect à l'état de faculté déjà développée.
Ensuite, Alexandre ne présente pas la saisie de cet intelligible
comme s'imposant à l'intellect humain du seul fait qu'un intelligible
en acte doit nécessairement faire passer à l'acte un intellect en
puissance; au contraire, il y voit le résultat d'un effort conscient
et délibéré: 'Ceux-là qui ont à coeur d'avoir en eux quelque chose
de divin, écrit-il en concluant son exposé sur le νοῦς θύραθεν, doivent s'appliquer à devenir capables de penser quelque chose qui possède cette qualité.'[87] La ὁμοίωσις θεῷ dont il parle n'est donc pas
une simple étape dans le développement de tout intellect humain, mais
un but auquel doit viser l'homme intelligent désireux d'acquérir
quelque chose de divin et d'immortel.

Alexandre considère, en effet, l'intellect matériel comme mortel
au même titre que les autres facultés de l'âme; mortel sera donc
aussi l'*habitus*, la perfection de cet intellect matériel. Quant aux
intelligibles que l'intelligence humaine tire de la matière, ils ces-
sent d'être dès qu'ils ne sont plus pensés; ils sont donc, eux aussi,
corruptibles. En revanche, l'intelligible qui est tel indépendamment
de notre pensée humaine est incorruptible. Par conséquent, l'intellect qui l'aura pensé et qui, en le pensant, sera devenu semblable à
lui, sera, lui aussi, incorruptible. Cet intellect est appelé 'celui
qui vient en nous du dehors et est incorruptible' (ὁ νοῦς ὁ θύραθέν
τε ἐν ἡμῖν γινόμενος καὶ ἄφθαρτος).[88] Tout n'est pas absolument
clair dans cet exposé d'Alexandre, mais nous ne pouvons nous étendre
ici sur les difficultés qu'il soulève. La principale découle à coup
sûr du fait que l'immortalité acquise en pensant l'intellect divin
ne change rien à la condition mortelle de notre faculté, mais n'est
manifestement liée qu'au seul intelligible-intellect suprême qui
s'est installé en nous du fait que nous l'avons pensé.

Tournons-nous maintenant vers le *De intellectu*. Averroès, qui

lisait en traduction arabe les deux traités d'Alexandre sur l'âme et
sur l'intellect, avait déjà noté que l'auteur se contredit parfois
de l'un à l'autre.[89] Mais ces contradictions, sur lesquelles j'ai
moi-même insisté dans mon étude de 1942 au point de contester l'authenticité du *De intellectu*, ne sont-elles pas plus apparentes que
réelles, et ne se laissant-elles pas éliminer très facilement, comme
la critique a tenté de le faire?[90] De prime abord, les problèmes,
la terminologie, les solutions sont, à peu de choses près, les mêmes
de part et d'autre. A y regarder de plus près, cependant, on constate certaines divergences. (1) Ainsi le νοῦς ὑλικός dans le *De
anima* apparaît avant tout comme une disposition à recevoir la faculté intellectuelle, disposition présente en l'homme dès sa naissance. Dans le *De intellectu*, il est décrit comme l'aptitude à recevoir les formes et les concepts. Il se trouve chez tous les êtres
qui ont une âme complète, c'est-à-dire chez tous les hommes. (2) De
part et d'autre vient ensuite l'intellect qui possède la ἕξις, l'*habitus* lui permettant de penser et de saisir par sa propre force les
formes intelligibles des objets sensibles. Ce second intellect n'est
autre que le νοῦς ὑλικός ayant reçu la ἕξις. Le *De intellectu* ne dit
rien du processus par lequel on passe du particulier à l'universel et
grâce auquel, d'après le *De anima*, se constitue la ἕξις. (3) Le νοῦς
ποιητικός (identifié dans les deux traités à l'intelligible-intellect
suprême, toujours en acte) est, d'après le *De intellectu*, la cause
qui implante dans l'intellect potentiel et matériel l'*habitus* noétique
et en fait réellement un intellect; il est agent de la pensée; il
mène l'intellect matériel à son acte. Si les formules, très nettes,
du *De intellectu* ne trompent pas, la causalité du νοῦς ποιητικός est
donc présentée assez différemment dans les deux traités: dans le *De
anima*, il est cause d'intelligibilité pour les formes engagées dans
la matière, rendant ainsi possible leur saisie par l'intellect pensant. Dans le *De intellectu*, il apparaît comme la cause donnant à
l'intellect matériel son plein développement de faculté. (4) Comment
s'opère, d'après le *De intellectu*, cette action de l'intellect agent?
Il peut être, en tant qu'intelligible pur, reçu directement par nous;
quand nous le pensons, il s'installe en nous en tant qu'intellect
agent venu de l'extérieur; il n'est ni une partie ni une faculté de
notre âme; séparé de nous, toujours en acte, substance sans matière,
c'est à bon droit qu'il est qualifié d'immortel par Aristote. Quant

à son rôle dans l'intellection, Alexandre n'y fait qu'une allusion:
'Ainsi donc, cet être intelligible de par sa propre nature et intellect en acte devient, pour l'intellect matériel, la cause qui le
porte à séparer, imiter et penser chaque forme intelligible engagée
dans la matière et à la rendre intelligible, en se référant à son
rapport avec la forme du genre qu'on a dit (c'est-à-dire: avec la
forme qui est, par soi, intelligible en acte).'[91] Il semble donc
que la capacité qu'acquiert le νοῦς ὑλικός d'abstraire et de connaître les formes matérielles intelligibles en puissance lui vient
du fait qu'ayant reçu en lui l'intelligible suprême, source de
toute intelligibilité, il peut, en s'y référant, mettre au jour ce
que les autres êtres ont en eux d'intelligible. La perspective
diffère sensiblement de celle du *De anima*.

Cela dit, on ne peut nier qu'il existe une foule de traits communs invitant à rapprocher les deux ouvrages. Je pense tout d'abord
à une certaine ambiguïté dans la conception du νοῦς ὑλικός ou δυνάμει: celui-ci est présenté tantôt comme l'état de l'âme antérieur à
l'acquisition de la faculté d'abstraire et de penser,[92] tantôt comme
la faculté en vertu de laquelle l'âme est capable d'accueillir
toutes les formes intelligibles, mais n'en possède encore aucune.[93]
Parallèlement, le νοῦς ἐν ἕξει apparaît tantôt comme celui qui possède, en fait, la capacité de penser, d'agir par lui-même, c'est-à-
dire de saisir par sa propre efficience les formes intelligibles,[94]
tantôt comme l'ensemble des intelligibles qui meublent la faculté
intellective, où ils sont présents d'une manière latente aussi longtemps que l'intellect ne fait pas retour sur lui-même pour les connaître et les utiliser.[95]

Dans l'esprit de l'auteur, les deux manières de présenter et le
νοῦς ὑλικός et le νοῦς ἐν ἕξει semblent bien avoir été compatibles
au point que l'une se laisse aisément ramener à l'autre: l'intellect
matériel, encore incapable d'abstraire et de saisir les formes engagées dans la matière, n'en renferme évidemment aucune; par ailleurs,
dès qu'il est entré en possession de la capacité d'abstraire et de
saisir l'intelligible, il se meuble immédiatement des formes qu'il
conserve en lui et sur lesquelles il peut alors faire retour à sa
guise. Ainsi, l'état du développement de l'intellect en tant que
faculté répond à une certaine relation de cet intellect avec les
intelligibles potentiels contenus dans les êtres sensibles. Dans

les deux traités enfin, le νοῦς ποιητικός, identifié avec le νοῦς-
νοητόν suprême du Λ de la *Métaphysique*, est donné comme la cause
qui confère sa ἕξις à l'intellect matériel. En le pensant, nous
nous identifions à lui; il devient notre νοῦς θύραθεν et, à la différence du νοῦς ὑλικός et du νοῦς ἐν ἕξει, ce νοῦς θύραθεν est divin
et incorruptible.

La réduction de l'intellect à son seul contenu, au détriment de
sa consistance propre en tant que faculté, apparaît comme l'une des
tendances les plus caractéristiques de la noétique d'Alexandre. Il
est hautement significatif que l'intellect potentiel soit comparé,
plutôt qu'à une tablette sur laquelle rien n'est écrit, à l'absence
même d'écriture sur cette tablette.[96] C'est sans doute aussi en
partant de là que s'explique, en fin de compte, l'étrange théorie
de l'immortalité du νοῦς θύραθεν: quard il est pensé par nous, celui-
ci ne confère l'immortalité ni au νοῦς ὑλικός ni non plus au νοῦς ἐν
ἕξει, du fait que les concepts qui meublent ce dernier sont eux-mêmes
'corruptibles'; c'est en lui-même qu'il est immortel. S'il est permis, pour éclairer la conception d'Alexandre, de reprendre et de développer la comparaison du νοῦς ὑλικός avec l'absence d'écriture sur
la tablette, on dira que l'intellect ἐν ἕξει, fait des concepts intelligibles tirés des êtres matériels, est comparable à des signes
d'écriture pouvant s'effacer et disparaître, tandis que le νοῦς θύραθεν serait analogue à une écriture indélébile.

Si l'on tient compte à la fois de la parenté doctrinale du *De
anima* et du *De intellectu* et des divergences qui les opposent, on
doit conclure que les deux traités proviennent bien de la même école
et qu'il n'existe aucune raison décisive de mettre en doute leur attribution traditionnelle au grand Alexandre d'Aphrodise. Mais lequel
des deux traités est alors le plus ancien, et lequel représente un
état plus avancé de la réflexion d'Alexandre? Il m'apparaît aujourd'hui que le *De intellectu* doit avoir précédé le *De anima*. En
effet: (1) Le *De anima*, postérieur aux commentaires sur la *Physique*,
le *De caelo*, les *Météorologiques*, le *De anima* et le *De sensu*, doit
certainement être situé assez tard dans la carrière d'Alexandre.
(2) Dans le *De intellectu*, l'auteur éprouve le besoin de rapporter
les thèses que soutenait un de ses maîtres, et de les critiquer ensuite; cette attitude s'explique mieux chez un penseur jeune encore
que chez un chercheur 'en fin de carrière'. (3) Contre B.C.Bazán[97]

et avec P.L.Donini,[98] quoique pour des raisons en partie différentes, je tiens le *De anima* pour un ouvrage plus achevé et plus mûr
que le *De intellectu*. Je suis assez porté à croire, aujourd'hui,
que le *De intellectu* a précédé le grand commentaire au *De anima*,
tandis que le *De anima* personnel d'Alexandre résumerait les résultats acquis dans ce commentaire.

   Nous ne savons rien des disciples d'Alexandre. Si nous cherchons
à découvrir quelle fut la contribution du troisième siècle à l'interprétation du *De anima* après les travaux de l'Aphrodisien, nous
devrons nous tourner avant tout vers Plotin et son disciple Porphyre. Il est bien connu que Plotin n'ignorait pas les thèses
d'Aristote et qu'à l'occasion, il a marqué ses réserves à leur égard
ou les a rejetées sans ambages. Sa polémique vise non seulement
les rapports entre l'intellect et l'intelligible et l'unité de l'intellect, mais aussi la conception aristotélicienne de l'âme en général,[99] le mode de présence de l'âme dans le corps, etc. Grâce au
témoignage de Porphyre, nous savons aussi que, dans ses séminaires
philosophiques, il lui arrivait de faire appel aux commentateurs
d'Aristote, Aspasius, Adraste et Alexandre d'Aphrodise notamment.[100]
Mais, qu'il critique Aristote ou consulte des commentateurs plus
tardifs, Plotin ne s'astreint pas à citer littéralement, à expliquer
le mot à mot d'un texte, à démonter pièce par pièce l'argumentation
qu'il trouve chez un auteur. Dans l'élaboration de sa propre doctrine, il repense les théories de ses prédécesseurs et les utilise
comme points de départ, sans chercher à éclairer dans le détail
l'expression écrite de ces théories. Son attitude n'est guère différente lorsqu'il entend plutôt faire oeuvre de critique: il vise
ce qu'il tient pour l'essentiel sans trop se préoccuper des nuances
qui donnent à chaque penseur son individualité.[101] Dans ces conditions, on ne saurait le ranger parmi les interprètes du *De anima*.
C'est ce qui m'autorise à ne pas m'arrêter davantage aux jugements
qu'il porte sur la psychologie d'Aristote et à la dette qu'il a pu
contracter envers elle.

   Les choses se présentent différemment chez Porphyre. Le disciple
de Plotin s'est intéressé de très près au *De anima*. S'il ne semble
pas en avoir commenté le texte entier, du moins en a-t-il analysé
certains passages.[102] A en juger par le témoignage de Thémistius,
il est certain qu'il soumettait plusieurs affirmations d'Aristote à

une critique sévère.[103] Ainsi, il voyait dans les lignes I 1, 403a
10-12 un raisonnement vicieux: après avoir noté que, si l'âme a
quelque opération ou quelque affection qui lui soit propre, elle
peut être séparable, Aristote n'était pas autorisé à dire que, si
aucune opération ou affection ne lui est propre, elle n'est pas séparable.[104] En fait, Porphyre s'en prend à la conception de l'âme
comme entéléchie et plaide en faveur de la thèse platonicienne selon
laquelle l'âme peut exister sans le corps.[105] Les objections for-
mulées par Aristote contre la théorie platonicienne de l'âme automotrice, et la thèse d'Aristote selon laquelle l'âme meut tout en
étant elle-même immobile, faisaient également l'objet de ses critiques. Contre *De An.* I 3, 406a30 - b3, il faisait valoir que les
mouvements propres à l'âme, jugements et assentiments, ne sont point
les mouvements locaux du corps, et qu'inversement les mouvements
imprimés au corps ne coïncident pas avec ceux dont est animée l'âme
elle-même, pas plus que le mouvement rectiligne ascensionnel de
l'exhalaison attirée par le soleil ne coïncide avec la révolution
circulaire du soleil lui-même.[106] Il contestait l'affirmation de
I 3, 406b3-5: il n'est pas légitime de dire que si l'âme, étant
animée d'un mouvement local, peut sortir du corps, elle pourra s'y
réintroduire à nouveau; ceux qui tiennent l'âme pour un *pneuma* et
lui confèrent ainsi un mouvement local ne sont pas disposés à
admettre qu'elle pourrait réintégrer le corps après s'en être
séparée.[107] A la thèse platonicienne, Aristote objectait qu'on ne
peut identifier les mouvements imprimés à l'âme de l'extérieur, ceux
des sensations, par exemple, avec les mouvements supposés constitutifs de l'essence de l'âme.[108] Porphyre répond que les sensibles
ne meuvent pas la sensation, mais n'en sont que la condition indispensable. De même, ce n'est pas la proie prise dans la toile de
l'araignée qui meut celle-ci; c'est l'élan propre à l'insecte qui
le conduit à sa proie.[109] Le visible est avec la vue dans la même
relation que le sol avec le marcheur: il est une condition, non une
cause.[110] Enfin, Aristote soulignait que, puisque tout mouvement
fait sortir le mû d'un état pour le mener à un autre, le mouvement
propre à l'essence de l'âme fera sortir celle-ci de sa propre essence.[111] Porphyre répond qu'au contraire, plus l'âme se meut, et
plus elle s'affirme dans son essence: son mouvement, c'est la vie,
et pour elle, se mouvoir équivaut à vivre.[112]

L'opinion de ceux qui, comme Galien et Alexandre, faisaient dépendre l'âme du mélange corporel, ne pouvait non plus manquer d'être
attaquée par Porphyre. Il la critiquait tout en répondant à une
question soulevée par Aristote lui-même:[113] ce n'est pas l'âme,
disait-il, qui est détruite quand le mélange se corrompt, mais
simplement l'animation (ἐμψυχία) que l'âme confère au corps; l'âme
elle-même est séparable, et elle donne au corps l'éclat de la vie
comme le soleil donne à l'air sa lumière.[114] D'autres aspects de
la doctrine de Porphyre peuvent sans doute être tirés de la longue
discussion que Thémistius consacre au fragment cité.[115] C'est
probablement l'âme universelle qui, d'après lui, 'illumine' les
corps organisés individuels et leur confère la 'puissance vitale',
l'animation; il en donnait comme preuve la génération spontanée
d'insectes ou de petits animaux.[116]

Rappelons enfin que Porphyre reprochait à Aristote d'avoir, dans
sa polémique contre la définition de l'âme proposée par Xénocrate,[117]
ergoté sur les mots plutôt que d'examiner la portée réelle de cette
définition.[118] Le ton de ces reproches devait être assez violent,
puisque Porphyre allait jusqu'à qualifier d'inintelligibles (ἀδιανό-
ητα) les considérations d'Aristote.[119]

On le voit: l'attitude de Porphyre en face du *De anima* diffère
totalement de celle qu'il avait adoptée envers les traités de l'*Organon*. Alors qu'il cherche à rendre accessible aux Platoniciens la
logique d'Aristote, en rédigeant une *Introduction aux catégories*
(l'*Isagoge*) ainsi que deux commentaires à ce traité et un au *De interpretatione*, il n'examine certains passages du *De anima* que pour en
faire la critique à la lumière de ses propres convictions. Ce qui
lui tient à coeur, c'est de défendre la conception platonicienne de
l'âme. Il combat donc et l'entéléchisme d'Aristote et les théories
naturalistes apparentées; il souligne que l'âme est active et cause
de son propre mouvement, même dans les cas où elle reçoit des impul-
sions de l'extérieur; en même temps, il cherche à renverser les objections d'Aristote contre la définition de l'âme comme une substance automotrice.

Porphyre était mort depuis une cinquantaine d'années (entre 301
et 305) quand, vers le milieu du quatrième siècle, Thémistius rédigea
sa paraphrase au *De anima*. Il se peut que cette paraphrase lui ait
été inspirée par l'enseignement de son père et de son beau-père, mais

naturellement nous sommes incapables d'en juger. En revanche, et
bien qu'une paraphrase ne laisse que peu de place aux considérations
personnelles et à la critique, il apparaît assez clairement que Thémistius s'appuie dans une certaine mesure sur les travaux d'exégètes
antérieurs, sans toujours accepter leurs vues. Il cite notamment
les apories de Théophraste sur l'intellect. Il recourt aussi, sans
le nommer, mais en marquant ses distances, au commentaire d'Alexandre. Certains difficultés soulevées par Plotin retiennent son attention.[120] Enfin, il s'attarde assez longuement à présenter et à
réfuter diverses interprétations avancées par Porphyre. De prime
abord, on pourrait le croire antiplatonicien, puisque aussi bien il
rejette la conception qui fait de l'âme une substance se mouvant
elle-même et nie que l'âme puisse être, en elle-même, le siège de
mouvements.[121] Pourtant, à diverses reprises, il laisse entendre
que le fossé entre Platon et Aristote est moins profond qu'il ne
semble, à condition que l'on comprenne bien ce qu'a voulu dire Platon. Quand Platon parle de l'âme, c'est en vérité à l'intellect
qu'il pense.[122] Les preuves qu'il donne de l'immortalité de l'âme
valent en réalité pour l'intellect, qui est quelque chose de l'âme.[123]
Comme Aristote, Platon a bien senti qu'il était difficile de déclarer certaines facultés de l'âme mortelles et d'autres immortelles,
et c'est pour cela que, dans la composition de l'âme, il accorde à
l'intellect un statut particulier, tandis qu'Aristote introduit
l'intellect 'du dehors', afin que son incorruptibilité ne soit point
battue en brèche par les parties ou facultés mortelles.[124] Enfin,
clôturant le long exposé qu'il consacre à la noétique, Thémistius
remarque que les positions qu'il vient de présenter furent celles
d'Aristote, de Théophraste et sans doute aussi de Platon.[125] Dans
une certaine mesure, donc, cette tendance de Thémistius à minimiser
l'opposition entre Aristote et Platon prépare la thèse que Simplicius placera au centre de son interprétation des traités du Stagirite.

La question de savoir si l'âme est séparable du corps, et, d'une
manière plus générale, le problème des rapports entre l'âme et le
corps, ne peuvent être résolus que si l'on tranche une autre question: toutes les activités et les affections du vivant sont-elles
communes à l'âme et au corps, ou en est-il qui appartiennent exclusivement à l'âme?[126] Thémistius distingue entre les πάθη qui appar-

tiennent au vivant du fait de l'âme: plaisir, peine, sensation, imagination, et celles qui sont propres à l'âme seule: intellection et
contemplation.[127] Dans les πάθη du premier groupe, l'interdépendance du psychique et du physique est manifeste. Il est clair que
le rapport de l'âme au corps n'y est pas comparable à celui de l'artisan à son outil; il arrive que le vivant se trouve en présence
d'une cause qui devrait provoquer une colère ou une crainte violen-
tes, mais qu'il n'éprouve cependant pas ces affections; et il arrive au contraire que des causes minimes et à peine perceptibles
déclenchent des affections très intenses: c'est le cas notamment
lorsque le corps est privé de nourriture et affaibli, ou que les
humeurs fondamentales se trouvent déséquilibrées; il est évident
alors, écrit Thémistius en reprenant la formule même qui avait servi
de titre à un petit traité de Galien, que ces affections sont la
conséquence des 'mélanges' du corps, τὰ πάθη ταῖς κράσεσιν ἕπεσθαι
τοῦ σώματος. Si le corps n'était qu'un simple instrument de l'activité psychique, il en irait dans le cas des πάθη comme dans celui
de la sensation, où le dérangement de l'organe fait obstacle à l'exercice normal de l'activité sensible. Au contraire, un mélange
vicieux (φαύλη κρᾶσις) du corps n'entrave point les πάθη, mais il
les provoque plutôt et les intensifie: preuve manifeste de l'étroite
interdépendance du corps et des πάθη, lesquels sont vraiment des
λόγοι ἔνυλοι.[128] Dans le même ordre d'idées, on peut dire que la
théorie faisant de l'âme une harmonie, sans être très proche de la
vérité, n'en est pourtant pas fort éloignée, car l'âme n'est pas
totalement étrangère à la constitution du mélange corporel; autrement, pourquoi périrait-elle quand le mélange vient à être détruit,
ou inversement pourquoi le mélange se corromprait-il lorsque l'âme
quitte le corps?[129]

Même au niveau de l'intelligence,[130] Thémistius admet une certaine
liaison entre le psychique et le somatique. Aristote ayant mentionné
un intellect passif, qui est corruptible,[131] le paraphraste se fonde
sur un autre texte - I 4, 408b25-9, qu'il comprend sans doute mal -
pour expliquer qu'il s'agit là du νοῦς κοινός, lequel est siège de
la pensée discursive et des passions et n'est présent en l'homme que
parce que celui-ci est fait d'âme et de corps.[132] Comme Platon l'a
bien vu, pour que l'intellect puisse être uni à un corps matériel,
il doit exister entre eux des intermédiaires qui les relient et les

adaptent l'un à l'autre: ce sont justement les πάθη qui jouent ce
rôle, car, conditionnés par l'état du corps, ils peuvent aussi participer à la raison; parler d'un παθητικὸς νοῦς revient à parler de
πάθη λογικά.[133]

Pourtant, Thémistius se garde bien de suivre Alexandre, qui déclarait l'intellect proprement humain mortel au même titre que les
autres facultés de l'âme. Les pages qu'il consacre à la question du
νοῦς sont, du reste, les plus intéressantes et les plus originales
de toute sa paraphrase; on dirait que, séduit par la difficulté de
la question et convaincu de son importance, il a jugé utile de lui
consacrer une véritable monographie, faisant éclater ainsi le cadre
trop étroit de la paraphrase. Nous ne pouvons ici qu'en indiquer
quelques aspects.

Mises à part la question de la liaison à l'organisme corporel et
celle de l'immortalité, Thémistius n'expose rien, touchant le νοῦς
δυνάμει et le νοῦς καθ' ἕξιν, qui ne se trouve déjà chez Alexandre
et ne corresponde, en fait, à l'exégèse traditionnellement admise
avant lui. L'intellect en puissance, propre à l'âme humaine, n'est,
en soi, aucune forme, mais il est capable de les recevoir toutes. Il
se trouve déjà chez les jeunes enfants. Au cours de son développement, grâce à son activité sur les sensibles et les phantasmes de
l'imagination, il s'exerce et devient capable de se mettre en quête
de l'universel, de collecter le semblable dans le dissemblable, de
découvrir l'identique au sein du différent; il possède, dès lors, une
perfection qui le rend pareil au savant qui a en lui les théorèmes
de la science sans les utiliser; il a acquis une sorte de faculté
visuelle qu'il n'avait pas auparavant: dorénavant, il peut oeuvrer
par lui-même, sans qu'un nouvel entraînement ou qu'un enseignement
étranger lui soient indispensables. L'*habitus* qu'il comporte alors
est comme une réserve de concepts latents (νοήματα ἀποκείμενα). Il
lui est ainsi loisible de passer de ce second stade de la puissance
à l'acte, en se pensant lui-même: à ce troisième stade, il y a identité entre le νοῦς ἐνεργείᾳ et les νοήματα ἐνεργείᾳ. En effet, les
formes engagées dans la matière ne sont pas intelligibles en soi,
elles ne comportent qu'une disposition à devenir objets de pensée;
c'est l'intellect qui, les coupant de la matière où elles sont en-
fouies, les rend pleinement intelligibles.[134]

L'intellect en puissance n'étant qu'une 'disposition favorable' (εὐφυΐα), il est clair que l'être humain, dans son développement naturel, ne peut s'y arrêter: il doit atteindre au τέλος auquel la nature le destine et l'a préparé. Or nul être ne peut se perfectionner par lui-même. Il devra donc exister un intellect en acte, qui se combinera avec l'intellect potentiel et fera de lui un καθ' ἕξιν νοῦς en perfectionnant sa disposition naturelle, en constituant son *habitus* noétique. Comment s'opère cette action de l'intellect en acte sur l'intellect potentiel? Elle est double, comme celle de la lumière qui fait passer à l'acte et la faculté visuelle et les couleurs. L'intellect actif (νοῦς ἐνεργείᾳ, νοῦς ποιητικός) se superpose à l'intellect potentiel au point de ne plus faire qu'un avec lui; il le façonne comme un artisan façonnerait son oeuvre si, au lieu d'agir sur elle de l'extérieur, il était présent au sein même de cette oeuvre. Grâce à lui, l'intellect humain devient capable d'opérer les passages, les rapprochements, les divisions et les abstractions qui constituent l'intellection. L'intellect avait en lui une réserve de 'concepts communs' (κοινὰ νοήματα), sorte de préconcepts récoltés à partir des sensibles particuliers. Désormais, il va pouvoir travailler sur ces matériaux issus de la sensation et de l'imagination et transformer les intelligibles en puissance en intelligibles en acte.[135]

Peut-on définir de manière plus précise les rapports entre cet intellect actif et la personne humaine? Le *moi* de l'homme, explique Thémistius, c'est l'intellect fait de la composition de l'intellect potentiel et de l'intellect actif, mais à ce moi, c'est l'intellect actif qui confère le ἐμοὶ εἶναι; il constitue donc le véritable εἶδος de l'homme:[136] de ce fait, nous sommes immortels. Pourtant, les activités proprement humaines du νοῦς ποιητικός, telles que la pensée discursive et le souvenir, sont conditionnées par sa liaison avec l'intellect commun, qui est passif et corruptible; c'est ce qui explique pourquoi nous ne nous souvenons pas de ce que fut l'activité du νοῦς ποιητικός alors qu'il était καθ' ἑαυτόν, avant qu'il vînt parfaire notre humaine constitution (σύστασις), et c'est pourquoi aussi, après la mort, l'intellect impassible et immortel ne se souvient pas des activités qu'il a exercées quand il était lié à un être corruptible.[137]

Les pages que Thémistius consacre à l'intellect actif sont sans aucun doute les plus importantes et les plus instructives de toute

sa paraphrase. Son étude est à la fois historique et philologique:
il mentionne et discute les thèses d'exégètes antérieurs, rassemble
et interprète plusieurs textes d'Aristote capables d'éclairer les
obscures affirmations du chapitre III 5 et fait appel aux apories
de Théophraste pour dégager et étayer sa propre position. Celle-ci
n'apparaît pas de prime abord avec la clarté et la précision que
l'on pourrait souhaiter; pourtant, derrière la complexité des remarques de détail, il n'est pas impossible d'en apercevoir les lignes
maîtresses.

Qu'est au juste l'intellect actif dont parle Aristote? D'aucuns
ont voulu l'identifier tout bonnement à l'ensemble des propositions
scientifiques et des sciences qui en dérivent, mais c'est là négliger les caractères que lui attribue Aristote quand il le déclare
divin, impassible, immortel, éternel, séparé, et fait de lui une
substance et un acte. D'autres croient qu'il est identique au 'premier Dieu'. Mais divers textes d'Aristote plaident contre cette
identification et montrent qu'il est 'dans l'âme', qu'il doit donc
être identique à nous ou être quelque chose de nous-mêmes.[138] Faut-
il le tenir pour unique ou le considérer comme multiple? Ici, divers arguments peuvent être avancés en faveur de l'une et de l'autre
thèse. En fin de compte, Thémistius paraît considérer que les deux
positions ne sont pas totalement inconciliables. S'il y a, par exemple, autant d'intellects actifs que d'intellects potentiels, on
ne voit pas comment expliquer cette multiplicité: c'est la matière
qui individualise des êtres spécifiquement identiques, et l'intellect actif est sans matière; et si chaque intellect actif est différent des autres, qu'est-ce qui déterminera leur répartition? La
comparaison avec la lumière suggère plutôt qu'on ne peut s'en tenir
à la multiplicité pure et simple des intellects actifs: la lumière
est une ou, plus exactement, le dispensateur de toute lumière, le
soleil, est un, mais les facultés visuelles qu'il fait passer à
l'acte et les objets qu'il éclaire sont néanmoins multiples. Du
reste, si l'être de chacun de nous ne dérivait pas d'un intellect
actif unique, comment pourrait-on expliquer l'origine des notions
communes à tous les hommes (κοιναὶ ἔννοιαι)? Comment se ferait-il
que nous ayons tous, et sans l'avoir apprise, une même connaissance
des premiers principes? L'enseignement lui-même cesserait d'être
possible si le maître et le disciple n'avaient point au départ les

mêmes concepts en commun.[139] Plus haut déjà, après avoir noté que
la thèse de Porphyre entraînait logiquement celle de l'unicité de
l'âme, Thémistius semblait prêt à admettre une double entéléchie
pour le diaphane, l'une, plus parfaite et unique, le soleil, correspondant à l'âme unique, l'autre, moins parfaite, la lumière dis-
tribuée dans les divers corps diaphanes, correspondant aux âmes individuelles. Pourtant, cette conception de l'âme à la fois une et
multiple ne lui paraissait pas exempte de difficultés.[140] En réalité, estime-t-il, la question de l'unicité de l'âme, soulevée par
les modernes et par les anciens, ce n'est pas pour l'âme, mais pour
l'intellect qu'elle doit être posée.[141] La solution qu'il suggère
vise, comme on l'a vu, à concilier unité et multiplicité.[142] Le
platonisme ou, plus exactement, le néoplatonisme de Porphyre en a
sans doute inspiré certains aspects.

Un dernier point mérite d'être souligné, sur lequel Thémistius
prend manifestement le contrepied d'une thèse d'Alexandre. Il reconnaît bien que l'intellect commun, dépendant du corps, de la
sensation et de l'imagination, est mortel, mais il le distingue
explicitement de l'intellect potentiel. Celui-ci est séparable, il
n'est pas mêlé au corps, il n'a pas d'organe, et son impassibilité
est d'un niveau supérieur à celle de la sensation. Loin d'appa-
raître comme la pure puissance qu'il était chez Alexandre, le νοῦς
δυνάμει comporte donc une certaine substantialité. Mais il a quelque chose d'incomplet, d'inachevé: il précède l'intellect actif
comme la lueur de l'aube précède la pleine lumière, comme la fleur
précède le fruit. Antériorité purement temporelle donc, car absolument, l'intellect actif lui est de loin supérieur et est χωριστός
à un degré bien plus éminent.[143] De l'intellect passif, corruptible, inséparable du corps, on doit distinguer l'intellect fait de
l'union de l'intellect potentiel et de l'intellect actif; cet intellect, à la fois double et un comme le sont les êtres faits de
matière et de forme, est, lui, séparable du corps, incorruptible
et exempt de génération.[144]

NOTES

1 Them. *De An.* 108, 11. Prisc. *Metaphr.* 22, 34.

2 Them. *De An.* 108, 8-10 ... μὴ μακρῶς εἰρημένα, ἀλλὰ λίαν συν-
τόμως τε καὶ βραχέως τῇ γε λέξει· τοῖς γὰρ πράγμασι μεστά ἐστι
πολλῶν μὲν ἀποριῶν, πολλῶν δὲ ἐπιστάσεων, πολλῶν δὲ λύσεων.
L'examen des fragments littéraux cités chez Thémistius et Priscien montre que Thémistius a parfaitement discerné les caractères essentiels de l'ouvrage.

3 Sur ces problèmes, voir E.Barbotin, *La théorie aristotélicienne
de l'intellect d'après Théophraste* (Louvain 1954).

4 Comme Aristote le laisse entendre en *GA* II 3, 736b27sqq.

5 Galen. *De plac. Hipp. et Plat.* VI 2, vol. V, p. 515 Kühn ὁ δ'
'Αριστοτέλης τε καὶ ὁ Ποσειδώνιος εἴδη μὲν ἢ μέρη ψυχῆς οὐκ
ὀνομάζουσι, δυνάμεις δ' εἶναί φασι μιᾶς οὐσίας ἐκ τῆς καρδίας
ὁρμωμένης.

6 Sur Andronicus et la définition de Xénocrate: Them. *De An.* 31, 1-5
et 32, 19-21. Sur la propre définition d'Andronicus: Galen, *Quod
animi mores* 44,12-45,3 Müller (*Scr. min.* II). On trouvera plus de
détails dans mon ouvrage *Der Aristotelismus bei den Griechen* I
(Berlin-New York 1973), 132-4. Il n'est pas exact que le nom
d'Andronicus, qui n'apparaît pas dans les manuscrits grecs de
Galien, soit le fruit d'une simple conjecture, comme on l'a répété
souvent (en dernier lieu P.L.Donini, 'L'anima e gli elementi nel
De anima di Alessandro di Afrodisia', *Atti dell'Accademia delle
Scienze di Torino* 105 (1970-1), 101-3, et *Tre studi sull'Aris-
totelismo nel II sec. d. C.* (Turin 1974), 139 n. 27): il est
attesté notamment par la traduction de Ḥunain ibn Isḥāq (9e s.).

7 Fragments chez Eusèbe.

8 Moraux (*op.cit. n.6*), I 172-6.

9 Stob. I 49, 1b, p. 320,5-8 = *Dox.* IV 3,10. Voir Moraux (*op.cit.
n.6*), I 207.

10 *De anima* 11,29-34 De Corte = 15,65-9 Verbeke.

11 Moraux (*op.cit. n.6*), I 207-8.

12 Them. *De An.* 108,6-7. Prisc. *Metaphr.* 26,1-6 = Fr. I^c Barbotin.
Voir Barbotin (*op.cit. n.3*), 134-6.

13 *De An. mant.* 106,20-3.

14 Diels, *Dox.* pp.448-57 et 854.

15 Fr. 15-17 Diels.

16 Étude de ces fragments dans Moraux (*op.cit. n.6*), I 299-305.

17 Détails dans Moraux (*op.cit. n.6*), I 299-300.

18 Diels, *Dox.* pp. 395 et 399.

19 *De An.* 60,1-65,21; *Quaest.* III 7 et 9; ap. Ps.-Philop. *De An.* 464,20-3; 465,23-7; 470,18-471,10.

20 Détails dans Moraux (*op.cit. n.6*), I 302-5.

21 Chez Stob. I 49, 25^a, p. 353,12-354,6.

22 Averroes, *Comm. magn. in De An.* III 14, 123-9, p. 432 Crawford.

23 Sur la psychologie de Nicolas, voir Moraux (*op.cit. n.6*), I 481-7.

24 *Leg. alleg.* III 29.

25 *Leg. alleg.* I 32; 88; 90.

26 *Leg. alleg.* I 32; 37; 40.

27 *Leg. alleg.* I 88.

28 *Leg. alleg.* I 90; *Quis rer. div. haer.* 64.

29 *De vita Mos.* I 27.

30 Voir notamment E.R.Goodenough, *By light, light: the mystic gospel of Hellenistic Judaism* (New Haven 1935), Appendice, et *An introduction to Philo Judaeus* (2e éd. Oxford 1962), 112-14. W. Völker, *Fortschritt und Vollendung bei Philo v. Alexandrien* (Leipzig 1938), 158-62.

31 Gen. I 26: Dieu dit: 'Faisons l'homme à notre image, selon notre ressemblance.' Gen. II 7: Dieu fit l'homme de la poussière du sol et il souffla dans ses narines un souffle de vie.

32 *De somn.* I 30-2 renferme des indications particulièrement révélatrices à ce sujet.

33 *Didask.* X 164,16-27 Hermann.

34 164,35-165,4.

35 Them. *De An.* 102,30-1 et 102,35-103,10 mentionne et combat les partisans de l'identité du νοῦς ποιητικός et du πρῶτος θεός.

36 Sur le problème de l'unicité de l'intellect agent, voir notamment Them. *De An.* 103,20-104,14.

37 *Didask.* IV 155,34.

38 Voir surtout le chapitre IX, et X 164,8-11.

39 VIII 162,28-163,9.

40 IV 155,35.

41 X 164,11-15.

42 X 164,34-5 et 165,18-25.

43 Plat. *R*. VI 507e - 509b.

44 *De An*. III 5, 430a15-17.

45 *Didask*. XXVI 179,17-29.

46 Voir *De An*. II 5, 417a22 - b2 et III 4, 429b5-9.

47 Dans l'ouvrage qu'il a consacré à Albinus (*Albinus and the his-
    tory of middle Platonism* (Cambridge 1937)), R.E.Witt souligne,
    après d'autres, le caractère parfois incohérent de son éclec-
    tisme; certains éléments dériveraient d'Arius Didymus, lequel
    se serait inspiré, mais en partie seulement, d'Antiochus. Sur
    l'identification du Démiurge platonicien avec le premier moteur
    d'Aristote, voir les pp. 122-44. En revanche, J.H.Loenen, 'Al-
    binus' Metaphysics. An attempt at rehabilitation', *Mnemosyne* 9
    (1956), 296-319, et 10 (1957), 35-56, s'efforce, sans toujours
    arriver à convaincre, de démontrer qu'Albinus n'est pas un éc-
    lectique, que son système n'est pas une combinaison syncrétiste
    de platonisme et d'aristotélisme, mais apparaît au contraire
    comme une interprétation du platonisme originale et parfaite-
    ment cohérente. Sur la question des rapports entre le premier
    intellect, l'intellect cosmique et l'âme, voir surtout les pp.
    304-11. Sur les éléments aristotéliciens et stoïciens chez
    Albinus, voir la p. 316, n. 1, où on lit: 'If eclecticism is
    taken in its specific sense, viz. as a conscious design, we are
    not justified in calling Albinus an eclecticist.' P.Merlan,
    Monopsychism mysticism metaconsciousness (The Hague 1963), qui
    cherche à montrer que Plotin a connu et utilisé la doctrine de
    l'intelligence élaborée par Alexandre d'Aphrodise, analyse aux
    pp. 61-7 les textes d'Albinus relatifs au νοῦς (réserves de W.
    Theiler, *Gnomon* 37 (1965), 21-3). Dans un ouvrage récent,
    Donini (*Tre Studi*, *op.cit. n.6*) s'appuie notamment sur le té-
    moignage d'Albinus pour étayer sa thèse selon laquelle la noéti-
    que d'Alexandre serait tributaire du platonisme moyen; voir sur-
    tout les pp. 26-48. On trouvera dans les ouvrages cités des in-
    dications bibliographiques plus abondantes sur Albinus: elles
    permettront de compléter la page trop brève que lui consacre E.
    des Places, 'Etudes fecentes (1953-1973) sur le platonisme moyen
    du IIe siècle après J.-C.', *Bull. Assoc. Budé* (1974), 347-58
    (sur Albinus: 350-1).

48 Att. ap. Eus. *PE* XV 9,5-14 = Fr. VII Baudry.

49 J'étudie plus en détail les jugements portés par Galien sur
    'l'image de l'homme' d'Aristote dans mon article ' Galien et
    Aristote', paru dans *Images of man in ancient and medieval
    thought. Studia Gerardo Verbeke ab amicis et collegis dicata*
    (Louvain 1976), 127-46.

50 *De usu partium* VII 8, p. 542 (III K.); *De util. resp.* 1, p. 472
   (IV K.); *De foet. format.* 6, pp. 700-2 (IV K.); *In Hippocr. epid.*
   VI, pp. 247-8 (XVII B K.).

51 *Quod animi mores* 32,1-13 M.

52 Texte fondamental: *Quod animi mores* 37,5-26 M. Voir aussi 44,
   20-45,3 M., où il est rappelé qu'en définissant l'âme comme ἡ
   κατὰ τὸ εἶδος οὐσία, Aristote n'a voulu parler de rien d'autre
   que du mélange.

53 *Quod animi mores* 51,12-57,13 M. Les textes cités sont: *PA* II 2,
   648a2-13 (les différences dans le sang déterminent chez les animaux des différences de sensibilité, de courage, d'intelligence);
   II 4, 650b14 - 651a17 (rapports entre la constitution du sang, le
   caractère et l'intelligence des animaux); *HA* I 9, 491b11-13; 14-
   18; 22-6; 34 - 492a4; 492a7-12 (physionomie et caractère).

54 Innombrables textes dans le *De plac. Hippocr. et Plat.*

55 *De plac. Hippocr. et Plat.* IX 9, pp. 793-5 (V K.): la tripartition de l'âme et la répartition des trois parties entre des organes différents peuvent être démontrées scientifiquement, alors
   qu'il n'existe aucun argument sérieux à faire valoir sur leur
   nature et sur la question de leur immortalité. *De foet. format.*
   6, p. 701 (IV K.): la tripartition de l'âme a été prouvée dans
   de nombreux traités, notamment dans le περὶ τῶν τῆς ψυχῆς εἰδῶν
   (aujourd'hui perdu).

56 Ici également, on ne peut donner toutes les références. On
   pourra se reporter notamment à *De plac. Hippocr. et Plat.* I 6,
   pp. 187-8 (V K.); 8, pp. 200-3; 10, pp. 206-8 (quoique n'ignorant pas entièrement l'anatomie, Aristote s'est mépris sur la
   nature des nerfs et l'organe d'où ils partent); IV 1, p. 363;
   VI 2, pp. 515-16; VII 8, p. 647; *De usu part.* VIII 3-4 (III K.)
   etc.

57 *De plac. Hippocr. et Plat.* VII 1, p. 587 (V K.).

58 *Ibid.* p. 591.

59 *Ibid.* IX 9, p. 794.

60 *De subst. fac. nat. fragm.* pp. 762-3 (IV K.).

61 *Quod animi mores* 37,16-38,22 M.

62 Voir le témoignage de Galien cité ci-dessus n. 51.

63 Alex. *De sensu* 10,2.

64 Lequel parle, *De sensu* 82,16, des ὑπομνηματισάμενοι τὸ βιβλίον.

65 Them. *De An.* 61,21-34.

66 Alex. *Meteor.* 143,12-14.

67 Alex. *De An. mant.* 110,4-113,12. On a proposé de corriger en
   Aristoclès le nom du maître d'Alexandre, qui, dans les manuscrits, est appelé *Aristoteles*. Mais il n'existe aucune preuve
   qu'Aristoclès de Messine ait jamais été le maître d'Alexandre.
   Par ailleurs, un péripatéticien Aristote de Mytilène jouissait,
   sous Galien, d'un certain renom. Sur la question, voir P.Moraux,
   Archiv Gesch. Philos. 49 (1967), 169-82.

68 Alex. *De An. mant.* 112,5sqq. Ces apories rappellent les questions embarrassantes qu'Atticus formulait à l'adresse d'Aristote, ap. Eus. *PE* XV 9,13 = Fr. VII Baudry.

69 B.C.Bazán, 'L'authenticité du *De intellectu* attribué à Alexandre
   d'Aphrodise', *Rev. Philos. Louvain* 71 (1973), 468-87.

70 On trouvera plus de détails dans le tome III de mon *Aristotelismus bei den Griechen*, en préparation.

71 On ne relève pas de divergences notables entre les fragments du
   commentaire et le *De anima* personnel. Par ailleurs, le *De anima*
   est postérieur au commentaire (conservé) au *De sensu*, qu'il cite
   textuellement à plusieurs reprises. Le commentaire au *De sensu*,
   de son côté, ne peut avoir été rédigé qu'après le commentaire au
   De anima, et il est certainement postérieur aux commentaires à
   la *Physique*, au *De caelo* et aux *Météorologiques*. Ainsi, le *De
   anima* d'Alexandre ne peut certainement pas être regardé comme un
   ouvrage de jeunesse.

72 *De An.* 2,4-9. Sur la théorie de l'âme chez Alexandre, voir maintenant Donini, 'L'anima ...' (*art.cit. n.6*), 61-107. L'auteur
   s'en prend à plusieurs erreurs d'appréciation que j'ai commises
   dans mon travail de 1942 sur Alexandre et que j'avais, du reste,
   reconnues moi-même depuis longtemps. J'ai peine à croire, pourtant, qu'on puisse admettre, comme l'écrit P.L.Donini, que l'exposé d'Alexandre se caractérise par son esprit de rigueur sys-
   tématique, la fermeté et la cohérence du dessein, ainsi que par
   la capacité de synthèse philosophique et les intuitions géniales
   de l'auteur.

73 *De An.* 2,10-25; 10,26-11,13.

74 Je résume *De An.* 2,25-13,8. Le texte traduit figure en 12,21-4.

75 *De An.* 24,18-26,30, surtout 24,21-3 οὐ γὰρ ἡ τοιάδε τῶν σωμάτων
   κρᾶσις ἡ ψυχή, ὅπερ ἦν ἡ ἁρμονία, ἀλλ' ἡ ἐπὶ τῇ τοιᾷδε κράσει
   δύναμις γεννωμένη. La formule évoque la définition de l'âme par
   Andronicus telle que la rapporte Galien, κρᾶσιν εἶναί φησιν ἢ
   δύναμιν ἐπομένην τῇ κράσει.

76 Mich. Eph. *Parva naturalia* 135,22-30. Après avoir critiqué la
   conception d'Alexandre d'après laquelle l'*intellectus possibilis*
   n'est rien d'autre qu'une disposition, S.Thomas, *S. c. gentil.*
   II 63 écrit: praedictae autem opinioni Alexandri de intellectu
   possibili propinqua est Galeni medici de anima. Dicit enim animam esse complexionem. - Il y a longtemps que m'est apparue la
   ressemblance entre les idées de Galien et celles d'Alexandre au

sujet de l'âme. Les pages qui lui seront consacrées aux tomes II et III de mon *Aristotelismus bei den Griechen* étaient en grande partie rédigées quand est paru l'article de P.L.Donini (*cité n.6*) où les conceptions d'Alexandre sont rapprochées de celles de Galien.

77 *De An.* 80,16-87,1.

78 87,25-88,10.

79 Merlan (*op.cit. n.47*), surtout 16-17. Donini, *Tre studi* (*op. cit. n.6*), surtout 26-33.

80 Voir *De An.* 88,2-5.

81 89,21-90,2.

82 88,17-24.

83 88,24-89,11.

84 Bazán (*art.cit. n.69*), surtout 483-4.

85 *De An.* 88,5-11; 89,21-90,2; 90,11-20; 91,3-4.

86 88,6; 91,3-4.

87 91,5-6.

88 90,2-91,6.

89 Averrois Cord. *Comm. magn. in Ar. de an. libros*, ed. F.S.Crawford (1953), p. 483: quod autem dixit in quodam tractatu quem fecit de intellectu secundum opinionem Aristotelis videtur contradicere ei quod dixit in libro *de anima*.

90 Bazán (*art.cit. n. 69*).

91 *De int.* 108,19-22.

92 *De An.* 81,13-15; 81,22-5; *De int.* 106,23-4; 110,20-4.

93 Cette conception prévaut dans le *De int.*; voir surtout 106,25-107,20, à comparer avec *De An.* 84,14-27; 85,5-10.

94 *De An.* 82,1-15; 85,20-5; 86,16-17; *De int.* 107,21-8; 107, 32-4; 111,31-2.

95 *De An.* 86,5-6.

96 *De An.* 84,24-6.

97 (*Art.cit. n.69*), pp. 482-4.

98 *Tre studi* (*op.cit. n.6*), 61.

99 Voir à ce sujet G.Verbeke, 'Les critiques de Plotin contre l'entéléchisme d'Aristote: essai d'interprétation de l'*Enn*. 4.7.8 ', *Philomathes. Studies ... in memory of Philip Merlan* (The Hague 1971), 194-222. Donini, *Tre studi* (*op.cit. n.6*), 9sqq.

100 Depuis quelques années, la critique s'est efforcée - avec un succès inégal - de déceler chez Plotin des réminiscences d'Alexandre d'Aphrodise. On pourra consulter notamment H.R.Schwyzer, Art. 'Plotinos', *RE* XXI (1952), 573-4. P.Henry, 'Une comparaison chez Aristote, Alexandre et Plotin', *Les sources de Plotin. Fondation Hardt. Entretiens* 5 (Vandoeuvres, Genève 1960), 429-44. A.H.Amstrong, 'The background of the doctrine "That the Intelligibles are not outside the Intellect"', *ibid.* 405-6. Merlan (*op.cit. n.47*), 13-16 et 39-40. F.P.Hager, 'Die Aristoteles-interpretation des Alexander von Aphrodisias und die Aristoteleskritik Plotins bezüglich der Lehre vom Geist', *Archiv Gesch. Philos.* 46 (1964), 174-87. J.M.Rist, 'On tracking Alexander of Aphrodisias', *Archiv Gesch. Philos.* 48 (1966), 82-90. H.J. Blumenthal, 'Plotinus *Ennead* IV.3.20-1 and his sources: Alexander, Aristotle and others', *Archiv Gesch. Philos.* 50 (1968), 254-61. Donini, *Tre studi* (*op.cit. n.6*), surtout 5-25. - La difficulté de ces recherches et la fragilité de certains rapprochements découlent du fait que nous n'avons plus grand-chose de la littérature exégétique aristotélicienne des premiers siècles. Certaines rencontres entre Plotin et Alexandre peuvent être fortuites et ne représenter qu'une opinion ou une formule courantes chez les péripatéticiens de l'époque, mais connues uniquement grâce à Alexandre.

101 Voir, dans le même sens, J.M.Rist (*art.cit. n.100*), 90.

102 L'existence d'un commentaire au *De anima* n'est pas attestée. En revanche, Suidas nous apprend (s. v. Πορφύριος) que Porphyre avait écrit un πρὸς ᾽Αριστοτέλην περὶ τοῦ εἶναι τὴν ψυχὴν ἐντελέχειαν (no 33 de la liste de J.Bidez). C'est sans doute dans cet ouvrage que Thémistius a trouvé les indications dont il va être question. Dans ce qui suit, nous ne pourrons examiner en détail les remarques de Porphyre. Il va sans dire que de nombreux rapprochements avec Plotin s'imposeraient.

103 Them. *De An.* 16,19 l'appelle ὁ τῶν ᾽Αριστοτέλους ἐξεταστής, le vérificateur, le scrutateur des oeuvres d'Aristote, sans doute pour laisser entendre qu'il y cherchait ce qui prêtait le flanc à la critique. Comme l'indique une notice marginale du *Laur.* 87,25, c'est bien Porphyre qui est visé, car la σύνοψις mentionnée en 16,30 est effectivement de lui: voir Simpl. *Ph.* 802,8 et 918,13.

104 Them. *De An.* 6,11-33. Porphyre est désigné comme ὁ ἐνιστάμενος πρὸς τοῦτον τὸν λόγον; comparer avec 16,19 ὁ ... ἐξεταστὴς ἐνίσταται τοῖς εἰλημμένοις, où il s'agit certainement de Porphyre. - La critique adressée par Porphyre à Aristote est résumée par Thémistius, *De An.* 6,12-14, et rapportée également par Philopon, *De An.* 46,10-18, qui l'attribue à des exégètes qu'il ne nomme pas. En voici la teneur. Il aurait fallu détruire (ἀνελεῖν) l'antécédent en prenant la contradictoire du conséquent, tandis

qu'Aristote s'efforce de détruire le conséquent en prenant la
contradictoire de l'antécédent. Autrement dit, Porphyre aurait
admis 'si A, alors B; mais non B; donc non A'; il reproche à
Aristote d'avoir raisonné de manière incorrecte en disant: 'si
A, alors B; mais non A; donc non B'. C'est évidemment fausser
la portée des indications d'Aristote dans les lignes incrimi-
nées. Comme l'avaient déjà noté les 'exégètes attiques' (Plutarque?) mentionnés par Philopon, De An. 46,18sqq. et comme me
le rappelle aimablement J.Brunschwig, que je remercie de ses
remarques et de son aide, Aristote n'introduit aucun lien de
consécution entre le conditionnel positif ('si l'âme possède
quelque opération ou affection propre, elle est séparable') et
le conditionnel négatif ('si l'âme n'a pas d'opération propre,
elle n'est pas séparable'). - Il est remarquable que Porphyre
prête à Aristote la volonté de détruire (πειρᾶται ἀναιρεῖν) la
thèse selon laquelle l'âme est séparable. Pour des raisons
qu'il me serait trop long d'exposer ici, je soupçonne que cette
interprétation du passage en cause remonte à Alexandre d'Aphrodise. - Thémistius, quant à lui, reproche à Porphyre de n'avoir
pas tenu compte du fait que, dans le conditionnel positif d'Aristote, la consécution n'est pas donnée comme nécessaire, mais
comme contingente (ἐνδέχοιτ' ἄν); or dans une consécution contingente, la destruction de l'antécédent entraîne avec elle
celle du conséquent. Thémistius donne les exemples suivants:
'Si Dion navigue, il se peut (ἐνδέχεται) qu'il ait une navigation heureuse; si Dion ne navigue pas, il ne se peut non plus
(οὐδ'... ἐνδέχεται) qu'il ait une navigation heureuse.' A rejeter: 'S'il ne se peut que Dion ait une navigation heureuse,
il ne se peut non plus qu'il navigue.' Autre exemple: 'Si ce
qui s'approche est un animal, il se peut que ce soit un cheval.' A rejeter: 'Si ce n'est pas un cheval, ce n'est pas non
plus un animal.' En consécution contingente, explique Thémistius, le rapport de l'antécédent au conséquent est comme celui
d'un tout à sa partie: en supprimant le tout, on supprime la
partie.

105 L'entéléchisme est également attaqué par Porphyre dans son Contra
    Boethum, Fr. 6 et 8 ap. Eus. PE XV 11,1 et 4, p. 374 Mras.

106 Them. De An. 16,19-25. Réfutation par Thémistius 16,25-36.

107 16,36-9. Réfutation 16,39-17,8.

108 De An. I 3, 406b5-11.

109 Them. De An. 17,25-9. La même opinion, mais illustrée différem-
    ment, se retrouve par exemple chez Porphyre, Sent. 18 Mommert:
    les οἰκειώσεις et les πάθη de l'âme sont en réalité des ἐνέρ-
    γειαι ne ressemblant en rien au réchauffement ou au refroidisse-
    ment des corps. Lors de la perception, l'âme ressemble à l'har-
    monie séparée que le musicien a en lui, tandis que l'élément
    corporel, qui 'subit', est analogue aux cordes bien accordées
    que meut le musicien. Cette comparaison est prise à Plotin III
    6, 4, 43-52.

110 Them. De An. 17,32-5.

111 *De An.* I 3, 406b11-15.

112 Them. *De An.* 18,16-20. Comparer avec Porph. *Sent.* 21 M., où on lit notamment que l'âme n'est pas composée de vie et de non-vie, mais n'est que vie, ce qu'a voulu exprimer Platon en donnant l'αὐτοκίνητον comme l'essence et le logos de l'âme.

113 *De An.* I 4, 408a24-9.

114 Them. *De An.* 25,33-6. Je tiens pour assuré que le sujet de φησίν est ici Porphyre, comme dans les passages cités plus haut: la pensée et le vocabulaire rappellent le *Contra Boethum* Fr. 7 ap. Eus. *PE* XV 11,2-3, p. 374 Mras, notamment παρουσίᾳ ... τῆς ψυχῆς ζωτικὸν γέγονε τὸ τοῦ ζῴου σῶμα, ὡς ... ἡλίου ἀνατολῇ πεφώτισταί γε ὁ ἀήρ, σκοτεινὸς ὢν ἄνευ τῆς τούτου ἐκ-λάμψεως, et un peu plus bas la distinction d'ἐμψυχία et de ψυχή.

115 Them. *De An.* 25,36-27,7.

116 Voir surtout Them. *De An.* 26,20-30. Les rapports entre l'âme universelle et les âmes individuelles sont présentés d'un point de vue assez différent chez Porph. *Sent.* 27 M. - On se rappel-lera que pour Plotin également, la nature de l'animal est faite du corps vivant et d'une sorte d'illumination (ἔλλαμψις) que lui donne l'âme, et que l'âme universelle illumine de ses re-flets celle qui est dans le corps. Voir notamment I 1,7; 8; 10; 11; 12; II 3, 9 etc.

117 *De An.* I 4, 408b32sqq.

118 Them. *De An.* 31,1-3.

119 32,19-22.

120 Dans la discussion de mon rapport, C. de Vogel a souligné, en citant de nombreux textes, que Plotin s'était, lui aussi, penché sur plusieurs des problèmes que soulève Thémistius, et qu'il avait, à plus d'une reprise, proposé des solutions assez sem-blables à celles du paraphraste. Les activités et affections du vivant sont-elles communes à l'âme et au corps, ou certaines d'entre elles appartiennent-elles à l'âme seule (Plot. I 1)? L'âme unie au corps se souvient-elle de son existence anté-rieure, et l'âme sortie du corps se souvient-elle de son séjour ici-bas (IV 3,25-4,17)? La pensée discursive dépend-elle du corps?, etc. Une comparaison détaillée des vues de Plotin et de Thémistius dépasserait le cadre du présent rapport. Même si, dans sa paraphrase, Thémistius ne cite pas Plotin nommé-ment, il est probable qu'il a connu ses idées, en partie peut-être à travers Porphyre, qu'il utilise.

121 Them. *De An.* 14,28-19,14.

122 20,19-26. Déjà Aristote, *De An.* I 3, 407a3sqq. notait à propos de l'âme du monde dont il est question dans le *Timée*: τὴν ... τοῦ παντὸς (ψυχὴν) δῆλον ὅτι τοιαύτην εἶναι βούλεται οἶόν ποτ' ἐστὶν ὁ καλούμενος νοῦς.

123 106,29-107,2.

124 37,20-8.

125 108,35-109,3.

126 5,31-5.

127 2,28-32.

128 7,1-25.

129 25,23-33.

130 Sur la doctrine de l'intelligence chez Thémistius, on pourra
consulter O.Balleriaux, 'D'Aristote à Thémistius. Contribution
à une histoire de la noétique après Aristote' (Thèse de Liège,
1943) (cet ouvrage de mon ancien condisciple est resté inédit,
et je ne l'ai pas sous la main), un chapitre d'O.Hamelin, *La
théorie de l'intellect d'après Aristote et ses commentateurs*
(Paris 1953), 38-43, et surtout l'étude de G.Verbeke dans son
édition de Thémistius, *Comm. sur le traité de l'âme d'Aristote.
Trad. de Guillaume de Moerbeke* (Louvain-Paris 1957), *(Corp.
lat. comm. in Arist. gr.* I), xxxix-lxii.

131 *De An.* III 5, 430a24.

132 Them. *De An.* 105,13-22. Voir aussi 101,5-9; 102,1-24; 108,28-
31.

133 107,7-29.

134 93,32-98,9. Thémistius fait allusion au problème des universaux
en 3,32-4,11; le genre n'est qu'un ἐννόημα; il n'est donc rien,
ou est postérieur au particulier; l'espèce, elle, est une nature
(φύσις), une forme (μορφή); on peut donc se demander si les
définitions sont des déterminations de concepts ou si elles correspondent à des natures présentes dans les particuliers.

135 98,12-100,15.

136 100,16-37. Rappelons que pour Platon, c'est l'âme qui est notre
moi véritable (*Alc.* I 130c; *Phd.* 115cd; *Lg.* XII 959ab). Pour
Aristote, c'est le λόγον ἔχον, le νοῦς (*Protr.* Fr. 6 Walzer et
Ross = B 62 Düring; *EN* IX 8, 1168b35-1169a2). Même opinion chez
Xénocrate (R.Heinze, *Xenokrates* (Leipzig 1892), 143), Cicéron
(*De rep.* VI 24 mens cuiusque is est quisque), Philon (*Quod det.
potiori insid. soleat* 22; *De agric.* 9) et d'autres (I.Heinemann,
Poseidonios' metaph. Schr. (Breslau 1921), 62-3). Plotin, quant
à lui, oppose assez souvent le moi inférieur, 'l'homme avec la
bête', c'est-à-dire le corps doué de vie, au moi supérieur, à
'ce qui est au-dessus de la bête', l'homme véritable, l'âme
raisonnable, qui vit dans l'intelligible (nombreux textes, notamment I 1,7; 10; I 4, 9; II 3, 9); mais notre raisonnement,
notre raison discursive ne sont pas l'intelligence pure; nous
ne sommes pas l'intelligence; celle-ci est supérieure à la raison

discursive, qui reçoit son empreinte (V 3,3); par notre âme,
nous participons à l'essence (οὐσία), nous sommes une certaine
essence, mais nous ne sommes pas l'essence elle-même (VI 8,12);
notre âme, qui est un composé, n'est pas identique à l'être de
l'âme (τὸ ψυχῇ εἶναι) (I 1,12). 'L'acte d'intellection a lieu
lorsque l'âme pense les objets intelligibles, et lorsque l'intelligence agit sur nous; car l'intelligence est à la fois une
partie de nous-mêmes et un être supérieur auquel nous nous éle-
vons' (I 1, 13, trad. E.Bréhier). Sur le problème du moi chez
Plotin, voir entre autres E.Zeller, *Philos. d. Gr.* III 2, 5e
éd. Leipzig, pp. 631sqq., et A.H.Armstrong, 'Plotinus', *The
Cambridge History of later Greek and early Medieval Philosophy*
(Cambridge 1967), 224-6. Il est assez probable que Thémistius
s'est inspiré de ces considérations, en les adaptant à ses
vues personnelles, lorsqu'il a distingué le *moi*, qui est l'intellect où sont unis l'intellect potentiel et l'intellect actif, et l'*être du moi*, qui vient uniquement de l'intellect
actif.

137 101,9-102,29. Heinze considère le texte de 101,36-7 comme in-
intelligible et suppose qu'il a dû être déformé par une lacune.
Il me paraît plus simple d'écrire en 101,37 ὅσοι κακῶς (καὶ
codd.) ἀπορεῖν κτλ. pour obtenir le sens attendu.

138 102,30-103,19.

139 103,20-104,14.

140 25,38-27,7.

141 104,14;16.

142 Sur la difficile question de l'unité ou de la pluralité des intellects agents selon Thémistius, voir Verbeke (*op.cit. n.130*),
xlii-lv et lxi, dont l'interprétation est très voisine de celle
que je viens d'esquisser. Au contraire, Merlan (*op.cit. n.47*),
50, n. 3, conjecture que le passage où est avancée la thèse de
la pluralité n'est qu'une glose postérieure.

143 105,13-106,14.

144 108,28-34.

INDEX I

(a) ARISTOTLE

II INDEX OF TECHNICAL TERMS

Cross-references are to Index III